Get the eBook FREE!

(PDF, ePub, Kindle, and liveBook all included)

We believe that once you buy a book from us, you should be able to read it in any format we have available. To get electronic versions of this book at no additional cost to you, purchase and then register this book at the Manning website.

Go to https://www.manning.com/freebook and follow the instructions to complete your pBook registration.

That's it!
Thanks from Manning!

100 Go Mistakes
and How to Avoid Them

100 Go Mistakes

AND HOW TO AVOID THEM

TEIVA HARSANYI

MANNING
SHELTER ISLAND

For online information and ordering of this and other Manning books, please visit
www.manning.com. The publisher offers discounts on this book when ordered in quantity.
For more information, please contact

> Special Sales Department
> Manning Publications Co.
> 20 Baldwin Road
> PO Box 761
> Shelter Island, NY 11964
> Email: orders@manning.com

Manning Publications Co.
20 Baldwin Road
PO Box 761
Shelter Island, NY 11964

Development editor:	Doug Rudder
Technical development editors:	Arthur Zubarev
Review editor:	Mihaela Batinić
Production editor:	Deirdre S. Hiam
Copy editors:	Frances Buran and Tiffany Taylor
Proofreader:	Katie Tennant
Technical proofreader:	Tim van Deurzen
Typesetter and cover designer:	Marija Tudor

ISBN 9781617299599
Printed in the United States of America

To Davy Harsanyi: Keep being the person you are, little brother; the stars are your limit.

À Mélissa, ma puce.

contents

3 Data types   56

preface

In 2019, I started my second professional experience with Go as the primary language. While working in this new context, I noticed some common patterns regarding Go coding mistakes. I started to think that perhaps writing about these frequent mistakes could help some developers.

So, I wrote a blog post called "The Top 10 Most Common Mistakes I've Seen in Go Projects." The post was very popular: it had more than 100,000 reads and was selected by the Golang Weekly newsletter as one of the top articles of 2019. Beyond that, I was pleased with the positive feedback I got from the Go community.

From that moment, I realized that communicating about common mistakes was a powerful tool. Accompanied by concrete examples, it can help people learn new skills efficiently and facilitate remembering the context of a mistake and how to avoid it.

I spent about a year compiling mistakes from various sources such as other professional projects, open source repositories, books, blogs, studies, and discussions with the Go community. To be transparent, I was also a decent source of inspiration regarding mistakes.

At the end of 2020, I reached 100 Go mistakes, which seemed to me like the right moment to propose my idea to a publisher. I contacted only one: Manning. I saw Manning as a top-level company known for publishing high-quality books, and to me, it was the perfect partner. It took me almost 2 years and countless iterations to frame each of the 100 mistakes alongside meaningful examples and multiple solutions where context is key.

I hope this book will help you avoid making these common mistakes and help you enhance your proficiency in the Go language.

acknowledgments

I want to thank a number of people. My parents, for pushing me when I was in a complete failure situation during my studies. My uncle Jean-Paul Demont, for helping me find the light. Pierre Gautier, for being a great source of inspiration and making me trust myself. Damien Chambon, for steadily setting the bar higher and pushing me to get better. Laurent Bernard, for being a role model and teaching me that soft skills and communication are crucial. Valentin Deleplace, for the consistency of his exceptional feedback. Doug Rudder, for teaching me the delicate art of conveying ideas in a written form. Tiffany Taylor and Katie Tennant, for the high-quality copy editing and proofreading, and Tim van Deurzen, for the depth and the quality of his technical review.

I also want to thank, Clara Chambon, my beloved little goddaughter; Virginie Chambon, the nicest person alive; the whole Harsanyi family; Afroditi Katika, my favorite PO; Sergio Garcez and Kasper Bentsen, two amazing engineers; and the entire Go community.

Lastly, I would like to thank the reviewers: Adam Wan, Alessandro Campeis, Allen Gooch, Andres Sacco, Anupam Sengupta, Borko Djurkovic, Brad Horrocks, Camal Cakar, Charles M. Shelton, Chris Allan, Clifford Thurber, Cosimo Damiano Prete, David Cronkite, David Jacobs, David Moravec, Francis Setash, Gianluigi Spagnuolo, Giuseppe Maxia, Hiroyuki Musha, James Bishop, Jerome Meyer, Joel Holmes, Jonathan R. Choate, Jort Rodenburg, Keith Kim, Kevin Liao, Lev Veyde, Martin Dehnert, Matt Welke, Neeraj Shah, Oscar Utbult, Peiti Li, Philipp Janertq, Robert Wenner, Ryan Burrowsq, Ryan Huber, Sanket Naik, Satadru Roy, Shon D. Vick, Thad Meyer, and Vadim Turkov. Your suggestions helped make this a better book.

about this book

100 Go Mistakes and How to Avoid Them contains 100 common mistakes made by Go developers when working with various aspects of the language. It focuses heavily on the core language and the standard library, not external libraries or frameworks. The discussions of most of the mistakes are accompanied by concrete examples to illustrate when we are likely to make such errors. It's not a dogmatic book: each solution is detailed to convey the context in which it should apply.

Who should read this book

This book is for developers with existing knowledge of the Go language. It doesn't review basic concepts such as syntax or keywords. Ideally, you have already worked on an existing Go project at work or home. But before delving into most topics, we make sure the foundations are clear.

How this book is organized: A roadmap

100 Go Mistakes and How to Avoid Them consists of 12 chapters:

- Chapter 1, "Go: Simple to learn but hard to master," describes why despite being considered a simple language, Go isn't easy to master. It also shows the different types of mistakes we cover in the book.
- Chapter 2, "Code and project organization," contains common mistakes that can prevent us from organizing a codebase in a clean, idiomatic, and maintainable manner.
- Chapter 3, "Data types," discusses mistakes related to basic types, slices, and maps.

- Chapter 4, "Control structures," explores common mistakes related to loops and other control structures.
- Chapter 5, "Strings," looks at the principle of string representation and common mistakes leading to code inaccuracy or inefficiency.
- Chapter 6, "Functions and methods," explores common problems related to functions and methods, such as choosing a receiver type and preventing common `defer` bugs.
- Chapter 7, "Error management," walks through idiomatic and accurate error handling in Go.
- Chapter 8, "Concurrency: Foundations," presents the fundamental concepts behind concurrency. We discuss topics such as why concurrency isn't always faster, the differences between concurrency and parallelism, and workload types.
- Chapter 9, "Concurrency: Practice," looks at concrete examples of mistakes related to applying concurrency when using Go channels, goroutines, and other primitives.
- Chapter 10, "The standard library," contains common mistakes made when using the standard library with HTTP, JSON, or (for example) the time API.
- Chapter 11, "Testing," discusses mistakes that make testing and benchmarking more brittle, less effective, and less accurate.
- Chapter 12, "Optimizations," closes the book by exploring how to optimize an application for performance, from understanding CPU fundamentals to Go-specific topics.

About the code

This book contains many examples of source code both in numbered listings and in line with normal text. In both cases, source code is formatted in a `fixed-width font like this` to separate it from ordinary text. Sometimes code is also in **bold** to highlight code that has changed from previous steps in the chapter, such as when a new feature adds to an existing line of code.

In many cases, the original source code has been reformatted; we've added line breaks and reworked indentation to accommodate the available page space in the book. In some cases, even this was not enough, and listings include line-continuation markers (➥). Additionally, comments in the source code have often been removed from the listings when the code is described in the text. Code annotations accompany many of the listings, highlighting important concepts.

You can get executable snippets of code from the liveBook (online) version of this book at https://livebook.manning.com/book/100-go-mistakes-how-to-avoid-them. The complete code for the examples in the book is available for download from the Manning website at https://www.manning.com/books/100-go-mistakes-how-to-avoid -them, and from GitHub at https://github.com/teivah/100-go-mistakes.

liveBook discussion forum

Purchase of *100 Go Mistakes and How to Avoid Them* includes free access to liveBook, Manning's online reading platform. Using liveBook's exclusive discussion features, you can attach comments to the book globally or to specific sections or paragraphs. It's a snap to make notes for yourself, ask and answer technical questions, and receive help from the author and other users. To access the forum, go to https://livebook .manning.com/book/100-go-mistakes-how-to-avoid-them/discussion. You can also learn more about Manning's forums and the rules of conduct at https://livebook .manning.com/discussion.

Manning's commitment to our readers is to provide a venue where a meaningful dialogue between individual readers and between readers and the author can take place. It is not a commitment to any specific amount of participation on the part of the author, whose contribution to the forum remains voluntary (and unpaid). We suggest you try asking the author some challenging questions lest his interest stray! The forum and the archives of previous discussions will be accessible from the publisher's website as long as the book is in print.

about the author

TEIVA HARSANYI is a senior software engineer at Docker. He has worked in various domains, including insurance, transportation, and safety-critical industries like air traffic management. He is very passionate about Go and how to design and implement reliable applications.

about the cover illustration

The figure on the cover of *100 Go Mistakes and How to Avoid Them* is "Femme de Buccari en Croatie," or "A woman from Bakar, Croatia," taken from a collection by Jacques Grasset de Saint-Sauveur, published in 1797. Each illustration is finely drawn and colored by hand.

In those days, it was easy to identify where people lived and what their trade or station in life was just by their dress. Manning celebrates the inventiveness and initiative of the computer business with book covers based on the rich diversity of regional culture centuries ago, brought back to life by pictures from collections such as this one.

Go: Simple to learn
but hard to master

This chapter covers

- What makes Go an efficient, scalable, and productive language
- Exploring why Go is simple to learn but hard to master
- Presenting the common types of mistakes made by developers

Making mistakes is part of everyone's life. As Albert Einstein once said,

> *A person who never made a mistake never tried anything new.*

What matters in the end isn't the number of mistakes we make, but our capacity to learn from them. This assertion also applies to programming. The seniority we acquire in a language isn't a magical process; it involves making many mistakes and learning from them. The purpose of this book is centered around this idea. It will help you, the reader, become a more proficient Go developer by looking at and learning from 100 common mistakes people make in many areas of the language.

This chapter presents a quick refresher as to why Go has become mainstream over the years. We'll discuss why, despite Go being considered simple to learn, mastering its nuances can be challenging. Finally, we'll introduce the concepts this book covers.

1.1 Go outline

If you are reading this book, it's likely that you're already sold on Go. Therefore, this section provides a brief reminder about what makes Go such a powerful language.

Software engineering has evolved considerably during the past decades. Most modern systems are no longer written by a single person but by teams consisting of multiple programmers—sometimes even hundreds, if not thousands. Nowadays, code must be readable, expressive, and maintainable to guarantee a system's durability over the years. Meanwhile, in our fast-moving world, maximizing agility and reducing the time to market is critical for most organizations. Programming should also follow this trend, and companies strive to ensure that software engineers are as productive as possible when reading, writing, and maintaining code.

In response to these challenges, Google created the Go programming language in 2007. Since then, many organizations have adopted the language to support various use cases: APIs, automation, databases, CLIs (command-line interfaces), and so on. Many today consider Go the language of the cloud.

Feature-wise, Go has no type inheritance, no exceptions, no macros, no partial functions, no support for lazy variable evaluation or immutability, no operator overloading, no pattern matching, and on and on. Why are these features missing from the language? The official Go FAQ (https://go.dev/doc/faq) gives us some insight:

> *Why does Go not have feature X? Your favorite feature may be missing because it doesn't fit, because it affects compilation speed or clarity of design, or because it would make the fundamental system model too difficult.*

Judging the quality of a programming language via its number of features is probably not an accurate metric. At least, it's not an objective of Go. Instead, Go utilizes a few essential characteristics when adopting a language at scale for an organization. These include the following:

- *Stability*—Even though Go receives frequent updates (including improvements and security patches), it remains a stable language. Some may even consider this one of the best features of the language.
- *Expressivity*—We can define expressivity in a programming language by how naturally and intuitively we can write and read code. A reduced number of keywords and limited ways to solve common problems make Go an expressive language for large codebases.
- *Compilation*—As developers, what can be more exasperating than having to wait for a build to test our application? Targeting fast compilation times has always been a conscious goal for the language designers. This, in turn, enables productivity.

- *Safety*—Go is a strong, statically typed language. Hence, it has strict compile-time rules, which ensure the code is type-safe in most cases.

Go was built from the ground up with solid features such as outstanding concurrency primitives with goroutines and channels. There's not a strong need to rely on external libraries to build efficient concurrent applications. Observing how important concurrency is these days also demonstrates why Go is such a suitable language for the present and probably for the foreseeable future.

Some also consider Go a simple language. And, in a sense, this isn't necessarily wrong. For example, a newcomer can learn the language's main features in less than a day. So why read a book centered on the concept of mistakes if Go is simple?

1.2 Simple doesn't mean easy

There is a subtle difference between simple and easy. *Simple*, applied to a technology, means not complicated to learn or understand. However, *easy* means that we can achieve anything without much effort. Go is simple to learn but not necessarily easy to master.

Let's take concurrency, for example. In 2019, a study focusing on concurrency bugs was published: "Understanding Real-World Concurrency Bugs in Go."[1] This study was the first systematic analysis of concurrency bugs. It focused on multiple popular Go repositories such as Docker, gRPC, and Kubernetes. One of the most important takeaways from this study is that most of the blocking bugs are caused by inaccurate use of the message-passing paradigm via channels, despite the belief that message passing is easier to handle and less error-prone than sharing memory.

What should be an appropriate reaction to such a takeaway? Should we consider that the language designers were wrong about message passing? Should we reconsider how we deal with concurrency in our project? Of course not.

It's not a question of confronting message passing versus sharing memory and determining the winner. However, it's up to us as Go developers to thoroughly understand how to use concurrency, its implications on modern processors, when to favor one approach over the other, and how to avoid common traps. This example highlights that although a concept such as channels and goroutines can be simple to learn, it isn't an easy topic in practice.

This leitmotif—simple doesn't mean easy—can be generalized to many aspects of Go, not only concurrency. Hence, to be proficient Go developers, we must have a thorough understanding of many aspects of the language, which requires time, effort, and mistakes.

This book aims to help accelerate our journey toward proficiency by delving into 100 Go mistakes.

---

[1] T. Tu, X. Liu, et al., "Understanding Real-World Concurrency Bugs in Go," presented at ASPLOS 2019, April 13–17, 2019.

1.3   100 Go mistakes

Why should we read a book about common Go mistakes? Why not deepen our knowledge with an ordinary book that would dig into different topics?

In a 2011 article, neuroscientists proved that the best time for brain growth is when we're facing mistakes.[2] Haven't we all experienced the process of learning from a mistake and recalling that occasion after months or even years, when some context related to it? As presented in another article, by Janet Metcalfe, this happens because mistakes have a facilitative effect.[3] The main idea is that we can remember not only the error but also the context surrounding the mistake. This is one of the reasons why learning from mistakes is so efficient.

To strengthen this facilitative effect, this book accompanies each mistake as much as possible with real-world examples. This book isn't only about theory; it also helps us get better at avoiding mistakes and making more well-informed, conscious decisions because we now understand the rationale behind them.

> *Tell me and I forget. Teach me and I remember. Involve me and I learn.*
>
> —Unknown

This book presents seven main categories of mistakes. Overall, the mistakes can be classified as

- Bugs
- Needless complexity
- Weaker readability
- Suboptimal or unidiomatic organization
- Lack of API convenience
- Under-optimized code
- Lack of productivity

We introduce each mistake category next.

1.3.1   Bugs

The first type of mistake and probably the most obvious is software bugs. In 2020, a study conducted by Synopsys estimated the cost of software bugs in the U.S. alone to be over $2 trillion.[4]

Furthermore, bugs can also lead to tragic impacts. We can, for example, mention cases such as Therac-25, a radiation therapy machine produced by Atomic Energy of Canada Limited (AECL). Because of a race condition, the machine gave its patients

---

[2] J. S. Moser, H. S. Schroder, et al., "Mind Your Errors: Evidence for a Neural Mechanism Linking Growth Mindset to Adaptive Posterror Adjustments," *Psychological Science*, vol. 22, no. 12, pp. 1484–1489, Dec. 2011.

[3] J. Metcalfe, "Learning from Errors," *Annual Review of Psychology*, vol. 68, pp. 465–489, Jan. 2017.

[4] Synopsys, "The Cost of Poor Software Quality in the US: A 2020 Report." 2020. https://news.synopsys.com/ 2021-01-06-Synopsys-Sponsored-CISQ-Research-Estimates-Cost-of-Poor-Software-Quality-in-the-US-2-08 -Trillion-in-2020.

radiation doses that were hundreds of times greater than expected, leading to the death of three patients. Hence, software bugs aren't only about money. As developers, we should remember how impactful our jobs are.

This book covers plenty of cases that could lead to various software bugs, including data races, leaks, logic errors, and other defects. Although accurate tests should be a way to discover such bugs as early as possible, we may sometimes miss cases because of different factors such as time constraints or complexity. Therefore, as a Go developer, it's essential to make sure we avoid common bugs.

1.3.2   Needless complexity

The next category of mistakes is related to unnecessary complexity. A significant part of software complexity comes from the fact that, as developers, we strive to think about imaginary futures. Instead of solving concrete problems right now, it can be tempting to build evolutionary software that could tackle whatever future use case arises. However, this leads to more drawbacks than benefits in most cases because it can make a codebase more complex to understand and reason about.

Getting back to Go, we can think of plenty of use cases where developers might be tempted to design abstractions for future needs, such as interfaces or generics. This book discusses topics where we should remain careful not to harm a codebase with needless complexity.

1.3.3   Weaker readability

Another kind of mistake is to weaken readability. As Robert C. Martin wrote in his book *Clean Code: A Handbook of Agile Software Craftsmanship*, the ratio of time spent reading versus writing is well over 10 to 1.[5] Most of us started to program on solo projects where readability wasn't that important. However, today's software engineering is programming with a time dimension: making sure we can still work with and maintain an application months, years, or perhaps even decades later.

When programming in Go, we can make many mistakes that can harm readability. These mistakes may include nested code, data type representations, or not using named result parameters in some cases. Throughout this book, we will learn how to write readable code and care for future readers (including our future selves).

1.3.4   Suboptimal or unidiomatic organization

Be it while working on a new project or because we acquire inaccurate reflexes, another type of mistake is organizing our code and a project suboptimally and unidiomatically. Such issues can make a project harder to reason about and maintain. This book covers some of these common mistakes in Go. For example, we'll look at how to structure a project and deal with utility packages or init functions. All in all, looking at these mistakes should help us organize our code and projects more efficiently and idiomatically.

---

[5] R. C. Martin, *Clean Code: A Handbook of Agile Software Craftsmanship.* Prentice Hall, 2008.

1.3.5   *Lack of API convenience*

Making common mistakes that weaken how convenient an API is for our clients is another type of mistake. If an API isn't user-friendly, it will be less expressive and, hence, harder to understand and more error-prone.

We can think about many situations such as overusing any types, using the wrong creational pattern to deal with options, or blindly applying standard practices from object-oriented programming that affect the usability of our APIs. This book covers common mistakes that prevent us from exposing convenient APIs for our users.

1.3.6   *Under-optimized code*

Under-optimized code is another type of mistake made by developers. It can happen for various reasons, such as not understanding language features or even a lack of fundamental knowledge. Performance is one of the most obvious impacts of this mistake, but not the only one.

We can think about optimizing code for other goals, such as accuracy. For example, this book provides some common techniques to ensure that floating-point operations are accurate. Meanwhile, we will cover plenty of cases that can negatively impact performance code because of poorly parallelized executions, not knowing how to reduce allocations, or the impacts of data alignment, for example. We will tackle optimization via different prisms.

1.3.7   *Lack of productivity*

In most cases, what's the best language we can choose when working on a new project? The one we're the most productive with. Being comfortable with how a language works and exploiting it to get the best out of it is crucial to reach proficiency.

In this book, we will cover many cases and concrete examples that will help us to be more productive while working in Go. For instance, we'll look at writing efficient tests to ensure that our code works, relying on the standard library to be more effective, and getting the best out of the profiling tools and linters. Now, it's time to delve into those 100 common Go mistakes.

Summary

- Go is a modern programming language that enables developer productivity, which is crucial for most companies today.
- Go is simple to learn but not easy to master. This is why we need to deepen our knowledge to make the most effective use of the language.
- Learning via mistakes and concrete examples is a powerful way to be proficient in a language. This book will accelerate our path to proficiency by exploring 100 common mistakes.

Code and project organization

This chapter covers

- Organizing our code idiomatically
- Dealing efficiently with abstractions: interfaces and generics
- Best practices regarding how to structure a project

Organizing a Go codebase in a clean, idiomatic, and maintainable manner isn't an easy task. It requires experience and even mistakes to understand all the best practices related to code and project organization. What are the traps to avoid (for example, variable shadowing and nested code abuse)? How do we structure packages? When and where do we use interfaces or generics, init functions, and utility packages? In this chapter, we examine common organizational mistakes.

2.1 #1: Unintended variable shadowing

The *scope* of a variable refers to the places a variable can be referenced: in other words, the part of an application where a name binding is valid. In Go, a variable name declared in a block can be redeclared in an inner block. This principle, called *variable shadowing*, is prone to common mistakes.

The following example shows an unintended side effect because of a shadowed variable. It creates an HTTP client in two different ways, depending on the value of a tracing Boolean:

```
var client *http.Client          Declares a
if tracing {                     client variable
    client, err := createClientWithTracing()    Creates an HTTP client with tracing
    if err != nil {                              enabled. (The client variable is
        return err                               shadowed in this block.)
    }
    log.Println(client)
} else {
    client, err := createDefaultClient()    Creates a default HTTP client.
    if err != nil {                         (The client variable is also
        return err                          shadowed in this block.)
    }
    log.Println(client)
}
// Use client
```

In this example, we first declare a `client` variable. Then, we use the short variable declaration operator (`:=`) in both inner blocks to assign the result of the function call to the inner `client` variables—not the outer one. As a result, the outer variable is always `nil`.

> **NOTE** This code compiles because the inner `client` variables are used in the logging calls. If not, we would have compilation errors such as `client declared and not used`.

How can we ensure that a value is assigned to the original `client` variable? There are two different options.

The first option uses temporary variables in the inner blocks this way:

```
var client *http.Client
if tracing {
    c, err := createClientWithTracing()    Creates a temporary
    if err != nil {                        variable c
        return err
    }
    client = c        Assigns this temporary
} else {              variable to client
    // Same logic
}
```

Here, we assign the result to a temporary variable, c, whose scope is only within the `if` block. Then, we assign it back to the `client` variable. Meanwhile, we do the same for the `else` part.

The second option uses the assignment operator (`=`) in the inner blocks to directly assign the function results to the `client` variable. However, this requires creating an `error` variable because the assignment operator works only if a variable name has already been declared. For example:

```
var client *http.Client
var err error                    ⟵――| Declares an err variable
if tracing {
    client, err = createClientWithTracing()  ⟵―┐  Uses the assignment operator to
    if err != nil {                              │  assign the *http.Client returned
        return err                               │  to the client variable directly
    }
} else {
    // Same logic
}
```

Instead of assigning to a temporary variable first, we can directly assign the result to
`client`.

Both options are perfectly valid. The main difference between the two alternatives
is that we perform only one assignment in the second option, which may be considered easier to read. Also, with the second option, we can mutualize and implement
error handling outside the `if/else` statements, as this example shows:

```
if tracing {
    client, err = createClientWithTracing()
} else {
    client, err = createDefaultClient()
}
if err != nil {
    // Common error handling
}
```

Variable shadowing occurs when a variable name is redeclared in an inner block, but we
saw that this practice is prone to mistakes. Imposing a rule to forbid shadowed variables
depends on personal taste. For example, sometimes it can be convenient to reuse an
existing variable name like `err` for errors. Yet, in general, we should remain cautious
because we now know that we can face a scenario where the code compiles, but the variable that receives the value is not the one expected. Later in this chapter, we will also see
how to detect shadowed variables, which may help us spot possible bugs.

The following section shows why it is important to avoid abusing nested code.

2.2   #2: Unnecessary nested code

A mental model applied to software is an internal representation of a system's behavior. While programming, we need to maintain mental models (about overall code
interactions and function implementations, for example). Code is qualified as readable based on multiple criteria such as naming, consistency, formatting, and so forth.
Readable code requires less cognitive effort to maintain a mental model; hence, it is
easier to read and maintain.

A critical aspect of readability is the number of nested levels. Let's do an exercise.
Suppose that we are working on a new project and need to understand what the following `join` function does:

```
func join(s1, s2 string, max int) (string, error) {
    if s1 == "" {
```

```
            return "", errors.New("s1 is empty")
    } else {
        if s2 == "" {
            return "", errors.New("s2 is empty")
        } else {
            concat, err := concatenate(s1, s2)     ◁─┐  Calls a concatenate
            if err != nil {                           │  function to perform some
                return "", err                        │  specific concatenation
            } else {                                  │  but may return errors
                if len(concat) > max {
                    return concat[:max], nil
                } else {
                    return concat, nil
                }
            }
        }
    }
}

func concatenate(s1 string, s2 string) (string, error) {
    // ...
}
```

This `join` function concatenates two strings and returns a substring if the length is greater than `max`. Meanwhile, it handles checks on `s1` and `s2` and whether the call to `concatenate` returns an error.

From an implementation perspective, this function is correct. However, building a mental model encompassing all the different cases is probably not a straightforward task. Why? Because of the number of nested levels.

Now, let's try this exercise again with the same function but implemented differently:

```
func join(s1, s2 string, max int) (string, error) {
    if s1 == "" {
        return "", errors.New("s1 is empty")
    }
    if s2 == "" {
        return "", errors.New("s2 is empty")
    }
    concat, err := concatenate(s1, s2)
    if err != nil {
        return "", err
    }
    if len(concat) > max {
        return concat[:max], nil
    }
    return concat, nil
}

func concatenate(s1 string, s2 string) (string, error) {
    // ...
}
```

You probably noticed that building a mental model of this new version requires less cognitive load despite doing the same job as before. Here we maintain only two nested levels. As mentioned by Mat Ryer, a panelist on the *Go Time* podcast (https://medium.com/@matryer/line-of-sight-in-code-186dd7cdea88):

> *Align the happy path to the left; you should quickly be able to scan down one column to see the expected execution flow.*

It was difficult to distinguish the expected execution flow in the first version because of the nested if/else statements. Conversely, the second version requires scanning down one column to see the expected execution flow and down the second column to see how the edge cases are handled, as figure 2.1 shows.

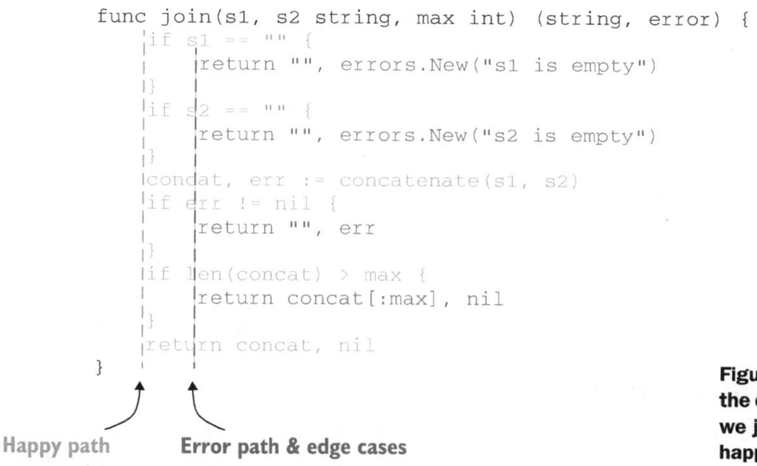

```
func join(s1, s2 string, max int) (string, error) {
    if s1 == "" {
        return "", errors.New("s1 is empty")
    }
    if s2 == "" {
        return "", errors.New("s2 is empty")
    }
    concat, err := concatenate(s1, s2)
    if err != nil {
        return "", err
    }
    if len(concat) > max {
        return concat[:max], nil
    }
    return concat, nil
}
```

Happy path   Error path & edge cases

Figure 2.1   To understand the expected execution flow, we just have to scan the happy path column.

In general, the more nested levels a function requires, the more complex it is to read and understand. Let's see some different applications of this rule to optimize our code for readability:

- When an if block returns, we should omit the else block in all cases. For example, we shouldn't write

```
if foo() {
    // ...
    return true
} else {
    // ...
}
```

Instead, we omit the else block like this:

```
if foo() {
    // ...
    return true
}
// ...
```

With this new version, the code living previously in the `else` block is moved to the top level, making it easier to read.

- We can also follow this logic with a non-happy path:

```
if s != "" {
    // ...
} else {
    return errors.New("empty string")
}
```

Here, an empty `s` represents the non-happy path. Hence, we should flip the condition like so:

```
if s == "" {
    return errors.New("empty string")        ◁──┐  Flips the if
}                                                │  condition
// ...
```

This new version is easier to read because it keeps the happy path on the left edge and reduces the number of blocks.

Writing readable code is an important challenge for every developer. Striving to reduce the number of nested blocks, aligning the happy path on the left, and returning as early as possible are concrete means to improve our code's readability.

In the next section, we discuss a common misuse in Go projects: init functions.

2.3   *#3: Misusing init functions*

Sometimes we misuse init functions in Go applications. The potential consequences are poor error management or a code flow that is harder to understand. Let's refresh our minds about what an init function is. Then, we will see when its usage is or isn't recommended.

2.3.1   *Concepts*

An init function is a function used to initialize the state of an application. It takes no arguments and returns no result (a `func()` function). When a package is initialized, all the constant and variable declarations in the package are evaluated. Then, the init functions are executed. Here is an example of initializing a `main` package:

```
package main

import "fmt"

var a = func() int {
    fmt.Println("var")        ◁──┤ Executed first
    return 0
}()

func init() {
    fmt.Println("init")       ◁──┤ Executed second
}
```

```
func main() {
    fmt.Println("main")    ◁—| Executed last
}
```

Running this example prints the following output:

```
var
init
main
```

An init function is executed when a package is initialized. In the following example, we define two packages, main and redis, where main depends on redis. First, main .go from the main package:

```
package main

import (
    "fmt"

    "redis"
)

func init() {
    // ...
}

func main() {
    err := redis.Store("foo", "bar")    ◁—| A dependency on
    // ...                                    the redis package
}
```

And then redis.go from the redis package:

```
package redis

// imports

func init() {
    // ...
}

func Store(key, value string) error {
    // ...
}
```

Because main depends on redis, the redis package's init function is executed first, followed by the init of the main package, and then the main function itself. Figure 2.2 shows this sequence.

We can define multiple init functions per package. When we do, the execution order of the init function inside the package is based on the source files' alphabetical order. For example, if a package contains an a.go file and a b.go file and both have an init function, the a.go init function is executed first.

Init functions example

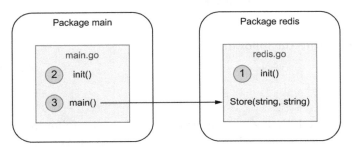

Figure 2.2 The init function of the redis package is executed first, then the init function of main, and finally the main function.

We shouldn't rely on the ordering of init functions within a package. Indeed, it can be dangerous as source files can be renamed, potentially impacting the execution order.

We can also define multiple init functions within the same source file. For example, this code is perfectly valid:

```go
package main

import "fmt"

func init() {                    First init function
    fmt.Println("init 1")
}

func init() {                    Second init function
    fmt.Println("init 2")
}

func main() {
}
```

The first init function executed is the first one in the source order. Here's the output:

```
init 1
init 2
```

We can also use init functions for side effects. In the next example, we define a main package that doesn't have a strong dependency on foo (for example, there's no direct use of a public function). However, the example requires the foo package to be initialized. We can do that by using the _ operator this way:

```go
package main

import (
    "fmt"

    _ "foo"              Imports foo for side effects
)

func main() {
    // ...
}
```

In this case, the `foo` package is initialized before `main`. Hence, the init functions of `foo` are executed.

Another aspect of an init function is that it can't be invoked directly, as in the following example:

```
package main

func init() {}

func main() {
    init()                    ◁─┤  Invalid reference
}
```

This code produces the following compilation error:

```
$ go build .
./main.go:6:2: undefined: init
```

Now that we've refreshed our minds about how init functions work, let's see when we should use or not use them. The following section sheds some light on this.

2.3.2   *When to use init functions*

First, let's look at an example where using an init function can be considered inappropriate: holding a database connection pool. In the `init` function in the example, we open a database using `sql.Open`. We make this database a global variable that other functions can later use:

```
var db *sql.DB

func init() {
    dataSourceName :=
        os.Getenv("MYSQL_DATA_SOURCE_NAME")    ◁─┤  Environment variable
    d, err := sql.Open("mysql", dataSourceName)
    if err != nil {
        log.Panic(err)
    }
    err = d.Ping()
    if err != nil {
        log.Panic(err)
    }                              ┌─  Assigns the DB connection
    db = d                    ◁───┘   to the global db variable
}
```

In this example, we open the database, check whether we can ping it, and then assign it to the global variable. What should we think about this implementation? Let's describe three main downsides.

First, error management in an init function is limited. Indeed, as an init function doesn't return an error, one of the only ways to signal an error is to panic, leading the application to be stopped. In our example, it might be OK to stop the application anyway if opening the database fails. However, it shouldn't necessarily be up to the package itself to decide whether to stop the application. Perhaps a caller might have preferred implementing a retry or using a fallback mechanism. In this case, opening the database within an init function prevents client packages from implementing their error-handling logic.

Another important downside is related to testing. If we add tests to this file, the init function will be executed before running the test cases, which isn't necessarily what we want (for example, if we add unit tests on a utility function that doesn't require this connection to be created). Therefore, the init function in this example complicates writing unit tests.

The last downside is that the example requires assigning the database connection pool to a global variable. Global variables have some severe drawbacks; for example:

- Any functions can alter global variables within the package.
- Unit tests can be more complicated because a function that depends on a global variable won't be isolated anymore.

In most cases, we should favor encapsulating a variable rather than keeping it global.

For these reasons, the previous initialization should probably be handled as part of a plain old function like so:

```
func createClient(dsn string) (*sql.DB, error) {      ◁─┐  Accepts a data source
    db, err := sql.Open("mysql", dsn)                      name and returns an
    if err != nil {                                        *sql.DB and an error
        return nil, err          ◁─┤ Returns an error
    }
    if err = db.Ping(); err != nil {
        return nil, err
    }
    return db, nil
}
```

Using this function, we tackled the main downsides discussed previously. Here's how:

- The responsibility of error handling is left up to the caller.
- It's possible to create an integration test to check that this function works.
- The connection pool is encapsulated within the function.

Is it necessary to avoid init functions at all costs? Not really. There are still use cases where init functions can be helpful. For example, the official Go blog (http://mng.bz/PW6w) uses an init function to set up the static HTTP configuration:

```
func init() {
    redirect := func(w http.ResponseWriter, r *http.Request) {
        http.Redirect(w, r, "/", http.StatusFound)
    }
    http.HandleFunc("/blog", redirect)
    http.HandleFunc("/blog/", redirect)

    static := http.FileServer(http.Dir("static"))
    http.Handle("/favicon.ico", static)
```

```
    http.Handle("/fonts.css", static)
    http.Handle("/fonts/", static)

    http.Handle("/lib/godoc/", http.StripPrefix("/lib/godoc/",
        http.HandlerFunc(staticHandler)))
}
```

In this example, the init function cannot fail (`http.HandleFunc` can panic, but only if the handler is `nil`, which isn't the case here). Meanwhile, there's no need to create any global variables, and the function will not impact possible unit tests. Therefore, this code snippet provides a good example of where init functions can be helpful. In summary, we saw that init functions can lead to some issues:

- They can limit error management.
- They can complicate how to implement tests (for example, an external dependency must be set up, which may not be necessary for the scope of unit tests).
- If the initialization requires us to set a state, that has to be done through global variables.

We should be cautious with init functions. They can be helpful in some situations, however, such as defining static configuration, as we saw in this section. Otherwise, and in most cases, we should handle initializations through ad hoc functions.

2.4   *#4: Overusing getters and setters*

In programming, data encapsulation refers to hiding the values or state of an object. Getters and setters are means to enable encapsulation by providing exported methods on top of unexported object fields.

In Go, there is no automatic support for getters and setters as we see in some languages. It is also considered neither mandatory nor idiomatic to use getters and setters to access struct fields. For example, the standard library implements structs in which some fields are accessible directly, such as the `time.Timer` struct:

```
timer := time.NewTimer(time.Second)
<-timer.C                              ⟵┤ C is a <-chan Time field
```

Although it's not recommended, we could even modify `C` directly (but we wouldn't receive events anymore). However, this example illustrates that the standard Go library doesn't enforce using getters and/or setters even when we shouldn't modify a field.

On the other hand, using getters and setters presents some advantages, including these:

- They encapsulate a behavior associated with getting or setting a field, allowing new functionality to be added later (for example, validating a field, returning a computed value, or wrapping the access to a field around a mutex).
- They hide the internal representation, giving us more flexibility in what we expose.

- They provide a debugging interception point for when the property changes at run time, making debugging easier.

If we fall into these cases or foresee a possible use case while guaranteeing forward compatibility, using getters and setters can bring some value. For example, if we use them with a field called `balance`, we should follow these naming conventions:

- The getter method should be named `Balance` (not `GetBalance`).
- The setter method should be named `SetBalance`.

Here's an example:

```
currentBalance := customer.Balance()    ⟵─┤ Getter
if currentBalance < 0 {
    customer.SetBalance(0)          ⟵─┤ Setter
}
```

In summary, we shouldn't overwhelm our code with getters and setters on structs if they don't bring any value. We should be pragmatic and strive to find the right balance between efficiency and following idioms that are sometimes considered indisputable in other programming paradigms.

Remember that Go is a unique language designed for many characteristics, including simplicity. However, if we find a need for getters and setters or, as mentioned, foresee a future need while guaranteeing forward compatibility, there's nothing wrong with using them.

Next, we will discuss the problem of overusing interfaces.

2.5   *#5: Interface pollution*

Interfaces are one of the cornerstones of the Go language when designing and structuring our code. However, like many tools or concepts, abusing them is generally not a good idea. Interface pollution is about overwhelming our code with unnecessary abstractions, making it harder to understand. It's a common mistake made by developers coming from another language with different habits. Before delving into the topic, let's refresh our minds about Go's interfaces. Then, we will see when it's appropriate to use interfaces and when it may be considered pollution.

2.5.1 *Concepts*

An interface provides a way to specify the behavior of an object. We use interfaces to create common abstractions that multiple objects can implement. What makes Go interfaces so different is that they are satisfied implicitly. There is no explicit keyword like `implements` to mark that an object X implements interface Y.

To understand what makes interfaces so powerful, we will dig into two popular ones from the standard library: `io.Reader` and `io.Writer`. The `io` package provides abstractions for I/O primitives. Among these abstractions, `io.Reader` relates to reading data from a data source and `io.Writer` to writing data to a target, as represented in figure 2.3.

io.Reader and io.Writer interfaces

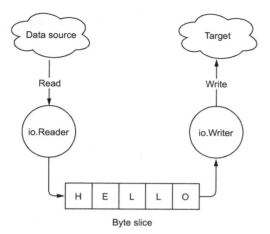

Figure 2.3 `io.Reader` reads from a data source and fills a byte slice, whereas `io.Writer` writes to a target from a byte slice.

The io.Reader contains a single Read method:

```
type Reader interface {
    Read(p []byte) (n int, err error)
}
```

Custom implementations of the io.Reader interface should accept a slice of bytes, filling it with its data and returning either the number of bytes read or an error.

On the other hand, io.Writer defines a single method, Write:

```
type Writer interface {
    Write(p []byte) (n int, err error)
}
```

Custom implementations of io.Writer should write the data coming from a slice to a target and return either the number of bytes written or an error. Therefore, both interfaces provide fundamental abstractions:

- io.Reader reads data from a source.
- io.Writer writes data to a target.

What is the rationale for having these two interfaces in the language? What is the point of creating these abstractions?

Let's assume we need to implement a function that should copy the content of one file to another. We could create a specific function that would take as input two *os.Files. Or, we can choose to create a more generic function using io.Reader and io.Writer abstractions:

```
func copySourceToDest(source io.Reader, dest io.Writer) error {
    // ...
}
```

This function would work with `*os.File` parameters (as `*os.File` implements both `io.Reader` and `io.Writer`) and any other type that would implement these interfaces. For example, we could create our own `io.Writer` that writes to a database, and the code would remain the same. It increases the genericity of the function; hence, its reusability.

Furthermore, writing a unit test for this function is easier because, instead of having to handle files, we can use the `strings` and `bytes` packages that provide helpful implementations:

```
func TestCopySourceToDest(t *testing.T) {
    const input = "foo"
    source := strings.NewReader(input)        ←─┤ Creates an io.Reader
    dest := bytes.NewBuffer(make([]byte, 0))  ←─┐ Creates an
                                                 │ io.Writer
    err := copySourceToDest(source, dest)     ←─┐ Calls copySourceToDest
    if err != nil {                              │ from a *strings.Reader
        t.FailNow()                              │ and a *bytes.Buffer
    }

    got := dest.String()
    if got != input {
        t.Errorf("expected: %s, got: %s", input, got)
    }
}
```

In the example, `source` is a `*strings.Reader`, whereas `dest` is a `*bytes.Buffer`. Here, we test the behavior of `copySourceToDest` without creating any files.

While designing interfaces, the granularity (how many methods the interface contains) is also something to keep in mind. A known proverb in Go (https://www.youtube.com/watch?v=PAAkCSZUG1c&t=318s) relates to how big an interface should be:

> *The bigger the interface, the weaker the abstraction.*
>
> —Rob Pike

Indeed, adding methods to an interface can decrease its level of reusability. `io.Reader` and `io.Writer` are powerful abstractions because they cannot get any simpler. Furthermore, we can also combine fine-grained interfaces to create higher-level abstractions. This is the case with `io.ReadWriter`, which combines the reader and writer behaviors:

```
type ReadWriter interface {
    Reader
    Writer
}
```

NOTE As Einstein said, "Everything should be made as simple as possible, but no simpler." Applied to interfaces, this denotes that finding the perfect granularity for an interface isn't necessarily a straightforward process.

Let's now discuss common cases where interfaces are recommended.

2.5.2 *When to use interfaces*

When should we create interfaces in Go? Let's look at three concrete use cases where interfaces are usually considered to bring value. Note that the goal isn't to be exhaustive because the more cases we add, the more they would depend on the context. However, these three cases should give us a general idea:

- Common behavior
- Decoupling
- Restricting behavior

COMMON BEHAVIOR

The first option we will discuss is to use interfaces when multiple types implement a common behavior. In such a case, we can factor out the behavior inside an interface. If we look at the standard library, we can find many examples of such a use case. For example, sorting a collection can be factored out via three methods:

- Retrieving the number of elements in the collection
- Reporting whether one element must be sorted before another
- Swapping two elements

Hence, the following interface was added to the `sort` package:

```
type Interface interface {
    Len() int                    ◁─┤ Number of elements
    Less(i, j int) bool                          ◁─┤ Checks two elements
    Swap(i, j int)   ◁─┤ Swaps two elements
}
```

This interface has a strong potential for reusability because it encompasses the common behavior to sort any collection that is index-based.

Throughout the `sort` package, we can find dozens of implementations. If at some point we compute a collection of integers, for example, and we want to sort it, are we necessarily interested in the implementation type? Is it important whether the sorting algorithm is a merge sort or a quicksort? In many cases, we don't care. Hence, the sorting behavior can be abstracted, and we can depend on the `sort.Interface`.

Finding the right abstraction to factor out a behavior can also bring many benefits. For example, the `sort` package provides utility functions that also rely on `sort.Interface`, such as checking whether a collection is already sorted. For instance,

```
func IsSorted(data Interface) bool {
    n := data.Len()
    for i := n - 1; i > 0; i-- {
        if data.Less(i, i-1) {
            return false
        }
    }
    return true
}
```

Because `sort.Interface` is the right level of abstraction, it makes it highly valuable.

Let's now see another main use case when using interfaces.

DECOUPLING

Another important use case is about decoupling our code from an implementation. If we rely on an abstraction instead of a concrete implementation, the implementation itself can be replaced with another without even having to change our code. This is the Liskov Substitution Principle (the *L* in Robert C. Martin's SOLID design principles).

One benefit of decoupling can be related to unit testing. Let's assume we want to implement a `CreateNewCustomer` method that creates a new customer and stores it. We decide to rely on the concrete implementation directly (let's say a `mysql.Store` struct):

```
type CustomerService struct {
    store mysql.Store          ◁─── Depends on the concrete
}                                    implementation

func (cs CustomerService) CreateNewCustomer(id string) error {
    customer := Customer{id: id}
    return cs.store.StoreCustomer(customer)
}
```

Now, what if we want to test this method? Because `customerService` relies on the actual implementation to store a `Customer`, we are obliged to test it through integration tests, which requires spinning up a MySQL instance (unless we use an alternative technique such as `go-sqlmock`, but this isn't the scope of this section). Although integration tests are helpful, that's not always what we want to do. To give us more flexibility, we should decouple `CustomerService` from the actual implementation, which can be done via an interface like so:

```
type customerStorer interface {       ◁─── Creates a storage
    StoreCustomer(Customer) error            abstraction
}

type CustomerService struct {
    storer customerStorer          ◁─── Decouples CustomerService from
}                                        the actual implementation

func (cs CustomerService) CreateNewCustomer(id string) error {
    customer := Customer{id: id}
    return cs.storer.StoreCustomer(customer)
}
```

Because storing a customer is now done via an interface, this gives us more flexibility in how we want to test the method. For instance, we can

- Use the concrete implementation via integration tests
- Use a mock (or any kind of test double) via unit tests
- Or both

Let's now discuss another use case: to restrict a behavior.

RESTRICTING BEHAVIOR

The last use case we will discuss can be pretty counterintuitive at first sight. It's about restricting a type to a specific behavior. Let's imagine we implement a custom configuration package to deal with dynamic configuration. We create a specific container for int configurations via an `IntConfig` struct that also exposes two methods: `Get` and `Set`. Here's how that code would look:

```
type IntConfig struct {
    // ...
}

func (c *IntConfig) Get() int {
    // Retrieve configuration
}

func (c *IntConfig) Set(value int) {
    // Update configuration
}
```

Now, suppose we receive an `IntConfig` that holds some specific configuration, such as a threshold. Yet, in our code, we are only interested in retrieving the configuration value, and we want to prevent updating it. How can we enforce that, semantically, this configuration is read-only, if we don't want to change our configuration package? By creating an abstraction that restricts the behavior to retrieving only a config value:

```
type intConfigGetter interface {
    Get() int
}
```

Then, in our code, we can rely on `intConfigGetter` instead of the concrete implementation:

```
type Foo struct {
    threshold intConfigGetter
}

func NewFoo(threshold intConfigGetter) Foo {      ◁──┐ Injects the
    return Foo{threshold: threshold}                 │ configuration getter
}

func (f Foo) Bar()  {
    threshold := f.threshold.Get()      ◁──┐ Reads the
    // ...                                  │ configuration
}
```

In this example, the configuration getter is injected into the `NewFoo` factory method. It doesn't impact a client of this function because it can still pass an `IntConfig` struct as it implements `intConfigGetter`. Then, we can only read the configuration in the `Bar` method, not modify it. Therefore, we can also use interfaces to restrict a type to a specific behavior for various reasons, such as semantics enforcement.

In this section, we saw three potential use cases where interfaces are generally considered as bringing value: factoring out a common behavior, creating some decoupling, and restricting a type to a certain behavior. Again, this list isn't exhaustive, but it should give us a general understanding of when interfaces are helpful in Go.

Now, let's finish this section and discuss the problems with interface pollution.

2.5.3 *Interface pollution*

It's fairly common to see interfaces being overused in Go projects. Perhaps the developer's background was C# or Java, and they found it natural to create interfaces before concrete types. However, this isn't how things should work in Go.

As we discussed, interfaces are made to create abstractions. And the main caveat when programming meets abstractions is remembering that abstractions *should be discovered, not created*. What does this mean? It means we shouldn't start creating abstractions in our code if there is no immediate reason to do so. We shouldn't design with interfaces but wait for a concrete need. Said differently, we should create an interface when we need it, not when we foresee that we could need it.

What's the main problem if we overuse interfaces? The answer is that they make the code flow more complex. Adding a useless level of indirection doesn't bring any value; it creates a worthless abstraction making the code more difficult to read, understand, and reason about. If we don't have a strong reason for adding an interface and it's unclear how an interface makes a code better, we should challenge this interface's purpose. Why not call the implementation directly?

> **NOTE** We may also experience performance overhead when calling a method through an interface. It requires a lookup in a hash table's data structure to find the concrete type an interface points to. But this isn't an issue in many contexts as the overhead is minimal.

In summary, we should be cautious when creating abstractions in our code—abstractions should be discovered, not created. It's common for us, software developers, to overengineer our code by trying to guess what the perfect level of abstraction is, based on what we think we might need later. This process should be avoided because, in most cases, it pollutes our code with unnecessary abstractions, making it more complex to read.

> *Don't design with interfaces, discover them.*
>
> —Rob Pike

Let's not try to solve a problem abstractly but solve what has to be solved now. Last, but not least, if it's unclear how an interface makes the code better, we should probably consider removing it to make our code simpler.

The following section continues with this thread and discusses a common interface mistake: creating interfaces on the producer side.

2.6 *#6: Interface on the producer side*

We saw in the previous section when interfaces are considered valuable. But Go developers often misunderstand one question: where should an interface live?

Before delving into this topic, let's make sure the terms we use throughout this section are clear:

- *Producer side*—An interface defined in the same package as the concrete implementation (see figure 2.4).
- *Consumer side*—An interface defined in an external package where it's used (see figure 2.5).

It's common to see developers creating interfaces on the producer side, alongside the concrete implementation. This design is perhaps a habit from developers having a C# or a Java background. But in Go, in most cases this is not what we should do.

Let's discuss the following example. Here, we create a specific package to store and retrieve customer data. Meanwhile,

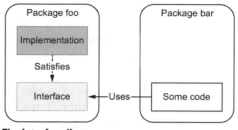

The interface lives on the producer side.

Figure 2.4   The interface is defined alongside the concrete implementation.

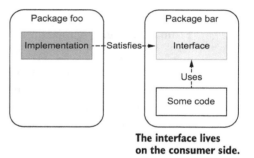

The interface lives on the consumer side.

Figure 2.5   The interface is defined where it's used.

still in the same package, we decide that all the calls have to go through the following interface:

```
package store

type CustomerStorage interface {
    StoreCustomer(customer Customer) error
    GetCustomer(id string) (Customer, error)
    UpdateCustomer(customer Customer) error
    GetAllCustomers() ([]Customer, error)
    GetCustomersWithoutContract() ([]Customer, error)
    GetCustomersWithNegativeBalance() ([]Customer, error)
}
```

We might think we have some excellent reasons to create and expose this interface on the producer side. Perhaps it's a good way to decouple the client code from the actual implementation. Or, perhaps we can foresee that it will help clients in creating test doubles. Whatever the reason, this isn't a best practice in Go.

As mentioned, interfaces are satisfied implicitly in Go, which tends to be a game-changer compared to languages with an explicit implementation. In most cases, the approach to follow is similar to what we described in the previous section: *abstractions should be discovered, not created.* This means that it's not up to the producer to force a given abstraction for all the clients. Instead, it's up to the client to decide whether it needs some form of abstraction and then determine the best abstraction level for its needs.

In the previous example, perhaps one client won't be interested in decoupling its code. Maybe another client wants to decouple its code but is only interested in the `GetAllCustomers` method. In this case, this client can create an interface with a single method, referencing the `Customer` struct from the external package:

```
package client

type customersGetter interface {
    GetAllCustomers() ([]store.Customer, error)
}
```

From a package organization, figure 2.6 shows the result. A couple of things to note:

- Because the `customersGetter` interface is only used in the `client` package, it can remain unexported.
- Visually, in the figure, it looks like circular dependencies. However, there's no dependency from `store` to `client` because the interface is satisfied implicitly. This is why such an approach isn't always possible in languages with an explicit implementation.

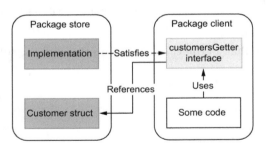

Figure 2.6   The `client` package defines the abstraction it needs by creating its own interface.

The main point is that the `client` package can now define the most accurate abstraction for its need (here, only one method). It relates to the concept of the Interface-Segregation Principle (the *I* in SOLID), which states that no client should be forced to depend on methods it doesn't use. Therefore, in this case, the best approach is to expose the concrete implementation on the producer side and let the client decide how to use it and whether an abstraction is needed.

For the sake of completeness, let's mention that this approach—interfaces on the producer side—is sometimes used in the standard library. For example, the `encoding` package defines interfaces implemented by other subpackages such as `encoding/json` or `encoding/binary`. Is the `encoding` package wrong about this? Definitely not. In this case, the abstractions defined in the `encoding` package are used across the standard library, and the language designers knew that creating these abstractions up front was valuable. We are back to the discussion in the previous section: don't create an abstraction if you think it might be helpful in an imaginary future or, at least, if you can't prove this abstraction is valid.

An interface should live on the consumer side in most cases. However, in particular contexts (for example, when we know—not foresee—that an abstraction will be helpful for consumers), we may want to have it on the producer side. If we do, we should strive to keep it as minimal as possible, increasing its reusability potential and making it more easily composable.

Let's continue the discussion about interfaces in the context of function signatures.

2.7   #7: Returning interfaces

While designing a function signature, we may have to return either an interface or a concrete implementation. Let's understand why returning an interface is, in many cases, considered a bad practice in Go.

We just presented why interfaces live, in general, on the consumer side. Figure 2.7 shows what would happen dependency-wise if a function returns an interface instead of a struct. We will see that it leads to issues.

We will consider two packages:

- `client`, which contains a `Store` interface
- `store`, which contains an implementation of `Store`

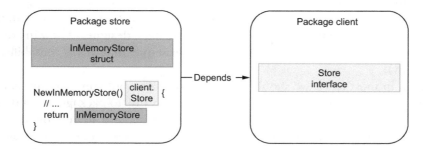

Figure 2.7   There's a dependency from the `store` package to the `client` package.

In the `store` package, we define an `InMemoryStore` struct that implements the `Store` interface. Meanwhile, we create a `NewInMemoryStore` function to return a `Store` interface. There's a dependency from the implementation package to the client package in this design, and that may already sound a bit odd.

For example, the `client` package can't call the `NewInMemoryStore` function anymore; otherwise, there would be a cyclic dependency. A possible solution could be to call this function from another package and to inject a `Store` implementation to client. However, being obliged to do that means that the design should be challenged.

Furthermore, what happens if another client uses the `InMemoryStore` struct? In that case, perhaps we would like to move the `Store` interface to another package, or back to the implementation package—but we discussed why, in most cases, this isn't a best practice. It looks like a code smell.

Hence, in general, returning an interface restricts flexibility because we force all the clients to use one particular type of abstraction. In most cases, we can get inspiration from Postel's law (https://datatracker.ietf.org/doc/html/rfc761):

> *Be conservative in what you do, be liberal in what you accept from others.*
>
> —Transmission Control Protocol

If we apply this idiom to Go, it means

- Returning structs instead of interfaces
- Accepting interfaces if possible

Of course, there are some exceptions. As software engineers, we are familiar with the fact that rules are never true 100% of the time. The most relevant one concerns the `error` type, an interface returned by many functions. We can also examine another exception in the standard library with the io package:

```
func LimitReader(r Reader, n int64) Reader {
    return &LimitedReader{r, n}
}
```

Here, the function returns an exported struct, `io.LimitedReader`. However, the function signature is an interface, `io.Reader`. What's the rationale for breaking the rule we've discussed so far? The `io.Reader` is an up-front abstraction. It's not one defined by clients, but it's one that is forced because the language designers knew in advance that this level of abstraction would be helpful (for example, in terms of reusability and composability).

All in all, in most cases, we shouldn't return interfaces but concrete implementations. Otherwise, it can make our design more complex due to package dependencies and can restrict flexibility because all the clients would have to rely on the same abstraction. Again, the conclusion is similar to the previous sections: if we know (not foresee) that an abstraction will be helpful for clients, we can consider returning an interface. Otherwise, we shouldn't force abstractions; they should be discovered by clients. If a client needs to abstract an implementation for whatever reason, it can still do that on the client's side.

In the next section, we will discuss a common mistake related to using any.

2.8 *#8: any says nothing*

In Go, an interface type that specifies zero methods is known as the empty interface, `interface{}`. With Go 1.18, the predeclared type any became an alias for an empty interface; hence, all the `interface{}` occurrences can be replaced by any. In many cases, any can be considered an overgeneralization; and as mentioned by Rob Pike, it doesn't convey anything (https://www.youtube.com/watch?v=PAAkCSZUG1c&t=7m 36s). Let's first remind ourselves of the core concepts, and then we can discuss the potential problems.

An any type can hold any value type:

```
func main() {
    var i any

    i = 42          ⟵——| An int
    i = "foo"                 ⟵——| A string
    i = struct {      ⟵——| A struct
        s string
    }{
        s: "bar",
    }
    i = f          ⟵——| A function

    _ = i              ⟵——| Assignment to the blank
}                                    identifier so that the
func f() {}                          example compiles
```

In assigning a value to an any type, we lose all type information, which requires a type assertion to get anything useful out of the i variable, as in the previous example. Let's look at another example, where using any isn't accurate. In the following, we implement a Store struct and the skeleton of two methods, Get and Set. We use these methods to store the different struct types, Customer and Contract:

```
package store

type Customer struct{
    // Some fields
}
type Contract struct{
    // Some fields
}

type Store struct{}

func (s *Store) Get(id string) (any, error) {      ⟵——| Returns any
    // ...
}

func (s *Store) Set(id string, v any) error {      ⟵——| Accepts any
    // ...
}
```

Although there is nothing wrong with Store compilation-wise, we should take a minute to think about the method signatures. Because we accept and return any arguments, the methods lack expressiveness. If future developers need to use the Store struct, they will probably have to dig into the documentation or read the code to understand how to use these methods. Hence, accepting or returning an any type doesn't convey meaningful information. Also, because there is no safeguard at compile time, nothing prevents a caller from calling these methods with whatever data type, such as an int:

```
s := store.Store{}
s.Set("foo", 42)
```

By using any, we lose some of the benefits of Go as a statically typed language. Instead, we should avoid any types and make our signatures explicit as much as possible. Regarding our example, this could mean duplicating the Get and Set methods per type:

```
func (s *Store) GetContract(id string) (Contract, error) {
    // ...
}

func (s *Store) SetContract(id string, contract Contract) error {
    // ...
}

func (s *Store) GetCustomer(id string) (Customer, error) {
    // ...
}

func (s *Store) SetCustomer(id string, customer Customer) error {
    // ...
}
```

In this version, the methods are expressive, reducing the risk of incomprehension. Having more methods isn't necessarily a problem because clients can also create their own abstraction using an interface. For example, if a client is interested only in the Contract methods, it could write something like this:

```
type ContractStorer interface {
    GetContract(id string) (store.Contract, error)
    SetContract(id string, contract store.Contract) error
}
```

What are the cases when any is helpful? Let's take a look at the standard library and see two examples where functions or methods accept any arguments. The first example is in the encoding/json package. Because we can marshal any type, the Marshal function accepts an any argument:

```
func Marshal(v any) ([]byte, error) {
    // ...
}
```

Another example is in the database/sql package. If the query is parameterized (for example, SELECT * FROM FOO WHERE id = ?), the parameters could be any kind. Hence, it also uses any arguments:

```
func (c *Conn) QueryContext(ctx context.Context, query string,
    args ...any) (*Rows, error) {
```

```
    // ...
}
```

In summary, any can be helpful if there is a genuine need for accepting or returning any possible type (for instance, when it comes to marshaling or formatting). In general, we should avoid overgeneralizing the code we write at all costs. Perhaps a little bit of duplicated code might occasionally be better if it improves other aspects such as code expressiveness.

Next, we will discuss another type of abstraction: generics.

2.9 #9: Being confused about when to use generics

Go 1.18 adds generics to the language. In a nutshell, this allows writing code with types that can be specified later and instantiated when needed. However, it can be confusing about when to use generics and when not to. Throughout this section, we will describe the concept of generics in Go and then look at common uses and misuses.

2.9.1 Concepts

Consider the following function that extracts all the keys from a map[string]int type:

```
func getKeys(m map[string]int) []string {
    var keys []string
    for k := range m {
        keys = append(keys, k)
    }
    return keys
}
```

What if we want to use a similar feature for another map type such as a map[int]string? Before generics, Go developers had a few options: using code generation, reflection, or duplicating code. For example, we could write two functions, one for each map type, or even try to extend getKeys to accept different map types:

```
func getKeys(m any) ([]any, error) {          ◁──┐ Accepts and returns
    switch t := m.(type) {                         any arguments
    default:
        return nil, fmt.Errorf("unknown type: %T", t)   ◁──┐ Handles run-time
    case map[string]int:                                      errors if a type isn't
        var keys []any                                        implemented yet
        for k := range t {
            keys = append(keys, k)
        }
        return keys, nil
    case map[int]string:
        // Copy the extraction logic
    }
}
```

With this example, we start to notice a few issues. First, it increases boilerplate code. Indeed, when we want to add a case, it requires duplicating the range loop. Meanwhile, the function now accepts an any type, which means we lose some of the benefits of Go as a typed language. Indeed, checking whether a type is supported is done at run time instead of compile time. Hence, we also need to return an error if the provided type is unknown. Finally, because the key type can be either int or string, we are obliged to return a slice of any type to factor out key types. This approach increases the effort on the caller side because the client may also need to perform a type check of the keys or an extra conversion. Thanks to generics, we can now refactor this code using type parameters.

Type parameters are generic types that we can use with functions and types. For example, the following function accepts a type parameter:

```
func foo[T any](t T) {          ◁─┐  T is a type
    // ...                          │  parameter.
}
```

When calling foo, we pass a type argument of any type. Supplying a type argument is called *instantiation,* and the work is done at compile time. This keeps type safety as part of the core language features and avoids run-time overhead.

Let's get back to the getKeys function and use type parameters to write a generic version that would accept any kind of map:

```
func getKeys[K comparable, V any](m map[K]V) []K {   ◁─┐  The keys are comparable,
    var keys []K              ◁─┐  Creates the            │  whereas values are of the
    for k := range m {           │  keys slice            │  any type.
        keys = append(keys, k)
    }
    return keys
}
```

To handle the map, we define two kinds of type parameters. First, the values can be of the any type: V any. However, in Go, the map keys can't be of the any type. For example, we cannot use slices:

```
var m map[[]byte]int
```

This code leads to a compilation error: invalid map key type []byte. Therefore, instead of accepting any key type, we are obliged to restrict type arguments so that the key type meets specific requirements. Here, the requirement is that the key type must be comparable (we can use == or !=). Hence, we defined K as comparable instead of any.

Restricting type arguments to match specific requirements is called a *constraint.* A constraint is an interface type that can contain

- A set of behaviors (methods)
- Arbitrary types

Let's check out a concrete example for the latter. Imagine we don't want to accept any comparable type for the map key type. For instance, we want to restrict it to either int or string types. We can define a custom constraint this way:

```
type customConstraint interface {
    ~int | ~string                    ◁─┐  Defines a custom type that
}                                        │  restricts types to int and string

func getKeys[K customConstraint,       ◁─┐  Changes the type parameter K
        V any](m map[K]V) []K {           │  to be a customConstraint type
    // Same implementation
}
```

First, we define a `customConstraint` interface to restrict the types to be either `int` or `string` using the union operator `|` (we will discuss the use of `~` a bit later). `K` is now a `customConstraint` instead of a `comparable` as before.

The signature of `getKeys` enforces that we can call it with a map of any value type, but the key type has to be an `int` or a `string`—for example, on the caller side:

```
m = map[string]int{
    "one":   1,
    "two":   2,
    "three": 3,
}
keys := getKeys(m)
```

Note that Go can infer that `getKeys` is called with a `string` type argument. The previous call is equivalent to this:

```
keys := getKeys[string](m)
```

~int vs. int

What's the difference between a constraint using `~int` or one using `int`? Using `int` restricts it to that type, whereas `~int` restricts all the types whose underlying type is an `int`. To illustrate, let's imagine a constraint where we would like to restrict a type to any `int` type implementing the `String() string` method:

```
type customConstraint interface {
    ~int
    String() string
}
```

Using this constraint restricts type arguments to custom types. For example,

```
type customInt int

func (i customInt) String() string {
    return strconv.Itoa(int(i))
}
```

Because `customInt` is an `int` and implements the `String() string` method, the `customInt` type satisfies the defined constraint. However, if we change the constraint to contain an `int` instead of an `~int`, using `customInt` leads to a compilation error because the `int` type doesn't implement `String() string`.

So far, we have discussed examples using generics for functions. However, we can also use generics with data structures. For example, we can create a linked list containing values of any type. For this, we will write an `Add` method to append a node:

```
type Node[T any] struct {          Uses a type
    Val   T                        parameter
    next *Node[T]
}

func (n *Node[T]) Add(next *Node[T]) {     Instantiates a
    n.next = next                          type receiver
}
```

In the example, we use type parameters to define `T` and use both fields in `Node`. Regarding the method, the receiver is instantiated. Indeed, because `Node` is generic, it has to follow the defined type parameter as well.

One last thing to note about type parameters is that they can't be used with method arguments, only with function arguments or method receivers. For example, the following method won't compile:

```
type Foo struct {}

func (Foo) bar[T any](t T) {}

./main.go:29:15: methods cannot have type parameters
```

If we want to use generics with methods, it's the receiver that needs to be a type parameter.

Now, let's examine concrete cases where we should and shouldn't use generics.

2.9.2   *Common uses and misuses*

When are generics useful? Let's discuss a few common uses where generics are recommended:

- *Data structures*—We can use generics to factor out the element type if we implement a binary tree, a linked list, or a heap, for example.
- *Functions working with slices, maps, and channels of any type*—A function to merge two channels would work with any channel type, for example. Hence, we could use type parameters to factor out the channel type:

```
func merge[T any](ch1, ch2 <-chan T) <-chan T {
    // ...
}
```

- *Factoring out behaviors instead of types*—The `sort` package, for example, contains a `sort.Interface` interface with three methods:

```
type Interface interface {
    Len() int
    Less(i, j int) bool
    Swap(i, j int)
}
```

This interface is used by different functions such as sort.Ints or sort
.Float64s. Using type parameters, we could factor out the sorting behavior
(for example, by defining a struct holding a slice and a comparison function):

```
type SliceFn[T any] struct {          ◁───┤ Uses a type parameter
    S        []T
    Compare func(T, T) bool     ◁──┐ Compares two
}                                  └ T elements

func (s SliceFn[T]) Len() int           { return len(s.S) }
func (s SliceFn[T]) Less(i, j int) bool { return s.Compare(s.S[i], s.S[j]) }
func (s SliceFn[T]) Swap(i, j int)      { s.S[i], s.S[j] = s.S[j], s.S[i] }
```

Then, because the SliceFn struct implements sort.Interface, we can sort the
provided slice using the sort.Sort(sort.Interface) function:

```
s := SliceFn[int]{
    S: []int{3, 2, 1},
    Compare: func(a, b int) bool {
        return a < b
    },
}
sort.Sort(s)
fmt.Println(s.S)

[1 2 3]
```

In this example, factoring out a behavior allows us to avoid creating one function per type.

Conversely, when is it recommended that we not use generics?

- *When calling a method of the type argument*—Consider a function that receives an
  io.Writer and calls the Write method, for example:

```
func foo[T io.Writer](w T) {
    b := getBytes()
    _, _ = w.Write(b)
}
```

In this case, using generics won't bring any value to our code whatsoever. We
should make the w argument an io.Writer directly.

- *When it makes our code more complex*—Generics are never mandatory, and as Go
  developers, we have lived without them for more than a decade. If we're writing
  generic functions or structures and we figure out that it doesn't make our code
  clearer, we should probably reconsider our decision for that particular use case.

Although generics can be helpful in particular conditions, we should be cautious
about when to use them and when not to use them. In general, if we want to answer
when not to use generics, we can find similarities with when not to use interfaces.
Indeed, generics introduce a form of abstraction, and we have to remember that
unnecessary abstractions introduce complexity.

Again, let's not pollute our code with needless abstractions, and let's focus on solving concrete problems for now. This means that we shouldn't use type parameters prematurely. Let's wait until we are about to write boilerplate code to consider using generics.

In the following section, we will discuss the possible problems while using type embedding.

2.10 #10: Not being aware of the possible problems with type embedding

When creating a struct, Go offers the option to embed types. But this can sometimes lead to unexpected behaviors if we don't understand all the implications of type embedding. Throughout this section, we look at how to embed types, what these bring, and the possible issues.

In Go, a struct field is called *embedded* if it's declared without a name. For example,

```
type Foo struct {
    Bar            ◁──┐ Embedded
}                     │ field

type Bar struct {
    Baz int
}
```

In the Foo struct, the Bar type is declared without an associated name; hence, it's an embedded field.

We use embedding to *promote* the fields and methods of an embedded type. Because Bar contains a Baz field, this field is promoted to Foo (see figure 2.8). Therefore, Baz becomes available from Foo:

```
foo := Foo{}
foo.Baz = 42
```

Note that Baz is available from two different paths: either from the promoted one using Foo.Baz or from the nominal one via Bar, Foo.Bar.Baz. Both relate to the same field.

```
Foo struct {                 Bar struct {
  Bar                          Baz int
  [Baz int]  ◁---- Promote ---- }
}
```

Figure 2.8 baz is promoted, hence accessible directly from s.

Interfaces and embedding

Embedding is also used within interfaces to compose an interface with others. In the following example, io.ReadWriter is composed of an io.Reader and an io.Writer:

```
type ReadWriter interface {
    Reader
    Writer
}
```

But the scope of this section is only related to embedded fields in structs.

Now that we've reminded ourselves what embedded types are, let's look at an example of a wrong usage. In the following, we implement a struct that holds some in-memory data, and we want to protect it against concurrent accesses using a mutex:

```
type InMem struct {
    sync.Mutex        ←┐  Embedded
    m map[string]int   │  field
}

func New() *InMem {
    return &InMem{m: make(map[string]int)}
}
```

We decided to make the map unexported so that clients can't interact with it directly but only via exported methods. Meanwhile, the mutex field is embedded. Therefore, we can implement a Get method this way:

```
func (i *InMem) Get(key string) (int, bool) {    ┐ Accesses the Lock
    i.Lock()                                   ←─┘ method directly
    v, contains := i.m[key]
    i.Unlock()              ←┐ The same goes for the
    return v, contains       │ Unlock method.
}
```

Because the mutex is embedded, we can directly access the Lock and Unlock methods from the i receiver.

We mentioned that such an example is a wrong usage of type embedding. What's the reason for this? Since sync.Mutex is an embedded type, the Lock and Unlock methods will be promoted. Therefore, both methods become visible to external clients using InMem:

```
m := inmem.New()
m.Lock() // ??
```

This promotion is probably not desired. A mutex is, in most cases, something that we want to encapsulate within a struct and make invisible to external clients. Therefore, we shouldn't make it an embedded field in this case:

```
type InMem struct {
    mu sync.Mutex      ←┐ Specifies that the sync.Mutex
    m map[string]int    │ field is not embedded
}
```

Because the mutex isn't embedded and is unexported, it can't be accessed from external clients. Let's now look at another example, but this time where embedding can be considered a correct approach.

We want to write a custom logger that contains an io.WriteCloser and exposes two methods, Write and Close. If io.WriteCloser wasn't embedded, we would need to write it like so:

```go
type Logger struct {
    writeCloser io.WriteCloser
}

func (l Logger) Write(p []byte) (int, error) {
    return l.writeCloser.Write(p)          ◁──┐ Forwards the call
}                                             │ to writeCloser

func (l Logger) Close() error {
    return l.writeCloser.Close()           ◁──┐ Forwards the call
}                                             │ to writeCloser

func main() {
    l := Logger{writeCloser: os.Stdout}
    _, _ = l.Write([]byte("foo"))
    _ = l.Close()
}
```

Logger would have to provide both a Write and a Close method that would *only* forward the call to io.WriteCloser. However, if the field now becomes embedded, we can remove these forwarding methods:

```go
type Logger struct {
    io.WriteCloser          ◁──┐ Makes io.Writer
}                              │ embedded

func main() {
    l := Logger{WriteCloser: os.Stdout}
    _, _ = l.Write([]byte("foo"))
    _ = l.Close()
}
```

It remains the same for clients with two exported Write and Close methods. But the example prevents implementing these additional methods simply to forward a call. Also, as Write and Close are promoted, it means that Logger satisfies the io.WriteCloser interface.

Embedding vs. OOP subclassing

Differentiating embedding from OOP subclassing can sometimes be confusing. The main difference is related to the identity of the receiver of a method. Let's look at the following figure. The left-hand side represents a type X being embedded in Y, whereas on the right-hand side, Y extends X.

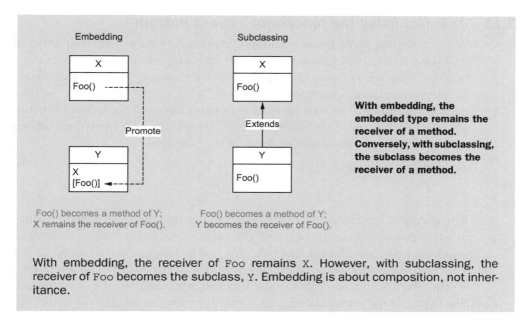

With embedding, the receiver of Foo remains X. However, with subclassing, the receiver of Foo becomes the subclass, Y. Embedding is about composition, not inheritance.

What should we conclude about type embedding? First, let's note that it's rarely a necessity, and it means that whatever the use case, we can probably solve it as well without type embedding. Type embedding is mainly used for convenience: in most cases, to promote behaviors.

If we decide to use type embedding, we need to keep two main constraints in mind:

- It shouldn't be used solely as some syntactic sugar to simplify accessing a field (such as `Foo.Baz()` instead of `Foo.Bar.Baz()`). If this is the only rationale, let's not embed the inner type and use a field instead.

- It shouldn't promote data (fields) or a behavior (methods) we want to hide from the outside: for example, if it allows clients to access a locking behavior that should remain private to the struct.

NOTE   Some may also argue that using type embedding could lead to extra efforts in terms of maintenance in the context of exported structs. Indeed, embedding a type inside an exported struct means remaining cautious when this type evolves. For example, if we add a new method to the inner type, we should ensure it doesn't break the latter constraint. Hence, to avoid this extra effort, teams can also prevent type embedding in public structs.

Using type embedding consciously by keeping these constraints in mind can help avoid boilerplate code with additional forwarding methods. However, let's make sure we don't do it solely for cosmetics and not promote elements that should remain hidden.

In the next section, we'll discuss common patterns to deal with optional configurations.

2.11   *#11: Not using the functional options pattern*

When designing an API, one question may arise: how do we deal with optional configurations? Solving this problem efficiently can improve how convenient our API will become. This section goes through a concrete example and covers different ways to handle optional configurations.

For this example, let's say we have to design a library that exposes a function to create an HTTP server. This function would accept different inputs: an address and a port. The following shows the skeleton of the function:

```
func NewServer(addr string, port int) (*http.Server, error) {
    // ...
}
```

The clients of our library have started to use this function, and everyone is happy. But at some point, our clients begin to complain that this function is somewhat limited and lacks other parameters (for example, a write timeout and a connection context). However, we notice that adding new function parameters breaks the compatibility, forcing the clients to modify the way they call `NewServer`. In the meantime, we would like to enrich the logic related to port management this way (figure 2.9):

- If the port isn't set, it uses the default one.
- If the port is negative, it returns an error.
- If the port is equal to 0, it uses a random port.
- Otherwise, it uses the port provided by the client.

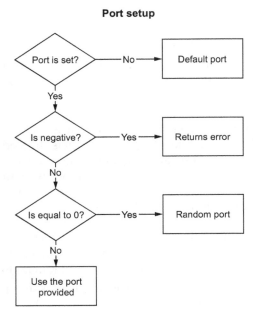

Figure 2.9   Logic related to the port option

How can we implement this function in an API-friendly way? Let's look at the different options.

2.11.1 *Config struct*

Because Go doesn't support optional parameters in function signatures, the first possible approach is to use a configuration struct to convey what's mandatory and what's optional. For example, the mandatory parameters could live as function parameters, whereas the optional parameters could be handled in the `Config` struct:

```
type Config struct {
    Port        int
}

func NewServer(addr string, cfg Config) {
}
```

This solution fixes the compatibility issue. Indeed, if we add new options, it will not break on the client side. However, this approach doesn't solve our requirement related to port management. Indeed, we should bear in mind that if a struct field isn't provided, it's initialized to its zero value:

- 0 for an integer
- 0.0 for a floating-point type
- `" "` for a string
- Nil for slices, maps, channels, pointers, interfaces, and functions

Therefore, in the following example, both structs are equal:

```
c1 := httplib.Config{
    Port: 0,                    ◁─┐ Initializes
}                                 │ Port to 0
c2 := httplib.Config{
                            ◁─┐ Port is missing, so
}                             │ it's initialized to 0.
```

In our case, we need to find a way to distinguish between a port purposely set to 0 and a missing port. Perhaps one option might be to handle all the parameters of the configuration struct as pointers in this way:

```
type Config struct {
    Port        *int
}
```

Using an integer pointer, semantically, we can highlight the difference between the value 0 and a missing value (a nil pointer).

This option would work, but it has a couple of downsides. First, it's not handy for clients to provide an integer pointer. Clients have to create a variable and then pass a pointer this way:

```
port := 0
config := httplib.Config{
    Port: &port,                    ⊲—| Provides an integer pointer
}
```

It's not a showstopper as such, but the overall API becomes a bit less convenient to use. Also, the more options we add, the more complex the code becomes.

The second downside is that a client using our library with the default configuration will need to pass an empty struct this way:

```
httplib.NewServer("localhost", httplib.Config{})
```

This code doesn't look great. Readers will have to understand what this magical struct's meaning is.

Another option is to use the classic builder pattern, as presented in the next section.

2.11.2 *Builder pattern*

Originally part of the Gang of Four design patterns, the *builder pattern* provides a flexible solution to various object-creation problems. The construction of Config is separated from the struct itself. It requires an extra struct, ConfigBuilder, which receives methods to configure and build a Config.

Let's see a concrete example and how it can help us in designing a friendly API that tackles all our requirements, including port management:

```
type Config struct {              ⊲—┐ Config
    Port int                         | struct
}

type ConfigBuilder struct {       ⊲—┐ Config builder struct,
    port *int                        | containing an optional port
}

func (b *ConfigBuilder) Port(
    port int) *ConfigBuilder {    ⊲—┐ Public method to
    b.port = &port                   | set up the port
    return b
}

func (b *ConfigBuilder) Build() (Config, error) {   ⊲—┐ Build method to create
    cfg := Config{}                                    | the config struct

    if b.port == nil {            ⊲—┐ Main logic related
        cfg.Port = defaultHTTPPort   | to port management
    } else {
        if *b.port == 0 {
            cfg.Port = randomPort()
        } else if *b.port < 0 {
            return Config{}, errors.New("port should be positive")
        } else {
            cfg.Port = *b.port
        }
    }
```

```
        return cfg, nil
}

func NewServer(addr string, config Config) (*http.Server, error) {
    // ...
}
```

The `ConfigBuilder` struct holds the client configuration. It exposes a `Port` method to set up the port. Usually, such a configuration method returns the builder itself so that we can use method chaining (for example, `builder.Foo("foo").Bar("bar")`). It also exposes a `Build` method that holds the logic on initializing the port value (whether the pointer was `nil`, etc.) and returns a `Config` struct once created.

> **NOTE** There isn't a single possible implementation of the builder pattern. For example, some may favor an approach where the logic to define the final port value is inside the `Port` method instead of `Build`. This section's scope is to present an overview of the builder pattern, not to look at all the different possible variations.

Then, a client would use our builder-based API in the following manner (we assume that we have put our code in an `httplib` package):

```
builder := httplib.ConfigBuilder{}          ⟵┐ Creates a
                                              ┘ builder config
builder.Port(8080)              ⟵┤ Sets the port
cfg, err := builder.Build()         ⟵┐
if err != nil {                      ┘ Builds the
    return err                         config struct
}

server, err := httplib.NewServer("localhost", cfg)   ⟵┤ Passes the config struct
if err != nil {
    return err
}
```

First, the client creates a `ConfigBuilder` and uses it to set up an optional field, such as the port. Then, it calls the `Build` method and checks for errors. If OK, the configuration is passed to `NewServer`.

   This approach makes port management handier. It's not required to pass an integer pointer, as the `Port` method accepts an integer. However, we still need to pass a config struct that can be empty if a client wants to use the default configuration:

```
server, err := httplib.NewServer("localhost", nil)
```

Another downside, in some situations, is related to error management. In programming languages where exceptions are thrown, builder methods such as `Port` can raise exceptions if the input is invalid. If we want to keep the ability to chain the calls, the function can't return an error. Therefore, we have to delay the validation in the `Build` method. If a client can pass multiple options, but we want to handle precisely the case that a port is invalid, it makes error handling more complex.

Let's now look at another approach called the functional options pattern, which relies on variadic arguments.

2.11.3 Functional options pattern

The last approach we will discuss is the *functional options pattern* (figure 2.10). Although there are different implementations with minor variations, the main idea is as follows:

- An unexported struct holds the configuration: `options`.
- Each option is a function that returns the same type: `type   Option func(options *options) error`. For example, `WithPort` accepts an `int` argument that represents the port and returns an `Option` type that represents how to update the `options` struct.

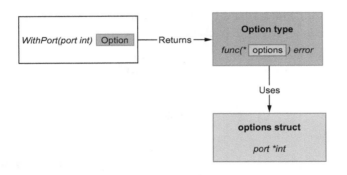

Figure 2.10   The `WithPort` option updates the final `options` struct.

Here's the Go implementation for the `options` struct, the `Option` type, and the `With-Port` option:

```
type options struct {          ⊲⎤ Configuration
    port *int                    ⎦ struct
}

type Option func(options *options) error     ⊲⎤ Represents a function type that
                                              ⎦ updates the configuration struct

func WithPort(port int) Option {       ⊲⎤ A configuration function
    return func(options *options) error {  ⎦ that updates the port
        if port < 0 {
            return errors.New("port should be positive")
        }
        options.port = &port
        return nil
    }
}
```

Here, `WithPort` returns a closure. A *closure* is an anonymous function that references variables from outside its body; in this case, the `port` variable. The closure respects the `Option` type and implements the port-validation logic. Each config field requires creating a public function (that starts with the `With` prefix by convention) containing similar logic: validating inputs if needed and updating the config struct.

Let's look at the last part on the provider side: the `NewServer` implementation. We'll pass the options as variadic arguments. Hence, we must iterate over these options to mutate the `options` config struct:

```
func NewServer(addr string, opts ...Option) (          ◄─┐  Accepts variadic
    *http.Server, error) {                                  Option arguments
    var options options                    ◄─────────────┘  Creates an empty
    for _, opt := range opts {                  ◄───┐          options struct
        err := opt(&options)    ◄─┐  Calls each option,   Iterates over all
        if err != nil {            which results in       the input options
            return nil, err        modifying the common
        }                          options struct
    }

    // At this stage, the options struct is built and contains the config
    // Therefore, we can implement our logic related to port configuration
    var port int
    if options.port == nil {
        port = defaultHTTPPort
    } else {
        if *options.port == 0 {
            port = randomPort()
        } else {
            port = *options.port
        }
    }

    // ...
}
```

We start by creating an empty `options` struct. Then, we iterate over each `Option` argument and execute them to mutate the `options` struct (bear in mind that the `Option` type is a function). Once the `options` struct is built, we can implement the final logic regarding port management.

Because `NewServer` accepts variadic `Option` arguments, a client can now call this API by passing multiple options following the mandatory address argument. For example,

```
server, err := httplib.NewServer("localhost",
        httplib.WithPort(8080),
        httplib.WithTimeout(time.Second))
```

However, if the client needs the default configuration, it doesn't have to provide an argument (for example, an empty struct, as we saw with the previous approaches). The client's call now might look something like this:

```
server, err := httplib.NewServer("localhost")
```

This pattern is the functional options pattern. It provides a handy and API-friendly way to handle options. Although the builder pattern can be a valid option, it has some minor downsides that tend to make the functional options pattern the idiomatic way to deal with this problem in Go. Let's also note that this pattern is used in different Go libraries such as gRPC.

The next section will discuss another common mistake: misorganization.

2.12   *#12: Project misorganization*

Organizing a Go project isn't an easy task. Because the Go language provides a lot of freedom in designing packages and modules, the best practices are not quite as ubiquitous as they should be. This section first discusses a common way of structuring a project and then discusses a few best practices, showing ways to improve how we organize a project.

2.12.1   *Project structure*

The Go language maintainer has no strong convention about structuring a project in Go. However, one layout has emerged over the years: project-layout (https:// github.com/golang-standards/project-layout).

If our project is small enough (only a few files), or if our organization has already created its standard, it may not be worth using or migrating to project-layout. Otherwise, it might be worth considering. Let's look at this layout and see what the main directories are:

- */cmd*—The main source files. The main.go of a `foo` application should live in /cmd/foo/main.go.
- */internal*—Private code that we don't want others importing for their applications or libraries.
- */pkg*—Public code that we want to expose to others.
- */test*—Additional external tests and test data. Unit tests in Go live in the same package as the source files. However, public API tests or integration tests, for example, should live in /test.
- */configs*—Configuration files.
- */docs*—Design and user documents.
- */examples*—Examples for our application and/or a public library.
- */api*—API contract files (Swagger, Protocol Buffers, etc.).
- */web*—Web application-specific assets (static files, etc.).
- */build*—Packaging and continuous integration (CI) files.
- */scripts*—Scripts for analysis, installation, and so on.
- */vendor*—Application dependencies (for example, Go modules dependencies).

There's no /src directory like in some other languages. The rationale is that /src is too generic; hence, this layout favors directories such as /cmd, /internal, or /pkg.

NOTE In 2021, Russ Cox, one of the core maintainers of Go, criticized this layout. Mainly, a project lives under the GitHub golang-standards organization despite not being an official standard. In any case, we must bear in mind that, regarding project structure, there's no mandatory convention. This layout may be helpful for you or not, but what's important here is that indecision is the only wrong decision. Hence, agree on a layout to keep things consistent in your organization so that developers don't waste time switching from one repository to another.

Now, let's discuss how to organize the main logic of a Go repository.

2.12.2 Package organization

In Go, there is no concept of subpackages. However, we can decide to organize packages within subdirectories. If we take a look at the standard library, the net directory is organized this way:

```
/net
    /http
        client.go
        ...
    /smtp
        auth.go
        ...
    addrselect.go
    ...
```

net acts both as a package and a directory that contains other packages. But net/http doesn't inherit from net or have specific access rights to the net package. Elements inside of net/http can only see exported net elements. The main benefit of subdirectories is to keep packages in a place where they live with high cohesion.

Regarding the overall organization, there are different schools of thought. For example, should we organize our application by context or by layer? It depends on our preferences. We may favor grouping code per context (such as the customer context, the contract context, etc.), or we may favor following hexagonal architecture principles and group per technical layer. If the decision we make fits our use case, it cannot be a wrong decision, as long as we remain consistent with it.

Regarding packages, there are multiple best practices that we should follow. First, we should avoid premature packaging because it might cause us to overcomplicate a project. Sometimes, it's better to use a simple organization and have our project evolve when we understand what it contains rather than forcing ourselves to make the perfect structure up front.

Granularity is another essential thing to consider. We should avoid having dozens of nano packages containing only one or two files. If we do, it's because we have probably missed some logical connections across these packages, making our project harder for readers to understand. Conversely, we should also avoid huge packages that dilute the meaning of a package name.

Package naming should also be considered with care. As we all know (as developers), naming is hard. To help clients understand a Go project, we should name our packages after what they provide, not what they contain. Also, naming should be meaningful. Therefore, a package name should be short, concise, expressive, and, by convention, a single lowercase word.

Regarding what to export, the rule is pretty straightforward. We should minimize what should be exported as much as possible to reduce the coupling between packages and keep unnecessary exported elements hidden. If we are unsure whether to export an element or not, we should default to not exporting it. Later, if we discover that we need to export it, we can adjust our code. Let's also keep in mind some exceptions, such as making fields exported so that a struct can be unmarshaled with encoding/json.

Organizing a project isn't straightforward, but following these rules should help make it easier to maintain. However, remember that consistency is also vital to ease maintainability. Therefore, let's make sure that we keep things as consistent as possible within a codebase.

In the next section, we will tackle utility packages.

2.13   *#13: Creating utility packages*

This section discusses a common bad practice: creating shared packages such as utils, common, and base. We will examine the problems with such an approach and learn how to improve our organization.

Let's look at an example inspired by the official Go blog. It's about implementing a set data structure (a map where the value is ignored). The idiomatic way to do this in Go is to handle it via a map[K]struct{} type with K that can be any type allowed in a map as a key, whereas the value is a struct{} type. Indeed, a map whose value type is struct{} conveys that we aren't interested in the value itself. Let's expose two methods in a util package:

```
package util

func NewStringSet(...string) map[string]struct{} {      ◁──┐ Creates a
    // ...                                                  │ string set
}

func SortStringSet(map[string]struct{}) []string {      ◁──┐ Returns a sorted
    // ...                                                  │ list of keys
}
```

A client will use this package like this:

```
set := util.NewStringSet("c", "a", "b")
fmt.Println(util.SortStringSet(set))
```

The problem here is that `util` is meaningless. We could call it `common`, `shared`, or base, but it remains a meaningless name that doesn't provide any insight about what the package provides.

Instead of a utility package, we should create an expressive package name such as `stringset`. For example,

```
package stringset

func New(...string) map[string]struct{} { ... }
func Sort(map[string]struct{}) []string { ... }
```

In this example, we removed the suffixes for `NewStringSet` and `SortStringSet`, which respectively became `New` and `Sort`. On the client side, it now looks like this:

```
set := stringset.New("c", "a", "b")
fmt.Println(stringset.Sort(set))
```

> **NOTE** In the previous section, we discussed the idea of nano packages. We mentioned how creating dozens of nano packages in an application can make the code path more complex to follow. However, the idea itself of a nano package isn't necessarily bad. If a small code group has high cohesion and doesn't really belong somewhere else, it's perfectly acceptable to organize it into a specific package. There isn't a strict rule to apply, and often, the challenge is finding the right balance.

We could even go a step further. Instead of exposing utility functions, we could create a specific type and expose `Sort` as a method this way:

```
package stringset

type Set map[string]struct{}
func New(...string) Set { ... }
func (s Set) Sort() []string { ... }
```

This change makes the client even simpler. There would only be one reference to the `stringset` package:

```
set := stringset.New("c", "a", "b")
fmt.Println(set.Sort())
```

With this small refactoring, we get rid of a meaningless package name to expose an expressive API. As Dave Cheney (a project member of Go) mentioned, we reasonably often find utility packages that handle common facilities. For example, if we decide to have a client and a server package, where should we put the common types? In this case, perhaps one solution is to combine the client, the server, and the common code into a single package.

Naming a package is a critical piece of application design, and we should be cautious about this as well. As a rule of thumb, creating shared packages without meaningful names isn't a good idea; this includes utility packages such as `utils`, `common`, or base. Also, bear in mind that naming a package after what it provides and not what it contains can be an efficient way to increase its expressiveness.

In the next section, we will discuss packages and package collisions.

2.14   *#14: Ignoring package name collisions*

Package collisions occur when a variable name collides with an existing package name, preventing the package from being reused. Let's look at a concrete example with a library exposing a Redis client:

```
package redis

type Client struct { ... }

func NewClient() *Client { ... }

func (c *Client) Get(key string) (string, error) { ... }
```

Now, let's jump on the client side. Despite the package name, redis, it's perfectly valid in Go to also create a variable named redis:

```
redis := redis.NewClient()      ◁──┐  Calls NewClient from
v, err := redis.Get("foo")          │  the redis package
                                ◁──┐  Uses the redis
                                   │  variable
```

Here, the redis variable name collides with the redis package name. Even though this is allowed, it should be avoided. Indeed, throughout the scope of the redis variable, the redis package won't be accessible.

Suppose that a qualifier references both a variable and a package name throughout a function. In that case, it might be ambiguous for a code reader to know what a qualifier refers to. What are the options to avoid such a collision? The first option is to use a different variable name. For example,

```
redisClient := redis.NewClient()
v, err := redisClient.Get("foo")
```

This is probably the most straightforward approach. However, if for some reason we prefer to keep our variable named redis, we can play with package imports. Using package imports, we can use an alias to change the qualifier to reference the redis package. For example,

```
import redisapi "mylib/redis"      ◁──┐  Creates an alias for
                                       │  the redis package
// ...

redis := redisapi.NewClient()      ◁──┐  Accesses the redis package
v, err := redis.Get("foo")             │  via the redisapi alias
```

Here, we used the redisapi import alias to reference the redis package so that we can keep our variable name redis.

> **NOTE** One option could also be to use dot imports to access all the public
> elements of a package without the package qualifier. However, this approach
> tends to increase confusion and should, in most cases, be avoided.

Also note that we should avoid naming collisions between a variable and a built-in
function. For example, we could do something like this:

```
copy := copyFile(src, dst)        ◁──┐ The copy variable collides with
                                     └─ the copy built-in function.
```

In this case, the `copy` built-in function wouldn't be accessible as long as the `copy` variable
lives. In summary, we should prevent variable name collisions to avoid ambiguity. If we
face a collision, we should either find another meaningful name or use an import alias.

In the next section, we will see a common mistake related to code documentation.

2.15 *#15: Missing code documentation*

Documentation is an important aspect of coding. It simplifies how clients can consume an API but can also help in maintaining a project. In Go, we should follow some
rules to make our code idiomatic. Let's examine these rules.

First, every exported element must be documented. Whether it is a structure, an
interface, a function, or something else, if it's exported, it must be documented. The
convention is to add comments, starting with the name of the exported element. For
example,

```
// Customer is a customer representation.
type Customer struct{}

// ID returns the customer identifier.
func (c Customer) ID() string { return "" }
```

As a convention, each comment should be a complete sentence that ends with punc-
tuation. Also bear in mind that when we document a function (or a method), we
should highlight what the function intends to do, not how it does it; this belongs to
the core of a function and comments, not documentation. Furthermore, the documentation should ideally provide enough information that the consumer does not
have to look at our code to understand how to use an exported element.

Deprecated elements

It's possible to deprecate an exported element using the `// Deprecated:` comment
this way:

```
// ComputePath returns the fastest path between two points.
// Deprecated: This function uses a deprecated way to compute
// the fastest path. Use ComputeFastestPath instead.
func ComputePath() {}
```

Then, if a developer uses the `ComputePath` function, they should get a warning.
(Most IDEs handle deprecated comments.)

When it comes to documenting a variable or a constant, we might be interested in conveying two aspects: its purpose and its content. The former should live as code documentation to be useful for external clients. The latter, though, shouldn't necessarily be public. For example,

```
// DefaultPermission is the default permission used by the store engine.
const DefaultPermission = 0o644 // Need read and write accesses.
```

This constant represents the default permission. The code documentation conveys its purpose, whereas the comment alongside the constant describes its actual content (read and write accesses).

To help clients and maintainers understand a package's scope, we should also document each package. The convention is to start the comment with `// Package` followed by the package name:

```
// Package math provides basic constants and mathematical functions.
//
// This package does not guarantee bit-identical results
// across architectures.
package math
```

The first line of a package comment should be concise. That's because it will appear in the package (figure 2.11 provides an example). Then, we can provide all the information we need in the following lines.

Name	Synopsis
archive	
tar	Package tar implements access to tar archives.
zip	Package zip provides support for reading and writing ZIP archives.
bufio	Package bufio implements buffered I/O. It wraps an io.Reader or io.Writer object, creating another object (Reader or Writer) that also implements the interface but provides buffering and some help for textual I/O.
builtin	Package builtin provides documentation for Go's predeclared identifiers.
bytes	Package bytes implements functions for the manipulation of byte slices.

Figure 2.11   An example of the generated Go standard library

Documenting a package can be done in any of the Go files; there is no rule. In general, we should put package documentation in a relevant file with the same name as the package or in a specific file such as doc.go.

One last thing to mention regarding package documentation is that comments not adjacent to the declaration are omitted. For example, the following copyright comment will not be visible in the produced documentation:

```
// Copyright 2009 The Go Authors. All rights reserved.
// Use of this source code is governed by a BSD-style
// license that can be found in the LICENSE file.
// Package math provides basic constants and mathematical functions.
//
```

Empty line. The previous comments will not be included in the documentation.

```
// This package does not guarantee bit-identical results
// across architectures.
package math
```

In summary, we should keep in mind that every exported element needs to be documented. Documenting our code shouldn't be a constraint. We should take the opportunity to make sure it helps clients and maintainers to understand the purpose of our code.

Finally, in the last section of this chapter, we will see a common mistake regarding tooling: not using linters.

2.16 *#16: Not using linters*

A *linter* is an automatic tool to analyze code and catch errors. The scope of this section isn't to give an exhaustive list of the existing linters; otherwise, it will become deprecated pretty quickly. But we should understand and remember why linters are essential for most Go projects.

To understand why linters are important, let's take one concrete example. In mistake #1, "Unintended variable shadowing," we discussed potential errors related to variable shadowing. Using vet, a standard linter from the Go toolset, and shadow, we can detect shadowed variables:

```
package main

import "fmt"

func main() {
    i := 0
    if true {
        i := 1               ◁──┐ Shadowed
        fmt.Println(i)          │ variable
    }
    fmt.Println(i)
}
```

Because vet is included with the Go binary, let's first install shadow, link it with Go vet, and then run it on the previous example:

```
$ go install \
  golang.org/x/tools/go/analysis/passes/shadow/cmd/shadow   ◁──┤ Installs shadow
$ go vet -vettool=$(which shadow)                         ◁──┐ Links to Go vet using
./main.go:8:3:                                               │ the vettol argument
    declaration of "i" shadows declaration at line 6   ◁──┐ Go vet detects the
                                                          │ shadow variable.
```

As we can see, vet informs us that the variable i is shadowed in this example. Using appropriate linters can help make our code more robust and detect potential errors.

> **NOTE** Linters don't cover all the mistakes in this book. Therefore, it's recommended that you just keep reading ;).

Again, this section's goal isn't to list all the available linters. However, if you're not a regular user of linters, here is a list that you may want to use daily:

- https://golang.org/cmd/vet/—A standard Go analyzer
- https://github.com/kisielk/errcheck—An error checker
- https://github.com/fzipp/gocyclo—A cyclomatic complexity analyzer
- https://github.com/jgautheron/goconst—A repeated string constants analyzer

Besides linters, we should also use code formatters to fix code style. Here is a list of some code formatters for you to try:

- https://golang.org/cmd/gofmt/—A standard Go code formatter
- https://godoc.org/golang.org/x/tools/cmd/goimports—A   standard   Go imports formatter

Meanwhile, we should also look at golangci-lint (https://github.com/golangci/golangci-lint). It's a linting tool that provides a facade on top of many useful linters and formatters. Also, it allows running the linters in parallel to improve analysis speed, which is quite handy.

Linters and formatters are a powerful way to improve the quality and consistency of our codebase. Let's take the time to understand which one we should use and make sure we automate their execution (such as a CI or Git precommit hook).

Summary

- Avoiding shadowed variables can help prevent mistakes like referencing the wrong variable or confusing readers.
- Avoiding nested levels and keeping the happy path aligned on the left makes building a mental code model easier.
- When initializing variables, remember that init functions have limited error handling and make state handling and testing more complex. In most cases, initializations should be handled as specific functions.
- Forcing the use of getters and setters isn't idiomatic in Go. Being pragmatic and finding the right balance between efficiency and blindly following certain idioms should be the way to go.
- Abstractions should be discovered, not created. To prevent unnecessary complexity, create an interface when you need it and not when you foresee needing it, or if you can at least prove the abstraction to be a valid one.
- Keeping interfaces on the client side avoids unnecessary abstractions.
- To prevent being restricted in terms of flexibility, a function shouldn't return interfaces but concrete implementations in most cases. Conversely, a function should accept interfaces whenever possible.
- Only use any if you need to accept or return any possible type, such as json.Marshal. Otherwise, any doesn't provide meaningful information and can lead to compile-time issues by allowing a caller to call methods with any data type.

- Relying on generics and type parameters can prevent writing boilerplate code to factor out elements or behaviors. However, do not use type parameters prematurely, but only when you see a concrete need for them. Otherwise, they introduce unnecessary abstractions and complexity.

- Using type embedding can also help avoid boilerplate code; however, ensure that doing so doesn't lead to visibility issues where some fields should have remained hidden.

- To handle options conveniently and in an API-friendly manner, use the functional options pattern.

- Following a layout such as project-layout can be a good way to start structuring Go projects, especially if you are looking for existing conventions to standardize a new project.

- Naming is a critical piece of application design. Creating packages such as `common`, `util`, and `shared` doesn't bring much value for the reader. Refactor such packages into meaningful and specific package names.

- To avoid naming collisions between variables and packages, leading to confusion or perhaps even bugs, use unique names for each one. If this isn't feasible, use an import alias to change the qualifier to differentiate the package name from the variable name, or think of a better name.

- To help clients and maintainers understand your code's purpose, document exported elements.

- To improve code quality and consistency, use linters and formatters.

Data types

3

Dealing with data types is a frequent operation for software engineers. This chapter delves into the most common mistakes related to basic types, slices, and maps. The only data type that we omit is strings because a later chapter deals with this type exclusively.

3.1 #17: Creating confusion with octal literals

Let's first look at a common misunderstanding with octal literal representation, which can lead to confusion or even bugs. What do you believe should be the output of the following code?

```
sum := 100 + 010
fmt.Println(sum)
```

At first glance, we may expect this code to print the result of 100 + 10 = 110. But it prints 108 instead. How is that possible?

In Go, an integer literal starting with 0 is considered an octal integer (base 8), so 10 in base 8 equals 8 in base 10. Thus, the sum in the previous example is equal to 100 + 8 = 108. This is an important property of integer literals to keep in mind—for example, to avoid confusion while reading existing code.

Octal integers are useful in different scenarios. For instance, suppose we want to open a file using `os.OpenFile`. This function requires passing a permission as a `uint32`. If we want to match a Linux permission, we can pass an octal number for readability instead of a base 10 number:

```
file, err := os.OpenFile("foo", os.O_RDONLY, 0644)
```

In this example, `0644` represents a specific Linux permission (read for all and write only for the current user). It's also possible to add an o character (the letter *o* in lower-case) following the zero:

```
file, err := os.OpenFile("foo", os.O_RDONLY, 0o644)
```

Using `0o` as a prefix instead of only `0` means the same thing. However, it can help make the code clearer.

> **NOTE**   We can also use an uppercase `O` character instead of a lowercase `o`. But passing `0O644` can increase confusion because, depending on the character font, `0` can look very similar to `O`.

We should also note the other integer literal representations:

- *Binary*—Uses a `0b` or `0B` prefix (for example, `0b100` is equal to 4 in base 10)
- *Hexadecimal*—Uses an `0x` or `0X` prefix (for example, `0xF` is equal to 15 in base 10)
- *Imaginary*—Uses an `i` suffix (for example, `3i`)

Finally, we can also use an underscore character (`_`) as a separator for readability. For example, we can write 1 billion this way: `1_000_000_000`. We can also use the underscore character with other representations (for example, `0b00_00_01`).

In summary, Go handles binary, hexadecimal, imaginary, and octal numbers. Octal numbers start with a 0. However, to improve readability and avoid potential mistakes for future code readers, make octal numbers explicit using a `0o` prefix.

The next section digs into integers, and we discuss how overflows are handled in Go.

3.2 *#18: Neglecting integer overflows*

Not understanding how integer overflows are handled in Go can lead to critical bugs. This section delves into this topic. But first, let's remind ourselves of a few concepts related to integers.

3.2.1   *Concepts*

Go provides a total of 10 integer types. There are four signed integer types and four unsigned integer types, as the following table shows.

Signed integers	Unsigned integers
int8 (8 bits)	uint8 (8 bits)
int16 (16 bits)	uint16 (16 bits)
int32 (32 bits)	uint32 (32 bits)
int64 (64 bits)	uint64 (64 bits)

The other two integer types are the most commonly used: int and uint. These two types have a size that depends on the system: 32 bits on 32-bit systems or 64 bits on 64-bit systems.

Let's now discuss overflow. Suppose we want to initialize an int32 to its maximum value and then increment it. What should be the behavior of this code?

```
var counter int32 = math.MaxInt32
counter++
fmt.Printf("counter=%d\n", counter)
```

This code compiles and doesn't panic at run time. However, the counter++ statement generates an integer overflow:

```
counter=-2147483648
```

An integer overflow occurs when an arithmetic operation creates a value outside the range that can be represented with a given number of bytes. An int32 is represented using 32 bits. Here is the binary representation of the maximum int32 value (math.MaxInt32):

```
01111111111111111111111111111111
 |------31 bits set to 1-------|
```

Because an int32 is a signed integer, the bit on the left represents the integer's sign: 0 for positive, 1 for negative. If we increment this integer, there is no space left to represent the new value. Hence, this leads to an integer overflow. Binary-wise, here's the new value:

```
10000000000000000000000000000000
 |------31 bits set to 0-------|
```

As we can see, the bit sign is now equal to 1, meaning negative. This value is the smallest possible value for a signed integer represented with 32 bits.

NOTE   The smallest possible negative value isn't 1111111111111111111111 11111111. Indeed, most systems rely on the two's complement operation to represent binary numbers (invert every bit and add 1). The main goal of this operation is to make $x + (-x)$ equal 0 regardless of x.

In Go, an integer overflow that can be detected at compile time generates a compilation error. For example,

```
var counter int32 = math.MaxInt32 + 1

constant 2147483648 overflows int32
```

However, at run time, an integer overflow or underflow is silent; this does not lead to an application panic. It is essential to keep this behavior in mind, because it can lead to sneaky bugs (for example, an integer increment or addition of positive integers that leads to a negative result).

   Before delving into how to detect an integer overflow with common operations, let's think about when to be concerned about it. In most contexts, like handling a counter of requests or basic additions/multiplications, we shouldn't worry too much if we use the right integer type. But in some cases, like memory-constrained projects using smaller integer types, dealing with large numbers, or doing conversions, we may want to check possible overflows.

> **NOTE** The Ariane 5 launch failure in 1996 (https://www.bugsnag.com/blog/bug-day-ariane-5-disaster) was due to an overflow resulting from converting a 64-bit floating-point to a 16-bit signed integer.

3.2.2 Detecting integer overflow when incrementing

If we want to detect an integer overflow during an increment operation with a type based on a defined size (`int8`, `int16`, `int32`, `int64`, `uint8`, `uint16`, `uint32`, or `uint64`), we can check the value against the `math` constants. For example, with an `int32`:

```
func Inc32(counter int32) int32 {
    if counter == math.MaxInt32 {          ◁──┐ Compares with
        panic("int32 overflow")                │ math.MaxInt32
    }
    return counter + 1
}
```

This function checks whether the input is already equal to `math.MaxInt32`. We know whether the increment leads to an overflow if that's the case.

   What about `int` and `uint` types? Before Go 1.17, we had to build these constants manually. Now, `math.MaxInt`, `math.MinInt`, and `math.MaxUint` are part of the `math` package. If we have to test an overflow on an `int` type, we can do it using `math.MaxInt`:

```
func IncInt(counter int) int {
    if counter == math.MaxInt {
        panic("int overflow")
    }
    return counter + 1
}
```

The logic is the same for a `uint`. We can use `math.MaxUint`:

```
func IncUint(counter uint) uint {
    if counter == math.MaxUint {
        panic("uint overflow")
    }
    return counter + 1
}
```

In this section, we learned how to check integer overflows following an increment operation. Now, what about addition?

3.2.3   *Detecting integer overflows during addition*

How can we detect an integer overflow during an addition? The answer is to reuse `math.MaxInt`:

```
func AddInt(a, b int) int {
    if a > math.MaxInt-b {          ◁──┐ Checks if an integer
        panic("int overflow")          │ overflow will occur
    }

    return a + b
}
```

In the example, a and b are the two operands. If a is greater than `math.MaxInt - b`, the operation will lead to an integer overflow. Now, let's look at the multiplication operation.

3.2.4   *Detecting an integer overflow during multiplication*

Multiplication is a bit more complex to handle. We have to perform checks against the minimal integer, `math.MinInt`:

```
func MultiplyInt(a, b int) int {
    if a == 0 || b == 0 {           ◁──┐ If one of the operands is equal
        return 0                       │ to 0, it directly returns 0.
    }

    result := a * b
    if a == 1 || b == 1 {           ◁──┐ Checks if one of the
        return result                  │ operands is equal to 1
    }
    if a == math.MinInt || b == math.MinInt {   ◁──┐ Checks if one of the operands
        panic("integer overflow")                   │ is equal to math.MinInt
    }
    if result/b != a {              ◁──┐ Checks if the multiplication
        panic("integer overflow")      │ leads to an integer overflow
    }
    return result
}
```

Checking an integer overflow with multiplication requires multiple steps. First, we need to test if one of the operands is equal to 0, 1, or `math.MinInt`. Then we divide the multiplication result by b. If the result isn't equal to the original factor (a), it means an integer overflow occurred.

In summary, integer overflows (and underflows) are silent operations in Go. If we want to check for overflows to avoid sneaky errors, we can use the utility functions described in this section. Also remember that Go provides a package to deal with large numbers: math/big. This might be an option if an int isn't enough.

We continue talking about basic Go types in the next section with floating points.

3.3   *#19: Not understanding floating points*

In Go, there are two floating-point types (if we omit imaginary numbers): float32 and float64. The concept of a floating point was invented to solve the major problem with integers: their inability to represent fractional values. To avoid bad surprises, we need to know that floating-point arithmetic is an approximation of real arithmetic. Let's examine the impact of working with approximations and how to increase accuracy. For that, we'll look at a multiplication example:

```
var n float32 = 1.0001
fmt.Println(n * n)
```

We may expect this code to print the result of 1.0001 * 1.0001 = 1.00020001, right? However, running it on most x86 processors prints 1.0002, instead. How do we explain that? We need to understand the arithmetic of floating points first.

Let's take the float64 type as an example. Note that there's an infinite number of real values between math.SmallestNonzeroFloat64 (the float64 minimum) and math.MaxFloat64 (the float64 maximum). Conversely, the float64 type has a finite number of bits: 64. Because making infinite values fit into a finite space isn't possible, we have to work with approximations. Hence, we may lose precision. The same logic goes for the float32 type.

Floating points in Go follow the IEEE-754 standard, with some bits representing a mantissa and other bits representing an exponent. A *mantissa* is a base value, whereas an *exponent* is a multiplier applied to the mantissa. In single-precision floating-point types (float32), 8 bits represent the exponent, and 23 bits represent the mantissa. In double-precision floating-point types (float64), the values are 11 and 52 bits, respectively, for the exponent and the mantissa. The remaining bit is for the sign. To convert a floating point into a decimal, we use the following calculation:

```
sign * 2^exponent * mantissa
```

Figure 3.1 illustrates the representation of 1.0001 as a float32. The exponent uses the 8-bit excess/bias notation: the 01111111 exponent value means 2^0, whereas the mantissa is equal to 1.000100016593933. (Note that the scope of this section isn't to explain how conversions work.) Hence, the decimal value equals $1 \times 2^0 \times$ 1.000100016593933. Thus, what we store in a single-precision floating-point value isn't 1.0001 but 1.000100016593933. A lack of precision affects the accuracy of the value stored.

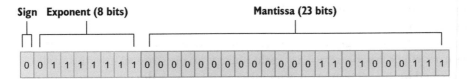

Figure 3.1   Representation of 1.0001 in `float32`

Once we understand that `float32` and `float64` are approximations, what are the implications for us as developers? The first implication is related to comparisons. Using the `==` operator to compare two floating-point numbers can lead to inaccuracies. Instead, we should compare their difference to see if it is less than some small error value. For example, the `testify` testing library (https://github.com/stretchr/testify) has an `InDelta` function to assert that two values are within a given delta of each other.

Also bear in mind that the result of floating-point calculations depends on the actual processor. Most processors have a floating-point unit (FPU) to deal with such calculations. There is no guarantee that the result executed on one machine will be the same on another machine with a different FPU. Comparing two values using a delta can be a solution for implementing valid tests across different machines.

Kinds of floating-point numbers

Go also has three special kinds of floating-point numbers:

- Positive infinite
- Negative infinite
- NaN (Not-a-Number), which is the result of an undefined or unrepresentable operation

According to IEEE-754, NaN is the only floating-point number satisfying `f != f`. Here's an example that constructs these special kinds of numbers, along with the output:

```
var a float64
positiveInf := 1 / a
negativeInf := -1 / a
nan := a / a
fmt.Println(positiveInf, negativeInf, nan)

+Inf -Inf NaN
```

We can check whether a floating-point number is infinite using `math.IsInf` and whether it is NaN using `math.IsNaN`.

So far, we have seen that decimal-to-floating-point conversions can lead to a loss of accuracy. This is the error due to conversion. Also note that the error can accumulate in a sequence of floating-point operations.

Let's look at an example with two functions that perform the same sequence of operations in a different order. In our example, f1 starts by initializing a float64 to 10,000 and then repeatedly adds 1.0001 to this result (n times). Conversely, f2 performs the same operations but in the opposite order (adding 10,000 in the end):

```
func f1(n int) float64 {
    result := 10_000.
    for i := 0; i < n; i++ {
        result += 1.0001
    }
    return result
}

func f2(n int) float64 {
    result := 0.
    for i := 0; i < n; i++ {
        result += 1.0001
    }
    return result + 10_000.
}
```

Now, let's run these functions on an x86 processor. This time, however, we'll vary n.

n	Exact result	f1	f2
10	10010.001	10010.000999999993	10010.001
1k	11000.1	11000.099999999293	11000.099999999982
1m	1.0101e+06	1.0100999999761417e+06	1.0100999999766762e+06

Notice that the bigger n is, the greater the imprecision. However, we can also see that the f2 accuracy is better than f1. Keep in mind that the order of floating-point calculations can affect the accuracy of the result.

When performing a chain of additions and subtractions, we should group the operations to add or subtract values with a similar order of magnitude before adding or subtracting those with magnitudes that aren't close. Because f2 adds 10,000, in the end it produces more accurate results than f1.

What about multiplications and divisions? Let's imagine that we want to compute the following:

```
a × (b + c)
```

As we know, this calculation is equal to

```
a × b + a × c
```

Let's run these two calculations with a having a different order of magnitude than b and c:

```
a := 100000.001
b := 1.0001
```

```
c := 1.0002

fmt.Println(a * (b + c))
fmt.Println(a*b + a*c)

200030.00200030004
200030.0020003
```

The exact result is 200,030.002. Hence, the first calculation has the worst accuracy. Indeed, when performing floating-point calculations involving addition, subtraction, multiplication, or division, we have to complete the multiplication and division operations first to get better accuracy. Sometimes, this may impact the execution time (in the previous example, it requires three operations instead of two). In that case, it's a choice between accuracy and execution time.

Go's `float32` and `float64` are approximations. Because of that, we have to bear a few rules in mind:

- When comparing two floating-point numbers, check that their difference is within an acceptable range.
- When performing additions or subtractions, group operations with a similar order of magnitude for better accuracy.
- To favor accuracy, if a sequence of operations requires addition, subtraction, multiplication, or division, perform the multiplication and division operations first.

The following section begins our examination of slices. It discusses two crucial concepts: a slice's length and capacity.

3.4   *#20: Not understanding slice length and capacity*

It's pretty common for Go developers to mix slice length and capacity or not understand them thoroughly. Assimilating these two concepts is essential for efficiently handling core operations such as slice initialization and adding elements with `append`, copying, or slicing. This misunderstanding can lead to using slices suboptimally or even to memory leaks (as we will see in later sections).

In Go, a slice is backed by an array. That means the slice's data is stored contiguously in an array data structure. A slice also handles the logic of adding an element if the backing array is full or shrinking the backing array if it's almost empty.

Internally, a slice holds a pointer to the backing array plus a length and a capacity. The length is the number of elements the slice contains, whereas the capacity is the number of elements in the backing array, counting from the first element in the slice. Let's go through a few examples to make things clearer. First, let's initialize a slice with a given length and capacity:

```
s := make([]int, 3, 6)        Three-length,
                              six-capacity slice
```

The first argument, representing the length, is mandatory. However, the second argument representing the capacity is optional. Figure 3.2 shows the result of this code in memory.

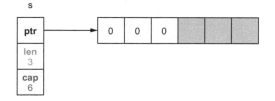

Figure 3.2 A three-length, six-capacity slice

In this case, make creates an array of six elements (the capacity). But because the length was set to 3, Go initializes only the first three elements. Also, because the slice is an []int type, the first three elements are initialized to the zeroed value of an int: 0. The grayed elements are allocated but not yet used.

If we print this slice, we get the elements within the range of the length, [0 0 0]. If we set s[1] to 1, the second element of the slice updates without impacting its length or capacity. Figure 3.3 illustrates this.

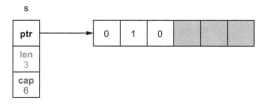

Figure 3.3 Updating the slice's second element: s[1] = 1

However, accessing an element outside the length range is forbidden, even though it's already allocated in memory. For example, s[4] = 0 would lead to the following panic:

```
panic: runtime error: index out of range [4] with length 3
```

How can we use the remaining space of the slice? By using the append built-in function:

```
s = append(s, 2)
```

This code appends to the existing s slice a new element. It uses the first grayed element (which was allocated but not yet used) to store element 2, as figure 3.4 shows.

The length of the slice is updated from 3 to 4 because the slice now contains four elements. Now, what happens if we add three more elements so that the backing array isn't large enough?

```
s = append(s, 3, 4, 5)
fmt.Println(s)
```

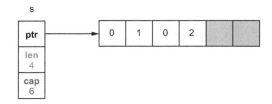

Figure 3.4 Appending an element to s

If we run this code, we see that the slice was able to cope with our request:

```
[0 1 0 2 3 4 5]
```

Because an array is a fixed-size structure, it can store the new elements until element 4. When we want to insert element 5, the array is already full: Go internally creates another array by doubling the capacity, copying all the elements, and then inserting element 5. Figure 3.5 shows this process.

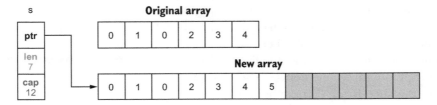

Figure 3.5 **Because the initial backing array is full, Go creates another array and copies all the elements.**

The slice now references the new backing array. What will happen to the previous backing array? If it's no longer referenced, it's eventually freed by the garbage collector (GC) if allocated on the heap. (We discuss heap memory in mistake #95, "Not understanding stack vs. heap," and we look at how the GC works in mistake #99, "Not understanding how the GC works.")

What happens with slicing? Slicing is an operation done on an array or a slice, providing a half-open range; the first index is included, whereas the second is excluded. The following example shows the impact, and figure 3.6 displays the result in memory:

```
s1 := make([]int, 3, 6)        Three-length,
                               six-capacity slice
s2 := s1[1:3]         Slicing from
                      indices 1 to 3
```

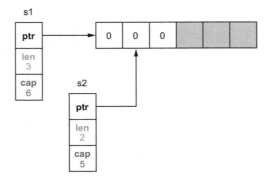

Figure 3.6 **The slices s1 and s2 reference the same backing array with different lengths and capacities.**

First, s1 is created as a three-length, six-capacity slice. When s2 is created by slicing s1, both slices reference the same backing array. However, s2 starts from a different index, 1. Therefore, its length and capacity (a two-length, five-capacity slice) differ from s1. If we update s1[1] or s2[0], the change is made to the same array, hence, visible in both slices, as figure 3.7 shows.

Now, what happens if we append an element to s2? Does the following code change s1 as well?

```
s2 = append(s2, 2)
```

The shared backing array is modified, but only the length of s2 changes. Figure 3.8 shows the result of appending an element to s2.

s1 remains a three-length, six-capacity slice. Therefore, if we print s1 and s2, the added element is only visible for s2:

```
s1=[0 1 0], s2=[1 0 2]
```

It's important to understand this behavior so that we don't make wrong assumptions while using append.

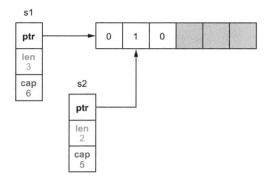

Figure 3.7 Because s1 and s2 are backed by the same array, updating a common element makes the change visible in both slices.

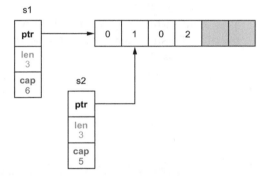

Figure 3.8 Appending an element to s2

NOTE In these examples, the backing array is internal and not available directly to the Go developer. The only exception is when a slice is created from slicing an existing array.

One last thing to note: what if we keep appending elements to s2 until the backing array is full? What will the state be, memory-wise? Let's add three more elements so that the backing array will not have enough capacity:

```
s2 = append(s2, 3)
s2 = append(s2, 4)      At this stage, the backing
s2 = append(s2, 5)  ⟵┘  array is already full.
```

This code leads to creating another backing array. Figure 3.9 displays the results in memory.

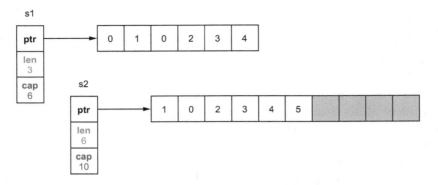

Figure 3.9   Appending elements to s2 until the backing array is full

s1 and s2 now reference two different arrays. As s1 is still a three-length, six-capacity slice, it still has some available buffer, so it keeps referencing the initial array. Also, the new backing array was made by copying the initial one from the first index of s2. That's why the new array starts with element 1, not 0.

To summarize, the *slice length* is the number of available elements in the slice, whereas the *slice capacity* is the number of elements in the backing array. Adding an element to a full slice (length == capacity) leads to creating a new backing array with a new capacity, copying all the elements from the previous array, and updating the slice pointer to the new array.

In the next section, we use the concepts of length and capacity with slice initialization.

3.5   *#21: Inefficient slice initialization*

While initializing a slice using make, we saw that we have to provide a length and an optional capacity. Forgetting to pass an appropriate value for both of these parameters when it makes sense is a widespread mistake. Let's see precisely when this is considered appropriate.

Suppose we want to implement a convert function that maps a slice of Foo into a slice of Bar, and both slices will have the same number of elements. Here is a first implementation:

```
func convert(foos []Foo) []Bar {        Creates the
    bars := make([]Bar, 0)    ⟵———   resulting slice

    for _, foo := range foos {
        bars = append(bars, fooToBar(foo))    ⟵┐  Converts a Foo into a Bar
    }                                           │  and adds it to the slice
    return bars
}
```

First, we initialize an empty slice of Bar elements using make([]Bar, 0). Then, we use append to add the Bar elements. At first, bars is empty, so adding the first element allocates a backing array of size 1. Every time the backing array is full, Go creates another array by doubling its capacity (discussed in the previous section).

This logic of creating another array because the current one is full is repeated multiple times when we add a third element, a fifth, a ninth, and so on. Assuming the input slice has 1,000 elements, this algorithm requires allocating 10 backing arrays and copying more than 1,000 elements in total from one array to another. This leads to additional effort for the GC to clean all these temporary backing arrays.

Performance-wise, there's no good reason not to give the Go runtime a helping hand. There are two different options for this. The first option is to reuse the same code but allocate the slice with a given capacity:

```go
func convert(foos []Foo) []Bar {
    n := len(foos)
    bars := make([]Bar, 0, n)        ⟵┘ Initializes with a zero length
                                         and a given capacity

    for _, foo := range foos {
        bars = append(bars, fooToBar(foo))    ⟵┐ Updates bars to append
    }                                            a new element
    return bars
}
```

The only change is to create `bars` with a capacity equal to n, the length of `foos`.

Internally, Go preallocates an array of *n* elements. Therefore, adding up to *n* elements means reusing the same backing array and hence reducing the number of allocations drastically. The second option is to allocate `bars` with a given length:

```go
func convert(foos []Foo) []Bar {
    n := len(foos)
    bars := make([]Bar, n)        ⟵┘ Initializes with
                                      a given length

    for i, foo := range foos {
        bars[i] = fooToBar(foo)    ⟵┐ Sets element i
    }                                 of the slice
    return bars
}
```

Because we initialize the slice with a length, *n* elements are already allocated and initialized to the zero value of `Bar`. Hence, to set elements, we have to use, not `append` but `bars[i]`.

Which option is best? Let's run a benchmark with the three solutions and an input slice of 1 million elements:

```
                                                              First solution with
                                                                 an empty slice
BenchmarkConvert_EmptySlice-4      22    49739882 ns/op    ⟵
BenchmarkConvert_GivenCapacity-4   86    13438544 ns/op    ⟵
BenchmarkConvert_GivenLength-4     91    12800411 ns/op
```

Third solution using a
given length and bars[i]

Second solution using a
given capacity and append

As we can see, the first solution has a significant impact performance-wise. When we keep allocating arrays and copying elements, the first benchmark is almost 400% slower than the other two. Comparing the second and the third solutions, the third is about 4% faster because we avoid repeated calls to the built-in append function, which has a small overhead compared to a direct assignment.

If setting a capacity and using append is less efficient than setting a length and assigning to a direct index, why do we see this approach being used in Go projects? Let's look at a concrete example in Pebble, an open source key-value store developed by Cockroach Labs (https://github.com/cockroachdb/pebble).

A function called collectAllUserKeys needs to iterate over a slice of structs to format a particular byte slice. The resulting slice will be twice the length of the input slice:

```
func collectAllUserKeys(cmp Compare,
    tombstones []tombstoneWithLevel) [][]byte {
    keys := make([][]byte, 0, len(tombstones)*2)
    for _, t := range tombstones {
        keys = append(keys, t.Start.UserKey)
        keys = append(keys, t.End)
    }
    // ...
}
```

Here, the conscious choice is to use a given capacity and append. What's the rationale? If we used a given length instead of a capacity, the code would be the following:

```
func collectAllUserKeys(cmp Compare,
    tombstones []tombstoneWithLevel) [][]byte {
    keys := make([][]byte, len(tombstones)*2)
    for i, t := range tombstones {
        keys[i*2] = t.Start.UserKey
        keys[i*2+1] = t.End
    }
    // ...
}
```

Notice how more complex the code to handle the slice index looks. Given that this function isn't performance sensitive, it was decided to favor the easiest option to read.

Slices and conditions

What if the future length of the slice isn't known precisely? For example, what if the length of the output slice depends on a condition?

```
func convert(foos []Foo) []Bar {
    // bars initialization

    for _, foo := range foos {
        if something(foo) {        ◁──┐ Add a Foo element
            // Add a bar element       │ only if a specific
        }                              │ condition is valid.
```

```
    }
    return bars
}
```

In this example, a `Foo` element is converted into a `Bar` and added to the slice only in a specific condition (`if something(foo)`). Should we initialize `bars` as an empty slice or with a given length or capacity?

There's no strict rule here. It's a traditional software problem: is it better to trade CPU or memory? Perhaps if `something(foo)` is true in 99% of the cases, it's worth initializing `bars` with a length or capacity. It depends on our use case.

Converting one slice type into another is a frequent operation for Go developers. As we have seen, if the length of the future slice is already known, there is no good reason to allocate an empty slice first. Our options are to allocate a slice with either a given capacity or a given length. Of these two solutions, we have seen that the second tends to be slightly faster. But using a given capacity and `append` can be easier to implement and read in some contexts.

The next section discusses the difference between nil and empty slices and why it matters for Go developers.

3.6   #22: Being confused about nil vs. empty slices

Go developers fairly frequently mix nil and empty slices. We may want to use one over the other depending on the use case. Meanwhile, some libraries make a distinction between the two. To be proficient with slices, we need to make sure we don't mix these concepts. Before looking at an example, let's discuss some definitions:

- A slice is empty if its length is equal to 0.
- A slice is nil if it equals `nil`.

Now, let's look at different ways to initialize a slice. Can you guess the output of the following code? Each time, we will print whether the slice is empty or nil:

```
func main() {
    var s []string        ◁──┤ Option 1 (a 0 value)
    log(1, s)

    s = []string(nil)     ◁──┤ Option 2
    log(2, s)

    s = []string{}        ◁──┤ Option 3
    log(3, s)

    s = make([]string, 0) ◁──┤ Option 4
    log(4, s)
}

func log(i int, s []string) {
    fmt.Printf("%d: empty=%t\tnil=%t\n", i, len(s) == 0, s == nil)
}
```

This example prints the following:

```
1: empty=true    nil=true
2: empty=true    nil=true
3: empty=true    nil=false
4: empty=true    nil=false
```

All the slices are empty, meaning the length equals 0. Therefore, a nil slice is also an empty slice. However, only the first two are nil slices. If we have multiple ways to initialize a slice, which option should we favor? There are two things to note:

- One of the main differences between a nil and an empty slice regards allocations. Initializing a nil slice doesn't require any allocation, which isn't the case for an empty slice.
- Regardless of whether a slice is nil, calling the append built-in function works. For example,

```
var s1 []string
fmt.Println(append(s1, "foo")) // [foo]
```

Consequently, if a function returns a slice, we shouldn't do as in other languages and return a non-nil collection for defensive reasons. Because a nil slice doesn't require any allocation, we should favor returning a nil slice instead of an empty slice. Let's look at this function, which returns a slice of strings:

```
func f() []string {
    var s []string
    if foo() {
        s = append(s, "foo")
    }
    if bar() {
        s = append(s, "bar")
    }
    return s
}
```

If both foo and bar are false, we get an empty slice. To prevent allocating an empty slice for no particular reason, we should favor option 1 (var s []string). We can use option 4 (make([]string, 0)) with a zero-length string, but doing so doesn't bring any value compared to option 1; and it requires an allocation.

However, in the case where we have to produce a slice with a known length, we should use option 4, s := make([]string, length), as this example shows:

```
func intsToStrings(ints []int) []string {
    s := make([]string, len(ints))
    for i, v := range ints {
        s[i] = strconv.Itoa(v)
    }
    return s
}
```

As discussed in mistake #21, "Inefficient slice initialization," we need to set the length (or capacity) in such a scenario to avoid extra allocations and copies. Now, two options remain from the example that looks at different ways to initialize a slice:

- Option 2: `s := []string(nil)`
- Option 3: `s := []string{}`

Option 2 isn't the most widely used. But it can be helpful as syntactic sugar because we can pass a nil slice in a single line—for example, using `append`:

```
s := append([]int(nil), 42)
```

If we had used option 1 (`var s []string`), it would have required two lines of code. This is probably not the most important readability optimization of all time, but it's still worth knowing.

> **NOTE**   In mistake #24, "Not making slice copies correctly," we will see one rationale to append to a nil slice.

Now, let's look at option 3: `s := []string{}`. This form is recommended to create a slice with initial elements:

```
s := []string{"foo", "bar", "baz"}
```

However, if we don't need to create a slice with initial elements, we shouldn't use this option. It brings the same benefits as option 1 (`var s []string`), except that the slice isn't nil; hence, it requires an allocation. Therefore, option 3 should be avoided without initial elements.

> **NOTE**   Some linters can catch option 3 without initial values and recommend changing it to option 1. However, we should remember that this also changes the semantics from a non-nil to a nil slice.

We should also mention that some libraries distinguish between nil and empty slices. This is the case, for example, with the `encoding/json` package. The following examples marshal two structs, one containing a nil slice and the second a non-nil, empty slice:

```
var s1 []float32          ◄───┤ Nil slice
customer1 := customer{
    ID:        "foo",
    Operations: s1,
}
b, _ := json.Marshal(customer1)
fmt.Println(string(b))

s2 := make([]float32, 0)      ◄───  Non-nil,
customer2 := customer{              empty slice
    ID:        "bar",
    Operations: s2,
}
b, _ = json.Marshal(customer2)
fmt.Println(string(b))
```

Running this example, notice that the marshaling results for these two structs are different:

```
{"ID":"foo","Operations":null}
{"ID":"bar","Operations":[]}
```

Here, a nil slice is marshaled as a `null` element, whereas a non-nil, empty slice is marshaled as an empty array. If we work in the context of strict JSON clients that differentiate between `null` and `[]`, it's essential to keep this distinction in mind.

The `encoding/json` package isn't the only package from the standard library to make this distinction. For example, `reflect.DeepEqual` returns `false` if we compare a nil and a non-nil empty slice, which is something to remember in the context of unit tests, for example. In any case, while working with the standard library or external libraries, we should ensure that when using one version or another, our code doesn't lead to unexpected results.

To summarize, in Go, there is a distinction between nil and empty slices. A nil slice equals `nil`, whereas an empty slice has a length of zero. A nil slice is empty, but an empty slice isn't necessarily `nil`. Meanwhile, a nil slice doesn't require any allocation. We have seen throughout this section how to initialize a slice depending on the context by using

- `var s []string` if we aren't sure about the final length and the slice can be empty
- `[]string(nil)` as syntactic sugar to create a nil and empty slice
- `make([]string, length)` if the future length is known

The last option, `[]string{}`, should be avoided if we initialize the slice without elements. Finally, let's check whether the libraries we use make the distinctions between nil and empty slices to prevent unexpected behaviors.

In the next section, we continue this discussion and see the best way to check for an empty slice after having called a function.

3.7 *#23: Not properly checking if a slice is empty*

We saw in the previous section that there is a distinction between nil and empty slices. Having these notions in mind, what's the idiomatic way to check if a slice contains elements? Not having a clear answer can lead to subtle bugs.

In this example, we call a `getOperations` function that returns a slice of `float32`. We want to call a `handle` function only if the slice contains elements. Here's a first (erroneous) version:

```
func handleOperations(id string) {
    operations := getOperations(id)
    if operations != nil {          ◁── Checks if the
        handle(operations)             operations slice is nil
    }
}
```

```
func getOperations(id string) []float32 {
    operations := make([]float32, 0)       ◁─┐ Initializes the
                                              │ operations slice
    if id == "" {
        return operations                  ◁─┐ Returns operations if the
    }                                         │ provided id is empty

    // Add elements to operations

    return operations
}
```

We determine whether the slice has elements by checking if the `operations` slice isn't `nil`. But there's a problem with this code: `getOperations` never returns a nil slice; instead, it returns an empty slice. Therefore, the `operations != nil` check will always be `true`.

What do we do in this situation? One approach might be to modify `getOperations` to return a nil slice if `id` is empty:

```
func getOperations(id string) []float32 {
    operations := make([]float32, 0)

    if id == "" {
        return nil       ◁─┐ Returns nil instead
    }                       │ of operations

    // Add elements to operations

    return operations
}
```

Instead of returning `operations` if `id` is empty, we return `nil`. This way, the check we implement about testing the slice nullity matches. However, this approach doesn't work in all situations—we're not always in a context where we can change the callee. For example, if we use an external library, we won't create a pull request just to change empty into nil slices.

How then can we check whether a slice is empty or nil? The solution is to check the length:

```
func handleOperations(id string) {
    operations := getOperations(id)
    if len(operations) != 0 {     ◁─┐ Checks the
        handle(operations)           │ slice length
    }
}
```

We mentioned in the previous section that an empty slice has, by definition, a length of zero. Meanwhile, nil slices are always empty. Therefore, by checking the length of the slice, we cover all the scenarios:

- If the slice is `nil`, `len(operations) != 0` is false.
- If the slice isn't `nil` but empty, `len(operations) != 0` is also false.

Hence, checking the length is the best option to follow as we can't always control the approach taken by the functions we call. Meanwhile, as the Go wiki states, when designing interfaces, we should avoid distinguishing nil and empty slices, which leads to subtle programming errors. When returning slices, it should make neither a semantic nor a technical difference if we return a nil or empty slice. Both should mean the same thing for the callers. This principle is the same with maps. To check if a map is empty, check its length, not whether it's `nil`.

In the next section, we see how to make slice copies correctly.

3.8   *#24: Not making slice copies correctly*

The `copy` built-in function allows copying elements from a source slice into a destination slice. Although it is a handy built-in function, Go developers sometimes misunderstand it. Let's look at a common mistake that results in copying the wrong number of elements.

In the following example, we create a slice and copy its elements to another slice. What should be the output of this code?

```
src := []int{0, 1, 2}
var dst []int
copy(dst, src)
fmt.Println(dst)
```

If we run this example, it prints `[]`, not `[0 1 2]`. What did we miss?

To use `copy` effectively, it's essential to understand that the number of elements copied to the destination slice corresponds to the minimum between:

- The source slice's length
- The destination slice's length

In the previous example, `src` is a three-length slice, but `dst` is a zero-length slice because it is initialized to its zero value. Therefore, the `copy` function copies the minimum number of elements (between 3 and 0): 0 in this case. The resulting slice is then empty.

If we want to perform a complete copy, the destination slice must have a length greater than or equal to the source slice's length. Here, we set up a length based on the source slice:

```
src := []int{0, 1, 2}
dst := make([]int, len(src))   ◁──┐  Creates a dst slice but
copy(dst, src)                     │  with a given length
fmt.Println(dst)
```

Because `dst` is now a slice initialized with a length equal to 3, it copies three elements. This time, if we run the code, it prints `[0 1 2]`.

NOTE Another common mistake is to invert the order of the arguments when calling `copy`. Remember that the destination is the former argument, whereas the source is the latter.

Let's also mention that using the `copy` built-in function isn't the only way to copy slice elements. There are different alternatives, the best known being probably the following, which uses `append`:

```
src := []int{0, 1, 2}
dst := append([]int(nil), src...)
```

We append the elements from the source slice to a nil slice. Hence, this code creates a three-length, three-capacity slice copy. This alternative has the advantage of being done in a single line. However, using `copy` is more idiomatic and, therefore, easier to understand, even though it takes an extra line.

Copying elements from one slice to another is a reasonably frequent operation. When using `copy`, we must recall that the number of elements copied to the destination corresponds to the minimum between the two slices' lengths. Also bear in mind that other alternatives exist to copy a slice, so we shouldn't be surprised if we find them in a codebase.

Let's continue discussing slices with a common mistake when using `append`.

3.9   #25: Unexpected side effects using slice append

This section discusses a common mistake when using `append`, which may have unexpected side effects in some situations. In the following example, we initialize an `s1` slice, create `s2` by slicing `s1`, and create `s3` by appending an element to `s2`:

```
s1 := []int{1, 2, 3}
s2 := s1[1:2]
s3 := append(s2, 10)
```

We initialize an `s1` slice containing three elements, and `s2` is created from slicing `s1`. Then we call `append` on `s3`. What should be the state of these three slices at the end of this code? Can you guess?

Following the second line, after `s2` is created, figure 3.10 shows the state of both slices in memory. `s1` is a three-length, three-capacity slice, and `s2` is a one-length, two-capacity slice, both backed by the same array we already mentioned. Adding an element using `append` checks whether the slice is full (length == capacity). If it is not full, the `append` function adds the element by updating the backing array and returning a slice having a length incremented by 1.

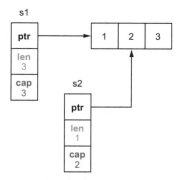

Figure 3.10   Both slices are backed by the same array but with a different length and capacity.

In this example, s2 isn't full; it can accept one more element. Figure 3.11 shows the final state of these three slices.

In the backing array, we updated the last element to store 10. Therefore, if we print all the slices, we get this output:

```
s1=[1 2 10], s2=[2], s3=[2 10]
```

The s1 slice's content was modified, even though we did not update s1[2] or s2[1] directly. We should keep this in mind to avoid unintended consequences.

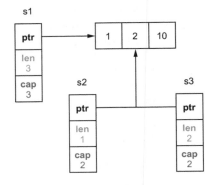

Figure 3.11 All the slices are backed by the same array.

Let's see one impact of this principle by passing the result of a slicing operation to a function. In the following, we initialize a slice with three elements and call a function with only the first two elements:

```
func main() {
    s := []int{1, 2, 3}

    f(s[:2])
    // Use s
}

func f(s []int) {
    // Update s
}
```

In this implementation, if f updates the first two elements, the changes are visible to the slice in main. However, if f calls append, it updates the third element of the slice, even though we pass only two elements. For example,

```
func main() {
    s := []int{1, 2, 3}

    f(s[:2])
    fmt.Println(s) // [1 2 10]
}

func f(s []int) {
    _ = append(s, 10)
}
```

If we want to *protect* the third element for defensive reasons, meaning to ensure that f doesn't update it, we have two options.

The first is to pass a copy of the slice and then construct the resulting slice:

```
func main() {
    s := []int{1, 2, 3}
```

```
    sCopy := make([]int, 2)
    copy(sCopy, s)          ◁────┐  Copies the first two
                                 │  elements of s into sCopy
    f(sCopy)
    result := append(sCopy, s[2])        ◁────┐  Appends s[2] to sCopy to
    // Use result                             │  construct the resulting slice
}

func f(s []int) {
    // Update s
}
```

Because we pass a copy to f, even if this function calls append, it will not lead to a side effect outside of the range of the first two elements. The downside of this option is that it makes the code more complex to read and adds an extra copy, which can be a problem if the slice is large.

The second option can be used to limit the range of potential side effects to the first two elements only. This option involves the so-called *full slice expression*: s[low:high:max]. This statement creates a slice similar to the one created with s[low:high], except that the resulting slice's capacity is equal to max - low. Here's an example when calling f:

```
func main() {
    s := []int{1, 2, 3}
    f(s[:2:2])          ◁────┐  Passes a subslice using
    // Use s                 │  the full slice expression
}

func f(s []int) {
    // Update s
}
```

Here, the slice passed to f isn't s[:2] but s[:2:2]. Hence, the slice's capacity is 2 − 0 = 2, as figure 3.12 shows.

When passing s[:2:2], we can limit the range of effects to the first two elements. Doing so also prevents us from having to perform a slice copy.

When using slicing, we must remember that we can face a situation leading to unintended side effects. If the resulting slice has a length smaller than its capacity, append can mutate the original slice. If we want to restrict the range of possible side effects, we can use either a slice copy or the full slice expression, which prevents us from doing a copy.

In the next section, we continue discussing slices but in the context of potential memory leaks.

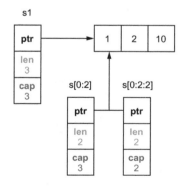

Figure 3.12 `s[0:2]` creates a two-length, three-capacity slice, whereas `s[0:2:2]` creates a two-length, two-capacity slice.

3.10 *#26: Slices and memory leaks*

This section shows that slicing an existing slice or array can lead to memory leaks in some conditions. We discuss two cases: one where the capacity is leaking and another that's related to pointers.

3.10.1 *Leaking capacity*

For the first case, leaking capacity, let's imagine implementing a custom binary protocol. A message can contain 1 million bytes, and the first 5 bytes represent the message type. In our code, we consume these messages, and for auditing purposes, we want to store the latest 1,000 message types in memory. This is the skeleton of our function:

```
func consumeMessages() {
    for {
        msg := receiveMessage()          ⟵  Receives a new []byte
        // Do something with msg              slice assigned to msg
        storeMessageType(getMessageType(msg))   ⟵  Stores the latest 1,000
    }                                                 message types in memory
}

func getMessageType(msg []byte) []byte {   ⟵  Computes the message
    return msg[:5]                              type by slicing msg
}
```

The getMessageType function computes the message type by slicing the input slice. We test this implementation, and everything is fine. However, when we deploy our application, we notice that our application consumes about 1 GB of memory. How is that possible?

The slicing operation on msg using msg[:5] creates a five-length slice. However, its capacity remains the same as the initial slice. The remaining elements are still allocated in memory, even if eventually msg is not referenced. Let's look at an example with a large message length of 1 million bytes, as shown in figure 3.13.

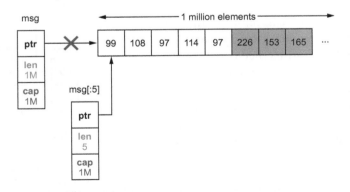

Figure 3.13   After a new loop iteration, msg is no longer used. However, its backing array will still be used by msg[:5].

The backing array of the slice still contains 1 million bytes after the slicing operation. Hence, if we keep 1,000 messages in memory, instead of storing about 5 KB, we hold about 1 GB.

What can we do to solve this issue? We can make a slice copy instead of slicing `msg`:

```
func getMessageType(msg []byte) []byte {
    msgType := make([]byte, 5)
    copy(msgType, msg)
    return msgType
}
```

Because we perform a copy, `msgType` is a five-length, five-capacity slice regardless of the size of the message received. Hence, we only store 5 bytes per message type.

Full slice expressions and capacity leakage

What about using the full slice expression to solve this issue? Let's look at this example:

```
func getMessageType(msg []byte) []byte {
    return msg[:5:5]
}
```

Here, `getMessageType` returns a shrunken version of the initial slice: a five-length, five-capacity slice. But would the GC be able to reclaim the inaccessible space from byte 5? The Go specification doesn't officially specify the behavior. However, by using `runtime.Memstats`, we can record statistics about the memory allocator, such as the number of bytes allocated on the heap:

```
func printAlloc() {
    var m runtime.MemStats
    runtime.ReadMemStats(&m)
    fmt.Printf("%d KB\n", m.Alloc/1024)
}
```

If we call this function following a call to `getMessageType` and `runtime.GC()` to force running a garbage collection, the inaccessible space isn't reclaimed. The whole backing array still lives in memory. Therefore, using the full slice expression isn't a valid option (unless a future update of Go tackles this).

As a rule of thumb, remember that slicing a large slice or array can lead to potential high memory consumption. The remaining space won't be reclaimed by the GC, and we can keep a large backing array despite using only a few elements. Using a slice copy is the solution to prevent such a case.

3.10.2 *Slice and pointers*

We have seen that slicing can cause a leak because of the slice capacity. But what about the elements, which are still part of the backing array but outside the length range? Does the GC collect them?

Let's examine this question using a `Foo` struct containing a byte slice:

```
type Foo struct {
    v []byte
}
```

We want to check the memory allocations after each step as follows:

1 Allocate a slice of 1,000 `Foo` elements.
2 Iterate over each `Foo` element, and for each one, allocate 1 MB for the `v` slice.
3 Call `keepFirstTwoElementsOnly`, which returns only the first two elements using slicing, and then call a GC.

We want to see how memory behaves following the call to `keepFirstTwoElementsOnly` and a garbage collection. Here's the scenario in Go (we reuse the `printAlloc` function mentioned previously):

```
func main() {
    foos := make([]Foo, 1_000)         ◁─┐ Allocates a slice of
    printAlloc()                          │ 1,000 elements

    for i := 0; i < len(foos); i++ {   ◁─┐ For each element,
        foos[i] = Foo{                    │ allocates a slice of 1 MB
            v: make([]byte, 1024*1024),
        }
    }
    printAlloc()
                                                    ┐ Keeps only the
    two := keepFirstTwoElementsOnly(foos)   ◁───────┘ first two elements
    runtime.GC()                       ◁─┐ Runs the GC to force
    printAlloc()                          │ cleaning the heap
    runtime.KeepAlive(two)    ◁─┐ Keeps a reference to
}                                │ the two variable

func keepFirstTwoElementsOnly(foos []Foo) []Foo {
    return foos[:2]
}
```

In this example, we allocate the `foos` slice, allocate a slice of 1 MB for each element, and then call `keepFirstTwoElementsOnly` and a GC. In the end, we use `runtime`
`.KeepAlive` to keep a reference to the `two` variable after the garbage collection so that it won't be collected.

We may expect the GC to collect the 998 remaining `Foo` elements and the data allocated for the slice because these elements can no longer be accessed. However, this isn't the case. For example, the code can output the following:

```
83 KB
1024072 KB        ┐ After the slicing
1024072 KB    ◁───┘ operation
```

The first output allocates about 83 KB of data. Indeed, we allocated 1,000 zero values of `Foo`. The second result allocates 1 MB per slice, which increases memory. However, notice that the GC did not collect the remaining 998 elements after the last step. What's the reason?

It's essential to keep this rule in mind when working with slices: if the element is a pointer or a struct with pointer fields, the elements won't be reclaimed by the GC. In our example, because `Foo` contains a slice (and a slice is a pointer on top of a backing array), the remaining 998 `Foo` elements and their slice aren't reclaimed. Therefore, even though these 998 elements can't be accessed, they stay in memory as long as the variable returned by `keepFirstTwoElementsOnly` is referenced.

What are the options to ensure that we don't leak the remaining `Foo` elements? The first option, again, is to create a copy of the slice:

```
func keepFirstTwoElementsOnly(foos []Foo) []Foo {
    res := make([]Foo, 2)
    copy(res, foos)
    return res
}
```

Because we copy the first two elements of the slice, the GC knows that the 998 elements won't be referenced anymore and can now be collected.

There's a second option if we want to keep the underlying capacity of 1,000 elements, which is to mark the slices of the remaining elements explicitly as `nil`:

```
func keepFirstTwoElementsOnly(foos []Foo) []Foo {
    for i := 2; i < len(foos); i++ {
        foos[i].v = nil
    }
    return foos[:2]
}
```

Here, we return a 2-length, 1,000-capacity slice, but we set the slices of the remaining elements to `nil`. Hence, the GC can collect the 998 backing arrays.

Which option is the best? If we don't want to keep the capacity at 1,000 elements, the first option is probably the best. However, the decision can also depend on the proportion of the elements. Figure 3.14 provides a visual example of the options we can choose, assuming a slice containing n elements where we want to keep i elements.

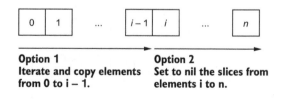

Option 1
Iterate and copy elements
from 0 to i – 1.

Option 2
Set to nil the slices from
elements i to n.

Figure 3.14   Option 1 iterates until `i`, whereas option 2 iterates from `i`.

The first option creates a copy of i elements. Hence, it must iterate from element 0 to i. The second option sets the remaining slices to nil, so it must iterate from element i to n. If performance is important and i is closer to n than 0, we may consider the second option. This requires iterating over fewer elements (at least, it's probably worth benchmarking the two options).

In this section, we saw two potential memory leak problems. The first was about slicing an existing slice or array to preserve the capacity. If we handle large slices and reslice them to keep only a fraction, a lot of memory will remain allocated but unused. The second problem is that when we use the slicing operation with pointers or structs with pointer fields, we need to know that the GC won't reclaim these elements. In that case, the two options are to either perform a copy or explicitly mark the remaining elements or their fields to nil.

Now, let's discuss maps in the context of initializations.

3.11   *#27: Inefficient map initialization*

This section discusses an issue similar to one we saw with slice initialization, but using maps. But first, we need to know the basics regarding how maps are implemented in Go to understand why tweaking map initialization is important.

3.11.1   *Concepts*

A *map* provides an unordered collection of key-value pairs in which all the keys are distinct. In Go, a map is based on the hash table data structure. Internally, a hash table is an array of buckets, and each bucket is a pointer to an array of key-value pairs, as figure 3.15 illustrates.

An array of four elements backs the hash table in figure 3.15. If we examine the array index, we notice one bucket consisting of a single key-value pair (element): "two"/2. Each bucket has a fixed size of eight elements.

Each operation (read, update, insert, delete) is done by associating a key to an array index. This step relies on a hash function. This function is stable because we want it to return the same bucket, given the same key, consistently. In the previous

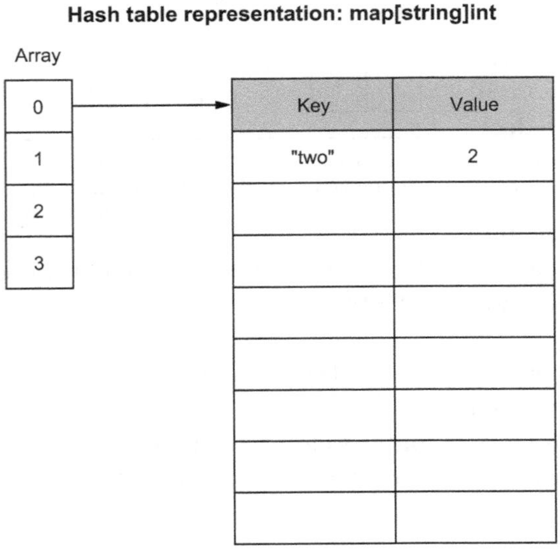

Hash table representation: map[string]int

Figure 3.15   **A hash table example with a focus on bucket 0**

example, hash("two") returns 0; hence, the element is stored in the bucket referenced by the array index 0.

If we insert another element, and hashing the key returns the same index, Go adds another element to the same bucket. Figure 3.16 shows this result.

Hash table representation: map[string]int

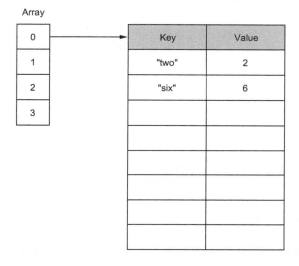

Figure 3.16 hash("six") returns 0; hence, the element is stored in the same bucket.

In the case of insertion into a bucket that is already full (bucket overflow), Go creates another bucket of eight elements and links the previous bucket to it. Figure 3.17 provides this result.

Hash table representation: map[string]int

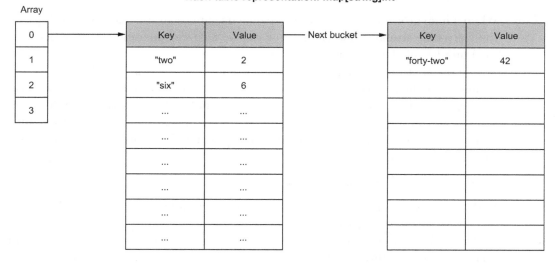

Figure 3.17 In case of a bucket overflow, Go allocates a new bucket and links the previous bucket to it.

Regarding reads, updates, and deletes, Go must calculate the corresponding array index. Then Go iterates sequentially over all the keys until it finds the provided one. Therefore, the worst-case time complexity for these three operations is $O(p)$, where p is the total number of elements in the buckets (one bucket by default, multiple buckets in case of overflows).

Let's now discuss why initializing a map efficiently is important.

3.11.2   *Initialization*

To understand the problems related to inefficient map initialization, let's create a `map[string]int` type containing three elements:

```
m := map[string]int{
    "1": 1,
    "2": 2,
    "3": 3,
}
```

Internally, this map is backed by an array consisting of a single entry: hence, a single bucket. What happens if we add 1 million elements? In this case, a single entry won't be enough because finding a key would mean, in the worst case, going over thousands of buckets. This is why a map should be able to grow automatically to cope with the number of elements.

When a map grows, it doubles its number of buckets. What are the conditions for a map to grow?

- The average number of items in the buckets (called the *load factor*) is greater than a constant value. This constant equals 6.5 (but it may change in future versions because it's internal to Go).
- Too many buckets have overflowed (containing more than eight elements).

When a map grows, all the keys are dispatched again to all the buckets. This is why, in the worst-case scenario, inserting a key can be an $O(n)$ operation, with n being the total number of elements in the map.

We saw that when using slices, if we knew up front the number of elements to be added to the slice, we could initialize it with a given size or capacity. This avoids having to keep repeating the costly slice growth operation. The idea is similar for maps. Indeed, we can use the `make` built-in function to provide an initial size when creating a map. For example, if we want to initialize a map that will contain 1 million elements, it can be done this way:

```
m := make(map[string]int, 1_000_000)
```

With a map, we can give the built-in function `make` only an initial size and not a capacity, as with slices: hence, a single argument.

By specifying a size, we provide a hint about the number of elements expected to go into the map. Internally, the map is created with an appropriate number of buckets to store 1 million elements. This saves a lot of computation time because the map won't have to create buckets on the fly and handle rebalancing buckets.

Also, specifying a size *n* doesn't mean making a map with a maximum number of *n* elements. We can still add more than *n* elements if needed. Instead, it means asking the Go runtime to allocate a map with room for at least *n* elements, which is helpful if we already know the size up front.

To understand why specifying a size is important, let's run two benchmarks. The first inserts 1 million elements in a map without setting an initial size, whereas we initialize the second map with a size:

```
BenchmarkMapWithoutSize-4    6    227413490 ns/op
BenchmarkMapWithSize-4      13     91174193 ns/op
```

The second version, with an initial size, is about 60% faster. By providing a size, we prevent the map from growing to cope with the inserted elements.

Therefore, just like with slices, if we know up front the number of elements a map will contain, we should create it by providing an initial size. Doing this avoids potential map growth, which is quite heavy computation-wise because it requires reallocating enough space and rebalancing all the elements.

Let's continue our discussion about maps and look at a common mistake that leads to memory leaks.

3.12   *#28: Maps and memory leaks*

When working with maps in Go, we need to understand some important characteristics of how a map grows and shrinks. Let's delve into this to prevent an issue that can cause memory leaks.

First, to view a concrete example of this problem, let's design a scenario where we will work with the following map:

```
m := make(map[int][128]byte)
```

Each value of m is an array of 128 bytes. We will do the following:

1. Allocate an empty map.
2. Add 1 million elements.
3. Remove all the elements, and run a GC.

After each step, we want to print the size of the heap (using MB this time). This shows us how this example behaves memory-wise:

```
n := 1_000_000
m := make(map[int][128]byte)
printAlloc()

for i := 0; i < n; i++ {        ⟵──┐ Adds 1 million
    m[i] = randBytes()                │ elements
}
```

```
printAlloc()

for i := 0; i < n; i++ {
    delete(m, i)
}
runtime.GC()
printAlloc()
runtime.KeepAlive(m)
```

Deletes 1 million elements

Triggers a manual GC

Keeps a reference to m so that the map isn't collected

We allocate an empty map, add 1 million elements, remove 1 million elements, and then run a GC. We also make sure to keep a reference to the map using `runtime.KeepAlive` so that the map isn't collected as well. Let's run this example:

```
0 MB
461 MB
293 MB
```

After m is allocated

After we add 1 million elements

After we remove 1 million elements

What can we observe? At first, the heap size is minimal. Then it grows significantly after having added 1 million elements to the map. But if we expected the heap size to decrease after removing all the elements, this isn't how maps work in Go. In the end, even though the GC has collected all the elements, the heap size is still 293 MB. So the memory shrunk, but not as we might have expected. What's the rationale?

We discussed in the previous section that a map is composed of eight-element buckets. Under the hood, a Go map is a pointer to a `runtime.hmap` struct. This struct contains multiple fields, including a B field, giving the number of buckets in the map:

```
type hmap struct {
    B uint8 // log_2 of # of buckets
            // (can hold up to loadFactor * 2^B items)
    // ...
}
```

After adding 1 million elements, the value of B equals 18, which means $2^{18} = 262,144$ buckets. When we remove 1 million elements, what's the value of B? Still 18. Hence, the map still contains the same number of buckets.

The reason is that the number of buckets in a map cannot shrink. Therefore, removing elements from a map doesn't impact the number of existing buckets; it just zeroes the slots in the buckets. A map can only grow and have more buckets; it never shrinks.

In the previous example, we went from 461 MB to 293 MB because the elements were collected, but running the GC didn't impact the map itself. Even the number of extra buckets (the buckets created because of overflows) remains the same.

Let's take a step back and discuss when the fact that a map cannot shrink can be a problem. Imagine building a cache using `map[int][128]byte`. This map holds per customer ID (the `int`), a sequence of 128 bytes. Now, suppose we want to save the last

1,000 customers. The map size will remain constant, so we shouldn't worry about the fact that a map cannot shrink.

However, let's say we want to store one hour of data. Meanwhile, our company has decided to have a big promotion for Black Friday: in one hour, we may have millions of customers connected to our system. But a few days after Black Friday, our map will contain the same number of buckets as during the peak time. This explains why we can experience high memory consumption that doesn't significantly decrease in such a scenario.

What are the solutions if we don't want to manually restart our service to clean the amount of memory consumed by the map? One solution could be to re-create a copy of the current map at a regular pace. For example, every hour, we can build a new map, copy all the elements, and release the previous one. The main drawback of this option is that following the copy and until the next garbage collection, we may consume twice the current memory for a short period.

Another solution would be to change the map type to store an array pointer: `map[int]*[128]byte`. It doesn't solve the fact that we will have a significant number of buckets; however, each bucket entry will reserve the size of a pointer for the value instead of 128 bytes (8 bytes on 64-bit systems and 4 bytes on 32-bit systems).

Coming back to the original scenario, let's compare the memory consumption for each map type following each step. The following table shows the comparison.

Step	`map[int][128]byte`	`map[int]*[128]byte`
Allocate an empty map.	0 MB	0 MB
Add 1 million elements.	461 MB	182 MB
Remove all the elements and run a GC.	293 MB	38 MB

As we can see, after removing all the elements, the amount of required memory is significantly less with a `map[int]*[128]byte` type. Also, in this case, the amount of required memory is less significant during peak times due to some optimizations to reduce the memory consumed.

> **NOTE** If a key or a value is over 128 bytes, Go won't store it directly in the map bucket. Instead, Go stores a pointer to reference the key or the value.

As we have seen, adding *n* elements to a map and then deleting all the elements means keeping the same number of buckets in memory. So, we must remember that because a Go map can only grow in size, so does its memory consumption. There is no automated strategy to shrink it. If this leads to high memory consumption, we can try different options such as forcing Go to re-create the map or using pointers to check if it can be optimized.

For the last section of this chapter, let's discuss comparing values in Go.

3.13   *#29: Comparing values incorrectly*

Comparing values is a common operation in software development. We frequently implement comparisons: writing a function to compare two objects, testing to compare a value against an expectation, and so on. Our first instinct might be to use the == operator everywhere. But as we will see in this section, this shouldn't always be the case. So when is it appropriate to use ==, and what are the alternatives?

To answer these questions, let's start with a concrete example. We create a basic customer struct and use == to compare two instances. What should be the output of this code, in your opinion?

```
type customer struct {
    id string
}

func main() {
    cust1 := customer{id: "x"}
    cust2 := customer{id: "x"}
    fmt.Println(cust1 == cust2)
}
```

Comparing these two customer structs is a valid operation in Go, and it will print true. Now, what happens if we make a slight modification to the customer struct to add a slice field?

```
type customer struct {
    id         string
    operations []float64      ⊲⎯⎯ New field
}

func main() {
    cust1 := customer{id: "x", operations: []float64{1.}}
    cust2 := customer{id: "x", operations: []float64{1.}}
    fmt.Println(cust1 == cust2)
}
```

We might expect this code to print true as well. However, it doesn't even compile:

```
invalid operation:
    cust1 == cust2 (struct containing []float64 cannot be compared)
```

The problem relates to how the == and != operators work. These operators don't work with slices or maps. Hence, because the customer struct contains a slice, it doesn't compile.

It's essential to understand how to use == and != to make comparisons effectively. We can use these operators on operands that are *comparable*:

- *Booleans*—Compare whether two Booleans are equal.
- *Numerics (int, float, and complex types)*—Compare whether two numerics are equal.

- *Strings*—Compare whether two strings are equal.
- *Channels*—Compare whether two channels were created by the same call to make or if both are nil.
- *Interfaces*—Compare whether two interfaces have identical dynamic types and equal dynamic values or if both are nil.
- *Pointers*—Compare whether two pointers point to the same value in memory or if both are nil.
- *Structs and arrays*—Compare whether they are composed of similar types.

NOTE We can also use the ?, >=, <, and > operators with numeric types to compare values and with strings to compare their lexical order.

In the last example, our code failed to compile as the struct was composed on a non-comparable type (a slice).

We also need to know the possible issues of using == and != with any types. For example, comparing two integers assigned to any types is allowed:

```
var a any = 3
var b any = 3
fmt.Println(a == b)
```

This code prints:

```
true
```

But what if we initialize two customer types (the latest version containing a slice field) and assign the values to any types? Here's an example:

```
var cust1 any = customer{id: "x", operations: []float64{1.}}
var cust2 any = customer{id: "x", operations: []float64{1.}}
fmt.Println(cust1 == cust2)
```

This code compiles. But as both types can't be compared because the customer struct contains a slice field, it leads to an error at run time:

```
panic: runtime error: comparing uncomparable type main.customer
```

With these behaviors in mind, what are the options if we have to compare two slices, two maps, or two structs containing noncomparable types? If we stick with the standard library, one option is to use run-time reflection with the reflect package.

Reflection is a form of metaprogramming, and it refers to the ability of an application to introspect and modify its structure and behavior. For example, in Go, we can use reflect.DeepEqual. This function reports whether two elements are *deeply equal* by recursively traversing two values. The elements it accepts are basic types plus arrays, structs, slices, maps, pointers, interfaces, and functions.

NOTE reflect.DeepEqual has a specific behavior depending on the type we provide. Before using it, read the documentation carefully.

Let's rerun the first example, adding `reflect.DeepEqual`:

```
cust1 := customer{id: "x", operations: []float64{1.}}
cust2 := customer{id: "x", operations: []float64{1.}}
fmt.Println(reflect.DeepEqual(cust1, cust2))
```

Even though the `customer` struct contains noncomparable types (slice), it operates as expected, printing `true`.

However, there are two things to keep in mind when using `reflect.DeepEqual`. First, it makes the distinction between an empty and a nil collection, as discussed in mistake #22, "Being confused about nil vs. empty slices." Is this a problem? Not necessarily; it depends on our use case. For example, if we want to compare the results of two unmarshaling operations (such as from JSON to a Go struct), we may want this difference to be raised. But it's worth keeping this behavior in mind to use `reflect.DeepEqual` effectively.

The other catch is something pretty standard in most languages. Because this function uses reflection, which introspects values at run time to discover how they are formed, it has a performance penalty. Doing a few benchmarks locally with structs of different sizes, on average, `reflect.DeepEqual` is about 100 times slower than `==`. This might be a reason to favor using it in the context of testing instead of at run time.

If performance is a crucial factor, another option might be to implement our own comparison method. Here's an example that compares two `customer` structs and returns a Boolean:

```
func (a customer) equal(b customer) bool {
    if a.id != b.id {                                    ⟵┐ Compares
        return false                                       │ the id fields
    }
    if len(a.operations) != len(b.operations) {          ⟵┐ Checks the length
        return false                                       │ of both slices
    }
    for i := 0; i < len(a.operations); i++ {             ⟵┐ Compares each
        if a.operations[i] != b.operations[i] {            │ element of both slices
            return false
        }
    }
    return true
}
```

In this code, we build our comparison method with custom checks on the different fields of the `customer` struct. Running a local benchmark on a slice composed of 100 elements shows that our custom `equal` method is about 96 times faster than `reflect.DeepEqual`.

In general, we should remember that the `==` operator is pretty limited. For example, it doesn't work with slices and maps. In most cases, using `reflect.DeepEqual` is a solution, but the main catch is the performance penalty. In the context of unit tests, some other options are possible, such as using external libraries with go-cmp (https://github.com/google/go-cmp) or testify (https://github.com/stretchr/testify).

However, if performance is crucial at run time, implementing our custom method might be the best solution.

One additional note: we must remember that the standard library has some existing comparison methods. For example, we can use the optimized `bytes.Compare` function to compare two slices of bytes. Before implementing a custom method, we need to make sure we don't reinvent the wheel.

Summary

- When reading existing code, bear in mind that integer literals starting with 0 are octal numbers. Also, to improve readability, make octal integers explicit by prefixing them with `0o`.
- Because integer overflows and underflows are handled silently in Go, you can implement your own functions to catch them.
- Making floating-point comparisons within a given delta can ensure that your code is portable.
- When performing addition or subtraction, group the operations with a similar order of magnitude to favor accuracy. Also, perform multiplication and division before addition and subtraction.
- Understanding the difference between slice length and capacity should be part of a Go developer's core knowledge. The slice length is the number of available elements in the slice, whereas the slice capacity is the number of elements in the backing array.
- When creating a slice, initialize it with a given length or capacity if its length is already known. This reduces the number of allocations and improves performance. The same logic goes for maps, and you need to initialize their size.
- Using copy or the full slice expression is a way to prevent `append` from creating conflicts if two different functions use slices backed by the same array. However, only a slice copy prevents memory leaks if you want to shrink a large slice.
- To copy one slice to another using the `copy` built-in function, remember that the number of copied elements corresponds to the minimum between the two slice's lengths.
- Working with a slice of pointers or structs with pointer fields, you can avoid memory leaks by marking as `nil` the elements excluded by a slicing operation.
- To prevent common confusions such as when using the `encoding/json` or the `reflect` package, you need to understand the difference between nil and empty slices. Both are zero-length, zero-capacity slices, but only a nil slice doesn't require allocation.
- To check if a slice doesn't contain any element, check its length. This check works regardless of whether the slice is `nil` or empty. The same goes for maps.
- To design unambiguous APIs, you shouldn't distinguish between nil and empty slices.

- A map can always grow in memory, but it never shrinks. Hence, if it leads to some memory issues, you can try different options, such as forcing Go to re-create the map or using pointers.
- To compare types in Go, you can use the == and != operators if two types are comparable: Booleans, numerals, strings, pointers, channels, and structs are composed entirely of comparable types. Otherwise, you can either use `reflect.DeepEqual` and pay the price of reflection or use custom implementations and libraries.

Control structures

This chapter covers

- How a `range` loop assigns the element values and evaluates the provided expression
- Dealing with `range` loops and pointers
- Preventing common map iteration and loop-breaking mistakes
- Using `defer` inside a loop

Control structures in Go are similar to those in C or Java but differ from them in significant ways. For example, there is no do or `while` loop in Go, only a generalized for. This chapter delves into the most common mistakes related to control structures, with a strong focus on the `range` loop, which is a common source of misunderstanding.

4.1 #30: Ignoring the fact that elements are copied in range loops

A range loop is a convenient way to iterate over various data structures. We don't have to handle an index and the termination state. Go developers may forget or be unaware of how a range loop assigns values, leading to common mistakes. First, let's remind ourselves how to use a range loop; then we'll look at how values are assigned.

4.1.1   Concepts

A range loop allows iterating over different data structures:

- String
- Array
- Pointer to an array
- Slice
- Map
- Receiving channel

Compared to a classic for loop, a range loop is a convenient way to iterate over all the elements of one of these data structures, thanks to its concise syntax. It's also less error-prone because we don't have to handle the condition expression and iteration variable manually, which may avoid mistakes such as off-by-one errors. Here is an example with an iteration over a slice of strings:

```
s := []string{"a", "b", "c"}
for i, v := range s {
    fmt.Printf("index=%d, value=%s\n", i, v)
}
```

This code loops over each element of the slice. In each iteration, as we iterate over a slice, range produces a pair of values: an index and an element value, assigned to i and v, respectively. In general, range produces two values for each data structure except a receiving channel, for which it produces a single element (the value).

In some cases, we may only be interested in the element value, not the index. Because not using a local variable would lead to a compilation error, we can instead use the blank identifier to replace the index variable, like so:

```
s := []string{"a", "b", "c"}
for _, v := range s {
    fmt.Printf("value=%s\n", v)
}
```

Thanks to the blank identifier, we iterate over each element by ignoring the index and assigning only the element value to v.

If we're not interested in the value, we can omit the second element:

```
for i := range s {}
```

Now that we've refreshed our minds on using a range loop, let's see what kind of value is returned during an iteration.

4.1.2   Value copy

Understanding how the value is handled during each iteration is critical for using a range loop effectively. Let's see how it works with a concrete example.

We create an `account` struct containing a single `balance` field:

```
type account struct {
    balance float32
}
```

Next, we create a slice of `account` structs and iterate over each element using a `range` loop. During each iteration, we increment the `balance` of each account:

```
accounts := []account{
    {balance: 100.},
    {balance: 200.},
    {balance: 300.},
}
for _, a := range accounts {
    a.balance += 1000
}
```

Following this code, which of the following two choices do you think shows the slice's content?

- `[{100} {200} {300}]`
- `[{1100} {1200} {1300}]`

The answer is `[{100} {200} {300}]`. In this example, the `range` loop does not affect the slice's content. Let's see why.

In Go, everything we assign is a copy:

- If we assign the result of a function returning a *struct*, it performs a copy of that struct.
- If we assign the result of a function returning a *pointer*, it performs a copy of the memory address (an address is 64 bits long on a 64-bit architecture).

It's crucial to keep this in mind to avoid common mistakes, including those related to range loops. Indeed, when a `range` loop iterates over a data structure, it performs a copy of each element to the value variable (the second item).

Coming back to our example, iterating over each `account` element results in a struct copy being assigned to the value variable a. Therefore, incrementing the balance with `a.balance += 1000` mutates only the value variable (a), not an element in the slice.

So, what if we want to update the slice elements? There are two main options. The first option is to access the element using the slice index. This can be achieved with either a classic `for` loop or a `range` loop using the index instead of the value variable:

```
for i := range accounts {
    accounts[i].balance += 1000
}
```
◁──┐ **Uses the index variable to
     access the element of the slice**

```
for i := 0; i < len(accounts); i++ {
    accounts[i].balance += 1000
}
```
◁──┐ **Uses the traditional
     for loop**

Both iterations have the same effect: updating the elements in the accounts slice.

Which one should we favor? It depends on the context. If we want to go over each element, the first loop is shorter to write and read. But if we need to control which element we want to update (such as one out of two), we should instead use the second loop.

Updating slice elements: A third option

Another option is to keep using the range loop and access the value but modify the slice type to a slice of account pointers:

```
accounts := []*account{        ◁──┐ Updates the slice
    {balance: 100.},               │ type to []*account
    {balance: 200.},
    {balance: 300.},
}
for _, a := range accounts {   ──┐ Updates the slice
    a.balance += 1000          ◁──┘ elements directly
}
```

In this case, as we mentioned, the a variable is a copy of the account pointer stored in the slice. But as both pointers reference the same struct, the a.balance += 1000 statement updates the slice element.

However, this option has two main downsides. First, it requires updating the slice type, which may not always be possible. Second, if performance is important, we should note that iterating over a slice of pointers may be less efficient for a CPU because of the lack of predictability (we will discuss this point in mistake #91, "Not understanding CPU caches").

In general, we should remember that the value element in a range loop is a copy. Therefore, if the value is a struct we need to mutate, we will only update the copy, not the element itself, unless the value or field we modify is a pointer. The favored options are to access the element via the index using a range loop or a classic for loop.

In the next section, we keep working with range loops and see how the provided expression is evaluated.

4.2   *#31: Ignoring how arguments are evaluated in range loops*

The range loop syntax requires an expression. For example, in for i, v := range exp, exp is the expression. As we have seen, it can be a string, an array, a pointer to an array, a slice, a map, or a channel. Now, let's discuss the following question: how is this expression evaluated? When using a range loop, this is an essential point to avoid common mistakes.

Let's look at the following example, which appends an element to a slice we iterate over. Do you believe the loop will terminate?

```
s := []int{0, 1, 2}
for range s {
    s = append(s, 10)
}
```

To understand this question, we should know that when using a range loop, the provided expression is evaluated only once, before the beginning of the loop. In this context, "evaluated" means the provided expression is copied to a temporary variable, and then range iterates over this variable. In this example, when the s expression is evaluated, the result is a slice copy, as shown in figure 4.1.

The range loop uses this temporary variable. The original slice s is also updated during each iteration. Hence, after three iterations, the state is as shown in figure 4.2.

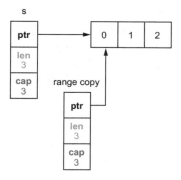

Figure 4.1   **s is copied to a temporary variable used by range.**

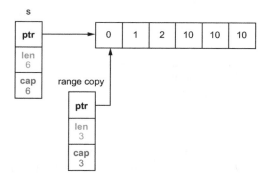

Figure 4.2   **The temporary variable remains a three-length slice; hence, the iteration completes.**

Each step results in appending a new element. However, after three steps, we have gone over all the elements. Indeed, the temporary slice used by range remains a three-length slice. Hence, the loop completes after three iterations.

The behavior is different with a classic for loop:

```
s := []int{0, 1, 2}
for i := 0; i < len(s); i++ {
    s = append(s, 10)
}
```

In this example, the loop never ends. The len(s) expression is evaluated during each iteration, and because we keep adding elements, we will never reach a termination state. It's essential to keep this difference in mind to use Go loops accurately.

Coming back to the range operator, we should know that the behavior we described (expression evaluated only once) also applies to all the data types provided.

As an example, let's look at the implication of this behavior with two other types: channels and arrays.

4.2.1   Channels

Let's see a concrete example based on iterating over a channel using a range loop. We create two goroutines, both sending elements to two distinct channels. Then, in the parent goroutine, we implement a consumer on one channel using a range loop that tries to switch to the other channel during the iteration:

```
ch1 := make(chan int, 3)          ◁─┐  Creates a first channel that will
go func() {                          │  contain elements 0, 1, and 2
    ch1 <- 0
    ch1 <- 1
    ch1 <- 2
    close(ch1)
}()

ch2 := make(chan int, 3)          ◁─┐  Creates a second channel that will
go func() {                          │  contain elements 10, 11, and 12
    ch2 <- 10
    ch2 <- 11
    ch2 <- 12
    close(ch2)
}()
                                 ┐ Assigns the first
ch := ch1         ◁──────────────┘ channel to ch    ┐ Creates a channel consumer
for v := range ch {              ◁─────────────────┘ by iterating over ch
    fmt.Println(v)
    ch = ch2      ◁─┐  Assigns the second
}                   │  channel to ch
```

In this example, the same logic applies regarding how the range expression is evaluated. The expression provided to range is a ch channel pointing to ch1. Hence, range evaluates ch, performs a copy to a temporary variable, and iterates over elements from this channel. Despite the ch = ch2 statement, range keeps iterating over ch1, not ch2:

```
0
1
2
```

The ch = ch2 statement isn't without effect, though. Because we assigned ch to the second variable, if we call close(ch) following this code, it will close the second channel, not the first.

Let's now see the impact of the range operator evaluating each expression only once when used with an array.

4.2.2   Array

What's the impact of using a range loop with an array? Because the range expression is evaluated before the beginning of the loop, what is assigned to the temporary loop variable is a copy of the array. Let's see this principle in action with the following example that updates a specific array index during the iteration:

```go
a := [3]int{0, 1, 2}          ← Creates an array
for i, v := range a {              of three elements   ← Iterates over
    a[2] = 10                  ←                             the array
    if i == 2 {               ←  Updates the
        fmt.Println(v)             last index
    }                         Prints the content
}                             of the last index
```

This code updates the last index to 10. However, if we run this code, it does not print 10; it prints 2, instead, as figure 4.3 shows.

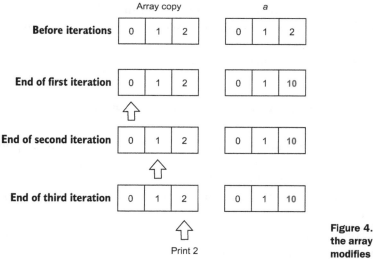

Array range iteration example

Figure 4.3   `range` iterates over the array copy (left) while the loop modifies a (right).

As we mentioned, the `range` operator creates a copy of the array. Meanwhile, the loop doesn't update the copy; it updates the original array: a. Therefore, the value of v during the last iteration is 2, not 10.

If we want to print the actual value of the last element, we can do so in two ways:

- By accessing the element from its index:

```go
a := [3]int{0, 1, 2}
for i := range a {
    a[2] = 10
    if i == 2 {                   ←  Accesses a[2] instead of
        fmt.Println(a[2])             the range value variable
    }
}
```

Because we access the original array, this code prints 2 instead of 10.

- Using an array pointer:

```
a := [3]int{0, 1, 2}
for i, v := range &a {        ◁─┐  Ranges over &a
    a[2] = 10                   │  instead of a
    if i == 2 {
        fmt.Println(v)
    }
}
```

We assign a copy of the array pointer to the temporary variable used by range. But because both pointers reference the same array, accessing v also returns 10.

Both options are valid. However, the second option doesn't lead to copying the whole array, which may be something to keep in mind in case the array is significantly large.

In summary, the range loop evaluates the provided expression only once, before the beginning of the loop, by doing a copy (regardless of the type). We should remember this behavior to avoid common mistakes that might, for example, lead us to access the wrong element.

In the next section, we see how to avoid common mistakes using range loops with pointers.

4.3   *#32: Ignoring the impact of using pointer elements in range loops*

This section looks at a specific mistake when using a range loop with pointer elements. If we're not cautious enough, it can lead us to an issue where we reference the wrong elements. Let's examine this problem and how to fix it.

Before we begin, let's clarify the rationale for using a slice or map of pointer elements. There are three main cases:

- In terms of semantics, storing data using pointer semantics implies sharing the element. For example, the following method holds the logic to insert an element into a cache:

```
type Store struct {
    m map[string]*Foo
}

func (s Store) Put(id string, foo *Foo) {
    s.m[id] = foo
    // ...
}
```

Here, using the pointer semantics implies that the Foo element is shared by both the caller of Put and the Store struct.

- Sometimes we already manipulate pointers. Hence, it can be handy to store pointers directly in our collection instead of values.

- If we store large structs, and these structs are frequently mutated, we can use pointers instead to avoid a copy and an insertion for each mutation:

```
func updateMapValue(mapValue map[string]LargeStruct, id string) {
    value := mapValue[id]
    value.foo = "bar"
    mapValue[id] = value
}
```

Copies ⟶ (pointing to `value := mapValue[id]`)

Inserts ⟵ (pointing to `mapValue[id] = value`)

```
func updateMapPointer(mapPointer map[string]*LargeStruct, id string) {
    mapPointer[id].foo = "bar"
}
```

Mutates the map element directly ⟵ (pointing to `mapPointer[id].foo = "bar"`)

Because `updateMapPointer` accepts a map of pointers, the mutation of the `foo` field can be done in a single step.

Now it's time to discuss the common mistake with pointer elements in `range` loops. We will consider the following two structs:

- A `Customer` struct representing a customer
- A `Store` that holds a map of `Customer` pointers

```
type Customer struct {
    ID      string
    Balance float64
}

type Store struct {
    m map[string]*Customer
}
```

The following method iterates over a slice of `Customer` elements and stores them in the `m` map:

```
func (s *Store) storeCustomers(customers []Customer) {
    for _, customer := range customers {
        s.m[customer.ID] = &customer
    }
}
```

Stores the customer pointer in the map ⟵ (pointing to `s.m[customer.ID] = &customer`)

In this example, we iterate over the input slice using the `range` operator and store `Customer` pointers in the map. But does this method do what we expect?

Let's give it a try by calling it with a slice of three different `Customer` structs:

```
s.storeCustomers([]Customer{
    {ID: "1", Balance: 10},
    {ID: "2", Balance: -10},
    {ID: "3", Balance: 0},
})
```

Here's the result of this code if we print the map:

```
key=1, value=&main.Customer{ID:"3", Balance:0}
key=2, value=&main.Customer{ID:"3", Balance:0}
key=3, value=&main.Customer{ID:"3", Balance:0}
```

As we can see, instead of storing three different `Customer` structs, all the elements stored in the map reference the same `Customer` struct: 3. What have we done wrong?

Iterating over the `customers` slice using the `range` loop, regardless of the number of elements, creates a single `customer` variable with a fixed address. We can verify this by printing the pointer address during each iteration:

```
func (s *Store) storeCustomers(customers []Customer) {
    for _, customer := range customers {
        fmt.Printf("%p\n", &customer)          ◁──┐  Prints the customer
        s.m[customer.ID] = &customer              │  address
    }
}

0xc000096020
0xc000096020
0xc000096020
```

Why is this important? Let's examine each iteration:

- During the first iteration, `customer` references the first element: `Customer 1`. We store a pointer to a `customer` struct.
- During the second iteration, `customer` now references another element: `Customer 2`. We also store a pointer to a `customer` struct.
- Finally, during the last iteration, `customer` references the last element: `Customer 3`. Again, the same pointer is stored in the map.

At the end of the iterations, we have stored the same pointer in the map three times (see figure 4.4). This pointer's last assignment is a reference to the slice's last element: `Customer 3`. This is why all the map elements reference the same `Customer`.

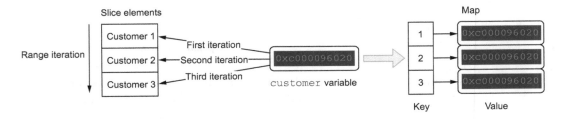

Figure 4.4 The `customer` variable has a constant address, so we store in the map the same pointer.

So, how do we fix this problem? There are two main solutions. The first is similar to what we saw in mistake #1, "Unintended variable shadowing." It requires creating a local variable:

```
func (s *Store) storeCustomers(customers []Customer) {
    for _, customer := range customers {           │  Creates a local
        current := customer              ◁─────────┘  current variable
```

```
        s.m[current.ID] = &current
    }
}
```
⟵ **Stores this pointer in the map**

In this example, we don't store a pointer referencing `customer`; instead, we store a pointer referencing `current`. `current` is a variable referencing a unique `Customer` during each iteration. Therefore, following the loop, we have stored different pointers referencing different `Customer` structs in the map. The other solution is to store a pointer referencing each element using the slice index:

```
func (s *Store) storeCustomers(customers []Customer) {
    for i := range customers {
        customer := &customers[i]
        s.m[customer.ID] = customer
    }
}
```
⟵ **Assigns to customer a pointer of the i element**
⟵ **Stores the customer pointer**

In this solution, `customer` is now a pointer. Because it's initialized during each iteration, it has a unique address. Therefore, we store different pointers in the maps.

When iterating over a data structure using a `range` loop, we must recall that all the values are assigned to a unique variable with a single unique address. Therefore, if we store a pointer referencing this variable during each iteration, we will end up in a situation where we store the same pointer referencing the same element: the latest one. We can overcome this issue by forcing the creation of a local variable in the loop's scope or creating a pointer referencing a slice element via its index. Both solutions are fine. Also note that we took a slice data structure as an input, but the problem would be similar with a map.

In the next section, we see common mistakes related to map iteration.

4.4   #33: Making wrong assumptions during map iterations

Iterating over a map is a common source of misunderstanding and mistakes, mostly because developers make wrong assumptions. In this section, we discuss two different cases:

- Ordering
- Map update during an iteration

We will see two common mistakes based on wrong assumptions while iterating over a map.

4.4.1   Ordering

Regarding ordering, we need to understand a few fundamental behaviors of the map data structure:

- It doesn't keep the data sorted by key (a map isn't based on a binary tree).
- It doesn't preserve the order in which the data was added. For example, if we insert pair A before pair B, we shouldn't make any assumptions based on this insertion order.

Furthermore, when iterating over a map, we shouldn't make any ordering assumptions at all. Let's examine the implications of this statement.

We will consider the map shown in figure 4.5, consisting of four buckets (the elements represent the key). Each index of the backing array references a given bucket.

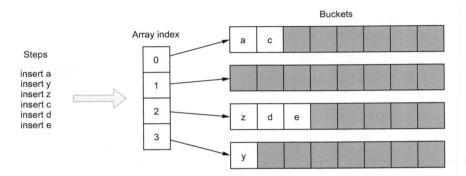

Figure 4.5   A map with four buckets

Now, let's iterate over this map using a `range` loop and print all the keys:

```
for k := range m {
    fmt.Print(k)
}
```

We mentioned that the data isn't sorted by key. Hence, we can't expect this code to print `acdeyz`. Meanwhile, we said the map doesn't preserve the insertion order. Hence, we also can't expect the code to print `ayzcde`.

But can we at least expect the code to print the keys in the order in which they are currently stored in the map, `aczdey`? No, not even this. In Go, the iteration order over a map is *not specified*. There is also no guarantee that the order will be the same from one iteration to the next. We should keep these map behaviors in mind so we don't base our code on wrong assumptions.

We can confirm all of these statements by running the previous loop twice:

```
zdyaec
czyade
```

As we can see, the order is different from one iteration to another.

> **NOTE** Although there is no guarantee about the iteration order, the iteration distribution isn't uniform. It's why the official Go specification states that the iteration is unspecified, not random.

So why does Go have such a surprising way to iterate over a map? It was a conscious choice by the language designers. They wanted to add some form of randomness to make sure developers never rely on any ordering assumptions while working with maps (see http://mng.bz/M2JW).

Hence, as Go developers, we should never make assumptions regarding ordering while iterating over a map. However, let's note that using packages from the standard library or external libraries can lead to different behaviors. For example, when the `encoding/json` package marshals a map into JSON, it reorders the data alphabetically by keys, regardless of the insertion order. But this isn't a property of the Go map itself. If ordering is necessary, we should rely on other data structures such as a binary heap (the GoDS library at https://github.com/emirpasic/gods contains helpful data structure implementations).

Let's now look at the second mistake related to updating a map while iterating over it.

4.4.2   *Map insert during iteration*

In Go, updating a map (inserting or deleting an element) during an iteration is allowed; it doesn't lead to a compilation error or a run-time error. However, there's another aspect we should consider when adding an entry in a map during an iteration, to avoid non-deterministic results.

Let's check the following example that iterates on a `map[int]bool`. If the pair value is true, we add another element. Can you guess what the output of this code will be?

```
m := map[int]bool{
    0: true,
    1: false,
    2: true,
}

for k, v := range m {
    if v {
        m[10+k] = true
    }
}

fmt.Println(m)
```

The result of this code is unpredictable. Here are some examples of results if we run this code multiple times:

```
map[0:true 1:false 2:true 10:true 12:true 20:true 22:true 30:true]
map[0:true 1:false 2:true 10:true 12:true 20:true 22:true 30:true 32:true]
map[0:true 1:false 2:true 10:true 12:true 20:true]
```

To understand the reason, we have to read what the Go specification says about a new map entry during an iteration:

> *If a map entry is created during iteration, it may be produced during the iteration or skipped. The choice may vary for each entry created and from one iteration to the next.*

Hence, when an element is added to a map during an iteration, it may be produced during a follow-up iteration, or it may not. As Go developers, we don't have any way to enforce the behavior. It also may vary from one iteration to another, which is why we got a different result three times.

It's essential to keep this behavior in mind to ensure that our code doesn't produce unpredictable outputs. If we want to update a map while iterating over it and make sure the added entries aren't part of the iteration, one solution is to work on a copy of the map, like so:

```
m := map[int]bool{
    0: true,
    1: false,
    2: true,
}
m2 := copyMap(m)          ⟵──┘ Creates a copy of
                               the initial map

for k, v := range m {
    m2[k] = v
    if v {
        m2[10+k] = true   ⟵──┘ Updates m2
    }                           instead of m
}

fmt.Println(m2)
```

In this example, we disassociate the map being read from the map being updated. Indeed, we keep iterating over m, but the updates are done on m2. This new version creates predictable and repeatable output:

```
map[0:true 1:false 2:true 10:true 12:true]
```

To summarize, when we work with a map, we shouldn't rely on the following:

- The data being ordered by keys
- Preservation of the insertion order
- A deterministic iteration order
- An element being produced during the same iteration in which it's added

Keeping these behaviors in mind should help us avoid common mistakes based on wrong assumptions.

In the next section, we see a mistake that is made fairly frequently while breaking loops.

4.5   *#34: Ignoring how the break statement works*

A break statement is commonly used to terminate the execution of a loop. When loops are used in conjunction with switch or select, developers frequently make the mistake of breaking the wrong statement.

Let's take a look at the following example. We implement a switch inside a for loop. If the loop index has the value 2, we want to break the loop:

```
for i := 0; i < 5; i++ {
    fmt.Printf("%d ", i)

    switch i {
```

```
        default:
        case 2:                      ┌─  If i equals 2,
            break      <─────┘   call break.
    }
}
```

This code may look right at first glance; however, it doesn't do what we expect. The break statement doesn't terminate the `for` loop: it terminates the `switch` statement, instead. Hence, instead of iterating from 0 to 2, this code iterates from 0 to 4: 0 1 2 3 4.

One essential rule to keep in mind is that a break statement terminates the execution of the innermost `for`, `switch`, or `select` statement. In the previous example, it terminates the `switch` statement.

So how can we write code that breaks the loop instead of the `switch` statement? The most idiomatic way is to use a label:

```
loop:                              ┌─  Defines a
    for i := 0; i < 5; i++ {   │   loop label
        fmt.Printf("%d ", i)

        switch i {
        default:
        case 2:
            break loop          ┌─  Terminates the loop attached to
        }                       │   the loop label, not the switch
    }
```

Here, we associate the `loop` label with the `for` loop. Then, because we provide the `loop` label to the break statement, it breaks the loop, not the switch. Therefore, this new version will print 0 1 2, as we expected.

Is a break with a label just like goto?

Some developers may challenge whether a break with a label is idiomatic and see it as a fancy goto statement. However, this isn't the case, and such code is used in the standard library. For example, we see this in the net/http package while reading lines from a buffer:

```
readlines:
    for {
        line, err := rw.Body.ReadString('\n')
        switch {
        case err == io.EOF:
            break readlines
        case err != nil:
            t.Fatalf("unexpected error reading from CGI: %v", err)
        }
        // ...
    }
```

This example uses an expressive label with readlines to emphasize the loop's goal. Hence, we should consider breaking a statement using labels an idiomatic approach in Go.

Breaking the wrong statement can also occur with a `select` inside a loop. In the following code, we want to use `select` with two cases and break the loop if the context cancels:

```
for {
    select {
    case <-ch:
        // Do something
    case <-ctx.Done():
        break          ◁⎯⎯  Breaks if the
    }                        context cancels
}
```

Here the innermost `for`, `switch`, or `select` statement is the `select` statement, not the `for` loop. So, the loop repeats. Again, to break the loop itself, we can use a label:

```
loop:                 ◁⎯⎯  Defines a
    for {                   loop label
        select {
        case <-ch:
            // Do something
        case <-ctx.Done():
            break loop    ◁⎯⎯  Terminates the loop attached to
        }                       the loop label, not the select
    }
```

Now, as expected, the `break` statement breaks the loop, not `select`.

> **NOTE** We can also use `continue` with a label to go to the next iteration of the labeled loop.

We should remain cautious while using a `switch` or `select` statement inside a loop. When using `break`, we should always make sure we know which statement it will affect. As we have seen, using labels is the idiomatic solution to enforce breaking a specific statement.

In the last section of this chapter, we keep discussing loops, but this time in conjunction with the `defer` keyword.

4.6   *#35: Using defer inside a loop*

The `defer` statement delays a call's execution until the surrounding function returns. It's mainly used to reduce boilerplate code. For example, if a resource has to be closed eventually, we can use `defer` to avoid repeating the closure calls before every single `return`. However, one common mistake is to be unaware of the consequences of using `defer` inside a loop. Let's look into this problem.

We will implement a function that opens a set of files where the file paths are received via a channel. Hence, we have to iterate over this channel, open the files, and handle the closure. Here's our first version:

```
func readFiles(ch <-chan string) error {    Iterates over
    for path := range ch {          ◁⎯⎯  the channel
```

```
file, err := os.Open(path)                    Opens
if err != nil {                               the file
    return err
}

defer file.Close()                            Defers the call
                                              to file.Close()
// Do something with file
    }
    return nil
}
```

NOTE We will discuss how to handle defer errors in mistake #54, "Not handling defer errors."

There is a significant problem with this implementation. We have to recall that defer schedules a function call when the *surrounding* function returns. In this case, the defer calls are executed not during each loop iteration but when the readFiles function returns. If readFiles doesn't return, the file descriptors will be kept open forever, causing leaks.

What are the options to fix this problem? One might be to get rid of defer and handle the file closure manually. But if we did that, we would have to abandon a convenient feature of the Go toolset just because we were in a loop. So, what are the options if we want to keep using defer? We have to create another surrounding function around defer that is called during each iteration.

For example, we can implement a readFile function holding the logic for each new file path received:

```
func readFiles(ch <-chan string) error {
    for path := range ch {
        if err := readFile(path); err != nil {     Calls the readFile function
            return err                              that contains the main logic
        }
    }
    return nil
}

func readFile(path string) error {
    file, err := os.Open(path)
    if err != nil {
        return err
    }

    defer file.Close()                              Keeps the
                                                    call to defer
    // Do something with file
    return nil
}
```

In this implementation, the defer function is called when readFile returns, meaning at the end of each iteration. Therefore, we do not keep file descriptors open until the parent readFiles function returns.

Another approach could be to make the `readFile` function a closure:

```
func readFiles(ch <-chan string) error {
    for path := range ch {
        err := func() error {
            // ...
            defer file.Close()
            // ...
        }()                          Runs the
        if err != nil {              provided closure
            return err
        }
    }
    return nil
}
```

But intrinsically, this remains the same solution: adding another surrounding function to execute the `defer` calls during each iteration. The plain old function has the advantage of probably being a bit clearer, and we can also write a specific unit test for it.

When using `defer`, we must remember that it schedules a function call when the surrounding function returns. Hence, calling `defer` within a loop will stack all the calls: they won't be executed during each iteration, which may cause memory leaks if the loop doesn't terminate, for example. The most convenient approach to solving this problem is introducing another function to be called during each iteration. But if performance is crucial, one downside is the overhead added by the function call. If we have such a case and we want to prevent this overhead, we should get rid of `defer` and handle the defer call manually before looping.

Summary

- The value element in a `range` loop is a copy. Therefore, to mutate a struct, for example, access it via its index or via a classic `for` loop (unless the element or the field you want to modify is a pointer).
- Understanding that the expression passed to the `range` operator is evaluated only once before the beginning of the loop can help you avoid common mistakes such as inefficient assignment in channel or slice iteration.
- Using a local variable or accessing an element using an index, you can prevent mistakes while copying pointers inside a loop.
- To ensure predictable outputs when using maps, remember that a map data structure
  - Doesn't order the data by keys
  - Doesn't preserve the insertion order
  - Doesn't have a deterministic iteration order
  - Doesn't guarantee that an element added during an iteration will be produced during this iteration
- Using `break` or `continue` with a label enforces breaking a specific statement. This can be helpful with `switch` or `select` statements inside loops.
- Extracting loop logic inside a function leads to executing a `defer` statement at the end of each iteration.

5

Strings

This chapter covers

- Understanding the fundamental concept of the rune in Go
- Preventing common mistakes with string iteration and trimming
- Avoiding inefficient code due to string concatenations or useless conversions
- Avoiding memory leaks with substrings

In Go, a string is an immutable data structure holding the following:

- A pointer to an immutable byte sequence
- The total number of bytes in this sequence

We will see in this chapter that Go has a pretty unique way to deal with strings. Go introduces a concept called *runes*; this concept is essential to understand and may confuse newcomers. Once we know how strings are managed, we can avoid common mistakes while iterating on a string. We will also look at common mistakes made by Go developers while using or producing strings. In addition, we will see that sometimes we can work directly with []byte, avoiding extra allocations. Finally, we will discuss how to avoid a common mistake that can create leaks from substrings. The primary goal of this chapter is to help you understand how strings work in Go by presenting common string mistakes.

5.1 *#36: Not understanding the concept of a rune*

We couldn't start this chapter about strings without discussing the concept of the rune in Go. As you will see in the following sections, this concept is key to thoroughly understanding how strings are handled and avoiding common mistakes. But before delving into Go runes, we need to make sure we are aligned about some fundamental programming concepts.

We should understand the distinction between a charset and an encoding:

- A charset, as the name suggests, is a set of characters. For example, the Unicode charset contains 2^21 characters.
- An encoding is the translation of a character's list in binary. For example, UTF-8 is an encoding standard capable of encoding all the Unicode characters in a variable number of bytes (from 1 to 4 bytes).

We mentioned characters to simplify the charset definition. But in Unicode, we use the concept of a *code point* to refer to an item represented by a single value. For example, the 汉 character is identified by the U+6C49 code point. Using UTF-8, 汉 is encoded using three bytes: 0xE6, 0xB1, and 0x89. Why is this important? Because in Go, a rune *is* a Unicode code point.

Meanwhile, we mentioned that UTF-8 encodes characters into 1 to 4 bytes, hence, up to 32 bits. This is why in Go, a rune is an alias of int32:

```
type rune = int32
```

Another thing to highlight about UTF-8: some people believe that Go strings are always UTF-8, but this isn't true. Let's consider the following example:

```
s := "hello"
```

We assign a string literal (a string constant) to s. In Go, a source code is encoded in UTF-8. So, all string literals are encoded into a sequence of bytes using UTF-8. However, a string is a sequence of arbitrary bytes; it's not necessarily based on UTF-8. Hence, when we manipulate a variable that wasn't initialized from a string literal (for example, reading from the filesystem), we can't necessarily assume that it uses the UTF-8 encoding.

> **NOTE** golang.org/x, a repository that provides extensions to the standard library, contains packages to work with UTF-16 and UTF-32.

Let's get back to the hello example. We have a string composed of five characters: *h, e, l, l,* and *o.*

These *simple* characters are encoded using a single byte each. This is why getting the length of s returns 5:

```
s := "hello"
fmt.Println(len(s)) // 5
```

But a character isn't always encoded into a single byte. Coming back to the 汉 character, we mentioned that with UTF-8, this character is encoded into three bytes. We can validate this with the following example:

```
s := "汉"
fmt.Println(len(s)) // 3
```

Instead of printing 1, this example prints 3. Indeed, the len built-in function applied on a string doesn't return the number of characters; it returns the number of bytes.

Conversely, we can create a string from a list of bytes. We mentioned that the 汉 character was encoded using three bytes, 0xE6, 0xB1, and 0x89:

```
s := string([]byte{0xE6, 0xB1, 0x89})
fmt.Printf("%s\n", s)
```

Here, we build a string composed of these three bytes. When we print the string, instead of printing three characters, the code prints a single one: 汉.

In summary:

- A charset is a set of characters, whereas an encoding describes how to translate a charset into binary.
- In Go, a string references an immutable slice of arbitrary bytes.
- Go source code is encoded using UTF-8. Hence, all string literals are UTF-8 strings. But because a string can contain arbitrary bytes, if it's obtained from somewhere else (not the source code), it isn't guaranteed to be based on the UTF-8 encoding.
- A rune corresponds to the concept of a Unicode code point, meaning an item represented by a single value.
- Using UTF-8, a Unicode code point can be encoded into 1 to 4 bytes.
- Using len on a string in Go returns the number of bytes, not the number of runes.

Having these concepts in mind is essential because runes are everywhere in Go. Let's see a concrete application of this knowledge involving a common mistake related to string iteration.

5.2   #37: Inaccurate string iteration

Iterating on a string is a common operation for developers. Perhaps we want to perform an operation for each rune in the string or implement a custom function to search for a specific substring. In both cases, we have to iterate on the different runes of a string. But it's easy to get confused about how iteration works.

Let's look at a concrete example. Here, we want to print the different runes in a string and their corresponding positions:

```
s := "hêllo"
for i := range s {
    fmt.Printf("position %d: %c\n", i, s[i])
}
fmt.Printf("len=%d\n", len(s))
```

⟵ **The string literal contains a special rune: ê.**

We use the `range` operator to iterate over `s`, and then we want to print each rune using its index in the string. Here's the output:

```
position 0: h
position 1: Ã
position 3: l
position 4: l
position 5: o
len=6
```

This code doesn't do what we want. Let's highlight three points:

- The second rune is Ã in the output instead of ê.
- We jumped from position 1 to position 3: what is at position 2?
- `len` returns a count of 6, whereas `s` contains only 5 runes.

Let's start with the last observation. We already mentioned that `len` returns the number of bytes in a string, not the number of runes. Because we assigned a string literal to `s`, `s` is a UTF-8 string. Meanwhile, the special character ê isn't encoded in a single byte; it requires 2 bytes. Therefore, calling `len(s)` returns 6.

Calculating the number of runes in a string

What if we want to get the number of runes in a string, not the number of bytes? How we can do this depends on the encoding.

In the previous example, because we assigned a string literal to `s`, we can use the `unicode/utf8` package:

```
fmt.Println(utf8.RuneCountInString(s)) // 5
```

Let's get back to the iteration to understand the remaining surprises:

```
for i := range s {
    fmt.Printf("position %d: %c\n", i, s[i])
}
```

We have to recognize that in this example, we don't iterate over each rune; instead, we iterate over each starting index of a rune, as shown in figure 5.1.

Printing `s[i]` doesn't print the *i*th rune; it prints the UTF-8 representation of the byte at index *i*. Hence, we printed hÃllo instead of hêllo. So how do we fix the code if we want to print all the different runes? There are two main options.

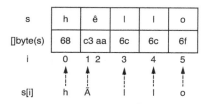

Figure 5.1   Printing s[i] prints the UTF-8 representation of each byte at index i.

We have to use the value element of the `range` operator:

```
s := "hêllo"
for i, r := range s {
    fmt.Printf("position %d: %c\n", i, r)
}
```

Instead of printing the rune using `s[i]`, we use the `r` variable. Using a `range` loop on a string returns two variables, the starting index of a rune and the rune itself:

```
position 0: h
position 1: ê
position 3: l
position 4: l
position 5: o
```

The other approach is to convert the string into a slice of runes and iterate over it:

```
s := "hêllo"
runes := []rune(s)
for i, r := range runes {
    fmt.Printf("position %d: %c\n", i, r)
}
```

```
position 0: h
position 1: ê
position 2: l
position 3: l
position 4: o
```

Here, we convert `s` into a slice of runes using `[]rune(s)`. Then we iterate over this slice and use the value element of the `range` operator to print all the runes. The only difference has to do with the position: instead of printing the starting index of the rune's byte sequence, the code prints the rune's index directly.

Note that this solution introduces a run-time overhead compared to the previous one. Indeed, converting a string into a slice of runes requires allocating an additional slice and converting the bytes into runes: an *O(n)* time complexity with *n* the number of bytes in the string. Therefore, if we want to iterate over all the runes, we should use the first solution.

However, if we want to access the *i*th rune of a string with the first option, we don't have access to the rune index; rather, we know the starting index of a rune in the byte sequence. Hence, we should favor the second option in most cases:

```
s := "hêllo"
r := []rune(s)[4]
fmt.Printf("%c\n", r) // o
```

This code prints the fourth rune by first converting the string into a rune slice.

> **A possible optimization to access a specific rune**
> One optimization is possible if a string is composed of single-byte runes: for example, if the string contains the letters A to Z and a to z. We can access the ith rune without converting the whole string into a slice of runes by accessing the byte directly using s[i]:
>
> ```
> s := "hello"
> fmt.Printf("%c\n", rune(s[4])) // o
> ```

In summary, if we want to iterate over a string's runes, we can use the range loop on the string directly. But we have to recall that the index corresponds not to the rune index but rather to the starting index of the byte sequence of the rune. Because a rune can be composed of multiple bytes, if we want to access the rune itself, we should use the value variable of range, not the index in the string. Meanwhile, if we are interested in getting the ith rune of a string, we should convert the string into a slice of runes in most cases.

In the next section, we look at a common source of confusion when using trim functions in the strings package.

5.3   *#38: Misusing trim functions*

One common mistake made by Go developers when using the strings package is to mix TrimRight and TrimSuffix. Both functions serve a similar purpose, and it can be fairly easy to confuse them. Let's take a look.

In the following example, we use TrimRight. What should be the output of this code?

```
fmt.Println(strings.TrimRight("123oxo", "xo"))
```

The answer is 123. Is that what you expected? If not, you were probably expecting the result of TrimSuffix, instead. Let's review both functions.

TrimRight removes all the trailing runes contained in a given set. In our example, we passed as a set xo, which contains two runes: x and o. Figure 5.2 shows the logic.

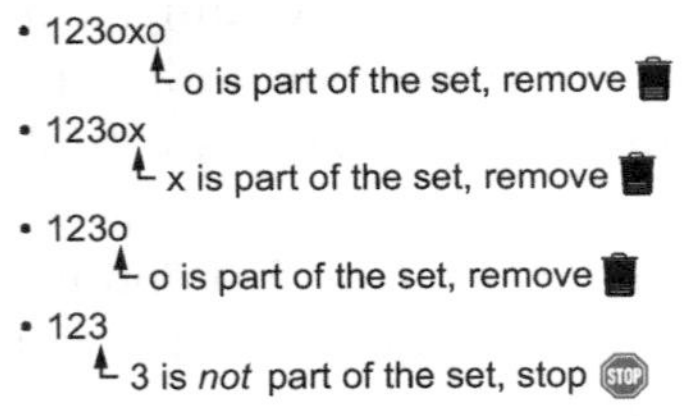

- 123oxo
  └ o is part of the set, remove 🗑
- 123ox
  └ x is part of the set, remove 🗑
- 123o
  └ o is part of the set, remove 🗑
- 123
  └ 3 is *not* part of the set, stop 🛑

Figure 5.2   TrimRight iterates backward until it finds a rune that is not part of the set.

`TrimRight` iterates backward over each rune. If a rune is part of the provided set, the function removes it. If not, the function stops its iteration and returns the remaining string. This is why our example returns 123.

On the other hand, `TrimSuffix` returns a string without a provided trailing suffix:

```
fmt.Println(strings.TrimSuffix("123oxo", "xo"))
```

Because 123oxo ends with xo, this code prints 123o. Also, removing the trailing suffix isn't a repeating operation, so `TrimSuffix("123xoxo", "xo")` returns 123xo.

The principle is the same for the left-hand side of a string with `TrimLeft` and `TrimPrefix`:

```
fmt.Println(strings.TrimLeft("oxo123", "ox")) // 123
fmt.Println(strings.TrimPrefix("oxo123", "ox")) /// o123
```

`strings.TrimLeft` removes all the leading runes contained in a set and hence prints 123. `TrimPrefix` removes the provided leading prefix, printing o123.

One last note related to this topic: `Trim` applies both `TrimLeft` and `TrimRight` on a string. So, it removes all the leading and trailing runes contained in a set:

```
fmt.Println(strings.Trim("oxo123oxo", "ox")) // 123
```

In summary, we have to make sure we understand the difference between `TrimRight`/`TrimLeft`, and `TrimSuffix`/`TrimPrefix`:

- `TrimRight`/`TrimLeft` removes the trailing/leading runes in a set.
- `TrimSuffix`/`TrimPrefix` removes a given suffix/prefix.

In the next section, we will delve into string concatenation.

5.4 *#39: Under-optimized string concatenation*

When it comes to concatenating strings, there are two main approaches in Go, and one of them can be really inefficient in some conditions. Let's examine this topic to understand which option we should favor and when.

Let's write a `concat` function that concatenates all the string elements of a slice using the += operator:

```
func concat(values []string) string {
    s := ""
    for _, value := range values {
        s += value
    }
    return s
}
```

During each iteration, the += operator concatenates s with the `value` string. At first sight, this function may not look wrong. But with this implementation, we forget one of the core characteristics of a string: its immutability. Therefore, each iteration doesn't update s; it reallocates a new string in memory, which significantly impacts the performance of this function.

Fortunately, there is a solution to deal with this problem, using the strings package and the Builder struct:

```go
func concat(values []string) string {
    sb := strings.Builder{}          // Creates a strings.Builder
    for _, value := range values {
        _, _ = sb.WriteString(value) // Appends a string
    }
    return sb.String()               // Returns the resulted string
}
```

First, we created a strings.Builder struct using its zero value. During each iteration, we constructed the resulting string by calling the WriteString method that appends the content of value to its internal buffer, hence minimizing memory copying.

Note that WriteString returns an error as the second output, but we purposely ignore it. Indeed, this method will never return a non-nil error. So what's the purpose of this method returning an error as part of its signature? strings.Builder implements the io.StringWriter interface, which contains a single method: WriteString(s string) (n int, err error). Hence, to comply with this interface, WriteString must return an error.

> **NOTE**　We will discuss ignoring errors idiomatically in mistake #53, "Not handling an error."

Using strings.Builder, we can also append

- A byte slice using Write
- A single byte using WriteByte
- A single rune using WriteRune

Internally, strings.Builder holds a byte slice. Each call to WriteString results in a call to append on this slice. There are two impacts. First, this struct shouldn't be used concurrently, as the calls to append would lead to race conditions. The second impact is something that we saw in mistake #21, "Inefficient slice initialization": if the future length of a slice is already known, we should preallocate it. For that purpose, strings.Builder exposes a method Grow(n int) to guarantee space for another *n* bytes.

Let's write another version of the concat method by calling Grow with the total number of bytes:

```go
func concat(values []string) string {
    total := 0
    for i := 0; i < len(values); i++ {      // Iterates over each string to compute
        total += len(values[i])             // the total number of bytes
    }

    sb := strings.Builder{}
    sb.Grow(total)                          // Calls Grow with this total
    for _, value := range values {
        _, _ = sb.WriteString(value)
```

```
    }
    return sb.String()
}
```

Before the iteration, we compute the total number of bytes the final string will contain and assign the result to total. Note that we're not interested in the number of runes but the number of bytes, so we use the len function. Then we call Grow to guarantee space for total bytes before iterating over the strings.

Let's run a benchmark to compare the three versions (v1 using +=; v2 using strings.Builder{} without preallocation; and v3 using strings.Builder{} with pre-allocation). The input slice contains 1,000 strings, and each string contains 1,000 bytes:

```
BenchmarkConcatV1-4              16      72291485 ns/op
BenchmarkConcatV2-4            1188        878962 ns/op
BenchmarkConcatV3-4            5922        190340 ns/op
```

As we can see, the latest version is by far the most efficient: 99% faster than v1 and 78% faster than v2. We may ask ourselves, how can iterating twice on the input slice make the code faster? The answer lies in mistake #21, "Inefficient slice initialization": if a slice isn't allocated with a given length or capacity, the slice will keep growing each time it becomes full, resulting in additional allocations and copies. Hence, iterating twice is the most efficient option in this case.

strings.Builder is the recommended solution to concatenate a list of strings. Usually, this solution should be used within a loop. Indeed, if we just have to concatenate a few strings (such as a name and a surname), using strings.Builder is not recommended as doing so will make the code a bit less readable than using the += operator or fmt.Sprintf.

As a general rule, we can remember that performance-wise, the strings.Builder solution is faster from the moment we have to concatenate more than about five strings. Even though this exact number depends on many factors, such as the size of the concatenated strings and the machine, this can be a rule of thumb to help us decide when to choose one solution over the other. Also, we shouldn't forget that if the number of bytes of the future string is known in advance, we should use the Grow method to preallocate the internal byte slice.

Next, we will discuss the bytes package and why it may prevent useless string conversions.

5.5   #40: Useless string conversions

When choosing to work with a string or a []byte, most programmers tend to favor strings for convenience. But most I/O is actually done with []byte. For example, io.Reader, io.Writer, and io.ReadAll work with []byte, not strings. Hence, working with strings means extra conversions, although the bytes package contains many of the same operations as the strings package.

Let's see an example of what we *shouldn't* do. We will implement a getBytes function that takes an io.Reader as an input, reads from it, and calls a sanitize function.

The sanitization will be done by trimming all the leading and trailing white spaces. Here's the skeleton of getBytes:

```go
func getBytes(reader io.Reader) ([]byte, error) {
    b, err := io.ReadAll(reader)            ←┐ b is a
    if err != nil {                          ┘ []byte.
        return nil, err
    }
    // Call sanitize
}
```

We call ReadAll and assign the byte slice to b. How can we implement the sanitize function? One option might be to create a sanitize(string) string function using the strings package:

```go
func sanitize(s string) string {
    return strings.TrimSpace(s)
}
```

Now, back to getBytes: as we manipulate a []byte, we must first convert it to a string before calling sanitize. Then we have to convert the results back into a []byte because getBytes returns a byte slice:

```go
return []byte(sanitize(string(b))), nil
```

What's the problem with this implementation? We have to pay the extra price of converting a []byte into a string and then converting a string into a []byte. Memory-wise, each of these conversions requires an extra allocation. Indeed, even though a string is backed by a []byte, converting a []byte into a string requires a copy of the byte slice. It means a new memory allocation and a copy of all the bytes.

String immutability

We can use the following code to test the fact that creating a string from a []byte leads to a copy:

```go
b := []byte{'a', 'b', 'c'}
s := string(b)
b[1] = 'x'
fmt.Println(s)
```

Running this code prints abc, not axc. Indeed, in Go, a string is immutable.

So, how should we implement the sanitize function? Instead of accepting and returning a string, we should manipulate a byte slice:

```go
func sanitize(b []byte) []byte {
    return bytes.TrimSpace(b)
}
```

The `bytes` package also has a `TrimSpace` function to trim all the leading and trailing white spaces. Then, calling the `sanitize` function doesn't require any extra conversions:

```
return sanitize(b), nil
```

As we mentioned, most I/O is done with `[]byte`, not strings. When we're wondering whether we should work with strings or `[]byte`, let's recall that working with `[]byte` isn't necessarily less convenient. Indeed, all the exported functions of the `strings` package also have alternatives in the `bytes` package: `Split`, `Count`, `Contains`, `Index`, and so on. Hence, whether we're doing I/O or not, we should first check whether we could implement a whole workflow using bytes instead of strings and avoid the price of additional conversions.

The last section of this chapter discusses how the substring operation can sometimes lead to memory leak situations.

5.6 *#41: Substrings and memory leaks*

In mistake #26, "Slices and memory leaks," we saw how slicing a slice or array may lead to memory leak situations. This principle also applies to string and substring operations. First, we will see how substrings are handled in Go to prevent memory leaks.

To extract a subset of a string, we can use the following syntax:

```
s1 := "Hello, World!"
s2 := s1[:5] // Hello
```

s2 is constructed as a substring of s1. This example creates a string from the first five bytes, not the first five runes. Hence, we shouldn't use this syntax in the case of runes encoded with multiple bytes. Instead, we should convert the input string into a `[]rune` type first:

```
s1 := "Hêllo, World!"
s2 := string([]rune(s1)[:5]) // Hêllo
```

Now that we have refreshed our minds regarding the substring operation, let's look at a concrete problem to illustrate possible memory leaks.

We will receive log messages as strings. Each log will first be formatted with a universally unique identifier (UUID; 36 characters) followed by the message itself. We want to store these UUIDs in memory: for example, to keep a cache of the latest *n* UUIDs. We should also note that these log messages can potentially be quite heavy (up to thousands of bytes). Here is our implementation:

```
func (s store) handleLog(log string) error {
    if len(log) < 36 {
        return errors.New("log is not correctly formatted")
    }
    uuid := log[:36]
    s.store(uuid)
    // Do something
}
```

To extract the UUID, we use a substring operation with `log[:36]` as we know that the UUID is encoded on 36 bytes. Then we pass this `uuid` variable to the `store` method that will store it in memory. Is this solution problematic? Yes, it is.

When doing a substring operation, the Go specification doesn't specify whether the resulting string and the one involved in the substring operation should share the same data. However, the standard Go compiler does let them share the same backing array, which is probably the best solution memory-wise and performance-wise as it prevents a new allocation and a copy.

We mentioned that log messages can be quite heavy. `log[:36]` will create a new string referencing the same backing array. Therefore, each `uuid` string that we store in memory will contain not just 36 bytes but the number of bytes in the initial `log` string: potentially, thousands of bytes.

How can we fix this? By making a deep copy of the substring so that the internal byte slice of `uuid` references a new backing array of only 36 bytes:

```go
func (s store) handleLog(log string) error {
    if len(log) < 36 {
        return errors.New("log is not correctly formatted")
    }
    uuid := string([]byte(log[:36]))      ⊲┐ Performs a []byte and
    s.store(uuid)                           │ then a string conversion
    // Do something
}
```

The copy is performed by converting the substring into a `[]byte` first and then into a string again. By doing this, we prevent a memory leak from occurring. The `uuid` string is backed by an array consisting of only 36 bytes.

Note that some IDEs or linters may warn that the `string([]byte(s))` conversions aren't necessary. For example, GoLand, the Go JetBrains IDE, warns about a redundant type conversion. This is true in the sense that we convert a string into a string, but this operation has an actual effect. As discussed, it prevents the new string from being backed by the same array as `uuid`. We need to be aware that the warnings raised by IDEs or linters may sometimes be inaccurate.

> **NOTE** Because a string is mostly a pointer, calling a function to pass a string doesn't result in a deep copy of the bytes. The copied string will still reference the same backing array.

As of Go 1.18, the standard library also includes a solution with `strings.Clone` that returns a fresh copy of a string:

```go
uuid := strings.Clone(log[:36])
```

Calling `strings.Clone` makes a copy of `log[:36]` into a new allocation, preventing a memory leak.

We need to keep two things in mind while using the substring operation in Go. First, the interval provided is based on the number of bytes, not the number of runes.

Second, a substring operation may lead to a memory leak as the resulting substring will share the same backing array as the initial string. The solutions to prevent this case from happening are to perform a string copy manually or to use `strings.Clone` from Go 1.18.

Summary

- Understanding that a rune corresponds to the concept of a Unicode code point and that it can be composed of multiple bytes should be part of the Go developer's core knowledge to work accurately with strings.

- Iterating on a string with the `range` operator iterates on the runes with the index corresponding to the starting index of the rune's byte sequence. To access a specific rune index (such as the third rune), convert the string into a `[]rune`.

- `strings.TrimRight`/`strings.TrimLeft` removes all the trailing/leading runes contained in a given set, whereas `strings.TrimSuffix`/`strings.TrimPrefix` returns a string without a provided suffix/prefix.

- Concatenating a list of strings should be done with `strings.Builder` to prevent allocating a new string during each iteration.

- Remembering that the `bytes` package offers the same operations as the `strings` package can help avoid extra byte/string conversions.

- Using copies instead of substrings can prevent memory leaks, as the string returned by a substring operation will be backed by the same byte array.

Functions and methods

This chapter covers

- When to use value or pointer receivers
- When to use named result parameters and their potential side effects
- Avoiding a common mistake while returning a nil receiver
- Why using functions that accept a filename isn't a best practice
- Handling `defer` arguments

A *function* wraps a sequence of statements into a unit that can be called elsewhere. It can take some input(s) and produces some output(s). On the other hand, a *method* is a function attached to a given type. The attached type is called a *receiver* and can be a pointer or a value. We start this chapter by discussing how to choose one receiver type or the other, as this is usually a source of debate. Then we discuss named parameters, when to use them, and why they can sometimes lead to mistakes. We also discuss common mistakes when designing a function or returning specific values such as a nil receiver.

6.1 #42: Not knowing which type of receiver to use

Choosing a receiver type for a method isn't always straightforward. When should we use value receivers? When should we use pointer receivers? In this section, we look at the conditions to make the right decision.

In chapter 12, we will thoroughly discuss values versus pointers. So, this section will only scratch the surface in terms of performance. Also, in many contexts, using a value or pointer receiver should be dictated not by performance but rather by other conditions that we will discuss. But first, let's refresh our memories about how receivers work.

In Go, we can attach either a value or a pointer receiver to a method. With a value receiver, Go makes a copy of the value and passes it to the method. Any changes to the object remain local to the method. The original object remains unchanged.

As an illustration, the following example mutates a value receiver:

```go
type customer struct {
    balance float64
}

func (c customer) add(v float64) {          ◁─┤ Value receiver
    c.balance += v
}

func main() {
    c := customer{balance: 100.}
    c.add(50.)                                    The customer balance
    fmt.Printf("balance: %.2f\n", c.balance)  ◁─┘ remains unchanged.
}
```

Because we use a value receiver, incrementing the balance in the add method doesn't mutate the balance field of the original customer struct:

```
100.00
```

On the other hand, with a pointer receiver, Go passes the address of an object to the method. Intrinsically, it remains a copy, but we only copy a pointer, not the object itself (passing by reference doesn't exist in Go). Any modifications to the receiver are done on the original object. Here is the same example, but now the receiver is a pointer:

```go
type customer struct {
    balance float64
}

func (c *customer) add(operation float64) {  ◁─┤ Pointer receiver
    c.balance += operation
}

func main() {
    c := customer{balance: 100.0}
    c.add(50.0)                                   The customer balance
    fmt.Printf("balance: %.2f\n", c.balance)  ◁─┘ is updated.
}
```

Because we use a pointer receiver, incrementing the balance mutates the `balance` field of the original `customer` struct:

```
150.00
```

Choosing between value and pointer receivers isn't always straightforward. Let's discuss some of the conditions to help us choose.

A receiver *must* be a pointer

- If the method needs to mutate the receiver. This rule is also valid if the receiver is a slice and a method needs to append elements:

```
type slice []int

func (s *slice) add(element int) {
    *s = append(*s, element)
}
```

- If the method receiver contains a field that cannot be copied: for example, a type part of the `sync` package (we will discuss this point in mistake #74, "Copying a sync type").

A receiver *should* be a pointer

- If the receiver is a large object. Using a pointer can make the call more efficient, as doing so prevents making an extensive copy. When in doubt about how large is large, benchmarking can be the solution; it's pretty much impossible to state a specific size, because it depends on many factors.

A receiver *must* be a value

- If we have to enforce a receiver's immutability.
- If the receiver is a map, function, or channel. Otherwise, a compilation error occurs.

A receiver *should* be a value

- If the receiver is a slice that doesn't have to be mutated.
- If the receiver is a small array or struct that is naturally a value type without mutable fields, such as `time.Time`.
- If the receiver is a basic type such as `int`, `float64`, or `string`.

One case needs more discussion. Let's say that we design a different `customer` struct. Its mutable fields aren't part of the struct directly but are inside another struct:

```
type customer struct {
    data *data        ◁──┐  balance isn't part of the customer struct directly
}                         │  but is in a struct referenced by a pointer field.

type data struct {
    balance float64
}
```

```
func (c customer) add(operation float64) {          ◁───┐  Uses a value
    c.data.balance += operation                          │  receiver
}

func main() {
    c := customer{data: &data{
        balance: 100,
    }}
    c.add(50.)
    fmt.Printf("balance: %.2f\n", c.data.balance)
}
```

Even though the receiver is a value, calling add changes the actual balance in the end:

```
150.00
```

In this case, we don't need the receiver to be a pointer to mutate balance. However, for clarity, we may favor using a pointer receiver to highlight that customer as a whole object is mutable.

Mixing receiver types

Are we allowed to mix receiver types, such as a struct containing multiple methods, some of which have pointer receivers and others of which have value receivers? The consensus tends toward forbidding it. However, there are some counterexamples in the standard library, for example, time.Time.

The designers wanted to enforce that a time.Time struct is immutable. Hence, most methods such as After, IsZero, and UTC have a value receiver. But to comply with existing interfaces such as encoding.TextUnmarshaler, time.Time has to implement the UnmarshalBinary([]byte) error method, which mutates the receiver given a byte slice. Thus, this method has a pointer receiver.

Consequently, mixing receiver types should be avoided in general but is not forbidden in 100% of cases.

We should now have a good understanding of whether to use value or pointer receivers. Of course, it's impossible to be exhaustive, as there will always be edge cases, but this section's goal was to provide guidance to cover most cases. By default, we can choose to go with a value receiver unless there's a good reason not to do so. In doubt, we should use a pointer receiver.

In the next section, we discuss named result parameters: what they are and when to use them.

6.2   *#43: Never using named result parameters*

Named result parameters are an infrequently used option in Go. This section looks at when it's considered appropriate to use named result parameters to make our API more convenient. But first, let's refresh our memory about how they work.

When we return parameters in a function or a method, we can attach names to these parameters and use them as regular variables. When a result parameter is named, it's initialized to its zero value when the function/method begins. With named result parameters, we can also call a naked return statement (without arguments). In that case, the current values of the result parameters are used as the returned values.

Here's an example that uses a named result parameter b:

```go
func f(a int) (b int) {      ◁─┐ Names the int
    b = a                      │ result parameter b
    return      ◁─┐ Returns the
}                  │ current value of b
```

In this example, we attach a name to the result parameter: b. When we call `return` without arguments, it returns the current value of b.

When is it recommended that we use named result parameters? First, let's consider the following interface, which contains a method to get the coordinates from a given address:

```go
type locator interface {
    getCoordinates(address string) (float32, float32, error)
}
```

Because this interface is unexported, documentation isn't mandatory. Just by reading this code, can you guess what these two `float32` results are? Perhaps they are a latitude and a longitude, but in which order? Depending on the conventions, latitude isn't always the first element. Therefore, we have to check the implementation to understand the results.

In that case, we should probably use named result parameters to make the code easier to read:

```go
type locator interface {
    getCoordinates(address string) (lat, lng float32, err error)
}
```

With this new version, we can understand the meaning of the method signature by looking at the interface: latitude first, longitude second.

Now, let's pursue the question of when to use named result parameters with the method implementation. Should we also use named result parameters as part of the implementation itself?

```go
func (l loc) getCoordinates(address string) (
    lat, lng float32, err error) {
    // ...
}
```

In this specific case, having an expressive method signature can also help code readers. Hence, we probably want to use named result parameters as well.

NOTE If we need to return multiple results of the same type, we can also think about creating an ad hoc struct with meaningful field names. However, this isn't always possible: for example, when satisfying an existing interface that we can't update.

Next, let's consider another function signature that allows us to store a `Customer` type in a database:

```
func StoreCustomer(customer Customer) (err error) {
    // ...
}
```

Here, naming the `error` parameter `err` isn't helpful and doesn't help readers. In this case, we should favor not using named result parameters.

So, when to use named result parameters depends on the context. In most cases, if it's not clear whether using them makes our code more readable, we shouldn't use named result parameters.

Also note that having the result parameters already initialized can be quite handy in some contexts, even though they don't necessarily help readability. The following example proposed in *Effective Go* (https://go.dev/doc/effective_go) is inspired by the `io.ReadFull` function:

```
func ReadFull(r io.Reader, buf []byte) (n int, err error) {
    for len(buf) > 0 && err == nil {
        var nr int
        nr, err = r.Read(buf)
        n += nr
        buf = buf[nr:]
    }
    return
}
```

In this example, having named result parameters doesn't really increase readability. However, because both `n` and `err` are initialized to their zero value, the implementation is shorter. On the other hand, this function can be slightly confusing for readers at first sight. Again, it's a question of finding the right balance.

One note regarding naked returns (returns without arguments): they are considered acceptable in short functions; otherwise, they can harm readability because the reader must remember the outputs throughout the entire function. We should also be consistent within the scope of a function, using either only naked returns or only returns with arguments.

So what are the rules regarding named result parameters? In most cases, using named result parameters in the context of an interface definition can increase readability without leading to any side effects. But there's no strict rule in the context of a method implementation. In some cases, named result parameters can also increase readability: for example, if two parameters have the same type. In other cases, they can also be used for convenience. Therefore, we should use named result parameters sparingly when there's a clear benefit.

NOTE In mistake #54, "Not handling defer errors," we will discuss another use case for using named result parameters in the context of defer calls.

Furthermore, if we're not careful enough, using named result parameters can lead to side effects and unintended consequences, as we see in the next section.

6.3 *#44: Unintended side effects with named result parameters*

We mentioned why named result parameters can be useful in some situations. But as these result parameters are initialized to their zero value, using them can sometimes lead to subtle bugs if we're not careful enough. This section illustrates such a case.

Let's enhance our previous example of a method that returns the latitude and longitude from a given address. Because we return two float32s, we decide to use named result parameters to make the latitude and longitude explicit. This function will first validate the given address and then get the coordinates. In between, it will perform a check on the input context to make sure it wasn't canceled and that its deadline hasn't passed.

NOTE We will delve into the concept of context in Go in mistake #60, "Misunderstanding Go contexts." If you're not familiar with contexts, briefly, a context can carry a cancellation signal or a deadline. We can check those by calling the Err method and testing that the returned error isn't nil.

Here's the new implementation of the getCoordinates method. Can you spot what's wrong with this code?

```
func (l loc) getCoordinates(ctx context.Context, address string) (
    lat, lng float32, err error) {
    isValid := l.validateAddress(address)        ◁─┐ Validates
    if !isValid {                                   │ the address
        return 0, 0, errors.New("invalid address")
    }

    if ctx.Err() != nil {      ◁─┐ Checks whether the
        return 0, 0, err          │ context was canceled or
    }                             │ the deadline has passed

    // Get and return coordinates
}
```

The error might not be obvious at first glance. Here, the error returned in the if ctx.Err() != nil scope is err. But we haven't assigned any value to the err variable. It's still assigned to the zero value of an error type: nil. Hence, this code will always return a nil error.

Furthermore, this code compiles because err was initialized to its zero value due to named result parameters. Without attaching a name, we would have gotten the following compilation error:

```
Unresolved reference 'err'
```

One possible fix is to assign `ctx.Err()` to `err` like so:

```
if err := ctx.Err(); err != nil {
    return 0, 0, err
}
```

We keep returning `err`, but we first assign it to the result of `ctx.Err()`. Note that `err` in this example shadows the result variable.

> **Using a naked return statement**
> Another option is to use a naked return statement:
> ```
> if err = ctx.Err(); err != nil {
>     return
> }
> ```
> However, doing so would break the rule stating that we shouldn't mix naked returns and returns with arguments. In this case, we should probably stick with the first option. Remember that using named result parameters doesn't necessarily mean using naked returns. Sometimes we can just use named result parameters to make a signature clearer.

We conclude this discussion by emphasizing that named result parameters can improve code readability in some cases (such as returning the same type multiple times) and be quite handy in others. But we must recall that each parameter is initialized to its zero value. As we have seen in this section, this can lead to subtle bugs that aren't always straightforward to spot while reading code. Therefore, let's remain cautious when using named result parameters, to avoid potential side effects.

In the next section, we discuss a common mistake made by Go developers when a function returns an interface.

6.4   *#45: Returning a nil receiver*

In this section, we discuss the impact of returning an interface and why doing so may lead to errors in some conditions. This mistake is probably one of the most widespread in Go because it may be considered counterintuitive, at least before we've made it.

Let's consider the following example. We will work on a `Customer` struct and implement a `Validate` method to perform sanity checks. Instead of returning the first error, we want to return a list of errors. To do that, we will create a custom error type to convey multiple errors:

```
type MultiError struct {
    errs []string
}

func (m *MultiError) Add(err error) {          ◁─┤ Adds an error
    m.errs = append(m.errs, err.Error())
}
```

```
func (m *MultiError) Error() string {
    return strings.Join(m.errs, ";")
}
```

◁— **Implements the error interface**

MultiError satisfies the error interface because it implements Error() string. Meanwhile, it exposes an Add method to append an error. Using this struct, we can implement a Customer.Validate method in the following manner to check the customer's age and name. If the sanity checks are OK, we want to return a nil error:

```
func (c Customer) Validate() error {
    var m *MultiError

    if c.Age < 0 {
        m = &MultiError{}
        m.Add(errors.New("age is negative"))
    }
    if c.Name == "" {
        if m == nil {
            m = &MultiError{}
        }
        m.Add(errors.New("name is nil"))
    }

    return m
}
```

◁— **Instantiates an empty *MultiError**

◁— **Appends an error if the age is negative**

◁— **Appends an error if the name is nil**

In this implementation, m is initialized to the zero value of *MultiError: hence, nil. When a sanity check fails, we allocate a new MultiError if needed and then append an error. In the end, we return m, which can be either a nil pointer or a pointer to a MultiError struct, depending on the checks.

Now, let's test this implementation by running a case with a valid Customer:

```
customer := Customer{Age: 33, Name: "John"}
if err := customer.Validate(); err != nil {
    log.Fatalf("customer is invalid: %v", err)
}
```

Here is the output:

```
2021/05/08 13:47:28 customer is invalid: <nil>
```

This result may be pretty surprising. The Customer was valid, yet the err != nil condition was true, and logging the error printed <nil>. So, what's the issue?

In Go, we have to know that a pointer receiver can be nil. Let's experiment by creating a dummy type and calling a method with a nil pointer receiver:

```
type Foo struct{}

func (foo *Foo) Bar() string {
    return "bar"
}
```

```
func main() {
    var foo *Foo
    fmt.Println(foo.Bar())        ⊲—|  foo is nil.
}
```

`foo` is initialized to the zero value of a pointer: `nil`. But this code compiles, and it prints `bar` if we run it. A nil pointer is a valid receiver.

But why is this the case? In Go, a method is just syntactic sugar for a function whose first parameter is the receiver. Hence, the `Bar` method we've seen is similar to this function:

```
func Bar(foo *Foo) string {
    return "bar"
}
```

We know that passing a nil pointer to a function is valid. Therefore, using a nil pointer as a receiver is also valid.

Let's get back to our initial example:

```
func (c Customer) Validate() error {
    var m *MultiError

    if c.Age < 0 {
        // ...
    }
    if c.Name == "" {
        // ...
    }

    return m
}
```

`m` is initialized to the zero value of a pointer: `nil`. Then, if all the checks are valid, the argument provided to the `return` statement isn't `nil` directly but a nil pointer. Because a nil pointer is a valid receiver, converting the result into an interface won't yield a nil value. In other words, the caller of `Validate` will always get a non-nil error.

To make this point clear, let's remember that in Go, an interface is a dispatch wrapper. Here, the wrappee is `nil` (the `MultiError` pointer), whereas the wrapper isn't (the `error` interface); see figure 6.1.

Therefore, regardless of the `Customer` provided, the caller of this function will always receive a non-nil error. Understanding this behavior is imperative, because it's a widespread Go mistake.

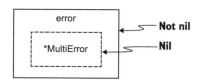

Figure 6.1 The `error` wrapper isn't `nil`.

So, what should we do to fix this example? The easiest solution is to return `m` only if it's not `nil`:

```
func (c Customer) Validate() error {
    var m *MultiError
```

```
if c.Age < 0 {
    // ...
}
if c.Name == "" {
    // ...
}

if m != nil {          Returns m only if there
    return m      ◁──  was at least one error
}
return nil     ◁──  Otherwise,
}                   returns nil
```

At the end of the method, we check whether m is not nil. If that is true, we return m; otherwise, we return nil explicitly. Hence, in the case of a valid Customer, we return a nil interface, not a nil receiver converted into a non-nil interface.

We've seen in this section that in Go, having a nil receiver is allowed, and an interface converted from a nil pointer isn't a nil interface. For that reason, when we have to return an interface, we should return not a nil pointer but a nil value directly. Generally, having a nil pointer isn't a desirable state and means a probable bug.

We saw an example with errors throughout this section because this is the most common case leading to this error. But this problem isn't only tied to errors: it can happen with any interface implemented using pointer receivers.

The next section discusses a common design mistake when using a filename as a function input.

6.5   #46: Using a filename as a function input

When creating a new function that needs to read a file, passing a filename isn't considered a best practice and can have negative effects, such as making unit tests harder to write. Let's delve into this problem and understand how to overcome it.

Suppose we want to implement a function to count the number of empty lines in a file. One way to implement this function would be to accept a filename and use bufio.NewScanner to scan and check every line:

```
func countEmptyLinesInFile(filename string) (int, error) {
    file, err := os.Open(filename)      ◁──  Opens
    if err != nil {                          filename
        return 0, err
    }
    // Handle file closure
                                              Creates a scanner from the *os.File
    scanner := bufio.NewScanner(file)   ◁──  variable that will split the input per line
    for scanner.Scan() {     ◁──  Iterates over
        // ...                     each line
    }
}
```

We open a file from the filename. Then we use bufio.NewScanner to scan every line (by default, it splits the input per line).

This function will do what we expect it to do. Indeed, as long as the provided filename is valid, we will read from it and return the number of empty lines. So what's the problem?

Let's say we want to implement unit tests to cover the following cases:

- A nominal case
- An empty file
- A file containing only empty lines

Each unit test will require creating a file in our Go project. The more complex the function is, the more cases we may want to add, and the more files we will create. We may have to create dozens of files in some cases, which can quickly become unmanageable.

Furthermore, this function isn't reusable. For example, if we had to implement the same logic but count the number of empty lines with an HTTP request, we would have to duplicate the main logic:

```
func countEmptyLinesInHTTPRequest(request http.Request) (int, error) {
    scanner := bufio.NewScanner(request.Body)
    // Copy the same logic
}
```

One way to overcome these limitations might be to make the function accept a `*bufio.Scanner` (the output returned by `bufio.NewScanner`). Both functions have the same logic from the moment we create the `scanner` variable, so this approach would work. But in Go, the idiomatic way is to start from the reader's abstraction.

Let's write a new version of the `countEmptyLines` function that receives an `io.Reader` abstraction instead:

```
func countEmptyLines(reader io.Reader) (int, error) {        ◁──┐ Accepts an io.Reader
                                                                │ as the input
    scanner := bufio.NewScanner(reader)      ◁──┐ Creates a *bufio.Scanner from
    for scanner.Scan() {                         │ an io.Reader, not an *os.File
        // ...
    }
}
```

Because `bufio.NewScanner` accepts an `io.Reader`, we can directly pass the `reader` variable.

What are the benefits of this approach? First, this function abstracts the data source. Is it a file? An HTTP request? A socket input? It's not important for the function. Because `*os.File` and the `Body` field of `http.Request` implement `io.Reader`, we can reuse the same function regardless of the input type.

Another benefit is related to testing. We mentioned that creating one file per test case could quickly become cumbersome. Now that `countEmptyLines` accepts an `io.Reader`, we can implement unit tests by creating an `io.Reader` from a string:

```
func TestCountEmptyLines(t *testing.T) {
    emptyLines, err := countEmptyLines(strings.NewReader(     ◁──┐ Passes an io.Reader
        `foo                                                      │ from a string
            bar
```

```
            baz
            `))
    // Test logic
}
```

In this test, we create an `io.Reader` using `strings.NewReader` from a string literal directly. Therefore, we don't have to create one file per test case. Each test case can be self-contained, improving the test readability and maintainability as we don't have to open another file to see the content.

Accepting a filename as a function input to read from a file should, in most cases, be considered a code smell (except in specific functions such as `os.Open`). As we've seen, it makes unit tests more complex because we may have to create multiple files. It also reduces the reusability of a function (although not all functions are meant to be reused). Using the `io.Reader` interface abstracts the data source. Regardless of whether the input is a file, a string, an HTTP request, or a gRPC request, the implementation can be reused and easily tested.

In the last section of the chapter, let's discuss a common mistake related to `defer`: how function/method arguments and method receivers are evaluated.

6.6   *#47: Ignoring how defer arguments and receivers are evaluated*

We mentioned in a previous section that the `defer` statement delays a call's execution until the surrounding function returns. A common mistake made by Go developers is not understanding how arguments are evaluated. We will delve into this problem with two subsections: one related to function and method arguments and the second related to method receivers.

6.6.1   *Argument evaluation*

To illustrate how arguments are evaluated with `defer`, let's work on a concrete example. A function needs to call two functions `foo` and `bar`. Meanwhile, it has to handle a status regarding execution:

- `StatusSuccess` if both `foo` and `bar` return no errors
- `StatusErrorFoo` if `foo` returns an error
- `StatusErrorBar` if `bar` returns an error

We will use this status for multiple actions: for example, to notify another goroutine and to increment counters. To avoid repeating these calls before every return statement, we will use `defer`. Here's our first implementation:

```
const (
    StatusSuccess  = "success"
    StatusErrorFoo = "error_foo"
    StatusErrorBar = "error_bar"
)
```

```
func f() error {
    var status string
    defer notify(status)              ⊲─┐  Defers the call to notify
    defer incrementCounter(status)    ⊲─┐  Defers the call to
                                           incrementCounter

    if err := foo(); err != nil {
        status = StatusErrorFoo       ⊲─┐  Sets the status
        return err                         to error foo
    }

    if err := bar(); err != nil {
        status = StatusErrorBar       ⊲─┐  Sets the status
        return err                         to error bar
    }

    status = StatusSuccess            ⊲─┐  Sets the status
    return nil                             to success
}
```

First we declare a status variable. Then we defer the calls to notify and increment-Counter using defer. Throughout this function, and depending on the execution path, we update status accordingly.

However, if we give this function a try, we see that regardless of the execution path, notify and incrementCounter are always called with the same status: an empty string. How is this possible?

We need to understand something crucial about argument evaluation in a defer function: the arguments are evaluated *right away*, not once the surrounding function returns. In our example, we call notify(status) and incrementCounter(status) as defer functions. Therefore, Go will delay these calls to be executed once f returns with the current value of status at the stage we used defer, hence passing an empty string. How can we solve this problem if we want to keep using defer? There are two leading solutions.

The first solution is to pass a string pointer to the defer functions:

```
func f() error {
    var status string
    defer notify(&status)             ⊲─┐  Passes a string
    defer incrementCounter(&status)   ⊲─┐  pointer to notify
                                      ⊲─┐  Passes a string pointer
                                           to incrementCounter
    // The rest of the function is unchanged
    if err := foo(); err != nil {
        status = StatusErrorFoo
        return err
    }

    if err := bar(); err != nil {
        status = StatusErrorBar
        return err
    }
```

```
    status = StatusSuccess
    return nil
}
```

We keep updating `status` depending on the cases, but now `notify` and `increment-Counter` receive a string pointer. Why does this approach work?

Using `defer` evaluates the arguments right away: here, the address of `status`. Yes, `status` itself is modified throughout the function, but its address remains constant, regardless of the assignments. Hence, if `notify` or `incrementCounter` uses the value referenced by the string pointer, it will work as expected. But this solution requires changing the signature of the two functions, which may not always be possible.

There's another solution: calling a closure as a `defer` statement. As a reminder, a closure is an anonymous function value that references variables from outside its body. The arguments passed to a `defer` function are evaluated right away. But we must know that the variables referenced by a `defer` closure are evaluated *during* the closure execution (hence, when the surrounding function returns).

Here is an example to clarify how `defer` closures work. A closure references two variables, one as a function argument and the second as a variable outside its body:

```
func main() {
    i := 0                          Calls as a defer function
    j := 0                          a closure that accepts
    defer func(i int) {        ◄──  an integer as an input
        fmt.Println(i, j)      ◄──┐ i is the function input, and
    }(i)        ◄──               └ j is an external variable.
    i++           Passes i to the closure
    j++           (evaluated right away)
}
```

Here, the closure uses `i` and `j` variables. `i` is passed as a function argument, so it's evaluated immediately. Conversely, `j` references a variable outside of the closure body, so it's evaluated when the closure is executed. If we run this example, it will print `0 1`.

Therefore, we can use a closure to implement a new version of our function:

```
                                Calls a closure as
func f() error {                the defer function
    var status string
    defer func() {      ◄──┘        Calls notify within the
        notify(status)        ◄──┘  closure and reference status
        incrementCounter(status)
    }()                            ◄──┐ Calls incrementCounter
                                      │ within the closure and
    // The rest of the function is unchanged   reference status
}
```

Here, we wrap the calls to both `notify` and `incrementCounter` within a closure. This closure references the `status` variable from outside its body. Therefore, `status` is evaluated once the closure is executed, not when we call `defer`. This solution also works and doesn't require `notify` and `incrementCounter` to change their signature.

Now, what about using `defer` on a method with a pointer or value receiver? Let's look at these questions.

6.6.2   *Pointer and value receivers*

In mistake #42, "Not knowing which type of receiver to use," we said that a receiver can be either a value or a pointer. The same logic related to argument evaluation applies when we use `defer` on a method: the receiver is also evaluated immediately. Let's understand the impact with both receiver types.

First, here's an example that calls a method on a value receiver using `defer` but mutates this receiver afterward:

```
func main() {
    s := Struct{id: "foo"}       | s is evaluated
    defer s.print()        <──┘  immediately.
    s.id = "bar"        <──┐
}                             | Updates s.id
                              | (not visible)

type Struct struct {
    id string
}

func (s Struct) print() {
    fmt.Println(s.id)       <──| foo
}
```

We defer the call to the `print` method. As with arguments, calling `defer` makes the receiver be evaluated immediately. Hence, `defer` delays the method's execution with a struct that contains an `id` field equal to `foo`. Therefore, this example prints `foo`.

Conversely, if the pointer is a receiver, the potential changes to the receiver after the call to `defer` are visible:

```
func main() {
    s := &Struct{id: "foo"}      | s is a pointer, so it is evaluated immediately
    defer s.print()        <──┘  | but may reference another variable when
    s.id = "bar"        <──┐     | the defer method is executed.
}                             | Updates s.id
                              | (visible)

type Struct struct {
    id string
}

func (s *Struct) print() {
    fmt.Println(s.id)       <──| bar
}
```

The `s` receiver is also evaluated immediately. However, calling the method leads to copying the pointer receiver. Hence, the changes made to the struct referenced by the pointer are visible. This example prints `bar`.

In summary, when we call `defer` on a function or method, the call's arguments are evaluated immediately. If we want to mutate the arguments provided to `defer` afterward, we can use pointers or closures. For a method, the receiver is also evaluated immediately; hence, the behavior depends on whether the receiver is a value or a pointer.

Summary

- The decision whether to use a value or a pointer receiver should be made based on factors such as the type, whether it has to be mutated, whether it contains a field that can't be copied, and how large the object is. When in doubt, use a pointer receiver.

- Using named result parameters can be an efficient way to improve the readability of a function/method, especially if multiple result parameters have the same type. In some cases, this approach can also be convenient because named result parameters are initialized to their zero value. But be cautious about potential side effects.

- When returning an interface, be cautious about returning not a nil pointer but an explicit nil value. Otherwise, unintended consequences may result because the caller will receive a non-nil value.

- Designing functions to receive io.Reader types instead of filenames improves the reusability of a function and makes testing easier.

- Passing a pointer to a defer function and wrapping a call inside a closure are two possible solutions to overcome the immediate evaluation of arguments and receivers.

Error management

This chapter covers

- Understanding when to panic
- Knowing when to wrap an error
- Comparing error types and error values efficiently since Go 1.13
- Handling errors idiomatically
- Understanding how to ignore an error
- Handling errors in `defer` calls

Error management is a fundamental aspect of building robust and observable applications, and it should be as important as any other part of a codebase. In Go, error management doesn't rely on the traditional try/catch mechanism as most programming languages do. Instead, errors are returned as normal return values.

This chapter will cover the most common mistakes related to errors.

7.1 #48: Panicking

It's pretty common for Go newcomers to be somewhat confused about error handling. In Go, errors are usually managed by functions or methods that return an error type as the last parameter. But some developers may find this approach surprising and be tempted to reproduce exception handling in languages such as Java or Python using `panic` and `recover`. So, let's refresh our minds about the concept of panic and discuss when it's considered appropriate or not to panic.

In Go, `panic` is a built-in function that stops the ordinary flow:

```go
func main() {
    fmt.Println("a")
    panic("foo")
    fmt.Println("b")
}
```

This code prints a and then stops before printing b:

```
a
panic: foo

goroutine 1 [running]:
main.main()
        main.go:7 +0xb3
```

Once a panic is triggered, it continues up the call stack until either the current goroutine has returned or panic is caught with `recover`:

```go
func main() {
    defer func() {
        if r := recover(); r != nil {          ◁──┐ Calls recover within
            fmt.Println("recover", r)              │ a defer closure
        }
    }()

    f()          ◁──┐ Calls f, which panics. This panic is
}                    │ caught by the previous recover.
func f() {
    fmt.Println("a")
    panic("foo")
    fmt.Println("b")
}
```

In the f function, once `panic` is called, it stops the current execution of the function and goes up the call stack: `main`. In `main`, because the panic is caught with `recover`, it doesn't stop the goroutine:

```
a
recover foo
```

Note that calling `recover()` to capture a goroutine panicking is only useful inside a `defer` function; otherwise, the function would return `nil` and have no other effect. This is because `defer` functions are also executed when the surrounding function panics.

Now, let's tackle this question: when is it appropriate to panic? In Go, `panic` is used to signal genuinely exceptional conditions, such as a programmer error. For example, if we look at the net/http package, we notice that in the WriteHeader method, there is a call to a checkWriteHeaderCode function to check whether the status code is valid:

```go
func checkWriteHeaderCode(code int) {
    if code < 100 || code > 999 {
        panic(fmt.Sprintf("invalid WriteHeader code %v", code))
    }
}
```

This function panics if the status code is invalid, which is a pure programmer error.

Another example based on a programmer error can be found in the database/sql package while registering a database driver:

```go
func Register(name string, driver driver.Driver) {
    driversMu.Lock()
    defer driversMu.Unlock()
    if driver == nil {                                      Panics if the
        panic("sql: Register driver is nil")     ◄──┘      driver is nil
    }
    if _, dup := drivers[name]; dup {
        panic("sql: Register called twice for driver " + name)   ◄──────────┐
    }
                                                      Panics if the driver is
    drivers[name] = driver                                already registered
}
```

This function panics if the driver is nil (driver.Driver is an interface) or has already been registered. Both cases would again be considered programmer errors. Also, in most cases (for example, with go-sql-driver/mysql [https://github.com/go-sql-driver/mysql], the most popular MySQL driver for Go), Register is called via an init function, which limits error handling. For all these reasons, the designers made the function panic in case of an error.

Another use case in which to panic is when our application requires a dependency but fails to initialize it. For example, let's imagine that we expose a service to create new customer accounts. At some stage, this service needs to validate the provided email address. To implement this, we decide to use a regular expression.

In Go, the regexp package exposes two functions to create a regular expression from a string: Compile and MustCompile. The former returns a *regexp.Regexp and an error, whereas the latter returns only a *regexp.Regexp but panics in case of an error. In this case, the regular expression is a mandatory dependency. Indeed, if we fail to compile it, we will never be able to validate any email input. Hence, we may favor using MustCompile and panicking in case of an error.

Panicking in Go should be used sparingly. We have seen two prominent cases, one to signal a programmer error and another where our application fails to create a mandatory dependency. Hence, there are exceptional conditions that lead us to stop the application. In most other cases, error management should be done with a function that returns a proper error type as the last return argument.

Let's now start our discussion of errors. In the next section, we see when to wrap an error.

7.2   *#49: Ignoring when to wrap an error*

Since Go 1.13, the `%w` directive allows us to wrap errors conveniently. But some developers may be confused about when to wrap an error (or not). So, let's remind ourselves what error wrapping is and then when to use it.

Error wrapping is about wrapping or packing an error inside a wrapper container that also makes the source error available (see figure 7.1). In general, the two main use cases for error wrapping are the following:

- Adding additional context to an error
- Marking an error as a specific error

Figure 7.1   Wrap the error inside a wrapper.

Regarding adding context, let's consider the following example. We receive a request from a specific user to access a database resource, but we get a "permission denied" error during the query. For debugging purposes, if the error is eventually logged, we want to add extra context. In this case, we can wrap the error to indicate who the user is and what resource is being accessed, as shown in figure 7.2.

Figure 7.2   Adding additional context to the "permission denied" error

Now let's say that instead of adding context, we want to mark the error. For example, we want to implement an HTTP handler that checks whether all the errors received while calling functions are of a `Forbidden` type so we can return a 403 status code. In that case, we can wrap this error inside `Forbidden` (see figure 7.3).

Figure 7.3   Marking the error `Forbidden`

In both cases, the source error remains available. Hence, a caller can also handle an error by unwrapping it and checking the source error. Also note that sometimes we want to combine both approaches: adding context and marking an error.

Now that we have clarified the main use cases in which to wrap an error, let's see different ways in Go to return an error we receive. We will consider the following piece of code and explore different options inside the `if err != nil` block:

```
func Foo() error {
    err := bar()
    if err != nil {
        // ?
    }
    // ...
}
```

How do we
return the error?

The first option is to return this error directly. If we don't want to mark the error and there's no helpful context we want to add, this approach is fine:

```
if err != nil {
    return err
}
```

Figure 7.4 shows that we return the same error returned by `bar`.

Before Go 1.13, to wrap an error, the only option without using an external library was to create a custom error type:

```
type BarError struct {
    Err error
}
```

Figure 7.4   We can return the error directly.

```
func (b BarError) Error() string {
    return "bar failed:" + b.Err.Error()
}
```

Then, instead of returning `err` directly, we wrapped the error into a `BarError` (see figure 7.5):

```
if err != nil {
    return BarError{Err: err}
}
```

Figure 7.5   Wrapping the error inside `BarError`

The benefit of this option is its flexibility. Because `BarError` is a custom struct, we can add any additional context if needed. However, being obliged to create a specific error type can quickly become cumbersome if we want to repeat this operation.

To overcome this situation, Go 1.13 introduced the `%w` directive:

```
if err != nil {
    return fmt.Errorf("bar failed: %w", err)
}
```

This code wraps the source error to add additional context without having to create another error type, as shown in figure 7.6.

Figure 7.6   Wrap an error into a standard error.

Because the source error remains available, a client can unwrap the parent error and then check whether the source error was of a specific type or value (we discuss these points in the following sections).

The last option we will discuss is to use the `%v` directive, instead:

```
if err != nil {
    return fmt.Errorf("bar failed: %v", err)
}
```

The difference is that the error itself isn't wrapped. We transform it into another error to add context, and the source error is no longer available, as shown in figure 7.7.

Figure 7.7   Converting the error

The information about the source of the problem remains available. However, a caller can't unwrap this error and check whether the source was bar error. So, in a sense, this option is more restrictive than `%w`. Should we prevent that, since the `%w` directive has been released? Not necessarily.

Wrapping an error makes the source error available for callers. Hence, it means introducing potential coupling. For example, imagine that we use wrapping and the caller of `Foo` checks whether the source error is `bar error`. Now, what if we change our implementation and use another function that will return another type of error? It will break the error check made by the caller.

To make sure our clients don't rely on something that we consider implementation details, the error returned should be transformed, not wrapped. In such a case, using `%v` instead of `%w` can be the way to go.

Let's review all the different options we tackled.

Option	Extra context	Marking an error	Source error available
Returning error directly	No	No	Yes
Custom error type	Possible (if the error type contains a string field, for example)	Yes	Possible (if the source error is exported or accessible via a method)
`fmt.Errorf` with `%w`	Yes	No	Yes
`fmt.Errorf` with `%v`	Yes	No	No

To summarize, when handling an error, we can decide to wrap it. Wrapping is about adding additional context to an error and/or marking an error as a specific type. If we need to mark an error, we should create a custom error type. However, if we just want to add extra context, we should use `fmt.Errorf` with the `%w` directive as it doesn't require creating a new error type. Yet, error wrapping creates potential coupling as it makes the source error available for the caller. If we want to prevent it, we shouldn't use error wrapping but error transformation, for example, using `fmt.Errorf` with the `%v` directive.

This section has shown how to wrap an error with the `%w` directive. But once we start using it, what's the impact of checking an error type?

7.3   *#50: Checking an error type inaccurately*

The previous section introduced a possible way to wrap errors using the `%w` directive. However, when we use that approach, it's also essential to change our way of checking for a specific error type; otherwise, we may handle errors inaccurately.

Let's discuss a concrete example. We will write an HTTP handler to return the transaction amount from an ID. Our handler will parse the request to get the ID and retrieve the amount from a database (DB). Our implementation can fail in two cases:

- If the ID is invalid (string length other than five characters)
- If querying the DB fails

In the former case, we want to return `StatusBadRequest` (`400`), whereas in the latter, we want to return `ServiceUnavailable` (`503`). To do so, we will create a `transient-Error` type to mark that an error is temporary. The parent handler will check the error type. If the error is a `transientError`, it will return a 503 status code; otherwise, it will return a 400 status code.

Let's first focus on the error type definition and the function the handler will call:

```
type transientError struct {
    err error
}
```

```
func (t transientError) Error() string {        ◁─┐ Creates a custom
    return fmt.Sprintf("transient error: %v", t.err)   │ transientError
}


func getTransactionAmount(transactionID string) (float32, error) {
    if len(transactionID) != 5 {
        return 0, fmt.Errorf("id is invalid: %s",
            transactionID)              ◁─┐ Returns a simple error if the
    }                                     │ transaction ID is invalid

    amount, err := getTransactionAmountFromDB(transactionID)
    if err != nil {
        return 0, transientError{err: err}    ◁─┐ Returns a transientError
    }                                           │ if we fail to query the DB
    return amount, nil
}
```

getTransactionAmount returns an error using fmt.Errorf if the identifier is invalid.
However, if getting the transaction amount from the DB fails, getTransactionAmount
wraps the error into a transientError type.

Now, let's write the HTTP handler that checks the error type to return the appropriate HTTP status code:

```
                                              Extracts the
                                              transaction ID

func handler(w http.ResponseWriter, r *http.Request) {        │ Calls
    transactionID := r.URL.Query().Get("transaction")   ◁──   │ getTransactionAmount
                                                              │ that contains
    amount, err := getTransactionAmount(transactionID)  ◁──┘ all the logic
    if err != nil {
        switch err := err.(type) {          ◁─────────
        case transientError:
            http.Error(w, err.Error(), http.StatusServiceUnavailable)
        default:
            http.Error(w, err.Error(), http.StatusBadRequest)
        }
        return                                      Checks the error type and
    }                                              returns a 503 if the error is a
                                                   transient one; otherwise, a 400
    // Write response
}
```

Using a switch on the error type, we return the appropriate HTTP status code: 400 in
the case of a bad request or 503 in the case of a transient error.

This code is perfectly valid. However, let's assume that we want to perform a small
refactoring of getTransactionAmount. The transientError will be returned by
getTransactionAmountFromDB instead of getTransactionAmount. getTransaction-
Amount now wraps this error using the %w directive:

```
func getTransactionAmount(transactionID string) (float32, error) {
    // Check transaction ID validity
```

```
    amount, err := getTransactionAmountFromDB(transactionID)
    if err != nil {
        return 0, fmt.Errorf("failed to get transaction %s: %w",
            transactionID, err)                     ⟵┐  Wraps the error instead of
    }                                                │  returning a transientError directly
    return amount, nil
}

func getTransactionAmountFromDB(transactionID string) (float32, error) {
    // ...
    if err != nil {
        return 0, transientError{err: err}      ⟵┐  This function now
    }                                            │  returns the transientError.
    // ...
}
```

If we run this code, it always returns a 400 regardless of the error case, so the `case`
`Transient` error will never be hit. How can we explain this behavior?

Before the refactoring, `transientError` was returned by `getTransactionAmount`
(see figure 7.8). After the refactoring, `transientError` is now returned by `get-`
`TransactionAmountFromDB` (figure 7.9).

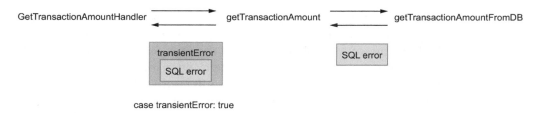

Figure 7.8 Because `getTransactionAmount` returned a `transientError` if the DB failed, the
case was true.

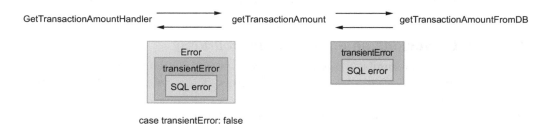

Figure 7.9 Now `getTransactionAmount` returns a wrapped error. Hence, `case transientError`
is false.

What `getTransactionAmount` returns isn't a `transientError` directly: it's an error
wrapping `transientError`. Therefore `case transientError` is now false.

For that exact purpose, Go 1.13 came with a directive to wrap an error and a way to check whether the wrapped error is of a certain type with `errors.As`. This function recursively unwraps an error and returns `true` if an error in the chain matches the expected type.

Let's rewrite our implementation of the caller using `errors.As`:

```go
func handler(w http.ResponseWriter, r *http.Request) {
    // Get transaction ID

    amount, err := getTransactionAmount(transactionID)    │ Calls errors.As by
    if err != nil {                                        │ providing a pointer
        if errors.As(err, &transientError{}) {        ◄───┘ to transientError
            http.Error(w, err.Error(),
                http.StatusServiceUnavailable)    ◄───┐ Returns a 503 if the
        } else {                                      │ error is transient
            http.Error(w, err.Error(),
                http.StatusBadRequest)    ◄───┐ Else returns
        }                                     │ a 400
        return
    }

    // Write response
}
```

We got rid of the `switch` case type in this new version, and we now use `errors.As`. This function requires the second argument (the target error) to be a pointer. Otherwise, the function will compile but panic at runtime. Regardless of whether the runtime error is directly a `transientError` type or an error wrapping `transientError`, `errors.As` returns `true`; hence, the handler will return a 503 status code.

In summary, if we rely on Go 1.13 error wrapping, we must use `errors.As` to check whether an error is a specific type. This way, regardless of whether the error is returned directly by the function we call or wrapped inside an error, `errors.As` will be able to recursively unwrap our main error and see if one of the errors is a specific type.

We have just seen how to compare an error type; now it's time to compare an error value.

7.4   #51: Checking an error value inaccurately

This section is similar to the previous one but with sentinel errors (error values). First, we will define what a sentinel error conveys. Then, we will see how to compare an error to a value.

A sentinel error is an error defined as a global variable:

```go
import "errors"

var ErrFoo = errors.New("foo")
```

In general, the convention is to start with `Err` followed by the error type: here, `ErrFoo`. A sentinel error conveys an *expected* error. But what do we mean by an expected error? Let's discuss it in the context of an SQL library.

We want to design a `Query` method that allows us to execute a query to a database. This method returns a slice of rows. How should we handle the case when no rows are found? We have two options:

- Return a sentinel value: for example, a nil slice (think about `strings.Index`, which returns the sentinel value −1 if a substring isn't present).
- Return a specific error that a client can check.

Let's take the second approach: our method can return a specific error if no rows are found. We can classify this as an *expected* error, because passing a request that returns no rows is allowed. Conversely, situations like network issues and connection polling errors are *unexpected* errors. It doesn't mean we don't want to handle unexpected errors; it means that semantically, those errors convey a different meaning.

If we take a look at the standard library, we can find many examples of sentinel errors:

- `sql.ErrNoRows`—Returned when a query doesn't return any rows (which was exactly our case)
- `io.EOF`—Returned by an `io.Reader` when no more input is available

That's the general principle behind sentinel errors. They convey an expected error that clients will expect to check. Therefore, as general guidelines,

- Expected errors should be designed as error values (sentinel errors): `var ErrFoo = errors.New("foo")`.
- Unexpected errors should be designed as error types: `type BarError struct { … }`, with `BarError` implementing the `error` interface.

Let's get back to the common mistake. How can we compare an error to a specific value? By using the `==` operator:

```
err := query()
if err != nil {
    if err == sql.ErrNoRows {        ◁─┐  Checks error against the
        // ...                          │  sql.ErrNoRows variable
    } else {
        // ...
    }
}
```

Here, we call a `query` function and get an error. Checking whether the error is an `sql.ErrNoRows` is done using the `==` operator.

However, just as we discussed in the previous section, a sentinel error can also be wrapped. If an `sql.ErrNoRows` is wrapped using `fmt.Errorf` and the `%w` directive, `err == sql.ErrNoRows` will always be false.

Again, Go 1.13 provides an answer. We have seen how `errors.As` is used to check an error against a type. With error values, we can use its counterpart: `errors.Is`. Let's rewrite the previous example:

```
err := query()
if err != nil {
```

```
    if errors.Is(err, sql.ErrNoRows) {
        // ...
    } else {
        // ...
    }
}
```

Using `errors.Is` instead of the `==` operator allows the comparison to work even if the error is wrapped using `%w`.

In summary, if we use error wrapping in our application with the `%w` directive and `fmt.Errorf`, checking an error against a specific value should be done using `errors.Is` instead of `==`. Thus, even if the sentinel error is wrapped, `errors.Is` can recursively unwrap it and compare each error in the chain against the provided value.

Now it's time to discuss one of the most important aspects of error handling: not handling an error twice.

7.5   *#52: Handling an error twice*

Handling an error multiple times is a mistake made frequently by developers, not specifically in Go. Let's understand why this is a problem and how to handle errors efficiently.

To illustrate the problem, let's write a `GetRoute` function to get the route from a pair of sources to a pair of target coordinates. Let's assume this function will call an unexported `getRoute` function that contains the business logic to calculate the best route. Before calling `getRoute`, we have to validate the source and target coordinates using `validateCoordinates`. We also want the possible errors to be logged. Here's a possible implementation:

```
func GetRoute(srcLat, srcLng, dstLat, dstLng float32) (Route, error) {
    err := validateCoordinates(srcLat, srcLng)
    if err != nil {
        log.Println("failed to validate source coordinates")      ◁──┐ Logs and returns
        return Route{}, err                                           │ the error
    }

    err = validateCoordinates(dstLat, dstLng)
    if err != nil {
        log.Println("failed to validate target coordinates")      ◁──┐ Logs and returns
        return Route{}, err                                           │ the error
    }

    return getRoute(srcLat, srcLng, dstLat, dstLng)
}

func validateCoordinates(lat, lng float32) error {
    if lat > 90.0 || lat < -90.0 {
        log.Printf("invalid latitude: %f", lat)           ◁──┐ Logs and returns
        return fmt.Errorf("invalid latitude: %f", lat)        │ the error
    }
    if lng > 180.0 || lng < -180.0 {                                 Logs and returns
        log.Printf("invalid longitude: %f", lng)          ◁──┘ the error
```

```
        return fmt.Errorf("invalid longitude: %f", lng)
    }
    return nil
}
```

What's the problem with this code? First, in `validateCoordinates`, it is cumbersome to repeat the `invalid latitude` or `invalid longitude` error messages in both logging and the error returned. Also, if we run the code with an invalid latitude, for example, it will log the following lines:

```
2021/06/01 20:35:12 invalid latitude: 200.000000
2021/06/01 20:35:12 failed to validate source coordinates
```

Having two log lines for a single error is a problem. Why? Because it makes debugging harder. For example, if this function is called multiple times concurrently, the two messages may not be one after the other in the logs, making the debugging process more complex.

As a rule of thumb, an error should be handled only once. Logging an error is handling an error, and so is returning an error. Hence, we should either log or return an error, never both.

Let's rewrite our implementation to handle errors only once:

```
func GetRoute(srcLat, srcLng, dstLat, dstLng float32) (Route, error) {
    err := validateCoordinates(srcLat, srcLng)
    if err != nil {
        return Route{}, err          ⊲─┐ Only returns
    }                                    │ an error

    err = validateCoordinates(dstLat, dstLng)
    if err != nil {
        return Route{}, err          ⊲─┐ Only returns
    }                                    │ an error

    return getRoute(srcLat, srcLng, dstLat, dstLng)
}

func validateCoordinates(lat, lng float32) error {
    if lat > 90.0 || lat < -90.0 {                            │ Only returns
        return fmt.Errorf("invalid latitude: %f", lat)  ⊲─┘ an error
    }
    if lng > 180.0 || lng < -180.0 {
        return fmt.Errorf("invalid longitude: %f", lng)  ⊲─┐ Only returns
    }                                                        │ an error
    return nil
}
```

In this version, each error is handled only once by being returned directly. Then, assuming the caller of `GetRoute` is handling the possible errors with logging, the code will output the following message in case of an invalid latitude:

```
2021/06/01 20:35:12 invalid latitude: 200.000000
```

Is this new Go version of the code perfect? Not really. For example, the first implementation led to two logs in case of an invalid latitude. Still, we knew which call to `validateCoordinates` was failing: either the source or the target coordinates. Here, we lose this information, so we need to add additional context to the error.

Let's rewrite the latest version of our code using Go 1.13 error wrapping (we omit `validateCoordinates` as it remains unchanged):

```
func GetRoute(srcLat, srcLng, dstLat, dstLng float32) (Route, error) {
    err := validateCoordinates(srcLat, srcLng)
    if err != nil {
        return Route{},
            fmt.Errorf("failed to validate source coordinates: %w",
                err)                    ◁─┐ Returns a
    }                                     │ wrapper error

    err = validateCoordinates(dstLat, dstLng)
    if err != nil {
        return Route{},
            fmt.Errorf("failed to validate target coordinates: %w",
                err)                    ◁─┐ Returns a
    }                                     │ wrapper error

    return getRoute(srcLat, srcLng, dstLat, dstLng)
}
```

Each error returned by `validateCoordinates` is now wrapped to provide additional context for the error: whether it's related to the source or target coordinates. So if we run this new version, here's what the caller logs in case of an invalid source latitude:

```
2021/06/01 20:35:12 failed to validate source coordinates:
    invalid latitude: 200.000000
```

With this version, we have covered all the different cases: a single log, without losing any valuable information. In addition, each error is handled only once, which simplifies our code by, for example, avoiding repeating error messages.

Handling an error should be done only once. As we have seen, logging an error is handling an error. Hence, we should either log or return an error. By doing this, we simplify our code and gain better insights into the error situation. Using error wrapping is the most convenient approach as it allows us to propagate the source error and add context to an error.

In the next section, we see the appropriate way to ignore an error in Go.

7.6   *#53: Not handling an error*

In some cases, we may want to ignore an error returned by a function. There should be only one way to do this in Go; let's understand why.

We will consider the following example, where we call a `notify` function that returns a single `error` argument. We're not interested in this error, so we purposely omit any error handling:

```
func f() {
    // ...
    notify()          ◁──┐  Error handling
}                        │  is omitted.

func notify() error {
    // ...
}
```

Because we want to ignore the error, in this example, we just call `notify` without assigning its output to a classic `err` variable. There's nothing wrong with this code from a functional standpoint: it compiles and runs as expected.

However, from a maintainability perspective, the code can lead to some issues. Let's consider a new reader looking at it. This reader notices that `notify` returns an error but that the error isn't handled by the parent function. How can they guess whether or not handling the error was intentional? How can they know whether the previous developer forgot to handle it or did it purposely?

For these reasons, when we want to ignore an error in Go, there's only one way to write it:

```
_ = notify()
```

Instead of not assigning the error to a variable, we assign it to the blank identifier. In terms of compilation and run time, this approach doesn't change anything compared to the first piece of code. But this new version makes explicit that we aren't interested in the error.

A comment can also accompany such code, but not a comment like the following that mentions ignoring the error:

```
// Ignore the error
_ = notify()
```

This comment just duplicates what the code does and should be avoided. But it may be a good idea to write a comment that indicates the rationale for why the error is ignored, like this:

```
// At-most once delivery.
// Hence, it's accepted to miss some of them in case of errors.
_ = notify()
```

Ignoring an error in Go should be the exception. In many cases, we may still favor logging them, even at a low log level. But if we are sure that an error can and should be ignored, we must do so explicitly by assigning it to the blank identifier. This way, a future reader will understand that we ignored the error intentionally.

The last section of this chapter discusses how to handle errors returned by `defer` functions.

7.7   *#54: Not handling defer errors*

Not handling errors in `defer` statements is a mistake that's frequently made by Go developers. Let's understand what the problem is and the possible solutions.

In the following example, we will implement a function to query a DB to get the balance given a customer ID. We will use `database/sql` and the `Query` method.

> **NOTE**   We won't delve too deep here into how this package works; we do that in mistake #78, "Common SQL mistakes."

Here's a possible implementation (we focus on the query itself, not the parsing of the results):

```
const query = "..."

func getBalance(db *sql.DB, clientID string) (
    float32, error) {
    rows, err := db.Query(query, clientID)
    if err != nil {
        return 0, err
    }
    defer rows.Close()         ◁──┐  Defers the call
                                  │  to rows.Close()
    // Use rows
}
```

`rows` is a `*sql.Rows` type. It implements the `Closer` interface:

```
type Closer interface {
    Close() error
}
```

This interface contains a single `Close` method that returns an error (we will also look at this topic in mistake #79, "Not closing transient resources"). We mentioned in the previous section that errors should always be handled. But in this case, the error returned by the `defer` call is ignored:

```
defer rows.Close()
```

As discussed in the previous section, if we don't want to handle the error, we should ignore it explicitly using the blank identifier:

```
defer func() { _ = rows.Close() }()
```

This version is more verbose but is better from a maintainability perspective as we explicitly mark that we are ignoring the error.

But in such a case, instead of blindly ignoring all errors from `defer` calls, we should ask ourselves whether that is the best approach. In this case, calling `Close()` returns an error when it fails to free a DB connection from the pool. Hence, ignoring this error is probably not what we want to do. Most likely, a better option would be to log a message:

```
defer func() {
    err := rows.Close()
    if err != nil {
        log.Printf("failed to close rows: %v", err)
    }
}()
```

Now, if closing `rows` fails, the code will log a message so we're aware of it.

What if, instead of handling the error, we prefer to propagate it to the caller of `getBalance` so that they can decide how to handle it?

```
defer func() {
    err := rows.Close()
    if err != nil {
        return err
    }
}()
```

This implementation doesn't compile. Indeed, the `return` statement is associated with the anonymous `func()` function, not `getBalance`.

If we want to tie the error returned by `getBalance` to the error caught in the `defer` call, we must use named result parameters. Let's write the first version:

```
func getBalance(db *sql.DB, clientID string) (
    balance float32, err error) {
    rows, err := db.Query(query, clientID)
    if err != nil {
        return 0, err
    }
    defer func() {
        err = rows.Close()          ◁──┐  Assigns the error to the
    }()                                │  output named parameter

    if rows.Next() {
        err := rows.Scan(&balance)
        if err != nil {
            return 0, err
        }
        return balance, nil
    }
    // ...
}
```

Once the `rows` variable has been correctly created, we defer the call to `rows.Close()` in an anonymous function. This function assigns the error to the `err` variable, which is initialized using named result parameters.

This code may look okay, but there's a problem with it. If `rows.Scan` returns an error, `rows.Close` is executed anyway; but because this call overrides the error returned by `getBalance`, instead of returning an error, we may return a nil error if `rows.Close` returns successfully. In other words, if the call to `db.Query` succeeds (the first line of the function), the error returned by `getBalance` will always be the one returned by `rows.Close`, which isn't what we want.

The logic we need to implement isn't straightforward:

- If `rows.Scan` succeeds,
  - If `rows.Close` succeeds, return no error.
  - If `rows.Close` fails, return this error.

And if `rows.Scan` fails, the logic is a bit more complex because we may have to handle two errors:

- If `rows.Scan` fails,
  - If `rows.Close` succeeds, return the error from `rows.Scan`.
  - If `rows.Close` fails . . . then what?

If both `rows.Scan` and `rows.Close` fail, what should we do? There are several options. For example, we can return a custom error that conveys two errors. Another option, which we will implement, is to return the `rows.Scan` error but log the `rows.Close` error. Here's our final implementation of the anonymous function:

```
defer func() {
    closeErr := rows.Close()        ◁──┐ Assigns the rows.Close
    if err != nil {            ◁──────────  error to another variable
        if closeErr != nil {                      ┌─ If err was already not
            log.Printf("failed to close rows: %v", err)   └─ nil, we prioritize it.
        }
        return
    }                          ┌─ Otherwise, we
    err = closeErr      ◁──────┘  return closeErr.
}()
```

The `rows.Close` error is assigned to another variable: `closeErr`. Before assigning it to `err`, we check whether `err` is different from `nil`. If that's the case, an error was already returned by `getBalance`, so we decide to log `err` and return the existing error.

As discussed, errors should always be handled. In the case of errors returned by `defer` calls, the very least we should do is ignore them explicitly. If this isn't enough, we can handle the error directly by logging it or propagating it up to the caller, as illustrated in this section.

Summary

- Using `panic` is an option to deal with errors in Go. However, it should only be used sparingly in unrecoverable conditions: for example, to signal a programmer error or when you fail to load a mandatory dependency.
- Wrapping an error allows you to mark an error and/or provide additional context. However, error wrapping creates potential coupling as it makes the source error available for the caller. If you want to prevent that, don't use error wrapping.
- If you use Go 1.13 error wrapping with the `%w` directive and `fmt.Errorf`, comparing an error against a type or a value has to be done using `errors.As` or

`errors.Is`, respectively. Otherwise, if the returned error you want to check is wrapped, it will fail the checks.

- To convey an expected error, use error sentinels (error values). An unexpected error should be a specific error type.

- In most situations, an error should be handled only once. Logging an error is handling an error. Therefore, you have to choose between logging or returning an error. In many cases, error wrapping is the solution as it allows you to provide additional context to an error and return the source error.

- Ignoring an error, whether during a function call or in a `defer` function, should be done explicitly using the blank identifier. Otherwise, future readers may be confused about whether it was intentional or a miss.

- In many cases, you shouldn't ignore an error returned by a `defer` function. Either handle it directly or propagate it to the caller, depending on the context. If you want to ignore it, use the blank identifier.

Concurrency: Foundations

This chapter covers

- Understanding concurrency and parallelism
- Why concurrency isn't always faster
- The impacts of CPU-bound and I/O-bound workloads
- Using channels vs. mutexes
- Understanding the differences between data races and race conditions
- Working with Go contexts

In recent decades, CPU vendors have stopped focusing only on clock speed. Instead, modern CPUs are designed with multiple cores and hyperthreading (multiple logical cores on the same physical core). Therefore, to leverage these architectures, concurrency has become critical for software developers. Even though Go provides *simple* primitives, this doesn't necessarily mean that writing concurrent code has become easy. This chapter discusses fundamental concepts related to concurrency; chapter 9 will then focus on practice.

8.1 #55: Mixing up concurrency and parallelism

Even after years of concurrent programming, developers may not clearly understand the differences between concurrency and parallelism. Before delving into Go-specific topics, it's first essential to understand these concepts so we share a common vocabulary. This section illustrates with a real-life example: a coffee shop.

In this coffee shop, one waiter is in charge of accepting orders and preparing them using a single coffee machine. Customers give their orders and then wait for their coffee (see figure 8.1).

Customer queue   **Accept orders and grind coffee**   **Coffee machine**

Figure 8.1 A simple coffee shop

If the waiter is having a hard time serving all the customers and the coffee shop wants to speed up the overall process, one idea might be to have a second waiter and a second coffee machine. A customer in the queue would wait for a waiter to be available (figure 8.2).

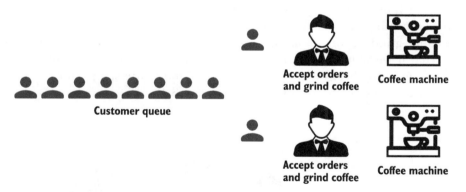

Accept orders and grind coffee   **Coffee machine**

Customer queue

Accept orders and grind coffee   **Coffee machine**

Figure 8.2 Duplicating everything in the coffee shop

In this new process, every part of the system is independent. The coffee shop should serve consumers twice as fast. This is a *parallel* implementation of a coffee shop.

If we want to scale, we can keep duplicating waiters and coffee machines over and over. However, this isn't the only possible coffee shop design. Another approach might be to split the work done by the waiters and have one in charge of accepting orders and another one who grinds the coffee beans, which are then brewed in a single machine. Also, instead of blocking the customer queue until a customer is served, we could introduce another queue for customers waiting for their orders (think about Starbucks) (figure 8.3).

Figure 8.3 Splitting the role of the waiters

With this new design, we don't make things parallel. But the overall structure is affected: we split a given role into two roles, and we introduce another queue. Unlike parallelism, which is about doing the same thing multiple times at once, *concurrency* is about structure.

Assuming one thread represents the waiter accepting orders and another represents the coffee machine, we have introduced yet another thread to grind the coffee beans. Each thread is independent but has to coordinate with others. Here, the waiter thread accepting orders has to communicate which coffee beans to grind. Meanwhile, the coffee-grinding threads must communicate with the coffee machine thread.

What if we want to increase throughput by serving more customers per hour? Because grinding beans takes longer than accepting orders, a possible change could be to hire another coffee-grinding waiter (figure 8.4).

Figure 8.4 Hiring another waiter to grind coffee beans

Here, the structure remains the same. It is still a three-step design: accept, grind, brew coffee. Hence, there are no changes in terms of concurrency. But we are back to adding parallelism, here for one particular step: the order preparation.

Now, let's assume that the part slowing down the whole process is the coffee machine. Using a single coffee machine introduces contentions for the coffee-grinding threads as they both wait for a coffee machine thread to be available. What could be a solution? Adding more coffee machine threads (figure 8.5).

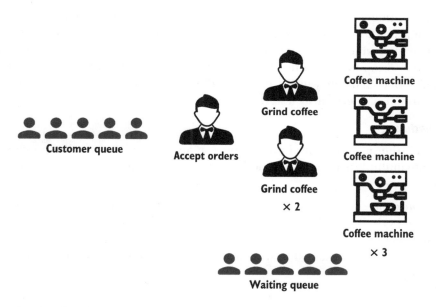

Figure 8.5 Adding more coffee machines

Instead of a single coffee machine, we have increased the level of parallelism by introducing more machines. Again, the structure hasn't changed; it remains a three-step design. But throughput should increase because the level of contention for the coffee-grinding threads should decrease.

With this design, we can notice something important: *concurrency enables parallelism.* Indeed, concurrency provides a structure to solve a problem with parts that may be parallelized.

> *Concurrency is about dealing with lots of things at once. Parallelism is about doing lots of things at once.*
>
> —Rob Pike

In summary, concurrency and parallelism are different. Concurrency is about structure, and we can change a sequential implementation into a concurrent one by introducing different steps that separate concurrent threads can tackle. Meanwhile, parallelism is about execution, and we can use it at the step level by adding more parallel threads. Understanding these two concepts is fundamental to being a proficient Go developer.

The next section discusses a prevalent mistake: believing that concurrency is always the way to go.

8.2   *#56: Thinking concurrency is always faster*

A misconception among many developers is believing that a concurrent solution is always faster than a sequential one. This couldn't be more wrong. The overall performance of a solution depends on many factors, such as the efficiency of our structure (concurrency), which parts can be tackled in parallel, and the level of contention among the computation units. This section reminds us about some fundamental knowledge of concurrency in Go; then we will see a concrete example where a concurrent solution isn't necessarily faster.

8.2.1   Go scheduling

A thread is the smallest unit of processing that an OS can perform. If a process wants to execute multiple actions simultaneously, it spins up multiple threads. These threads can be

- *Concurrent*—Two or more threads can start, run, and complete in overlapping time periods, like the waiter thread and the coffee machine thread in the previous section.
- *Parallel*—The same task can be executed multiple times at once, like multiple waiter threads.

The OS is responsible for scheduling the thread's processes optimally so that

- All the threads can consume CPU cycles without being starved for too much time.
- The workload is distributed as evenly as possible among the different CPU cores.

> **NOTE**   The word *thread* can also have a different meaning at a CPU level. Each physical core can be composed of multiple logical cores (the concept of hyperthreading), and a logical core is also called a thread. In this section, when we use the word *thread*, we mean the unit of processing, not a logical core.

A CPU core executes different threads. When it switches from one thread to another, it executes an operation called *context switching*. The active thread consuming CPU cycles was in an *executing* state and moves to a *runnable* state, meaning it's ready to be executed pending an available core. Context switching is considered an expensive operation because the OS needs to save the current execution state of a thread before the switch (such as the current register values).

As Go developers, we can't create threads directly, but we can create goroutines, which can be thought of as application-level threads. However, whereas an OS thread is context-switched on and off a CPU core by the OS, a goroutine is context-switched on and off an OS thread by the Go runtime. Also, compared to an OS thread, a goroutine has a smaller memory footprint: 2 KB for goroutines from Go 1.4. An OS thread depends on the OS, but, for example, on Linux/x86-32, the default size is 2 MB (see http://mng.bz/DgMw). Having a smaller size makes context switching faster.

NOTE Context switching a goroutine versus a thread is about 80% to 90% faster, depending on the architecture.

Let's now discuss how the Go scheduler works to overview how goroutines are handled. Internally, the Go scheduler uses the following terminology (see http://mng.bz/N611):

- *G*—Goroutine
- *M*—OS thread (stands for *machine*)
- *P*—CPU core (stands for *processor*)

Each OS thread (M) is assigned to a CPU core (P) by the OS scheduler. Then, each goroutine (G) runs on an M. The GOMAXPROCS variable defines the limit of Ms in charge of executing user-level code simultaneously. But if a thread is blocked in a system call (for example, I/O), the scheduler can spin up more Ms. As of Go 1.5, GOMAXPROCS is by default equal to the number of available CPU cores.

A goroutine has a simpler lifecycle than an OS thread. It can be doing one of the following:

- *Executing*—The goroutine is scheduled on an M and executing its instructions.
- *Runnable*—The goroutine is waiting to be in an executing state.
- *Waiting*—The goroutine is stopped and pending something completing, such as a system call or a synchronization operation (such as acquiring a mutex).

There's one last stage to understand about the implementation of Go scheduling: when a goroutine is created but cannot be executed yet; for example, all the other Ms are already executing a G. In this scenario, what will the Go runtime do about it? The answer is queuing. The Go runtime handles two kinds of queues: one local queue per P and a global queue shared among all the Ps.

Figure 8.6 shows a given scheduling situation on a four-core machine with GOMAXPROCS equal to 4. The parts are the logical cores (Ps), goroutines (Gs), OS threads (Ms), local queues, and global queue.

First, we can see five Ms, whereas GOMAXPROCS is set to 4. But as we mentioned, if needed, the Go runtime can create more OS threads than the GOMAXPROCS value.

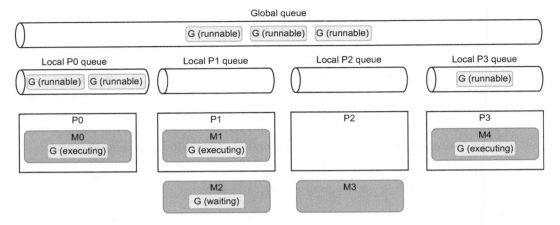

Figure 8.6   An example of the current state of a Go application executed on a four-core machine. Goroutines that aren't in an executing state are either runnable (pending being executed) or waiting (pending a blocking operation).

P0, P1, and P3 are currently busy executing Go runtime threads. But P2 is presently idle as M3 is switched off P2, and there's no goroutine to be executed. This isn't a good situation because six runnable goroutines are pending being executed, some in the global queue and some in other local queues. How will the Go runtime handle this situation? Here's the scheduling implementation in pseudocode (see http:// mng.bz/lxY8):

```
runtime.schedule() {
    // Only 1/61 of the time, check the global runnable queue for a G.
    // If not found, check the local queue.
    // If not found,
    //      Try to steal from other Ps.
    //      If not, check the global runnable queue.
    //      If not found, poll network.
}
```

Every sixty-first execution, the Go scheduler will check whether goroutines from the global queue are available. If not, it will check its local queue. Meanwhile, if both the global and local queues are empty, the Go scheduler can pick up goroutines from other local queues. This principle in scheduling is called *work stealing*, and it allows an underutilized processor to actively look for another processor's goroutines and *steal* some.

One last important thing to mention: prior to Go 1.14, the scheduler was cooperative, which meant a goroutine could be context-switched off a thread only in specific blocking cases (for example, channel send or receive, I/O, waiting to acquire a mutex). Since Go 1.14, the Go scheduler is now preemptive: when a goroutine is running for a specific amount of time (10 ms), it will be marked preemptible and can be context-switched off to be replaced by another goroutine. This allows a long-running job to be forced to share CPU time.

Now that we understand the fundamentals of scheduling in Go, let's look at a concrete example: implementing a merge sort in a parallel manner.

8.2.2   *Parallel merge sort*

First, let's briefly review how the merge sort algorithm works. Then we will implement a parallel version. Note that the objective isn't to implement the most efficient version but to support a concrete example showing why concurrency isn't always faster.

The merge sort algorithm works by breaking a list repeatedly into two sublists until each sublist consists of a single element and then merging these sublists so that the result is a sorted list (see figure 8.7). Each split operation splits the list into two sublists, whereas the merge operation merges two sublists into a sorted list.

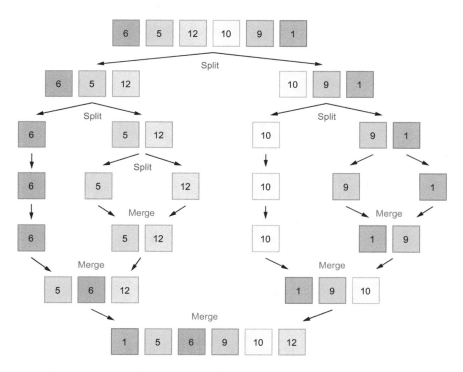

Figure 8.7   Applying the merge sort algorithm repeatedly breaks each list into two sublists. Then the algorithm uses a merge operation such that the resulting list is sorted.

Here is the sequential implementation of this algorithm. We don't include all of the code as it's not the main point of this section:

```
func sequentialMergesort(s []int) {
    if len(s) <= 1 {
        return
    }
```

```
    middle := len(s) / 2
    sequentialMergesort(s[:middle])        ⟵⊣ First half
    sequentialMergesort(s[middle:])              ⟵⊣ Second half
    merge(s, middle)                   ⟵⊣ Merges the
}                                          two halves

func merge(s []int, middle int) {
    // ...
}
```

This algorithm has a structure that makes it open to concurrency. Indeed, as each `sequentialMergesort` operation works on an independent set of data that doesn't need to be fully copied (here, an independent view of the underlying array using slicing), we could distribute this workload among the CPU cores by spinning up each `sequentialMergesort` operation in a different goroutine. Let's write a first parallel implementation:

```
func parallelMergesortV1(s []int) {
    if len(s) <= 1 {
        return
    }

    middle := len(s) / 2

    var wg sync.WaitGroup
    wg.Add(2)
                              Spins up the first half of
    go func() {          ⟵⊣  the work in a goroutine
        defer wg.Done()
        parallelMergesortV1(s[:middle])
    }()
                              Spins up the second half of
    go func() {          ⟵⊣  the work in a goroutine
        defer wg.Done()
        parallelMergesortV1(s[middle:])
    }()

    wg.Wait()            Merges
    merge(s, middle)  ⟵⊣ the halves
}
```

In this version, each half of the workload is handled in a separate goroutine. The parent goroutine waits for both parts by using `sync.WaitGroup`. Hence, we call the `Wait` method before the merge operation.

> **NOTE** If you're not yet familiar with `sync.WaitGroup`, we will look at it in more detail in mistake #71, "Misusing sync.WaitGroup." In a nutshell, it allows us to wait for *n* operations to complete: usually goroutines, as in the previous example.

We now have a parallel version of the merge sort algorithm. Therefore, if we run a benchmark to compare this version against the sequential one, the parallel version should be faster, correct? Let's run it on a four-core machine with 10,000 elements:

```
Benchmark_sequentialMergesort-4        2278993555 ns/op
Benchmark_parallelMergesortV1-4       17525998709 ns/op
```

Surprisingly, the parallel version is almost an order of magnitude slower. How can we explain this result? How is it possible that a parallel version that distributes a workload across four cores is slower than a sequential version running on a single machine? Let's analyze the problem.

If we have a slice of, say, 1,024 elements, the parent goroutine will spin up two goroutines, each in charge of handling a half consisting of 512 elements. Each of these goroutines will spin up two new goroutines in charge of handling 256 elements, then 128, and so on, until we spin up a goroutine to compute a single element.

If the workload that we want to parallelize is too small, meaning we're going to compute it too fast, the benefit of distributing a job across cores is destroyed: the time it takes to create a goroutine and have the scheduler execute it is much too high compared to directly merging a tiny number of items in the current goroutine. Although goroutines are lightweight and faster to start than threads, we can still face cases where a workload is too small.

NOTE   We will discuss how to recognize when an execution is poorly parallelized in mistake #98, "Not using Go diagnostics tooling."

So what can we conclude from this result? Does it mean the merge sort algorithm cannot be parallelized? Wait, not so fast.

Let's try another approach. Because merging a tiny number of elements within a new goroutine isn't efficient, let's define a threshold. This threshold will represent how many elements a half should contain in order to be handled in a parallel manner. If the number of elements in the half is fewer than this value, we will handle it sequentially. Here's a new version:

```
const max = 2048          ⭠┤ Defines the threshold

func parallelMergesortV2(s []int) {
    if len(s) <= 1 {
        return
    }

    if len(s) <= max {                   │ Calls our initial
        sequentialMergesort(s)     ⭠┘ sequential version
    } else {                        ⭠  If bigger than the threshold,
        middle := len(s) / 2        │ keeps the parallel version

        var wg sync.WaitGroup
        wg.Add(2)

        go func() {
            defer wg.Done()
            parallelMergesortV2(s[:middle])
        }()

        go func() {
            defer wg.Done()
```

```
            parallelMergesortV2(s[middle:])
        }()

        wg.Wait()
        merge(s, middle)
    }
}
```

If the number of elements in the s slice is smaller than max, we call the sequential version. Otherwise, we keep calling our parallel implementation. Does this approach impact the result? Yes, it does:

```
Benchmark_sequentialMergesort-4        2278993555 ns/op
Benchmark_parallelMergesortV1-4       17525998709 ns/op
Benchmark_parallelMergesortV2-4        1313010260 ns/op
```

Our v2 parallel implementation is more than 40% faster than the sequential one, thanks to this idea of defining a threshold to indicate when parallel should be more efficient than sequential.

> **NOTE** Why did I set the threshold to 2,048? Because it was the optimal value for this specific workload on my machine. In general, such magic values should be defined carefully with benchmarks (running on an execution environment similar to production). It's also pretty interesting to note that running the same algorithm in a programming language that doesn't implement the concept of goroutines has an impact on the value. For example, running the same example in Java using threads means an optimal value closer to 8,192. This tends to illustrate how goroutines are more efficient than threads.

We have seen throughout this chapter the fundamental concepts of scheduling in Go: the differences between a thread and a goroutine and how the Go runtime schedules goroutines. Meanwhile, using the parallel merge sort example, we illustrated that concurrency isn't always necessarily faster. As we have seen, spinning up goroutines to handle minimal workloads (merging only a small set of elements) demolishes the benefit we could get from parallelism.

So, where should we go from here? We must keep in mind that concurrency isn't always faster and shouldn't be considered the default way to go for all problems. First, it makes things more complex. Also, modern CPUs have become incredibly efficient at executing sequential code and predictable code. For example, a superscalar processor can parallelize instruction execution over a single core with high efficiency.

Does this mean we shouldn't use concurrency? Of course not. However, it's essential to keep these conclusions in mind. If we're not sure that a parallel version will be faster, the right approach may be to start with a simple sequential version and build from there using profiling (mistake #98, "Not using Go diagnostics tooling") and benchmarks (mistake #89, "Writing inaccurate benchmarks"), for example. It can be the only way to ensure that concurrency is worth it.

The following section discusses a frequently asked question: when should we use channels or mutexes?

8.3 #57: Being puzzled about when to use channels or mutexes

Given a concurrency problem, it may not always be clear whether we can implement a solution using channels or mutexes. Because Go promotes sharing memory by communication, one mistake could be to always force the use of channels, regardless of the use case. However, we should see the two options as complementary. This section clarifies when we should favor one option over the other. The goal is not to discuss every possible use case (that would probably take an entire chapter) but to give general guidelines that can help us decide.

First, a brief reminder about channels in Go: channels are a communication mechanism. Internally, a channel is a pipe we can use to send and receive values and that allows us to *connect* concurrent goroutines. A channel can be either of the following:

- *Unbuffered*—The sender goroutine blocks until the receiver goroutine is ready.
- *Buffered*—The sender goroutine blocks only when the buffer is full.

Let's get back to our initial problem. When should we use channels or mutexes? We will use the example in figure 8.8 as a backbone. Our example has three different goroutines with specific relationships:

- G1 and G2 are parallel goroutines. They may be two goroutines executing the same function that keeps receiving messages from a channel, or perhaps two goroutines executing the same HTTP handler at the same time.
- On the other hand, G1 and G3 are concurrent goroutines, as are G2 and G3. All the goroutines are part of an overall concurrent structure, but G1 and G2 perform the first step, whereas G3 does the next step.

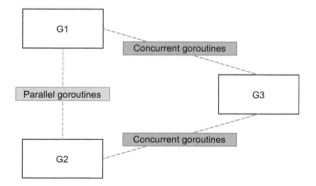

Figure 8.8   Goroutines G1 and G2 are parallel, whereas G2 and G3 are concurrent.

In general, parallel goroutines have to *synchronize*: for example, when they need to access or mutate a shared resource such as a slice. Synchronization is enforced with mutexes but not with any channel types (not with buffered channels). Hence, in general, synchronization between parallel goroutines should be achieved via mutexes.

Conversely, in general, concurrent goroutines have to *coordinate and orchestrate*. For example, if G3 needs to aggregate results from both G1 and G2, G1 and G2 need to signal to G3 that a new intermediate result is available. This coordination falls under the scope of communication—therefore, channels.

Regarding concurrent goroutines, there's also the case where we want to transfer the ownership of a resource from one step (G1 and G2) to another (G3); for example, if G1 and G2 are enriching a shared resource and at some point, we consider this job as complete. Here, we should use channels to signal that a specific resource is ready and handle the ownership transfer.

Mutexes and channels have different semantics. Whenever we want to share a state or access a shared resource, mutexes ensure exclusive access to this resource. Conversely, channels are a mechanic for signaling with or without data (chan struct{} or not). Coordination or ownership transfer should be achieved via channels. It's important to know whether goroutines are parallel or concurrent because, in general, we need mutexes for parallel goroutines and channels for concurrent ones.

Let's now discuss a widespread issue regarding concurrency: race problems.

8.4   *#58: Not understanding race problems*

Race problems can be among the hardest and most insidious bugs a programmer can face. As Go developers, we must understand crucial aspects such as data races and race conditions, their possible impacts, and how to avoid them. We will go through these topics by first discussing data races versus race conditions and then examining the Go memory model and why it matters.

8.4.1   *Data races vs. race conditions*

Let's first focus on data races. A data race occurs when two or more goroutines simultaneously access the same memory location and at least one is writing. Here is an example where two goroutines increment a shared variable:

```
i := 0

go func() {
    i++                      ⬅── Increments i
}()

go func() {
    i++
}()
```

If we run this code using the Go race detector (-race option), it warns us that a data race has occurred:

```
==================
WARNING: DATA RACE
Write at 0x00c00008e000 by goroutine 7:
  main.main.func2()
```

```
Previous write at 0x00c00008e000 by goroutine 6:
  main.main.func1()
===================
```

The final value of i is also unpredictable. Sometimes it can be 1, and sometimes 2.

What's the issue with this code? The i++ statement can be decomposed into three operations:

1. Read i.
2. Increment the value.
3. Write back to i.

If the first goroutine executes and completes before the second one, here's what happens.

Goroutine 1	Goroutine 2	Operation	i
			0
Read		<-	0
Increment			0
Write back		->	1
	Read	<-	1
	Increment		1
	Write back	->	2

The first goroutine reads, increments, and writes the value 1 back to i. Then the second goroutine performs the same set of actions but starts from 1. Hence, the final result written to i is 2.

However, there's no guarantee that the first goroutine will either start or complete before the second one in the previous example. We can also face the case of an interleaved execution where both goroutines run concurrently and compete to access i. Here's another possible scenario.

Goroutine 1	Goroutine 2	Operation	i
			0
Read		<-	0
	Read	<-	0
Increment			0
	Increment		0
Write back		->	1
	Write back	->	1

First, both goroutines read from i and get the value 0. Then, both increment it and write back their local result: 1, which isn't the expected result.

This is a possible impact of a data race. If two goroutines simultaneously access the same memory location with at least one writing to that memory location, the result can be hazardous. Even worse, in some situations, the memory location may end up holding a value containing a meaningless combination of bits.

> **NOTE** In mistake #83, "Not enabling the -race flag," we will see how Go can help us detect data races.

How can we prevent a data race from happening? Let's look at some different techniques. The scope here isn't to present all the possible options (for example, we will omit atomic.Value) but to show the main ones.

The first option is to make the increment operation atomic, meaning it's done in a single operation. This prevents entangled running operations.

Goroutine 1	Goroutine 2	Operation	i
			0
Read and increment		<->	1
	Read and increment	<->	2

Even if the second goroutine runs before the first one, the result remains 2.

Atomic operations can be done in Go using the sync/atomic package. Here's an example of how we can increment atomically an int64:

```
var i int64

go func() {
    atomic.AddInt64(&i, 1)          ⊲──┐  Increments i
}()                                    │  atomically

go func() {
    atomic.AddInt64(&i, 1)          ⊲──┤  Same
}()
```

Both goroutines update i atomically. An atomic operation can't be interrupted, thus preventing two accesses at the same time. Regardless of the goroutines' execution order, i will eventually equal 2.

> **NOTE** The sync/atomic package provides primitives for int32, int64, uint32, and uint64 but not for int. This is why i is an int64 in this example.

Another option is to synchronize the two goroutines with an ad hoc data structure like a mutex. *Mutex* stands for *mutual exclusion*; a mutex ensures that at most one goroutine accesses a so-called critical section. In Go, the sync package provides a Mutex type:

```
i := 0
mutex := sync.Mutex{}

go func() {
    mutex.Lock()        ◁─┘  Start of the
    i++          ◁─┤  Increments i      critical section
    mutex.Unlock()      ◁──┐
}()                          End of the
                             critical section

go func() {
    mutex.Lock()
    i++
    mutex.Unlock()
}()
```

In this example, incrementing `i` is the critical section. Regardless of the goroutines' ordering, this example also produces a deterministic value for `i`: 2.

Which approach works best? The boundary is pretty straightforward. As we mentioned, the `sync/atomic` package works only with specific types. If we want something else (for example, slices, maps, and structs), we can't rely on `sync/atomic`.

Another possible option is to prevent sharing the same memory location and instead favor communication across the goroutines. For example, we can create a channel that each goroutine uses to produce the value of the increment:

```
i := 0
ch := make(chan int)

go func() {
    ch <- 1       ◁──┐  Notifies the goroutine
}()                    to increment by 1

go func() {
    ch <- 1
}()
                       Increments i from what's
i += <-ch     ◁─┘  received from the channel
i += <-ch
```

Each goroutine sends a notification via the channel that we should increment `i` by 1. The parent goroutine collects the notifications and increments `i`. Because it's the only goroutine writing to `i`, this solution is also free of data races.

Let's sum up what we have seen so far. Data races occur when multiple goroutines access the same memory location simultaneously (for example, the same variable) and at least one of them is writing. We have also seen how to prevent this issue with three synchronization approaches:

- Using atomic operations
- Protecting a critical section with a mutex
- Using communication and channels to ensure that a variable is updated by only one goroutine

With these three approaches, the value of i will eventually be set to 2, regardless of the execution order of the two goroutines. But depending on the operation we want to perform, does a data-race-free application necessarily mean a deterministic result? Let's explore this question with another example.

Instead of having two goroutines increment a shared variable, now each one makes an assignment. We will follow the approach of using a mutex to prevent data races:

```
i := 0
mutex := sync.Mutex{}

go func() {
    mutex.Lock()
    defer mutex.Unlock()
    i = 1          ◁─┐  The first goroutine
} ()                 │  assigns 1 to i.

go func() {
    mutex.Lock()
    defer mutex.Unlock()   │  The second goroutine
    i = 2          ◁─┘  assigns 2 to i.
} ()
```

The first goroutine assigns 1 to i, whereas the second one assigns 2.

Is there a data race in this example? No, there isn't. Both goroutines access the same variable, but not at the same time, as the mutex protects it. But is this example deterministic? No, it isn't.

Depending on the execution order, i will eventually equal either 1 or 2. This example doesn't lead to a data race. But it has a *race condition*. A race condition occurs when the behavior depends on the sequence or the timing of events that can't be controlled. Here, the timing of events is the goroutines' execution order.

Ensuring a specific execution sequence among goroutines is a question of coordination and orchestration. If we want to ensure that we first go from state 0 to state 1, and then from state 1 to state 2, we should find a way to guarantee that the goroutines are executed in order. Channels can be a way to solve this problem. Coordinating and orchestrating can also ensure that a particular section is accessed by only one goroutine, which can also mean removing the mutex in the previous example.

In summary, when we work in concurrent applications, it's essential to understand that a data race is different from a race condition. A data race occurs when multiple goroutines simultaneously access the same memory location and at least one of them is writing. A data race means unexpected behavior. However, a data-race-free application doesn't necessarily mean deterministic results. An application can be free of data races but still have behavior that depends on uncontrolled events (such as goroutine execution, how fast a message is published to a channel, or how long a call to a database lasts); this is a race condition. Understanding both concepts is crucial to becoming proficient in designing concurrent applications.

Let's now examine the Go memory model and understand why it matters.

8.4.2 *The Go memory model*

The previous section discussed three main techniques to synchronize goroutines: atomic operations, mutexes, and channels. However, there are some core principles we should be aware of as Go developers. For example, buffered and unbuffered channels offer differ guarantees. To avoid unexpected races caused by a lack of understanding of the core specifications of the language, we have to look at the Go memory model.

The Go memory model (https://go.dev/ref/mem) is a specification that defines the conditions under which a read from a variable in one goroutine can be guaranteed to happen after a write to the same variable in a different goroutine. In other words, it provides guarantees that developers should keep in mind to avoid data races and force deterministic output.

Within a single goroutine, there's no chance of unsynchronized access. Indeed, the happens-before order is guaranteed by the order expressed by our program.

However, within multiple goroutines, we should bear in mind some of these guarantees. We will use the notation A < B to denote that event A happens before event B. Let's examine these guarantees (some copied from the Go memory model):

- Creating a goroutine happens before the goroutine's execution begins. Therefore, reading a variable and then spinning up a new goroutine that writes to this variable doesn't lead to a data race:

```
i := 0
go func() {
    i++
}()
```

- Conversely, the exit of a goroutine isn't guaranteed to happen before any event. Thus, the following example has a data race:

```
i := 0
go func() {
    i++
}()
fmt.Println(i)
```

Again, if we want to prevent the data race from happening, we should synchronize these goroutines.

- A send on a channel happens before the corresponding receive from that channel completes. In the next example, a parent goroutine increments a variable before a send, while another goroutine reads it after a channel read:

```
i := 0
ch := make(chan struct{})
go func() {
    <-ch
    fmt.Println(i)
```

```
}()
i++
ch <- struct{}{}
```

The order is as follows:

```
variable increment < channel send < channel receive < variable read
```

By transitivity, we can ensure that accesses to i are synchronized and hence free from data races.

- Closing a channel happens before a receive of this closure. The next example is similar to the previous one, except that instead of sending a message, we close the channel:

```
i := 0
ch := make(chan struct{})
go func() {
    <-ch
    fmt.Println(i)
}()
i++
close(ch)
```

Therefore, this example is also free from data races.

- The last guarantee regarding channels may be counterintuitive at first sight: a receive from an unbuffered channel happens *before* the send on that channel completes.

  First, let's look at an example with a buffered channel instead of an unbuffered channel. We have two goroutines, and the parent sends a message and reads a variable while the child updates this variable and receives from the channel:

```
i := 0
ch := make(chan struct{}, 1)
go func() {
    i = 1
    <-ch
}()
ch <- struct{}{}
fmt.Println(i)
```

This example leads to a data race. We can see in figure 8.9 that both the read and the write to i may occur simultaneously; therefore, i isn't synchronized.

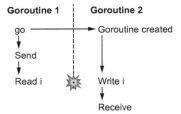

Figure 8.9   If the channel is buffered, it leads to a data race.

Now, let's change the channel to an unbuffered one to illustrate the memory model guarantee:

```
i := 0
ch := make(chan struct{})
go func() {
    i = 1
    <-ch
}()
ch <- struct{}{}
fmt.Println(i)
```

Makes the channel unbuffered

Changing the channel type makes this example data-race-free (see figure 8.10). Here we can see the main difference: the write is guaranteed to happen before the read. Note that the arrows don't represent causality (of course, a receive is caused by a send); they represent the ordering guarantees of the Go memory model. Because a receive from an unbuffered channel happens before a send, the write to i will always occur before the read.

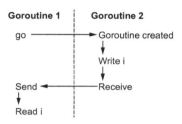

Figure 8.10   If the channel is unbuffered, it doesn't lead to a data race.

Throughout this section, we have covered the main guarantees of the Go memory model. Understanding these guarantees should be part of our core knowledge when writing concurrent code and can prevent us from making wrong assumptions that can lead to data races and/or race conditions.

The following section discusses why it's important to understand a workload type.

8.5   #59: Not understanding the concurrency impacts of a workload type

This section looks at the impacts of a workload type in a concurrent implementation. Depending on whether a workload is CPU- or I/O-bound, we may need to tackle the problem differently. Let's first define these concepts and then discuss the impacts.

In programming, the execution time of a workload is limited by one of the following:

- *The speed of the CPU*—For example, running a merge sort algorithm. The workload is called *CPU-bound*.
- *The speed of I/O*—For example, making a REST call or a database query. The workload is called *I/O-bound*.
- *The amount of available memory*—The workload is called *memory-bound*.

NOTE   The last is the rarest nowadays, given that memory has become very cheap in recent decades. Hence, this section focuses on the two first workload types: CPU- and I/O-bound.

Why is it important to classify a workload in the context of a concurrent application? Let's understand this alongside one concurrency pattern: worker pooling.

The following example implements a `read` function that accepts an `io.Reader` and reads 1,024 bytes from it repeatedly. We pass these 1,024 bytes to a `task` function that performs some tasks (we will see what kind of tasks later). This `task` function returns an integer, and we have to return the sum of all the results. Here's a sequential implementation:

```
func read(r io.Reader) (int, error) {
    count := 0
    for {
        b := make([]byte, 1024)        ─┐  Reads
        _, err := r.Read(b)         ◄──┘  1,024 bytes
        if err != nil {
            if err == io.EOF {      ◄──┐ Stops the loop when
                break                  │ we reach the end
            }
            return 0, err
        }
        count += task(b)            ◄──┐ Increments count based on
    }                                  │ the result of the task function
    return count, nil
}
```

This function creates a `count` variable, reads from the `io.Reader` input, calls `task`, and increments `count`. Now, what if we want to run all the `task` functions in a parallel manner?

One option is to use the so-called *worker-pooling pattern*. Doing so involves creating workers (goroutines) of a fixed size that poll tasks from a common channel (see figure 8.11).

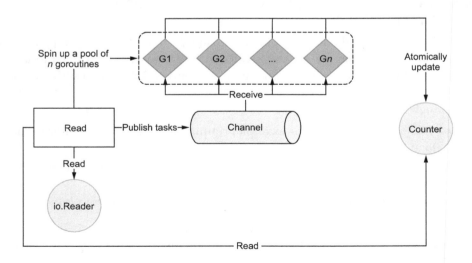

Figure 8.11   Each goroutine from the fixed pool receives from a shared channel.

First, we spin up a fixed pool of goroutines (we'll discuss how many afterward). Then we create a shared channel to which we publish tasks after each read to the `io.Reader`. Each goroutine from the pool receives from this channel, performs its work, and then atomically updates a shared counter.

Here is a possible way to write this in Go, with a pool size of 10 goroutines. Each goroutine atomically updates a shared counter:

```go
func read(r io.Reader) (int, error) {
    var count int64
    wg := sync.WaitGroup{}
    var n = 10

    ch := make(chan []byte, n)        // Creates a channel with a
                                      // capacity equal to the pool
    wg.Add(n)                         // Adds n to the wait group
    for i := 0; i < n; i++ {          // Creates a pool of n goroutines
        go func() {
            defer wg.Done()           // Calls the Done method once
                                      // the goroutine has received
                                      // from the channel
            for b := range ch {       // Each goroutine receives
                v := task(b)          // from the shared channel.
                atomic.AddInt64(&count, int64(v))
            }
        }()
    }

    for {
        b := make([]byte, 1024)
        // Read from r to b
        ch <- b                       // Publishes a new task to the
                                      // channel after every read
    }
    close(ch)
    wg.Wait()                         // Waits for the wait group to
                                      // complete before returning
    return int(count), nil
}
```

In this example, we use n to define the pool size. We create a channel with the same capacity as the pool and a wait group with a delta of n. This way, we reduce potential contention in the parent goroutine while publishing messages. We iterate n times to create a new goroutine that receives from the shared channel. Each message received is handled by executing `task` and incrementing the shared counter atomically. After reading from the channel, each goroutine decrements the wait group.

In the parent goroutine, we keep reading from `io.Reader` and publish each task to the channel. Last but not least, we close the channel and wait for the wait group to complete (meaning all the child goroutines have completed their jobs) before returning.

Having a fixed number of goroutines limits the downsides we discussed; it narrows the resources' impact and prevents an external system from being flooded. Now the golden question: what should be the value of the pool size? The answer depends on the workload type.

If the workload is I/O-bound, the answer mainly depends on the external system. How many concurrent accesses can the system cope with if we want to maximize throughput?

If the workload is CPU-bound, a best practice is to rely on GOMAXPROCS. GOMAXPROCS is a variable that sets the number of OS threads allocated to running goroutines. By default, this value is set to the number of logical CPUs.

> ### Using runtime.GOMAXPROCS
> We can use the `runtime.GOMAXPROCS(int)` function to update the value of GOMAX-PROCS. Calling it with 0 as an argument doesn't change the value; it just returns the current value:
>
> ```
> n := runtime.GOMAXPROCS(0)
> ```

So, what's the rationale for mapping the size of the pool to GOMAXPROCS? Let's take a concrete example and say that we will run our application on a four-core machine; thus Go will instantiate four OS threads where goroutines will be executed. At first, things may not be ideal: we may face a scenario with four CPU cores and four goroutines but only one goroutine being executed, as shown in figure 8.12.

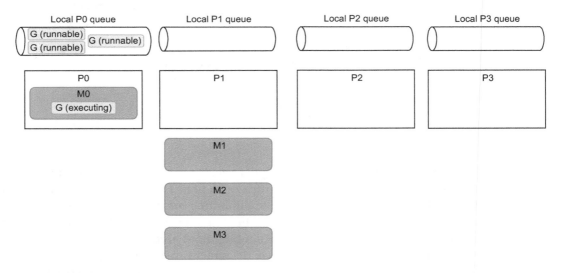

Figure 8.12   At most one goroutine is running.

M0 is currently running a goroutine of the worker pool. Hence, these goroutines start to receive messages from the channel and execute their jobs. But the three other goroutines from the pool aren't yet assigned to an M; hence, they are in a runnable state. M1, M2, and M3 don't have any goroutines to run, so they remain off a core. Thus only one goroutine is running.

Eventually, given the work-stealing concept we already described, P1 may steal goroutines from the local P0 queue. In figure 8.13, P1 stole three goroutines from P0. In this situation, the Go scheduler may also eventually assign all the goroutines to a different OS thread, but there's no guarantee about when this should occur. However, since one of the main goals of the Go scheduler is to optimize resources (here, the distribution of the goroutines), we should end up in such a scenario given the nature of the workloads.

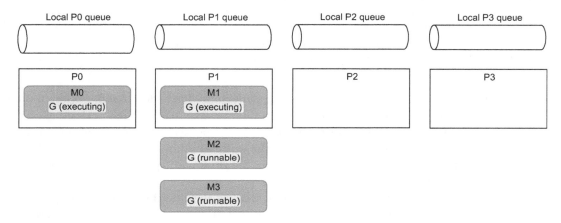

Figure 8.13   At most two goroutines are running.

This scenario is still not optimal, because at most two goroutines are running. Let's say the machine is running only our application (other than the OS processes), so P2 and P3 are free. Eventually, the OS should move M2 and M3 as shown in figure 8.14.

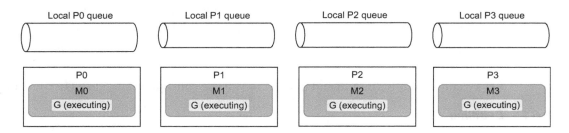

Figure 8.14   At most four goroutines are now running.

Here, the OS scheduler decided to move M2 to P2 and M3 to P3. Again, there is no guarantee about when this situation will happen. But given a machine executing only our four-thread application, this should be the final picture.

The situation has changed; it has become optimal. The four goroutines are running in separate threads and the threads on separate cores. This approach reduces the amount of context switching at both the goroutine and thread levels.

This global picture cannot be designed and requested by us (Go developers). However, as we have seen, we can enable it with favorable conditions in the case of CPU-bound workloads: having a worker pool based on GOMAXPROCS.

> **NOTE** If, given particular conditions, we want the number of goroutines to be bound to the number of CPU cores, why not rely on runtime.NumCPU(), which returns the number of logical CPU cores? As we mentioned, GOMAX-PROCS can be changed and can be less than the number of CPU cores. In the case of a CPU-bound workload, if the number of cores is four but we have only three threads, we should spin up three goroutines, not four. Otherwise, a thread will share its execution time among two goroutines, increasing the number of context switches.

When implementing the worker-pooling pattern, we have seen that the optimal number of goroutines in the pool depends on the workload type. If the workload executed by the workers is I/O-bound, the value mainly depends on the external system. Conversely, if the workload is CPU-bound, the optimal number of goroutines is close to the number of available threads. Knowing the workload type (I/O or CPU) is crucial when designing concurrent applications.

Last but not least, let's bear in mind that we should validate our assumptions via benchmarks in most cases. Concurrency isn't straightforward, and it can be pretty easy to make hasty assumptions that turn out to be invalid.

In the last section of this chapter, we discuss a crucial topic that we must understand to be proficient in Go: contexts.

8.6   *#60: Misunderstanding Go contexts*

Developers sometimes misunderstand the context.Context type despite it being one of the key concepts of the language and a foundation of concurrent code in Go. Let's look at this concept and be sure we understand why and how to use it efficiently.

According to the official documentation (https://pkg.go.dev/context):

> *A Context carries a deadline, a cancellation signal, and other values across API boundaries.*

Let's examine this definition and understand all the concepts related to a Go context.

8.6.1   *Deadline*

A deadline refers to a specific point in time determined with one of the following:

- A time.Duration from now (for example, in 250 ms)
- A time.Time (for example, 2023-02-07 00:00:00 UTC)

The semantics of a deadline convey that an ongoing activity should be stopped if this deadline is met. An activity is, for example, an I/O request or a goroutine waiting to receive a message from a channel.

Let's consider an application that receives flight positions from a radar every four seconds. Once we receive a position, we want to share it with other applications that are only interested in the latest position. We have at our disposal a `publisher` interface containing a single method:

```
type publisher interface {
    Publish(ctx context.Context, position flight.Position) error
}
```

This method accepts a context and a position. We assume that the concrete implementation calls a function to publish a message to a broker (such as using Sarama to publish a Kafka message). This function is *context aware*, meaning it can cancel a request once the context is canceled.

Assuming we don't receive an existing context, what should we provide to the `Publish` method for the context argument? We have mentioned that the applications are interested only in the latest position. Hence, the context that we build should convey that after 4 seconds, if we haven't been able to publish a flight position, we should stop the call to `Publish`:

```
type publishHandler struct {
    pub publisher
}

func (h publishHandler) publishPosition(position flight.Position) error {
    ctx, cancel := context.WithTimeout(context.Background(), 4*time.Second)    ◁──┘
    defer cancel()    ◁──────────────────────────────┐   Defers the
    return h.pub.Publish(ctx, position)    ◁──┐       │   cancellation
}
                      Passes the created context │
```

Creates the context that will
time out after 4 seconds

This code creates a context using the `context.WithTimeout` function. This function accepts a timeout and a context. Here, as `publishPosition` doesn't receive an existing context, we create one from an empty context with `context.Background`. Meanwhile, `context.WithTimeout` returns two variables: the context created and a cancellation `func()` function that will cancel the context once called. Passing the context created to the `Publish` method should make it return in at most 4 seconds.

What's the rationale for calling the `cancel` function as a `defer` function? Internally, `context.WithTimeout` creates a goroutine that will be retained in memory for 4 seconds or until `cancel` is called. Therefore, calling `cancel` as a `defer` function means that when we exit the parent function, the context will be canceled, and the goroutine created will be stopped. It's a safeguard so that when we return, we don't leave retained objects in memory.

Let's now move to the second aspect of Go contexts: cancellation signals.

8.6.2 Cancellation signals

Another use case for Go contexts is to carry a cancellation signal. Let's imagine that we want to create an application that calls `CreateFileWatcher(ctx context.Context, filename string)` within another goroutine. This function creates a specific file watcher that keeps reading from a file and catches updates. When the provided context expires or is canceled, this function handles it to close the file descriptor.

Finally, when `main` returns, we want things to be handled gracefully by closing this file descriptor. Therefore, we need to propagate a signal.

A possible approach is to use `context.WithCancel`, which returns a context (first variable returned) that will cancel once the `cancel` function (second variable returned) is called:

```go
func main() {
    ctx, cancel := context.WithCancel(context.Background())    ⟵┐ Creates a
    defer cancel()         ⟵┐ Defers the call                   │ cancellable
                            │ to cancel                          │ context
    go func() {
        CreateFileWatcher(ctx, "foo.txt")    ⟵┐ Calls the function using
    }()                                       │ the created context

    // ...
}
```

When `main` returns, it calls the `cancel` function to cancel the context passed to `CreateFileWatcher` so that the file descriptor is closed gracefully.

Next, let's discuss the last aspects of Go contexts: values.

8.6.3 *Context values*

The last use case for Go contexts is to carry a key-value list. Before understanding the rationale behind it, let's first see how to use it.

A context conveying values can be created this way:

```go
ctx := context.WithValue(parentCtx, "key", "value")
```

Just like `context.WithTimeout`, `context.WithDeadline`, and `context.WithCancel`, `context.WithValue` is created from a parent context (here, `parentCtx`). In this case, we create a new `ctx` context containing the same characteristics as `parentCtx` but also conveying a key and a value.

We can access the value using the `Value` method:

```go
ctx := context.WithValue(context.Background(), "key", "value")
fmt.Println(ctx.Value("key"))
```

```
value
```

The key and values provided are any types. Indeed, for the value, we want to pass any types. But why should the key be an empty interface as well and not a string, for example? That could lead to collisions: two functions from different packages could use the same string value as a key. Hence, the latter would override the former value. Consequently, a best practice while handling context keys is to create an unexported custom type:

```go
package provider

type key string

const myCustomKey key = "key"
```

```go
func f(ctx context.Context) {
    ctx = context.WithValue(ctx, myCustomKey, "foo")
    // ...
}
```

The myCustomKey constant is unexported. Hence, there's no risk that another package using the same context could override the value that is already set. Even if another package creates the same myCustomKey based on a key type as well, it will be a different key.

So what's the point of having a context carrying a key-value list? Because Go contexts are generic and mainstream, there are infinite use cases.

For example, if we use tracing, we may want different subfunctions to share the same correlation ID. Some developers may consider this ID too invasive to be part of the function signature. In this regard, we could also decide to include it as part of the provided context.

Another example is if we want to implement an HTTP middleware. If you're not familiar with such a concept, a middleware is an intermediate function executed before serving a request. For example, in figure 8.15, we have configured two middlewares that must be executed before executing the handler itself. If we want middlewares to communicate, they have to go through the context handled in the *http.Request.

Let's write an example of a middleware that marks whether the source host is valid:

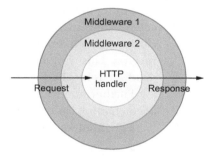

Figure 8.15   Before reaching the handler, a request goes through the configured middleware.

```go
type key string

const isValidHostKey key = "isValidHost"    // Creates the context key

func checkValid(next http.Handler) http.Handler {
    return http.HandlerFunc(func(w http.ResponseWriter, r *http.Request) {
        validHost := r.Host == "acme"                                    // Checks whether the host is valid
        ctx := context.WithValue(r.Context(), isValidHostKey, validHost) // Creates a new context with a value to convey whether the source host is valid

        next.ServeHTTP(w, r.WithContext(ctx))    // Calls the next step with the new context
    })
}
```

First, we define a specific context key called isValidHostKey. Then the checkValid middleware checks whether the source host is valid. This information is conveyed in a new context, passed to the next HTTP step using next.ServeHTTP (the next step can be another HTTP middleware or the final HTTP handler).

This example has shown how context with values can be used in concrete Go applications. We have seen in the previous sections how to create a context to carry a deadline, a cancellation signal, and/or values. We can use this context and pass it to *context-aware* libraries, meaning libraries exposing functions accepting a context. But now, suppose we have to create a library, and we want external clients to provide a context that could be canceled.

8.6.4   *Catching a context cancellation*

The context.Context type exports a Done method that returns a receive-only notification channel: <-chan struct{}. This channel is closed when the work associated with the context should be canceled. For example,

- The Done channel related to a context created with context.WithCancel is closed when the cancel function is called.
- The Done channel related to a context created with context.WithDeadline is closed when the deadline has expired.

One thing to note is that the internal channel should be closed when a context is canceled or has met a deadline, instead of when it receives a specific value, because the closure of a channel is the only channel action that all the consumer goroutines will receive. This way, all the consumers will be notified once a context is canceled or a deadline is reached.

Furthermore, context.Context exports an Err method that returns nil if the Done channel isn't yet closed. Otherwise, it returns a non-nil error explaining why the Done channel was closed: for example,

- A context.Canceled error if the channel was canceled
- A context.DeadlineExceeded error if the context's deadline passed

Let's see a concrete example in which we want to keep receiving messages from a channel. Meanwhile, our implementation should be context aware and return if the provided context is done:

```
func handler(ctx context.Context, ch chan Message) error {
    for {
        select {
        case msg := <-ch:                    Keeps receiving
            // Do something with msg         messages from ch
        case <-ctx.Done():                   If the context is done, returns
            return ctx.Err()                 the error associated with it
        }
    }
}
```

We create a for loop and use select with two cases: receiving messages from ch or receiving a signal that the context is done and we have to stop our job. While dealing with channels, this is an example of how to make a function context aware.

Implementing a function that receives a context

Within a function that receives a context conveying a possible cancellation or time-out, the action of receiving or sending a message to a channel shouldn't be done in a blocking way. For example, in the following function, we send a message to a channel and receive one from another channel:

```go
func f(ctx context.Context) error {
    // ...
    ch1 <- struct{}{}        <——| Send

    v := <-ch2               <——| Receive
    // ...
}
```

The problem with this function is that if the context is canceled or times out, we may have to wait until a message is sent or received, without benefit. Instead, we should use `select` to either wait for the channel actions to complete or wait for the context cancellation:

```go
func f(ctx context.Context) error {
    // ...
    select {                      <——  Sends a message to ch1 or waits
    case <-ctx.Done():                  for the context to be canceled
        return ctx.Err()
    case ch1 <- struct{}{}:
    }

    select {                      <——  Receives a message from ch2 or waits
    case <-ctx.Done():                  for the context to be canceled
        return ctx.Err()
    case v := <-ch2:
        // ...
    }
}
```

With this new version, if `ctx` is canceled or times out, we return immediately, without blocking the channel send or receive.

In summary, to be a proficient Go developer, we have to understand what a context is and how to use it. In Go, `context.Context` is everywhere in the standard library and external libraries. As we mentioned, a context allows us to carry a deadline, a cancellation signal, and/or a list of keys-values. In general, a function that users wait for should take a context, as doing so allows upstream callers to decide when calling this function should be aborted.

When in doubt about which context to use, we should use `context.TODO()` instead of passing an empty context with `context.Background`. `context.TODO()` returns an empty context, but semantically, it conveys that the context to be used is either unclear or not yet available (not yet propagated by a parent, for example).

Finally, let's note that the available contexts in the standard library are all safe for concurrent use by multiple goroutines.

Summary

- Understanding the fundamental differences between concurrency and parallelism is a cornerstone of the Go developer's knowledge. Concurrency is about structure, whereas parallelism is about execution.
- To be a proficient developer, you must acknowledge that concurrency isn't always faster. Solutions involving parallelization of minimal workloads may not necessarily be faster than a sequential implementation. Benchmarking sequential versus concurrent solutions should be the way to validate assumptions.
- Being aware of goroutine interactions can also be helpful when deciding between channels and mutexes. In general, parallel goroutines require synchronization and hence mutexes. Conversely, concurrent goroutines generally require coordination and orchestration and hence channels.
- Being proficient in concurrency also means understanding that data races and race conditions are different concepts. Data races occur when multiple goroutines simultaneously access the same memory location and at least one of them is writing. Meanwhile, being data-race-free doesn't necessarily mean deterministic execution. When a behavior depends on the sequence or the timing of events that can't be controlled, this is a race condition.
- Understanding the Go memory model and the underlying guarantees in terms of ordering and synchronization is essential to prevent possible data races and/or race conditions.
- When creating a certain number of goroutines, consider the workload type. Creating CPU-bound goroutines means bounding this number close to the GOMAXPROCS variable (based by default on the number of CPU cores on the host). Creating I/O-bound goroutines depends on other factors, such as the external system.
- Go contexts are also one of the cornerstones of concurrency in Go. A context allows you to carry a deadline, a cancellation signal, and/or a list of keys-values.

$$9$$

Concurrency: Practice

This chapter covers

- Preventing common mistakes with goroutines and channels
- Understanding the impacts of using standard data structures alongside concurrent code
- Using the standard library and some extensions
- Avoiding data races and deadlocks

In the previous chapter, we discussed the foundations of concurrency. Now it's time to look at practical mistakes made by Go developers when working with the concurrency primitives.

9.1   #61: Propagating an inappropriate context

Contexts are omnipresent when working with concurrency in Go, and in many situations, it may be recommended to propagate them. However, context propagation can sometimes lead to subtle bugs, preventing subfunctions from being correctly executed.

Let's consider the following example. We expose an HTTP handler that performs some tasks and returns a response. But just before returning the response, we also want to send it to a Kafka topic. We don't want to penalize the HTTP consumer latency-wise, so we want the publish action to be handled asynchronously within a new goroutine. We assume that we have at our disposal a `publish` function that accepts a context so the action of publishing a message can be interrupted if the context is canceled, for example. Here is a possible implementation:

```go
func handler(w http.ResponseWriter, r *http.Request) {
    response, err := doSomeTask(r.Context(), r)        // Performs some task to
    if err != nil {                                     // compute the HTTP response
        http.Error(w, err.Error(), http.StatusInternalServerError)
        return
    }

    go func() {                                         // Creates a goroutine to publish
        err := publish(r.Context(), response)           // the response to Kafka
        // Do something with err
    }()

    writeResponse(response)                             // Writes the
}                                                       // HTTP response
```

First we call a `doSomeTask` function to get a `response` variable. It's used within the goroutine calling `publish` and to format the HTTP response. Also, when calling `publish`, we propagate the context attached to the HTTP request. Can you guess what's wrong with this piece of code?

We have to know that the context attached to an HTTP request can cancel in different conditions:

- When the client's connection closes
- In the case of an HTTP/2 request, when the request is canceled
- When the response has been written back to the client

In the first two cases, we probably handle things correctly. For example, if we get a response from `doSomeTask` but the client has closed the connection, it's probably OK to call `publish` with a context already canceled so the message isn't published. But what about the last case?

When the response has been written to the client, the context associated with the request will be canceled. Therefore, we are facing a race condition:

- If the response is written after the Kafka publication, we both return a response and publish a message successfully.
- However, if the response is written before or during the Kafka publication, the message shouldn't be published.

In the latter case, calling `publish` will return an error because we returned the HTTP response quickly.

How can we fix this issue? One idea is to not propagate the parent context. Instead, we would call `publish` with an empty context:

```
err := publish(context.Background(), response)
```
◁─┐ **Uses an empty context instead
   │ of the HTTP request context**

Here, that would work. Regardless of how long it takes to write back the HTTP response, we can call `publish`.

But what if the context contained useful values? For example, if the context contained a correlation ID used for distributed tracing, we could correlate the HTTP request and the Kafka publication. Ideally, we would like to have a new context that is detached from the potential parent cancellation but still conveys the values.

The standard package doesn't provide an immediate solution to this problem. Hence, a possible solution is to implement our own Go context similar to the context provided, except that it doesn't carry the cancellation signal.

A `context.Context` is an interface containing four methods:

```
type Context interface {
    Deadline() (deadline time.Time, ok bool)
    Done() <-chan struct{}
    Err() error
    Value(key any) any
}
```

The context's deadline is managed by the `Deadline` method and the cancellation signal is managed via the `Done` and `Err` methods. When a deadline has passed or the context has been canceled, `Done` should return a closed channel, whereas `Err` should return an error. Finally, the values are carried via the `Value` method.

Let's create a custom context that detaches the cancellation signal from a parent context:

```
type detach struct {
    ctx context.Context
}
```
◁─┐ **Custom struct acting as a wrapper
   │ on top of the initial context**

```
func (d detach) Deadline() (time.Time, bool) {
    return time.Time{}, false
}

func (d detach) Done() <-chan struct{} {
    return nil
}

func (d detach) Err() error {
    return nil
}

func (d detach) Value(key any) any {
    return d.ctx.Value(key)
}
```
┌─ **Delegates the get value call
│ to the parent context**
◁─┘

Except for the `Value` method that calls the parent context to retrieve a value, the other methods return a default value so the context is never considered expired or canceled.

Thanks to our custom context, we can now call `publish` and detach the cancellation signal:

```
err := publish(detach{ctx: r.Context()}, response)
```
> Uses detach on top
> of the HTTP context

Now the context passed to `publish` will never expire or be canceled, but it will carry the parent context's values.

In summary, propagating a context should be done cautiously. We illustrated that in this section with an example of handling an asynchronous action based on a context associated with an HTTP request. Because the context is canceled once we return the response, the asynchronous action can also be stopped unexpectedly. Let's bear in mind the impacts of propagating a given context and, if necessary, that it is always possible to create a custom context for a specific action.

The following section discusses a common concurrency mistake: starting a goroutine without plans to stop it.

9.2 #62: Starting a goroutine without knowing when to stop it

Goroutines are easy and cheap to start—so easy and cheap that we may not necessarily have a plan for when to stop a new goroutine, which can lead to leaks. Not knowing when to stop a goroutine is a design issue and a common concurrency mistake in Go. Let's understand why and how to prevent it.

First, let's quantify what a goroutine leak means. In terms of memory, a goroutine starts with a minimum stack size of 2 KB, which can grow and shrink as needed (the maximum stack size is 1 GB on 64-bit and 250 MB on 32-bit). Memory-wise, a goroutine can also hold variable references allocated to the heap. Meanwhile, a goroutine can hold resources such as HTTP or database connections, open files, and network sockets that should eventually be closed gracefully. If a goroutine is leaked, these kinds of resources will also be leaked.

Let's look at an example in which the point where a goroutine stops is unclear. Here, a parent goroutine calls a function that returns a channel and then creates a new goroutine that will keep receiving messages from this channel:

```
ch := foo()
go func() {
    for v := range ch {
        // ...
    }
}()
```

The created goroutine will exit when `ch` is closed. But do we know exactly when this channel will be closed? It may not be evident, because `ch` is created by the `foo` function. If the channel is never closed, it's a leak. So, we should always be cautious about the exit points of a goroutine and make sure one is eventually reached.

Let's discuss a concrete example. We will design an application that needs to watch some external configuration (for example, using a database connection). Here's a first implementation:

```
func main() {
    newWatcher()

    // Run the application
}

type watcher struct { /* Some resources */ }

func newWatcher() {
    w := watcher{}
    go w.watch()
}
```

Creates a goroutine that watches some external configuration — points to `go w.watch()`

We call `newWatcher`, which creates a `watcher` struct and spins up a goroutine in charge of watching the configuration. The problem with this code is that when the main goroutine exits (perhaps because of an OS signal or because it has a finite workload), the application is stopped. Hence, the resources created by `watcher` aren't closed gracefully. How can we prevent this from happening?

One option could be to pass to `newWatcher` a context that will be canceled when `main` returns:

```
func main() {
    ctx, cancel := context.WithCancel(context.Background())
    defer cancel()

    newWatcher(ctx)

    // Run the application
}

func newWatcher(ctx context.Context) {
    w := watcher{}
    go w.watch(ctx)
}
```

Passes to newWatcher a context that will eventually cancel — points to `newWatcher(ctx)`

Propagates this context — points to `go w.watch(ctx)`

We propagate the context created to the `watch` method. When the context is canceled, the `watcher` struct should close its resources. However, can we guarantee that `watch` will have time to do so? Absolutely not—and that's a design flaw.

The problem is that we used signaling to convey that a goroutine had to be stopped. We didn't block the parent goroutine until the resources had been closed. Let's make sure we do:

```
func main() {
    w := newWatcher()
    defer w.close()
```

Defers the call to the close method — points to `defer w.close()`

```
    // Run the application
}

func newWatcher() watcher {
    w := watcher{}
    go w.watch()
    return w
}

func (w watcher) close() {
    // Close the resources
}
```

watcher has a new method: close. Instead of signaling watcher that it's time to close its resources, we now call this close method, using defer to guarantee that the resources are closed before the application exits.

In summary, let's be mindful that a goroutine is a resource like any other that must eventually be closed to free memory or other resources. Starting a goroutine without knowing when to stop it is a design issue. Whenever a goroutine is started, we should have a clear plan about when it will stop. Last but not least, if a goroutine creates resources and its lifetime is bound to the lifetime of the application, it's probably safer to wait for this goroutine to complete before exiting the application. This way, we can ensure that the resources can be freed.

Let's now discuss one of the most common mistakes while working in Go: mishandling goroutines and loop variables.

9.3   *#63: Not being careful with goroutines and loop variables*

Mishandling goroutines and loop variables is probably one of the most common mistakes made by Go developers when writing concurrent applications. Let's look at a concrete example; then we will define the conditions of such a bug and how to prevent it.

In the following example, we initialize a slice. Then, within a closure executed as a new goroutine, we access this element:

```
s := []int{1, 2, 3}

for _, i := range s {          Iterates over
    go func() {                each element
        fmt.Print(i)
    }()                        Accesses the
}                              loop variable
```

We might expect this code to print 123 in no particular order (as there is no guarantee that the first goroutine created will complete first). However, the output of this code isn't deterministic. For example, sometimes it prints 233 and other times 333. What's the reason?

In this example, we create new goroutines from a closure. As a reminder, a closure is a function value that references variables from outside its body: here, the i variable. We have to know that when a closure goroutine is executed, it doesn't capture the values when the goroutine is created. Instead, all the goroutines refer to the exact same variable. When a goroutine runs, it prints the value of i at the time fmt.Print is executed. Hence, i may have been modified since the goroutine was launched.

Figure 9.1 shows a possible execution when the code prints 233. Over time, the value of i varies: 1, 2, and then 3. In each iteration, we spin up a new goroutine. Because there's no guarantee when each goroutine will start and complete, the result varies as well. In this example, the first goroutine prints i when it's equal to 2. Then the other goroutines print i when the value is already equal to 3. Therefore, this example prints 233. The behavior of this code isn't deterministic.

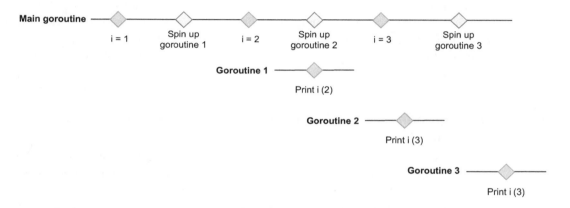

Figure 9.1 The goroutines access an i variable that isn't fixed but varies over time.

What are the solutions if we want each closure to access the value of i when the goroutine is created? The first option, if we want to keep using a closure, involves creating a new variable:

```
for _, i := range s {
    val := i                    ◁——  Creates a variable local
    go func() {                       to each iteration
        fmt.Print(val)
    }()
}
```

Why does this code work? In each iteration, we create a new local val variable. This variable captures the current value of i before the goroutine is created. Hence, when each closure goroutine executes the print statement, it does so with the expected value. This code prints 123 (again, in no particular order).

The second option no longer relies on a closure and instead uses an actual function:

```
for _, i := range s {
    go func(val int) {          ← Executes a function that takes
        fmt.Print(val)            an integer as an argument
    }(i)          ← Calls this function and passes
}                   the current value of i
```

We still execute an anonymous function within a new a goroutine (we don't run `go f(i)`, for example), but this time it isn't a closure. The function doesn't reference `val` as a variable from outside its body; `val` is now part of the function input. By doing so, we fix `i` in each iteration and make our application work as expected.

We have to be cautious with goroutines and loop variables. If the goroutine is a closure that accesses an iteration variable declared from outside its body, that's a problem. We can fix it either by creating a local variable (for example, as we have seen using `val := i` before executing the goroutine) or by making the function no longer a closure. Both options work, and there isn't one that we should favor over the other. Some developers may find the closure approach handier, whereas others may find the function approach more expressive.

What happens with a `select` statement on multiple channels? Let's find out.

9.4 #64: Expecting deterministic behavior using select and channels

One common mistake made by Go developers while working with channels is to make wrong assumptions about how `select` behaves with multiple channels. A false assumption can lead to subtle bugs that may be hard to identify and reproduce.

Let's imagine that we want to implement a goroutine that needs to receive from two channels:

- `messageCh` for new messages to be processed.
- `disconnectCh` to receive notifications conveying disconnections. In that case, we want to return from the parent function.

Of these two channels, we want to prioritize `messageCh`. For example, if a disconnection occurs, we want to ensure that we have received all the messages before returning.

We may decide to handle the prioritization like so:

```
for {
    select {          ← Uses the select statement to
    case v := <-messageCh:   receive from multiple channels
        fmt.Println(v)          ← Receives new
    case <-disconnectCh:         messages
        fmt.Println("disconnection, return")    ← Receives
        return                                     disconnections
    }
}
```

We use `select` to receive from multiple channels. Because we want to prioritize `messageCh`, we might assume that we should write the `messageCh` case first and the `disconnectCh` case next. But does this code even work? Let's give it a try by writing a dummy producer goroutine that sends 10 messages and then sends a disconnection notification:

```
for i := 0; i < 10; i++ {
    messageCh <- i
}
disconnectCh <- struct{}{}
```

If we run this example, here is a possible output if `messageCh` is buffered:

```
0
1
2
3
4
disconnection, return
```

Instead of consuming the 10 messages, we only received 5 of them. What's the reason? It lies in the specification of the `select` statement with multiple channels (https://go.dev/ref/spec):

> *If one or more of the communications can proceed, a single one that can proceed is chosen via a uniform pseudo-random selection.*

Unlike a `switch` statement, where the first case with a match wins, the `select` statement selects randomly if multiple options are possible.

This behavior might look odd at first, but there's a good reason for it: to prevent possible starvation. Suppose the first possible communication chosen is based on the source order. In that case, we may fall into a situation where, for example, we only receive from one channel because of a fast sender. To prevent this, the language designers decided to use a random selection.

Coming back to our example, even though `case v := <-messageCh` is first in source order, if there's a message in both `messageCh` and `disconnectCh`, there is no guarantee about which case will be chosen. For that reason, the example's behavior isn't deterministic. We may receive 0 messages, or 5, or 10.

How can we overcome this situation? There are different possibilities if we want to receive all the messages before returning in case of a disconnection.

If there's a single producer goroutine, we have two options:

- Make `messageCh` an unbuffered channel instead of a buffered channel. Because the sender goroutine blocks until the receiver goroutine is ready, this approach guarantees that all the messages from `messageCh` are received before the disconnection from `disconnectCh`.
- Use a single channel instead of two channels. For example, we can define a `struct` that conveys either a new message or a disconnection. Channels

guarantee that the order for the messages sent is the same as for the messages received, so we can ensure that the disconnection is received last.

If we fall into the case where we have multiple producer goroutines, it may be impossible to guarantee which one writes first. Hence, whether we have an unbuffered messageCh channel or a single channel, it will lead to a race condition among the producer goroutines. In that case, we can implement the following solution:

1 Receive from either messageCh or disconnectCh.
2 If a disconnection is received
   – Read all the existing messages in messageCh, if any.
   – Then return.

Here is the solution:

```
for {
    select {
    case v := <-messageCh:
        fmt.Println(v)
    case <-disconnectCh:
        for {                    ⟵—┤ Inner for/select
            select {
            case v := <-messageCh:    ⟵—┘ Reads the remaining
                fmt.Println(v)             messages
            default:              ⟵─────────────────┐ Then
                fmt.Println("disconnection, return")  │ returns
                return
            }
        }
    }
}
```

This solution uses an inner for/select with two cases: one on messageCh and a default case. Using default in a select statement is chosen only if none of the other cases match. In this case, it means we will return only after we have received all the remaining messages in messageCh.

Let's look at an example of how this code works. We will consider the case where we have two messages in messageCh and one disconnection in disconnectCh, as shown in figure 9.2.

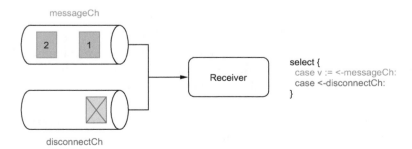

Figure 9.2
Initial state

In this situation, as we have said, `select` chooses one case or the other randomly. Let's assume `select` chooses the second case; see figure 9.3.

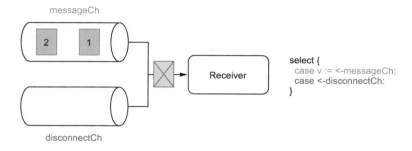

Figure 9.3   Receiving the disconnection

So, we receive the disconnection and enter in the inner `select` (figure 9.4). Here, as long as messages remain in `messageCh`, `select` will always prioritize the first case over `default` (figure 9.5).

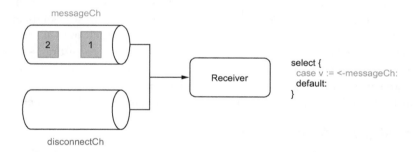

Figure 9.4   Inner `select`

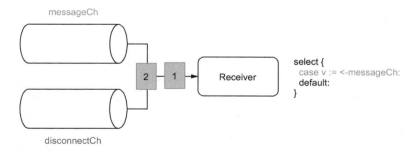

Figure 9.5   Receiving the remaining messages

Once we have received all the messages from messageCh, select does not block and chooses the default case (figure 9.6). Hence, we return and stop the goroutine.

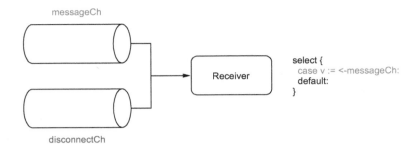

Figure 9.6   Default case

This is a way to ensure that we receive all the remaining messages from a channel with a receiver on multiple channels. Of course, if a messageCh is sent after the goroutine has returned (for example, if we have multiple producer goroutines), we will miss this message.

When using select with multiple channels, we must remember that if multiple options are possible, the first case in the source order does not automatically win. Instead, Go selects randomly, so there's no guarantee about which option will be chosen. To overcome this behavior, in the case of a single producer goroutine, we can use either unbuffered channels or a single channel. In the case of multiple producer goroutines, we can use inner selects and default to handle prioritizations.

The following section discusses a common type of channel: notification channels.

9.5   *#65: Not using notification channels*

Channels are a mechanism for communicating across goroutines via signaling. A signal can be either with or without data. But for Go programmers, it's not always straightforward how to tackle the latter case.

Let's look at a concrete example. We will create a channel that will notify us whenever a certain disconnection occurs. One idea is to handle it as a chan bool:

```
disconnectCh := make(chan bool)
```

Now, let's say we interact with an API that provides us with such a channel. Because it's a channel of Booleans, we can receive either true or false messages. It's probably clear what true conveys. But what does false mean? Does it mean we haven't been disconnected? And in this case, how frequently will we receive such a signal? Does it mean we have reconnected?

Should we even expect to receive false? Perhaps we should only expect to receive true messages. If that's the case, meaning we don't need a specific value to convey some information, we need a channel *without* data. The idiomatic way to handle it is a channel of empty structs: `chan struct{}`.

In Go, an empty struct is a struct without any fields. Regardless of the architecture, it occupies zero bytes of storage, as we can verify using `unsafe.Sizeof`:

```
var s struct{}
fmt.Println(unsafe.Sizeof(s))

0
```

> **NOTE** Why not use an empty interface (`var i interface{}`)? Because an empty interface isn't free; it occupies 8 bytes on 32-bit architecture and 16 bytes on 64-bit architecture.

An empty struct is a de facto standard to convey an absence of meaning. For example, if we need a hash set structure (a collection of unique elements), we should use an empty struct as a value: `map[K]struct{}`.

Applied to channels, if we want to create a channel to send notifications without data, the appropriate way to do so in Go is a `chan struct{}`. One of the best-known utilizations of a channel of empty structs comes with Go contexts, which we discuss in this chapter.

A channel can be with or without data. If we want to design an idiomatic API in regard to Go standards, let's remember that a channel without data should be expressed with a `chan struct{}` type. This way, it clarifies for receivers that they shouldn't expect any meaning from a message's content—only the fact that they have received a message. In Go, such channels are called *notification channels.*

The next section discusses how Go behaves with nil channels and its rationale for using them.

9.6 *#66: Not using nil channels*

A common mistake while working with Go and channels is forgetting that nil channels can sometimes be helpful. So what are nil channels, and why should we care about them? That is the scope of this section.

Let's start with a goroutine that creates a nil channel and waits to receive a message. What should this code do?

```
var ch chan int      ⟵―|  Nil channel
<-ch
```

`ch` is a `chan int` type. The zero value of a channel being nil, `ch` is `nil`. The goroutine won't panic; however, it will block forever.

The principle is the same if we send a message to a nil channel. This goroutine blocks forever:

```
var ch chan int
ch <- 0
```

Then what's the purpose of Go allowing messages to be received from or sent to a nil channel? We will discuss this question with a concrete example.

We will implement a `func merge(ch1, ch2 <-chan int) <-chan int` function to merge two channels into a single channel. By merging them (see figure 9.7), we mean each message received in either `ch1` or `ch2` will be sent to the channel returned.

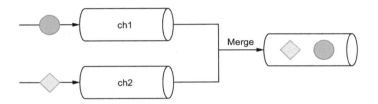

Figure 9.7   Merging two channels into one

How can we do this in Go? Let's first write a naive implementation that spins up a goroutine and receives from both channels (the resulting channel will be a buffered channel with one element):

```go
func merge(ch1, ch2 <-chan int) <-chan int {
    ch := make(chan int, 1)

    go func() {
        for v := range ch1 {         │ Receives from ch1 and publishes
            ch <- v                  ←┘ to the merged channel
        }
        for v := range ch2 {         ←┐ Receives from ch2 and publishes
            ch <- v                   │ to the merged channel
        }
        close(ch)
    }()

    return ch
}
```

Within another goroutine, we receive from both channels, and each message ends up being published in `ch`.

The main issue with this first version is that we receive from `ch1` and *then* we receive from `ch2`. It means we won't receive from `ch2` until `ch1` is closed. This doesn't fit our use case, as `ch1` may be open forever, so we want to receive from both channels simultaneously.

Let's write an improved version with concurrent receivers using `select`:

```go
func merge(ch1, ch2 <-chan int) <-chan int {
    ch := make(chan int, 1)

    go func() {
        for {                        │ Receives concurrently
            select {                 ←┘ to both ch1 and ch2
```

```
        case v := <-ch1:
            ch <- v
        case v := <-ch2:
            ch <- v
        }
    }
    close(ch)
}()

return ch
}
```

The `select` statement lets a goroutine wait on multiple operations at the same time. Because we wrap it inside a `for` loop, we should repeatedly receive messages from one or the other channel, correct? But does this code even work?

One problem is that the `close(ch)` statement is unreachable. Looping over a channel using the `range` operator breaks when the channel is closed. However, the way we implemented a `for/select` doesn't catch when either `ch1` or `ch2` is closed. Even worse, if at some point `ch1` or `ch2` is closed, here's what a receiver of the merged channel will receive when logging the value:

```
received: 0
received: 0
received: 0
received: 0
received: 0
...
```

So a receiver will repeatedly receive an integer equal to zero. Why? Receiving from a closed channel is a non-blocking operation:

```
ch1 := make(chan int)
close(ch1)
fmt.Print(<-ch1, <-ch1)
```

Whereas we may expect this code to either panic or block, instead it runs and prints `0 0`. What we catch here is the closure event, not an actual message. To check whether we receive a message or a closure signal, we must do it this way:

```
ch1 := make(chan int)
close(ch1)
v, open := <-ch1         ←──┐  Assigns to open whether
fmt.Print(v, open)           │  or not the channel is open
```

Using the `open` Boolean, we can now see whether `ch1` is still open:

```
0 false
```

Meanwhile, we also assign `0` to `v` because it's the zero value of an integer.

Let's get back to our second solution. We said that it doesn't work very well if `ch1` is closed; for example, because the `select` case is `case v := <-ch1`, we will keep entering this case and publishing a zero integer to the merged channel.

Let's take a step back and see what the best way would be to deal with this problem (see figure 9.8). We have to receive from both channels. Then, either

- ch1 is closed first, so we have to receive from ch2 until it is closed.
- ch2 is closed first, so we have to receive from ch1 until it is closed.

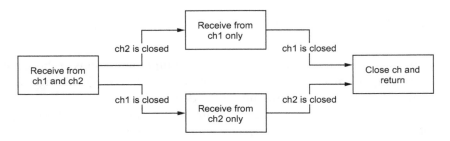

Figure 9.8   Handling different cases depending on whether ch1 or ch2 is closed first

How can we implement this in Go? Let's write a version like what we might do using a state machine approach and Booleans:

```go
func merge(ch1, ch2 <-chan int) <-chan int {
    ch := make(chan int, 1)
    ch1Closed := false
    ch2Closed := false

    go func() {
        for {
            select {
            case v, open := <-ch1:
                if !open {                    // Handles if ch1
                    ch1Closed = true          // is closed
                    break
                }
                ch <- v
            case v, open := <-ch2:
                if !open {                    // Handles if
                    ch2Closed = true          // ch2 is closed
                    break
                }
                ch <- v
            }

            if ch1Closed && ch2Closed {       // Closes and returns if both
                close(ch)                     // channels are closed
                return
            }
        }
    }()

    return ch
}
```

We define two Booleans ch1Closed and ch2Closed. Once we receive a message from a channel, we check whether it's a closure signal. If so, we handle it by marking the channel as closed (for example, ch1Closed = true). After both channels are closed, we close the merged channel and stop the goroutine.

What is the problem with this code, apart from the fact that it's starting to get complex? There is one major issue: when one of the two channels is closed, the for loop will act as a busy-waiting loop, meaning it will keep looping even though no new message is received in the other channel. We have to keep in mind the behavior of the select statement in our example. Let's say ch1 is closed (so we won't receive any new messages here); when we reach select again, it will wait for one of these three conditions to happen:

- ch1 is closed.
- ch2 has a new message.
- ch2 is closed.

The first condition, ch1 is closed, will always be valid. Therefore, as long as we don't receive a message in ch2 and this channel isn't closed, we will keep looping over the first case. This will lead to wasting CPU cycles and must be avoided. Therefore, our solution isn't viable.

We could try to enhance the state machine part and implement sub-for/select loops within each case. But this would make our code even more complex and harder to understand.

It's the right time to come back to nil channels. As we mentioned, receiving from a nil channel will block forever. How about using this idea in our solution? Instead of setting a Boolean after a channel is closed, we will assign this channel to nil. Let's write the final version:

```
func merge(ch1, ch2 <-chan int) <-chan int {
    ch := make(chan int, 1)

    go func() {
        for ch1 != nil || ch2 != nil {      ◁──┐ Continues if at least
            select {                              one channel isn't nil
            case v, open := <-ch1:
                if !open {
                    ch1 = nil          ◁──┐ Assigns ch1 to a nil
                    break                   channel once closed
                }
                ch <- v
            case v, open := <-ch2:
                if !open {
                    ch2 = nil          ◁──┐ Assigns ch2 to a nil
                    break                   channel once closed
                }
                ch <- v
            }
        }
        close(ch)
    }()
```

```
    return ch
}
```

First, we loop as long as at least one channel is still open. Then, for example, if ch1 is closed, we assign ch1 to nil. Hence, during the next loop iteration, the select statement will only wait for two conditions:

- ch2 has a new message.
- ch2 is closed.

ch1 is no longer part of the equation as it's a nil channel. Meanwhile, we keep the same logic for ch2 and assign it to nil after it's closed. Finally, when both channels are closed, we close the merged channel and return. Figure 9.9 shows a model of this implementation.

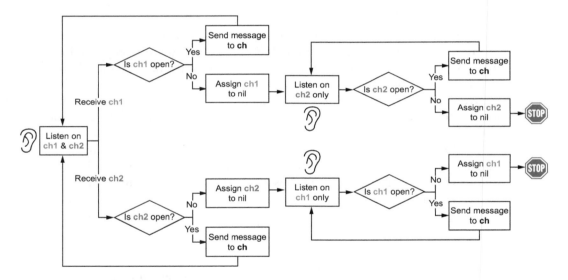

Figure 9.9   Receiving from both channels. If one is closed, we assign it to nil so we only receive from one channel.

This is the implementation we've been waiting for. We cover all the different cases, and it doesn't require a busy loop that will waste CPU cycles.

In summary, we have seen that waiting or sending to a nil channel is a blocking action, and this behavior isn't useless. As we have seen throughout the example of merging two channels, we can use nil channels to implement an elegant state machine that will *remove* one case from a select statement. Let's keep this idea in mind: nil channels are useful in some conditions and should be part of the Go developer's toolset when dealing with concurrent code.

In the next section, we discuss what size to set when creating a channel.

9.7   #67: Being puzzled about channel size

When we create a channel using the `make` built-in function, the channel can be either unbuffered or buffered. Related to this topic, two mistakes happen fairly frequently: being confused about when to use one or the other; and, if we use a buffered channel, what size to use. Let's examine these points.

First, let's remember the core concepts. An unbuffered channel is a channel *without* any capacity. It can be created by either omitting the size or providing a 0 size:

```
ch1 := make(chan int)
ch2 := make(chan int, 0)
```

Using an unbuffered channel (sometimes called a *synchronous channel*), the sender will block until the receiver receives data from the channel.

Conversely, a buffered channel has a capacity, and it must be created with a size greater than or equal to 1:

```
ch3 := make(chan int, 1)
```

With a buffered channel, a sender can send messages while the channel isn't full. Once the channel is full, it will block until a receiver goroutine receives a message. For example:

```
ch3 := make(chan int, 1)
ch3 <-1                    ⇠─┤  Non-blocking
ch3 <-2          ⇠─┤  Blocking
```

The first send isn't blocking, whereas the second one is, as the channel is full at this stage.

Let's take a step back and discuss the fundamental differences between these two channel types. Channels are a concurrency abstraction to enable communication among goroutines. But what about synchronization? In concurrency, synchronization means we can guarantee that multiple goroutines will be in a known state at some point. For example, a mutex provides synchronization because it ensures that only one goroutine can be in a critical section at the same time. Regarding channels:

- An unbuffered channel enables synchronization. We have the guarantee that two goroutines will be in a known state: one receiving and another sending a message.

- A buffered channel doesn't provide any strong synchronization. Indeed, a producer goroutine can send a message and then continue its execution if the channel isn't full. The only guarantee is that a goroutine won't receive a message before it is sent. But this is only a guarantee because of causality (you don't drink your coffee before you prepare it).

It's essential to keep in mind this fundamental distinction. Both channel types enable communication, but only one provides synchronization. If we need synchronization, we must use unbuffered channels. Unbuffered channels may also be easier to reason about: buffered channels can lead to obscure deadlocks that would be immediately apparent with unbuffered channels.

There are other cases where unbuffered channels are preferable: for example, in the case of a notification channel where the notification is handled via a channel closure (`close(ch)`). Here, using a buffered channel wouldn't bring any benefits.

But what if we need a buffered channel? What size should we provide? The default value we should use for buffered channels is its minimum: 1. So, we may approach the problem from this standpoint: is there any good reason *not* to use a value of 1? Here's a list of possible cases where we should use another size:

- While using a worker pooling-like pattern, meaning spinning a fixed number of goroutines that need to send data to a shared channel. In that case, we can tie the channel size to the number of goroutines created.
- When using channels for rate-limiting problems. For example, if we need to enforce resource utilization by bounding the number of requests, we should set up the channel size according to the limit.

If we are outside of these cases, using a different channel size should be done cautiously. It's pretty common to see a codebase using magic numbers for setting a channel size:

```
ch := make(chan int, 40)
```

Why 40? What's the rationale? Why not 50 or even 1000? Setting such a value should be done for a good reason. Perhaps it was decided following a benchmark or performance tests. In many cases, it's probably a good idea to comment on the rationale for such a value.

Let's bear in mind that deciding about an accurate queue size isn't an easy problem. First, it's a balance between CPU and memory. The smaller the value, the more CPU contention we can face. But the bigger the value, the more memory will need to be allocated.

Another point to consider is the one mentioned in a 2011 white paper about LMAX Disruptor (Martin Thompson et al.; https://lmax-exchange.github.io/disruptor/files/Disruptor-1.0.pdf):

> *Queues are typically always close to full or close to empty due to the differences in pace between consumers and producers. They very rarely operate in a balanced middle ground where the rate of production and consumption is evenly matched.*

So, it's rare to find a channel size that will be steadily accurate, meaning an accurate value that won't lead to too much contention or a waste of memory allocation.

This is why, except for the cases described, it's usually best to start with a default channel size of 1. When unsure, we can still measure it using benchmarks, for example.

As with almost any topic in programming, exceptions can be found. Therefore, the goal of this section isn't to be exhaustive but to give directions about what size we should use while creating channels. Synchronization is a guarantee with unbuffered channels, not buffered channels. Furthermore, if we need a buffered channel, we should remember to use one as the default value for the channel size. We should only decide to use another value with care using an accurate process, and the rationale should probably be commented. Last but not least, let's remember that choosing buffered channels may also lead to obscure deadlocks that would be easier to spot with unbuffered channels.

In the next section, we discuss possible side effects when dealing with string formatting.

9.8   *#68: Forgetting about possible side effects with string formatting*

Formatting strings is a common operation for developers, whether to return an error or log a message. However, it's pretty easy to forget the potential side effects of string formatting while working in a concurrent application. This section will see two concrete examples: one taken from the etcd repository leading to a data race and another leading to a deadlock situation.

9.8.1   *etcd data race*

etcd is a distributed key-value store implemented in Go. It is used in many projects, including Kubernetes, to store all cluster data. It provides an API to interact with a cluster. For example, the `Watcher` interface is used to be notified of data changes:

```
type Watcher interface {
    // Watch watches on a key or prefix. The watched events will be returned
    // through the returned channel.
    // ...
    Watch(ctx context.Context, key string, opts ...OpOption) WatchChan
    Close() error
}
```

The API relies on gRPC streaming. If you're not familiar with it, it's a technology to continuously exchange data between a client and a server. The server has to maintain a list of all the clients using this feature. Hence, the `Watcher` interface is implemented by a `watcher` struct containing all the active streams:

```
type watcher struct {
    // ...

    // streams hold all the active gRPC streams keyed by ctx value.
    streams map[string]*watchGrpcStream
}
```

The map's key is based on the context provided when calling the `Watch` method:

```
func (w *watcher) Watch(ctx context.Context, key string,
    opts ...OpOption) WatchChan {
    // ...
```

```
ctxKey := fmt.Sprintf("%v", ctx)        ◁──┐ Formats the map key depending
// ...                                        │ on the provided context
wgs := w.streams[ctxKey]
// ...
```

ctxKey is the map's key, formatted from the context provided by the client. When formatting a string from a context created with values (context.WithValue), Go will read all the values in this context. In this case, the etcd developers found that the context provided to Watch was a context containing mutable values (for example, a pointer to a struct) in some conditions. They found a case where one goroutine was updating one of the context values, whereas another was executing Watch, hence reading all the values in this context. This led to a data race.

The fix (https://github.com/etcd-io/etcd/pull/7816) was to not rely on fmt.Sprintf to format the map's key to prevent traversing and reading the chain of wrapped values in the context. Instead, the solution was to implement a custom streamKeyFromCtx function to extract the key from a specific context value that wasn't mutable.

> **NOTE** A potentially mutable value in a context can introduce additional complexity to prevent data races. This is probably a design decision to be considered with care.

This example illustrates that we have to be careful about the side effects of string formatting in concurrent applications—in this case, a data race. In the following example, we will see a side effect leading to a deadlock situation.

9.8.2 *Deadlock*

Let's say we have to deal with a Customer struct that can be accessed concurrently. We will use a sync.RWMutex to protect the accesses, whether reading or writing. We will implement an UpdateAge method to update the customer's age and check that the age is positive. Meanwhile, we will implement the Stringer interface.

Can you see what the problem is in this code with a Customer struct exposing an UpdateAge method and implementing the fmt.Stringer interface?

```
type Customer struct {
    mutex sync.RWMutex        ◁──┐ Uses a sync.RWMutex to
    id    string                  │ protect concurrent accesses
    age   int
}

func (c *Customer) UpdateAge(age int) error {
    c.mutex.Lock()            ◁──┐ Locks and defers unlock
    defer c.mutex.Unlock()        │ as we update Customer
                                                              ┐ Returns an error
    if age < 0 {                                          ◁──┘ if age is negative
        return fmt.Errorf("age should be positive for customer %v", c)
    }
```

```
    c.age = age
    return nil
}

func (c *Customer) String() string {        Locks and defers unlock
    c.mutex.RLock()                          as we read Customer
    defer c.mutex.RUnlock()
    return fmt.Sprintf("id %s, age %d", c.id, c.age)
}
```

The problem here may not be straightforward. If the provided age is negative, we return an error. Because the error is formatted, using the %s directive on the receiver, it will call the String method to format Customer. But because UpdateAge already acquires the mutex lock, the String method won't be able to acquire it (see figure 9.10).

Hence, this leads to a deadlock situation. If all goroutines are also asleep, it leads to a panic:

```
fatal error: all goroutines are asleep - deadlock!

goroutine 1 [semacquire]:
sync.runtime_SemacquireMutex(0xc00009818c, 0x10b7d00, 0x0)
...
```

How should we deal with this situation? First, it illustrates how unit testing is important. In that case, we may argue that creating a test with a negative age isn't worth it, as the logic is quite simple. However, without proper test coverage, we might miss this issue.

One thing that could be improved here is to restrict the scope of the mutex locking. In UpdateAge, we first acquire the lock and check whether the input is valid. We should do the opposite: first check the input, and if the input is valid, acquire the lock. This has the benefit of reducing the potential side effects but can also have an impact performance-wise—a lock is acquired only when it's required, not before:

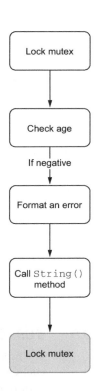

Figure 9.10
UpdateAge
execution if age
is negative

```
func (c *Customer) UpdateAge(age int) error {
    if age < 0 {
        return fmt.Errorf("age should be positive for customer %v", c)
    }

    c.mutex.Lock()          Locks the mutex only when
    defer c.mutex.Unlock()  input has been validated

    c.age = age
    return nil
}
```

In our case, locking the mutex only after the age has been checked avoids the deadlock situation. If the age is negative, `String` is called without locking the mutex beforehand.

In some conditions, though, it's not straightforward or possible to restrict the scope of a mutex lock. In these conditions, we have to be extremely careful with string formatting. Perhaps we want to call another function that doesn't try to acquire the mutex, or we only want to change the way we format the error so that it doesn't call the `String` method. For example, the following code doesn't lead to a deadlock because we only log the customer ID in accessing the `id` field directly:

```go
func (c *Customer) UpdateAge(age int) error {
    c.mutex.Lock()
    defer c.mutex.Unlock()

    if age < 0 {
        return fmt.Errorf("age should be positive for customer id %s", c.id)
    }

    c.age = age
    return nil
}
```

We have seen two concrete examples, one formatting a key from a context and another returning an error that formats a struct. In both cases, formatting a string leads to a problem: a data race and a deadlock situation, respectively. Therefore, in concurrent applications, we should remain cautious about the possible side effects of string formatting.

The following section discusses the behavior of `append` when it is called concurrently.

9.9   *#69: Creating data races with append*

We mentioned earlier what a data race is and what the impacts are. Now, let's look at slices and whether adding an element to a slice using `append` is data-race-free. Spoiler? It depends.

In the following example, we will initialize a slice and create two goroutines that will use `append` to create a new slice with an additional element:

```go
s := make([]int, 1)

go func() {                    ◁──┐  In a new goroutine, appends
    s1 := append(s, 1)            │  a new element on s
    fmt.Println(s1)
}()

go func() {                    ◁──┤  Same
    s2 := append(s, 1)
    fmt.Println(s2)
}()
```

Do you believe this example has a data race? The answer is no.

We have to recall some slice fundamentals described in chapter 3. A slice is backed by an array and has two properties: length and capacity. The length is the number of available elements in the slice, whereas the capacity is the total number of elements in the backing array, counting from the first element in the slice. When we use `append`, the behavior depends on whether the slice is full (length == capacity). If it is, the Go runtime creates a new backing array to add the new element; otherwise, the runtime adds it to the existing backing array.

In this example, we create a slice with `make([]int, 1)`. The code creates a one-length, one-capacity slice. Thus, because the slice is full, using `append` in each goroutine returns a slice backed by a new array. It doesn't mutate the existing array; hence, it doesn't lead to a data race.

Now, let's run the same example with a slight change in how we initialize `s`. Instead of creating a slice with a length of 1, we create it with a length of 0 but a capacity of 1:

```
s := make([]int, 0, 1)        ◁──┐ Changes the way the
                                  │ slice is initialized
// Same
```

How about this new example? Does it contain a data race? The answer is yes:

```
==================
WARNING: DATA RACE
Write at 0x00c00009e080 by goroutine 10:
  ...

Previous write at 0x00c00009e080 by goroutine 9:
  ...
==================
```

We create a slice with `make([]int, 0, 1)`. Therefore, the array isn't full. Both goroutines attempt to update the same index of the backing array (index 1), which is a data race.

How can we prevent the data race if we want both goroutines to work on a slice containing the initial elements of s plus an extra element? One solution is to create a copy of s:

```
s := make([]int, 0, 1)

go func() {
    sCopy := make([]int, len(s), cap(s))
    copy(sCopy, s)                      ◁── Makes a copy and uses
                                            append on the copied slice
    s1 := append(sCopy, 1)
    fmt.Println(s1)
}()

go func() {
    sCopy := make([]int, len(s), cap(s))
    copy(sCopy, s)                      ◁── Same

    s2 := append(sCopy, 1)
    fmt.Println(s2)
}()
```

Both goroutines make a copy of the slice. Then they use append on the slice copy, not the original slice. This prevents a data race because both goroutines work on isolated data.

Data races with slices and maps

How much do data races impact slices and maps? When we have multiple goroutines the following is true:

- Accessing the same slice index with at least one goroutine updating the value is a data race. The goroutines access the same memory location.
- Accessing different slice indices regardless of the operation isn't a data race; different indices mean different memory locations.
- Accessing the same map (regardless of whether it's the same or a different key) with at least one goroutine updating it is a data race. Why is this different from a slice data structure? As we mentioned in chapter 3, a map is an array of buckets, and each bucket is a pointer to an array of key-value pairs. A hashing algorithm is used to determine the array index of the bucket. Because this algorithm contains some randomness during the map initialization, one execution may lead to the same array index, whereas another execution may not. The race detector handles this case by raising a warning regardless of whether an actual data race occurs.

While working with slices in concurrent contexts, we must recall that using append on slices isn't always race-free. Depending on the slice and whether it's full, the behavior will change. If the slice is full, append is race-free. Otherwise, multiple goroutines may compete to update the same array index, resulting in a data race.

In general, we shouldn't have a different implementation depending on whether the slice is full. We should consider that using append on a shared slice in concurrent applications can lead to a data race. Hence, it should be avoided.

Now, let's discuss a common mistake with inaccurate mutex locks on top of slices and maps.

9.10   *#70: Using mutexes inaccurately with slices and maps*

While working in concurrent contexts where data is both mutable and shared, we often have to implement protected accesses around data structures using mutexes. A common mistake is to use mutexes inaccurately when working with slices and maps. Let's look at a concrete example and understand the potential problems.

We will implement a Cache struct used to handle caching for customer balances. This struct will contain a map of balances per customer ID and a mutex to protect concurrent accesses:

```
type Cache struct {
    mu       sync.RWMutex
    balances map[string]float64
}
```

NOTE This solution uses a sync.RWMutex to allow multiple readers as long as there are no writers.

Next, we add an AddBalance method that mutates the balances map. The mutation is done in a critical section (within a mutex lock and a mutex unlock):

```go
func (c *Cache) AddBalance(id string, balance float64) {
    c.mu.Lock()
    c.balances[id] = balance
    c.mu.Unlock()
}
```

Meanwhile, we have to implement a method to calculate the average balance for all the customers. One idea is to handle a minimal critical section this way:

```go
func (c *Cache) AverageBalance() float64 {
    c.mu.RLock()
    balances := c.balances            ◁──┐ Creates a copy of
    c.mu.RUnlock()                        │ the balances map

    sum := 0.
    for _, balance := range balances {  ◁──┐ Iterates over the copy, outside
        sum += balance                      │ of the critical section
    }
    return sum / float64(len(balances))
}
```

First we create a copy of the map to a local balances variable. Only the copy is done in the critical section to iterate over each balance and calculate the average outside of the critical section. Does this solution work?

If we run a test using the -race flag with two concurrent goroutines, one calling AddBalance (hence mutating balances) and another calling AverageBalance, a data race occurs. What's the problem here?

Internally, a map is a runtime.hmap struct containing mostly metadata (for example, a counter) and a pointer referencing data buckets. So, balances := c.balances doesn't copy the actual data. It's the same principle with a slice:

```go
s1 := []int{1, 2, 3}
s2 := s1
s2[0] = 42
fmt.Println(s1)
```

Printing s1 returns [42 2 3] even though we modify s2. The reason is that s2 := s1 creates a new slice: s2 has the same length and the same capacity and is backed by the same array as s1.

Coming back to our example, we assign to balances a new map referencing the same data buckets as c.balances. Meanwhile, the two goroutines perform operations on the same data set, and one of them mutates it. Hence, it's a data race. How can we fix the data race? We have two options.

If the iteration operation isn't heavy (that's the case here, as we perform an increment operation), we should protect the whole function:

```go
func (c *Cache) AverageBalance() float64 {
    c.mu.RLock()
    defer c.mu.RUnlock()          ◁─┐ Unlocks when
                                     │ the function returns
    sum := 0.
    for _, balance := range c.balances {
        sum += balance
    }
    return sum / float64(len(c.balances))
}
```

The critical section now encompasses the whole function, including the iterations. This prevents data races.

Another option, if the iteration operation isn't lightweight, is to work on an actual copy of the data and protect only the copy:

```go
func (c *Cache) AverageBalance() float64 {
    c.mu.RLock()
    m := make(map[string]float64, len(c.balances))   ◁─┐ Copies
    for k, v := range c.balances {                      │ the map
        m[k] = v
    }
    c.mu.RUnlock()

    sum := 0.
    for _, balance := range m {
        sum += balance
    }
    return sum / float64(len(m))
}
```

Once we have made a deep copy, we release the mutex. The iterations are done on the copy outside of the critical section.

Let's think about this solution. We have to iterate twice on the map values: once to copy and once to perform the operations (here, the increments). But the critical section is only the map copy. Therefore, this solution can be a good fit if and only if an operation isn't *fast*. For example, if an operation requires calling an external database, this solution will probably be more efficient. It's impossible to define a threshold when choosing one solution or the other as the choice depends on factors such as the number of elements and the average size of the struct.

In summary, we have to be careful with the boundaries of a mutex lock. In this section, we have seen why assigning an existing map (or an existing slice) to a map isn't enough to protect against data races. The new variable, whether a map or a slice, is backed by the same data set. There are two leading solutions to prevent this: protect the whole function, or work on a copy of the actual data. In all cases, let's be cautious when designing critical sections and make sure the boundaries are accurately defined.

Let's now discuss a common mistake while using sync.WaitGroup.

9.11 #71: Misusing sync.WaitGroup

sync.WaitGroup is a mechanism to wait for n operations to complete; generally, we use it to wait for n goroutines to complete. Let's first recall the public API; then we will look at a pretty frequent mistake leading to non-deterministic behavior.

A wait group can be created with the zero value of sync.WaitGroup:

```
wg := sync.WaitGroup{}
```

Internally, a sync.WaitGroup holds an internal counter initialized by default to 0. We can increment this counter using the Add(int) method and decrement it using Done() or Add with a negative value. If we want to wait for the counter to be equal to 0, we have to use the Wait() method that is blocking.

NOTE The counter cannot be negative, or the goroutine will panic.

In the following example, we will initialize a wait group, start three goroutines that will update a counter atomically, and then wait for them to complete. We want to wait for these three goroutines to print the value of the counter (which should be 3). Can you guess whether there's an issue with this code?

```
wg := sync.WaitGroup{}
var v uint64

for i := 0; i < 3; i++ {          Creates
    go func() {                   a goroutine      Increments the wait
        wg.Add(1)                                  group counter
        atomic.AddUint64(&v, 1)                        Atomically
        wg.Done()                                      increments v
    }()                           Decrements the
}                                 wait group counter

wg.Wait()                         Waits until all the goroutines have
fmt.Println(v)                    incremented v before printing it
```

If we run this example, we get a non-deterministic value: the code can print any value from 0 to 3. Also, if we enable the -race flag, Go will even catch a data race. How is this possible, given that we are using the sync/atomic package to update v? What's wrong with this code?

The problem is that wg.Add(1) is called within the newly created goroutine, not in the parent goroutine. Hence, there is no guarantee that we have indicated to the wait group that we want to wait for three goroutines before calling wg.Wait().

Figure 9.11 shows a possible scenario when the code prints 2. In this scenario, the main goroutine spins up three goroutines. But the last goroutine is executed after the two first goroutines have already called wg.Done(), so, the parent goroutine is already unlocked. Therefore, in this scenario, when the main goroutine reads v, it's equal to 2. The race detector can also detect unsafe accesses to v.

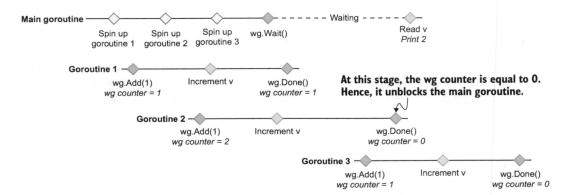

Figure 9.11 The last goroutine calls `wg.Add(1)` after the main goroutine is already unblocked.

When dealing with goroutines, it's crucial to remember that the execution isn't deterministic without synchronization. For example, the following code could print either ab or ba:

```
go func() {
    fmt.Print("a")
}()
go func() {
    fmt.Print("b")
}()
```

Both goroutines can be assigned to different threads, and there's no guarantee which thread will be executed first.

The CPU has to use a *memory fence* (also called a *memory barrier*) to ensure order. Go provides different synchronization techniques for implementing memory fences: for example, `sync.WaitGroup` enables a happens-before relationship between `wg.Add` and `wg.Wait`.

Coming back to our example, there are two options to fix our issue. First, we can call `wg.Add` before the loop with 3:

```
wg := sync.WaitGroup{}
var v uint64

wg.Add(3)
for i := 0; i < 3; i++ {
    go func() {
        // ...
    }()
}

// ...
```

Or, second, we can call `wg.Add` during each loop iteration before spinning up the child goroutines:

```
wg := sync.WaitGroup{}
var v uint64

for i := 0; i < 3; i++ {
    wg.Add(1)
    go func() {
        // ...
    }()
}

// ...
```

Both solutions are fine. If the value we want to set eventually to the wait group counter is known in advance, the first solution prevents us from having to call `wg.Add` multiple times. However, it requires making sure the same count is used everywhere to avoid subtle bugs.

Let's be cautious not to reproduce this common mistake made by Go developers. When using a `sync.WaitGroup`, the `Add` operation must be done before spinning up a goroutine in the parent goroutine, whereas the `Done` operation must be done within the goroutine.

The following section discusses another primitive of the `sync` package: `sync.Cond`.

9.12 #72: Forgetting about sync.Cond

Among the synchronization primitives in the `sync` package, `sync.Cond` is probably the least used and understood. However, it provides features that we can't achieve with channels. This section goes through a concrete example to show when `sync.Cond` can be helpful and how to use it.

The example in this section implements a donation goal mechanism: an application that raises alerts whenever specific goals are reached. We will have one goroutine in charge of incrementing a balance (an updater goroutine). In contrast, other goroutines will receive updates and print a message whenever a specific goal is reached (listener goroutines). For example, one goroutine is waiting for a $10 donation goal, whereas another is waiting for a $15 donation goal.

One first naive solution uses mutexes. The updater goroutine increments the balance every second. On the other side, the listener goroutines loop until their donation goal is met:

```
type Donation struct {                ◁─┐  Creates and instantiates a
    mu              sync.RWMutex         │  Donation struct containing the
    balance int                          │  current balance and a mutex
}
donation := &Donation{}

// Listener goroutines            ┐  Creates
f := func(goal int) {          ◁──┘  a closure
    donation.mu.RLock()
    for donation.balance < goal {      ◁─┐  Checks if the goal
        donation.mu.RUnlock()            │  is reached
        donation.mu.RLock()
```

```
        }
        fmt.Printf("$%d goal reached\n", donation.balance)
        donation.mu.RUnlock()
    }
}
go f(10)
go f(15)

// Updater goroutine
go func() {                          ┌── Keeps incrementing
    for {                        ◁───┘   the balance
        time.Sleep(time.Second)
        donation.mu.Lock()
        donation.balance++
        donation.mu.Unlock()
    }
}()
```

We protect the accesses to the shared `donation.balance` variable using the mutex. If we run this example, it works as expected:

```
$10 goal reached
$15 goal reached
```

The main issue—and what makes this a terrible implementation—is the busy loop. Each listener goroutine keeps looping until its donation goal is met, which wastes a lot of CPU cycles and makes the CPU usage gigantic. We need to find a better solution.

Let's take a step back. We have to find a way to signal from the updater goroutine whenever the balance is updated. If we think about signaling in Go, we should consider channels. So, let's try another version using the channel primitive:

```
type Donation struct {
    balance int                      ┌── Updates Donation so
    ch      chan int             ◁───┘   it contains a channel
}

donation := &Donation{ch: make(chan int)}

// Listener goroutines
f := func(goal int) {                        ┌── Receives channel
    for balance := range donation.ch {   ◁───┘   updates
        if balance >= goal {
            fmt.Printf("$%d goal reached\n", balance)
            return
        }
    }
}
go f(10)
go f(15)

// Updater goroutine
for {
    time.Sleep(time.Second)
    donation.balance++                            ┌── Sends a message whenever
    donation.ch <- donation.balance           ◁──┘   the balance is updated
}
```

Each listener goroutine receives from a shared channel. Meanwhile, the updater goroutine sends messages whenever the balance is updated. But if we give this solution a try, here is a possible output:

```
$11 goal reached
$15 goal reached
```

The first goroutine should have been notified when the balance was $10, not $11. What happened?

A message sent to a channel is received by only one goroutine. In our example, if the first goroutine receives from the channel before the second one, figure 9.12 shows what could happen.

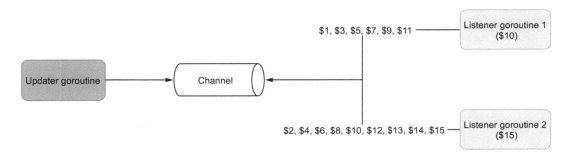

Figure 9.12   The first goroutine receives the $1 message, then the second goroutine receives the $2 message, then the first goroutine receives the $3 message, and so forth.

The default distribution mode with multiple goroutines receiving from a shared channel is round-robin. It can change if one goroutine isn't ready to receive messages (not in a waiting state on the channel); in that case, Go distributes the message to the next available goroutine.

Each message is received by a single goroutine. Therefore, the first goroutine didn't receive the $10 message in this example, but the second one did. Only a channel closure event can be broadcast to multiple goroutines. But here we don't want to close the channel, because then the updater goroutine couldn't send messages.

There's another issue with using channels in this situation. The listener goroutines return whenever their donation goal is met. Hence, the updater goroutine has to know when all the listeners stop receiving messages to the channel. Otherwise, the channel will eventually become full and block the sender. A possible solution could be to add a `sync.WaitGroup` to the mix, but doing so would make the solution more complex.

Ideally, we need to find a way to repeatedly broadcast notifications whenever the balance is updated to multiple goroutines. Fortunately, Go has a solution: `sync.Cond`. Let's first discuss the theory; then we will see how to solve our problem using this primitive.

According to the official documentation (https://pkg.go.dev/sync),

Cond implements a condition variable, a rendezvous point for goroutines waiting for or announcing the occurrence of an event.

A condition variable is a container of threads (here, goroutines) waiting for a certain condition. In our example, the condition is a balance update. The updater goroutine broadcasts a notification whenever a balance is updated, and the listener goroutine waits until an update. Furthermore, sync.Cond relies on a sync.Locker (a *sync .Mutex or *sync.RWMutex) to prevent data races. Here is a possible implementation:

```go
type Donation struct {
    cond    *sync.Cond          // Adds a
    balance int                 // *sync.Cond
}

donation := &Donation{                    // sync.Cond relies
    cond: sync.NewCond(&sync.Mutex{}),    // on a mutex.
}

// Listener goroutines
f := func(goal int) {
    donation.cond.L.Lock()
    for donation.balance < goal {         // Waits for a condition (balance
        donation.cond.Wait()              // updated) within lock/unlock
    }
    fmt.Printf("%d$ goal reached\n", donation.balance)
    donation.cond.L.Unlock()
}
go f(10)
go f(15)

// Updater goroutine
for {
    time.Sleep(time.Second)
    donation.cond.L.Lock()
    donation.balance++               // Increments the balance
    donation.cond.L.Unlock()         // within lock/unlock
    donation.cond.Broadcast()        // Broadcasts the fact that a condition
}                                    // was met (balance updated)
```

First we create a *sync.Cond using sync.NewCond and provide a *sync.Mutex. What about the listener and updater goroutines?

The listener goroutines loop until the donation balance is met. Within the loop, we use the Wait method that blocks until the condition is met.

NOTE Let's make sure the term *condition* is understood here. In this context, we're talking about the balance being updated, not the donation goal condition. So, it's a single condition variable shared by two listener goroutines.

The call to `Wait` must happen within a critical section, which may sound odd. Won't the lock prevent other goroutines from waiting for the same condition? Actually, the implementation of `Wait` is the following:

1 Unlock the mutex.
2 Suspend the goroutine, and wait for a notification.
3 Lock the mutex when the notification arrives.

So, the listener goroutines have two critical sections:

- When accessing `donation.balance` in `for donation.balance < goal`
- When accessing `donation.balance` in `fmt.Printf`

This way, all the accesses to the shared `donation.balance` variable are protected.

Now, what about the updater goroutine? The balance update is done within a critical section to prevent data races. Then we call the `Broadcast` method, which wakes all the goroutines waiting on the condition each time the balance is updated.

Hence, if we run this example, it prints what we expect:

```
10$ goal reached
15$ goal reached
```

In our implementation, the condition variable is based on the balance being updated. Therefore, the listener variables wake each time a new donation is made, to check whether their donation goal is met. This solution prevents us from having a busy loop that burns CPU cycles in repeated checks.

Let's also note one possible drawback when using `sync.Cond`. When we send a notification—for example, to a `chan struct`—even if there's no active receiver, the message is buffered, which guarantees that this notification will be received eventually. Using `sync.Cond` with the `Broadcast` method wakes all goroutines currently waiting on the condition; if there are none, the notification will be missed. This is also an essential principle that we have to keep in mind.

> **Signal() vs. Broadcast()**
>
> We can wake a single goroutine using `Signal()` instead of `Broadcast()`. In terms of semantics, it is the same as sending a message in a `chan struct` in a non-blocking fashion:
>
> ```
> ch := make(chan struct{})
> select {
> case ch <- struct{}{}:
> default:
> }
> ```

Signaling in Go can be achieved with channels. The only event that multiple goroutines can catch is a channel closure, but this can happen just once. Therefore, if we repeatedly send notifications to multiple goroutines, `sync.Cond` is a solution. This primitive is based on condition variables that set up containers of threads waiting for a specific condition. Using `sync.Cond`, we can broadcast signals that wake all the goroutines waiting on a condition.

Let's extend our knowledge of concurrency primitives using `golang.org/x` and the `errgroup` package.

9.13   *#73: Not using errgroup*

Regardless of the programming language, reinventing the wheel is rarely a good idea. It's also pretty common for codebases to reimplement how to spin up multiple goroutines and aggregate the errors. But a package in the Go ecosystem is designed to support this frequent use case. Let's look at it and understand why it should be part of the toolset of Go developers.

`golang.org/x` is a repository providing extensions to the standard library. The `sync` sub-repository contains a handy package: `errgroup`.

Suppose we have to handle a function, and we receive as an argument some data that we want to use to call an external service. Due to constraints, we can't make a single call; we make multiple calls with a different subset each time. Also, these calls are made in parallel (see figure 9.13).

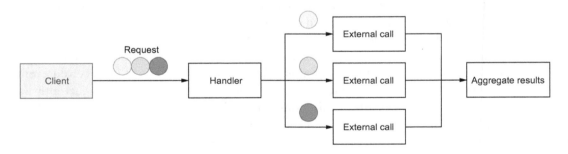

Figure 9.13   Each circle results in a parallel call.

In case of one error during a call, we want to return it. In case of multiple errors, we want to return only one of them. Let's write the skeleton of the implementation using only the standard concurrency primitives:

```
func handler(ctx context.Context, circles []Circle) ([]Result, error) {
    results := make([]Result, len(circles))
    wg := sync.WaitGroup{}
    wg.Add(len(results))

    for i, circle := range circles {
        i := i
        circle := circle
```

Creates a wait group to wait for all the goroutines that we spin up

Creates a new i variable used in the goroutine (see mistake #63, "Not being careful with goroutines and loop variables")

Same for circle

```
                    go func() {                  ┌─ Triggers a
  Indicates    ┌─▷      defer wg.Done()          │  goroutine per Circle
  when the     │
  goroutine is │        result, err := foo(ctx, circle)
  complete     │        if err != nil {
               │            // ?
               │        }
               │        results[i] = result     ┌─ Aggregates
               └─     }()                        │  the results
                }

        wg.Wait()
        // ...
    }
```

We decided to use a `sync.WaitGroup` to wait until all the goroutines are completed and handle the aggregations in a slice. This is one way to do it; another would be to send each partial result to a channel and aggregate them in another goroutine. The main challenge would be to reorder the incoming messages if ordering was required. Therefore, we decided to go with the easiest approach and a shared slice.

> **NOTE** Because each goroutine writes to a specific index, this implementation is data-race-free.

However, there's one crucial case we haven't tackled. What if `foo` (the call made within a new goroutine) returns an error? How should we handle it? There are various options, including these:

- Just like the `results` slice, we could have a slice of errors shared among the goroutines. Each goroutine would write to this slice in case of an error. We would have to iterate over this slice in the parent goroutine to determine whether an error occurred (O(n) time complexity).
- We could have a single error variable accessed by the goroutines via a shared mutex.
- We could think about sharing a channel of errors, and the parent goroutine would receive and handle these errors.

Regardless of the option chosen, it starts to make the solution pretty complex. For that reason, the `errgroup` package was designed and developed.

It exports a single `WithContext` function that returns a `*Group` struct given a context. This struct provides synchronization, error propagation, and context cancellation for a group of goroutines and exports only two methods:

- `Go` to trigger a call in a new goroutine.
- `Wait` to block until all the goroutines have completed. It returns the first non-nil error, if any.

Let's rewrite the solution using `errgroup`. First we need to import the `errgroup` package:

```
$ go get golang.org/x/sync/errgroup
```

And here's the implementation:

```go
func handler(ctx context.Context, circles []Circle) ([]Result, error) {
    results := make([]Result, len(circles))
    g, ctx := errgroup.WithContext(ctx)          Creates an *errgroup.Group
                                                  given the parent context
    for i, circle := range circles {
        i := i
        circle := circle
        g.Go(func() error {                       Calls Go to spin up the logic of
            result, err := foo(ctx, circle)       handling the error and aggregating
            if err != nil {                       the results in a new goroutine
                return err
            }
            results[i] = result
            return nil
        })
    }

    if err := g.Wait(); err != nil {              Calls Wait to wait
        return nil, err                           for all the goroutines
    }
    return results, nil
}
```

First, we create an `*errgroup.Group` by providing the parent context. In each iteration, we use `g.Go` to trigger a call in a new goroutine. This method takes a `func() error` as an input, with a closure wrapping the call to `foo` and handling the result and error. As the main difference from our first implementation, if we get an error, we return it from this closure. Then, `g.Wait` allows us to wait for all the goroutines to complete.

This solution is inherently more straightforward than the first one (which was partial, as we didn't handle the error). We don't have to rely on extra concurrency primitives, and the `errgroup.Group` is sufficient to tackle our use case.

Another benefit that we haven't tackled yet is the shared context. Let's imagine we have to trigger three parallel calls:

- The first returns an error in 1 millisecond.
- The second and third calls return a result or an error in 5 seconds.

We want to return an error, if any. Hence, there's no point in waiting until the second and third calls are complete. Using `errgroup.WithContext` creates a shared context used in all the parallel calls. Because the first call returns an error in 1 millisecond, it will cancel the context and thus the other goroutines. So, we won't have to wait 5 seconds to return an error. This is another benefit when using `errgroup`.

NOTE   The process invoked by `g.Go` must be *context aware*. Otherwise, canceling the context won't have any effect.

In summary, when we have to trigger multiple goroutines and handle errors plus context propagation, it may be worth considering whether `errgroup` could be a solution.

As we have seen, this package enables synchronization for a group of goroutines and provides an answer to deal with errors and shared contexts.

The last section of this chapter discusses a common mistake made by Go developers when copying a sync type.

9.14   *#74: Copying a sync type*

The sync package provides basic synchronization primitives such as mutexes, condition variables, and wait groups. For all these types, there's a hard rule to follow: they should never be copied. Let's understand the rationale and the possible problems.

We will create a thread-safe data structure to store counters. It will contain a map[string]int representing the current value for each counter. We will also use a sync.Mutex because the accesses have to be protected. And let's add an increment method to increment a given counter name:

```go
type Counter struct {
    mu       sync.Mutex
    counters map[string]int
}

func NewCounter() Counter {              Factory
    return Counter{counters: map[string]int{}}    function
}

func (c Counter) Increment(name string) {
    c.mu.Lock()                          Increments the counter
    defer c.mu.Unlock()                  in a critical section
    c.counters[name]++
}
```

The increment logic is done in a critical section: between c.mu.Lock() and c.mu.Unlock(). Let's give our method a try by using the -race option to run the following example that spins up two goroutines and increments their respective counters:

```go
counter := NewCounter()

go func() {
    counter.Increment("foo")
}()
go func() {
    counter.Increment("bar")
}()
```

If we run this example, it raises a data race:

```
==================
WARNING: DATA RACE
...
```

The problem in our Counter implementation is that the mutex is copied. Because the receiver of Increment is a value, whenever we call Increment, it performs a copy of the

`Counter` struct, which also copies the mutex. Therefore, the increment isn't done in a shared critical section.

sync types shouldn't be copied. This rule applies to the following types:

- `sync.Cond`
- `sync.Map`
- `sync.Mutex`
- `sync.RWMutex`
- `sync.Once`
- `sync.Pool`
- `sync.WaitGroup`

Therefore, the mutex shouldn't have been copied. What are the alternatives?

The first is to modify the receiver type for the `Increment` method:

```
func (c *Counter) Increment(name string) {
    // Same code
}
```

Changing the receiver type avoids copying `Counter` when `Increment` is called. Therefore, the internal mutex isn't copied.

If we want to keep a value receiver, the second option is to change the type of the `mu` field in `Counter` to be a pointer:

```
type Counter struct {
    mu       *sync.Mutex      ◁──┐ Changes the
    counters map[string]int      │ type of mu
}

func NewCounter() Counter {
    return Counter{
        mu: &sync.Mutex{},                    ◁──┐ Changes the way
        counters: map[string]int{},              │ mu is initialized
    }
}
```

If `Increment` has a value receiver, it still copies the `Counter` struct. However, as `mu` is now a pointer, it will perform a pointer copy only, not an actual copy of a `sync.Mutex`. Hence, this solution also prevents data races.

NOTE We also changed the way `mu` was initialized. Because `mu` is a pointer, if we omit it when creating `Counter`, it will be initialized to the zero value of a pointer: `nil`. This will cause to the goroutine to panic when `c.mu.Lock()` is called.

We may face the issue of unintentionally copying a sync field in the following conditions:

- Calling a method with a value receiver (as we have seen)
- Calling a function with a sync argument
- Calling a function with an argument that contains a sync field

In each case, we should remain very cautious. Also, let's note that some linters can catch this issue—for example, using `go vet`:

```
$ go vet .
./main.go:19:9: Increment passes lock by value: Counter contains sync.Mutex
```

As a rule of thumb, whenever multiple goroutines have to access a common `sync` element, we must ensure that they all rely on the same instance. This rule applies to all the types defined in the `sync` package. Using pointers is a way to solve this problem: we can have either a pointer to a `sync` element or a pointer to a struct containing a `sync` element.

Summary

- Understanding the conditions when a context can be canceled should matter when propagating it: for example, an HTTP handler canceling the context when the response has been sent.
- Avoiding leaks means being mindful that whenever a goroutine is started, you should have a plan to stop it eventually.
- To avoid bugs with goroutines and loop variables, create local variables or call functions instead of closures.
- Understanding that `select` with multiple channels chooses the case randomly if multiple options are possible prevents making wrong assumptions that can lead to subtle concurrency bugs.
- Send notifications using a `chan struct{}` type.
- Using nil channels should be part of your concurrency toolset because it allows you to *remove* cases from `select` statements, for example.
- Carefully decide on the right channel type to use, given a problem. Only unbuffered channels provide strong synchronization guarantees.
- You should have a good reason to specify a channel size other than one for buffered channels.
- Being aware that string formatting may lead to calling existing functions means watching out for possible deadlocks and other data races.
- Calling `append` isn't always data-race-free; hence, it shouldn't be used concurrently on a shared slice.
- Remembering that slices and maps are pointers can prevent common data races.
- To accurately use `sync.WaitGroup`, call the `Add` method before spinning up goroutines.
- You can send repeated notifications to multiple goroutines with `sync.Cond`.
- You can synchronize a group of goroutines and handle errors and contexts with the `errgroup` package.
- `sync` types shouldn't be copied.

The standard library

10

This chapter covers

- Providing a correct time duration
- Understanding potential memory leaks while using `time.After`
- Avoiding common mistakes in JSON handling and SQL
- Closing transient resources
- Remembering the `return` statement in HTTP handlers
- Why production-grade applications shouldn't use default HTTP clients and servers

The Go standard library is a set of core packages that enhance and extend the language. For example, Go developers can write HTTP clients or servers, handle JSON data, or interact with SQL databases. All of these features are provided by the standard library. However, it can be easy to misuse the standard library, or we may have a limited understanding of its behavior, which can lead to bugs and writing applications that shouldn't be considered production-grade. Let's look at some of the most common mistakes while using the standard library.

10.1   *#75: Providing a wrong time duration*

The standard library provides common functions and methods that accept a
time.Duration. However, because time.Duration is an alias for the int64 type, newcomers to the language can get confused and provide a wrong duration. For example,
developers with a Java or JavaScript background are used to passing numeric types.

To illustrate this common error, let's create a new time.Ticker that will deliver the
ticks of a clock every second:

```
ticker := time.NewTicker(1000)
for {
    select {
    case <-ticker.C:
        // Do something
    }
}
```

If we run this code, we notice that ticks aren't delivered every second; they are delivered every microsecond.

Because time.Duration is based on the int64 type, the previous code is correct
since 1000 is a valid int64. But time.Duration represents the elapsed time between
two instants in *nanoseconds*. Therefore, we provided NewTicker with a duration of
1,000 nanoseconds = 1 microsecond.

This mistake happens frequently. Indeed, standard libraries in languages such as
Java and JavaScript sometimes ask developers to provide durations in milliseconds.

Furthermore, if we want to purposely create a time.Ticker with an interval of 1
microsecond, we shouldn't pass an int64 directly. We should instead always use the
time.Duration API to avoid possible confusion:

```
ticker = time.NewTicker(time.Microsecond)
// Or
ticker = time.NewTicker(1000 * time.Nanosecond)
```

This is not the most complex mistake in this book, but developers with a background
in other languages can easily fall into the trap of believing that milliseconds are
expected for the functions and methods in the time package. We must remember to
use the time.Duration API and provide an int64 alongside a time unit.

Now, let's discuss a common mistake when using the time package with
time.After.

10.2   *#76: time.After and memory leaks*

time.After(time.Duration) is a convenient function that returns a channel and
waits for a provided duration to elapse before sending a message to this channel. Usually, it's used in concurrent code; otherwise, if we want to sleep for a given duration,
we can use time.Sleep(time.Duration). The advantage of time.After is that it can

be used to implement scenarios such as "If I don't receive any message in this channel for 5 seconds, I will … ." But codebases often include calls to `time.After` in a loop, which, as we describe in this section, may be a root cause of memory leaks.

Let's consider the following example. We will implement a function that repeatedly consumes messages from a channel. We also want to log a warning if we haven't received any messages for more than 1 hour. Here is a possible implementation:

```go
func consumer(ch <-chan Event) {
    for {
        select {
        case event := <-ch:          Handles
                                     the event
            handle(event)
                                                  Increments the
        case <-time.After(time.Hour):             idle counter
            log.Println("warning: no messages received")
        }
    }
}
```

Here, we use `select` in two cases: receiving a message from `ch` and after 1 hour without messages (`time.After` is evaluated during each iteration, so the timeout is *reset* every time). At first sight, this code looks OK. However, it may lead to memory usage issues.

As we said, `time.After` returns a channel. We may expect this channel to be closed during each loop iteration, but this isn't the case. The resources created by `time.After` (including the channel) are released once the timeout expires and use memory until that happens. How much memory? In Go 1.15, about 200 bytes of memory are used per call to `time.After`. If we receive a significant volume of messages, such as 5 million per hour, our application will consume 1 GB of memory to store the `time.After` resources.

Can we fix this issue by closing the channel programmatically during each iteration? No. The returned channel is a `<-chan time.Time`, meaning it is a receive-only channel that can't be closed.

We have several options to fix our example. The first is to use a context instead of `time.After`:

```go
func consumer(ch <-chan Event) {        Main
    for {                               loop
                                                              Creates a context
                                                              with timeout
        ctx, cancel := context.WithTimeout(context.Background(), time.Hour)
        select {
        case event := <-ch:      Cancels context if we
            cancel()             receive a message
            handle(event)
                                             Context
        case <-ctx.Done():                   cancellation
            log.Println("warning: no messages received")
        }
    }
}
```

The downside of this approach is that we have to re-create a context during every single loop iteration. Creating a context isn't the most lightweight operation in Go: for example, it requires creating a channel. Can we do better?

The second option comes from the `time` package: `time.NewTimer`. This function creates a `time.Timer` struct that exports the following:

- A `C` field, which is the internal timer channel
- A `Reset(time.Duration)` method to reset the duration
- A `Stop()` method to stop the timer

---

time.After internals

We should note that `time.After` also relies on `time.Timer`. However, it only returns the `C` field, so we don't have access to the `Reset` method:

```
package time

func After(d Duration) <-chan Time {        Creates a new time.Timer and
    return NewTimer(d).C              <──┘   returns the channel field
}
```

Let's implement a new version using `time.NewTimer`:

```
func consumer(ch <-chan Event) {
    timerDuration := 1 * time.Hour                     Creates a
    timer := time.NewTimer(timerDuration)     <──┘     new timer

    for {                                               Resets
        timer.Reset(timerDuration)            <──┘      the duration
        select {
        case event := <-ch:
            handle(event)                          Timer
        case <-timer.C:                   <──┘     expiration
            log.Println("warning: no messages received")
        }
    }
}
```

(Main loop → `for {` block)

In this implementation, we keep a recurring action during each loop iteration: calling the `Reset` method. However, calling `Reset` is less cumbersome than having to create a new context every time. It's faster and puts less pressure on the garbage collector because it doesn't require any new heap allocation. Therefore, using `time.Timer` is the best possible solution for our initial problem.

> **NOTE** For the sake of simplicity, in the example, the previous goroutine doesn't stop. As we mentioned in mistake #62, "Starting a goroutine without knowing when to stop it," this isn't a best practice. In production-grade code, we should find an exit condition such as a context that can be cancelled. In that case, we should also remember to stop the `time.Timer` using `defer timer.Stop()`, for example, right after the `timer` creation.

Using `time.After` in a loop isn't the only case that may lead to a peak in memory consumption. The problem relates to code that is repeatedly called. A loop is one case, but using `time.After` in an HTTP handler function can lead to the same issues because the function will be called multiple times.

In general, we should be cautious when using `time.After`. Remember that the resources created will only be released when the timer expires. When the call to `time.After` is repeated (for example, in a loop, a Kafka consumer function, or an HTTP handler), it may lead to a peak in memory consumption. In this case, we should favor `time.NewTimer`.

The following section discusses the most common mistakes during JSON handling.

10.3 *#77: Common JSON-handling mistakes*

Go has excellent support for JSON with the `encoding/json` package. This section covers three common mistakes related to encoding (marshaling) and decoding (unmarshaling) JSON data.

10.3.1 *Unexpected behavior due to type embedding*

In mistake #10, "Not being aware of the possible problems with type embedding," we looked at issues related to type embedding. In the context of JSON handling, let's discuss another potential impact of type embedding that can lead to unexpected marshaling/unmarshaling results.

In the following example, we create an `Event` struct containing an ID and an embedded timestamp:

```
type Event struct {
    ID int
    time.Time      ⊲—| Embedded field
}
```

Because `time.Time` is embedded, in the same way we described previously, we can access the `time.Time` methods directly at the `Event` level: for example, `event .Second()`.

What are the possible impacts of embedded fields with JSON marshaling? Let's find out in the following example. We will instantiate an `Event` and marshal it into JSON. What should be the output of this code?

```
event := Event{
    ID:   1234,
    Time: time.Now(),      ⊲——   The name of an anonymous field
}                                 during a struct instantiation is
b, err := json.Marshal(event)     the name of the struct (Time).
if err != nil {
    return err
}

fmt.Println(string(b))
```

We may expect this code to print something like the following:

```
{"ID":1234,"Time":"2021-05-18T21:15:08.381652+02:00"}
```

Instead, it prints this:

```
"2021-05-18T21:15:08.381652+02:00"
```

How can we explain this output? What happened to the `ID` field and the `1234` value? Because this field is exported, it should have been marshaled. To understand this problem, we have to highlight two points.

First, as discussed in mistake #10, if an embedded field type implements an interface, the struct containing the embedded field will also implement this interface. Second, we can change the default marshaling behavior by making a type implement the `json.Marshaler` interface. This interface contains a single `MarshalJSON` function:

```go
type Marshaler interface {
    MarshalJSON() ([]byte, error)
}
```

Here is an example with custom marshaling:

```go
type foo struct{}        ⟵—| Defines the struct

                                                   Implements the
func (foo) MarshalJSON() ([]byte, error) {    ⟵—| MarshalJSON method
    return []byte(`"foo"`), nil    ⟵—| Returns a static
}                                       response

func main() {
    b, err := json.Marshal(foo{})    ⟵  json.Marshal then relies
    if err != nil {                      on the custom MarshalJSON
        panic(err)                       implementation.
    }
    fmt.Println(string(b))
}
```

Because we have changed the default JSON marshaling behavior by implementing the `Marshaler` interface, this code prints `"foo"`.

Having clarified these two points, let's get back to the initial problem with the `Event` struct:

```go
type Event struct {
    ID int
    time.Time
}
```

We have to know that `time.Time` *implements* the `json.Marshaler` interface. Because `time.Time` is an embedded field of `Event`, the compiler promotes its methods. Therefore, `Event` also implements `json.Marshaler`.

Consequently, passing an `Event` to `json.Marshal` uses the marshaling behavior provided by `time.Time` instead of the default behavior. This is why marshaling an `Event` leads to ignoring the `ID` field.

NOTE   We would also face the issue the other way around if we were unmarshaling an `Event` using `json.Unmarshal`.

To fix this issue, there are two main possibilities. First, we can add a name so the time.Time field is no longer embedded:

```
type Event struct {
    ID   int
    Time time.Time        ⟵┐ time.Time is no longer
}                             an embedded type.
```

This way, if we marshal a version of this Event struct, it will print something like this:

```
{"ID":1234,"Time":"2021-05-18T21:15:08.381652+02:00"}
```

If we want or have to keep the time.Time field embedded, the other option is to make Event implement the json.Marshaler interface:

```
func (e Event) MarshalJSON() ([]byte, error) {
    return json.Marshal(
        struct {           ⟵┐ Creates an
            ID   int            anonymous struct
            Time time.Time
        }{
            ID:   e.ID,
            Time: e.Time,
        },
    )
}
```

In this solution, we implement a custom MarshalJSON method while defining an anonymous struct reflecting the structure of Event. But this solution is more cumbersome and requires that we ensure that the MarshalJSON method is always up to date with the Event struct.

We should be careful with embedded fields. While promoting the fields and methods of an embedded field type can sometimes be convenient, it can also lead to subtle bugs because it can make the parent struct implement interfaces without a clear signal. Again, when using embedded fields, we should clearly understand the possible side effects.

In the next section, we see another common JSON mistake related to using time.Time.

10.3.2 *JSON and the monotonic clock*

When marshaling or unmarshaling a struct that contains a time.Time type, we can sometimes face unexpected comparison errors. It's helpful to examine time.Time to refine our assumptions and prevent possible mistakes.

An OS handles two different clock types: wall and monotonic. This section looks first at these clock types and then at a possible impact while working with JSON and time.Time.

The wall clock is used to determine the current time of day. This clock is subject to variations. For example, if the clock is synchronized using the Network Time Protocol

(NTP), it can jump backward or forward in time. We shouldn't measure durations using the wall clock because we may face strange behavior, such as negative durations. This is why OSs provide a second clock type: monotonic clocks. The monotonic clock guarantees that time always moves forward and is not impacted by jumps in time. It can be affected by frequency adjustments (for example, if the server detects that the local quartz clock is moving at a different pace than the NTP server) but never by jumps in time.

In the following example, we consider an `Event` struct containing a single `time.Time` field (not embedded):

```
type Event struct {
    Time time.Time
}
```

We instantiate an `Event`, marshal it into JSON, and unmarshal it into another struct. Then we compare both structs. Let's find out if the marshaling/unmarshaling process is always symmetric:

```
t := time.Now()        ◁── Gets the current local time
event1 := Event{       ◁
    Time: t,              Instantiates an Event struct
}

b, err := json.Marshal(event1)   ◁── Marshals into JSON
if err != nil {
    return err
}

var event2 Event
err = json.Unmarshal(b, &event2)   ◁── Unmarshals JSON
if err != nil {
    return err
}

fmt.Println(event1 == event2)
```

What should be the output of this code? It prints `false`, not `true`. How can we explain this?

First, let's print the contents of `event1` and `event2`:

```
fmt.Println(event1.Time)
fmt.Println(event2.Time)

2021-01-10 17:13:08.852061 +0100 CET m=+0.000338660
2021-01-10 17:13:08.852061 +0100 CET
```

The code prints different contents for `event1` and `event2`. They are the same except for the `m=+0.000338660` part. What does this mean?

In Go, instead of splitting the two clocks into two different APIs, `time.Time` may contain both a wall clock and a monotonic time. When we get the local time using `time.Now()`, it returns a `time.Time` with both times:

```
2021-01-10 17:13:08.852061 +0100 CET m=+0.000338660
------------------------------------ --------------
           Wall time                 Monotonic time
```

Conversely, when we unmarshal the JSON, the `time.Time` field doesn't contain the monotonic time—only the wall time. Therefore, when we compare the structs, the result is `false` because of a monotonic time difference; this is also why we see a difference when we print both structs. How can we fix this problem? There are two main options.

When we use the `==` operator to compare both `time.Time` fields, it compares all the struct fields, including the monotonic part. To avoid this, we can use the `Equal` method instead:

```
fmt.Println(event1.Time.Equal(event2.Time))

true
```

The `Equal` method doesn't consider monotonic time; therefore, this code prints `true`. But in this case, we only compare the `time.Time` fields, not the parent `Event` structs.

The second option is to keep the `==` to compare the two structs but strip away the monotonic time using the `Truncate` method. This method returns the result of rounding the `time.Time` value down to a multiple of a given duration. We can use it by providing a zero duration like so:

```
t := time.Now()
event1 := Event{
    Time: t.Truncate(0),      ◁──┤ Strips away the
}                                   monotonic time

b, err := json.Marshal(event1)
if err != nil {
    return err
}

var event2 Event
err = json.Unmarshal(b, &event2)
if err != nil {
    return err
}
                                   Performs the comparison
fmt.Println(event1 == event2)  ◁──┤ using the == operator
```

With this version, the two `time.Time` fields are equal. Therefore, this code prints `true`.

time.Time and location

Let's also note that each `time.Time` is associated with a `time.Location` that represents the time zone. For example:

```
t := time.Now() // 2021-01-10 17:13:08.852061 +0100 CET
```

Here, the location is set to CET because I used `time.Now()`, which returns my current local time. The JSON marshaling result depends on the location. To prevent this, we can stick to a particular location:

```
location, err := time.LoadLocation("America/New_York")    ◁─────────┐
if err != nil {                                    Gets the current location
    return err                                      for America/New_York
}
t := time.Now().In(location) // 2021-05-18 22:47:04.155755 -0500 EST
```

Alternatively, we can get the current time in UTC:

```
t := time.Now().UTC() // 2021-05-18 22:47:04.155755 +0000 UTC
```

In summary, the marshaling/unmarshaling process isn't always symmetric, and we faced this case with a struct containing a `time.Time`. We should keep this principle in mind so we don't, for example, write erroneous tests.

10.3.3 *Map of any*

When unmarshaling data, we can provide a map instead of a struct. The rationale is that when the keys and values are uncertain, passing a map gives us some flexibility instead of a static struct. However, there's a rule to bear in mind to avoid wrong assumptions and possible goroutine panics.

Let's write an example that unmarshals a message into a map:

```
b := getMessage()
var m map[string]any
err := json.Unmarshal(b, &m)    ◁─┐  Provides
if err != nil {                   │  a map pointer
    return err
}
```

Let's provide the following JSON to the previous code:

```
{
    "id": 32,
    "name": "foo"
}
```

Because we use a generic `map[string]any`, it parses all the different fields automatically:

```
map[id:32 name:foo]
```

However, there's an important gotcha to remember if we use a map of any: any numeric value, regardless of whether it contains a decimal, is converted into a float64 type. We can observe this by printing the type of m["id"]:

```
fmt.Printf("%T\n", m["id"])
```

```
float64
```

We should be sure we don't make the wrong assumption and expect numeric values without decimals to be converted into integers by default. Making incorrect assumptions with type conversions could lead, for example, to goroutine panics.

The following section discusses the most common mistakes while writing applications that interact with SQL databases.

10.4   #78: Common SQL mistakes

The database/sql package provides a generic interface around SQL (or SQL-like) databases. It's also fairly common to see some patterns or mistakes while using this package. Let's delve into five common mistakes.

10.4.1   Forgetting that sql.Open doesn't necessarily establish connections to a database

When using sql.Open, one common misconception is expecting this function to establish connections to a database:

```
db, err := sql.Open("mysql", dsn)
if err != nil {
    return err
}
```

But this isn't necessarily the case. According to the documentation (https://pkg.go.dev/database/sql),

> *Open may just validate its arguments without creating a connection to the database.*

Actually, the behavior depends on the SQL driver used. For some drivers, sql.Open doesn't establish a connection: it's only a preparation for later use (for example, with db.Query). Therefore, the first connection to the database may be established lazily.

Why do we need to know about this behavior? For example, in some cases, we want to make a service ready only after we know that all the dependencies are correctly set up and reachable. If we don't know this, the service may accept traffic despite an erroneous configuration.

If we want to ensure that the function that uses sql.Open also guarantees that the underlying database is reachable, we should use the Ping method:

```
db, err := sql.Open("mysql", dsn)
if err != nil {
```

```
        return err
    }
if err := db.Ping(); err != nil {        ◁─────┐  Calls the Ping method
        return err                               │  following sql.Open
    }
```

`Ping` forces the code to establish a connection that ensures that the data source name is valid and the database is reachable. Note that an alternative to `Ping` is `PingContext`, which asks for an additional context conveying when the ping should be canceled or time out.

Despite being perhaps counterintuitive, let's remember that `sql.Open` doesn't necessarily establish a connection, and the first connection can be opened lazily. If we want to test our configuration and be sure a database is reachable, we should follow `sql.Open` with a call to the `Ping` or `PingContext` method.

10.4.2 *Forgetting about connections pooling*

Just as the default HTTP client and server provide default behaviors that may not be effective in production (see mistake #81, "Using the default HTTP client and server"), it's essential to understand how database connections are handled in Go. `sql.Open` returns an `*sql.DB` struct. This struct doesn't represent a single database connection; instead, it represents a pool of connections. This is worth noting so we're not tempted to implement it manually. A connection in the pool can have two states:

- Already used (for example, by another goroutine that triggers a query)
- Idle (already created but not in use for the time being)

It's also important to remember that creating a pool leads to four available config parameters that we may want to override. Each of these parameters is an exported method of `*sql.DB`:

- `SetMaxOpenConns`—Maximum number of open connections to the database (default value: `unlimited`)
- `SetMaxIdleConns`—Maximum number of idle connections (default value: `2`)
- `SetConnMaxIdleTime`—Maximum amount of time a connection can be idle before it's closed (default value: `unlimited`)
- `SetConnMaxLifetime`—Maximum amount of time a connection can be held open before it's closed (default value: `unlimited`)

Figure 10.1 shows an example with a maximum of five connections. It has four ongoing connections: three idle and one in use. Therefore, one slot remains available for an extra connection. If a new query comes in, it will pick one of the idle connections (if still available). If there are no more idle connections, the pool will create a new connection if an extra slot is available; otherwise, it will wait until a connection is available.

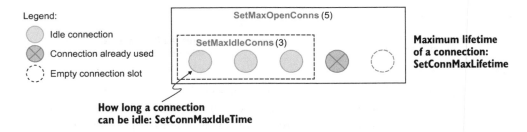

Figure 10.1   **A connection pool with five connections**

So, why should we tweak these config parameters?

- Setting `SetMaxOpenConns` is important for production-grade applications. Because the default value is unlimited, we should set it to make sure it fits what the underlying database can handle.
- The value of `SetMaxIdleConns` (default: 2) should be increased if our application generates a significant number of concurrent requests. Otherwise, the application may experience frequent reconnects.
- Setting `SetConnMaxIdleTime` is important if our application may face a burst of requests. When the application returns to a more peaceful state, we want to make sure the connections created are eventually released.
- Setting `SetConnMaxLifetime` can be helpful if, for example, we connect to a load-balanced database server. In that case, we want to ensure that our application never uses a connection for too long.

For production-grade applications, we must consider these four parameters. We can also use multiple connection pools if an application faces different use cases.

10.4.3   *Not using prepared statements*

A prepared statement is a feature implemented by many SQL databases to execute a repeated SQL statement. Internally, the SQL statement is precompiled and separated from the data provided. There are two main benefits:

- *Efficiency*—The statement doesn't have to be recompiled (compilation means parsing + optimization + translation).
- *Security*—This approach reduces the risks of SQL injection attacks.

Therefore, if a statement is repeated, we should use prepared statements. We should also use prepared statements in untrusted contexts (such as exposing an endpoint on the internet, where the request is mapped to an SQL statement).

To use prepared statements, instead of calling the `Query` method of `*sql.DB`, we call `Prepare`:

```
stmt, err := db.Prepare("SELECT * FROM ORDER WHERE ID = ?")    ◁──┐  Prepares the
if err != nil {                                                   │  statement
    return err
```

```
}
rows, err := stmt.Query(id)        ◁──┐ Executes the
// ...                                 │ prepared query
```

We prepare the statement and then execute it while providing the arguments. The
first output of the `Prepare` method is an `*sql.Stmt`, which can be reused and run
concurrently. When the statement is no longer needed, it must be closed using the
`Close()` method.

> **NOTE** The `Prepare` and `Query` methods have alternatives to provide an addi-
> tional context: `PrepareContext` and `QueryContext`.

For efficiency and security, we need to remember to use prepared statements when it
makes sense.

10.4.4 *Mishandling null values*

The next mistake is to mishandle null values with queries. Let's write an example
where we retrieve the department and age of an employee:

```
rows, err := db.Query("SELECT DEP, AGE FROM EMP WHERE ID = ?", id)   ◁──┐
if err != nil {
    return err                                                   Executes
}                                                                the query
// Defer closing rows

var (
    department string
    age int
)
for rows.Next() {
    err := rows.Scan(&department, &age)    ◁──┤ Scans each row
    if err != nil {
        return err
    }
    // ...
}
```

We use `Query` to execute a query. Then, we iterate over the rows and use `Scan` to copy
the column into the values pointed to by the `department` and `age` pointers. If we run
this example, we may get the following error while calling `Scan`:

```
2021/10/29 17:58:05 sql: Scan error on column index 0, name "DEPARTMENT":
converting NULL to string is unsupported
```

Here, the SQL driver raises an error because the department value is equal to `NULL`. If
a column can be nullable, there are two options to prevent `Scan` from returning an error.

The first approach is to declare `department` as a string pointer:

```
var (
    department *string     ◁──┐ Changing the type
    age        int            │ from string to *string
)
```

```
for rows.Next() {
    err := rows.Scan(&department, &age)
    // ...
}
```

We provide scan with the address of a pointer, not the address of a string type directly. By doing so, if the value is NULL, department will be nil.

The other approach is to use one of the sql.NullXXX types, such as sql.Null-String:

```
var (
    department sql.NullString        ⟵┐ Changes the type
    age        int                      │ to sql.NullString
)
for rows.Next() {
    err := rows.Scan(&department, &age)
    // ...
}
```

sql.NullString is a wrapper on top of a string. It contains two exported fields: String contains the string value, and Valid conveys whether the string isn't NULL. The following wrappers are accessible:

- sql.NullString
- sql.NullBool
- sql.NullInt32
- sql.NullInt64
- sql.NullFloat64
- sql.NullTime

Both approaches work, with sql.NullXXX expressing the intent more clearly, as mentioned by Russ Cox, a core Go maintainer (http://mng.bz/rJNX):

> *There's no effective difference. We thought people might want to use NullString because it is so common and perhaps expresses the intent more clearly than *string. But either will work.*

So, the best practice with a nullable column is to either handle it as a pointer or use an sql.NullXXX type.

10.4.5 *Not handling row iteration errors*

Another common mistake is to miss possible errors from iterating over rows. Let's look at a function where error handling is misused:

```
func get(ctx context.Context, db *sql.DB, id string) (string, int, error) {
    rows, err := db.QueryContext(ctx,
        "SELECT DEP, AGE FROM EMP WHERE ID = ?", id)
    if err != nil {                          ⟵┐ Handles errors while
        return "", 0, err                       │ executing the query
```

```
    }
    defer func() {                          Handles errors while
        err := rows.Close()           ←──── closing the rows
        if err != nil {
            log.Printf("failed to close rows: %v\n", err)
        }
    }()

    var (
        department string
        age        int
    )
    for rows.Next() {
        err := rows.Scan(&department, &age)   ←──┐  Handles errors while
        if err != nil {                          │  scanning a row
            return "", 0, err
        }
    }

    return department, age, nil
}
```

In this function, we handle three errors: while executing the query, closing the rows, and scanning a row. But this isn't enough. We have to know that the `for rows .Next() {}` loop can break either when there are no more rows or when an error happens while preparing the next row. Following a row iteration, we should call `rows.Err` to distinguish between the two cases:

```
func get(ctx context.Context, db *sql.DB, id string) (string, int, error) {
    // ...
    for rows.Next() {
        // ...
    }

    if err := rows.Err(); err != nil {    ←──┐  Checks rows.Err to determine
        return "", 0, err                     │  whether the previous loop
    }                                          │  stopped because of an error

    return department, age, nil
}
```

This is the best practice to keep in mind: because `rows.Next` can stop either when we have iterated over all the rows or when an error happens while preparing the next row, we should check `rows.Err` following the iteration.

Let's now discuss a frequent mistake: forgetting to close transient resources.

10.5   *#79: Not closing transient resources*

Pretty frequently, developers work with transient (temporary) resources that must be closed at some point in the code: for example, to avoid leaks on disk or in memory. Structs can generally implement the `io.Closer` interface to convey that a transient resource has to be closed. Let's look at three common examples of what happens when resources aren't correctly closed and how to handle them properly.

10.5.1 *HTTP body*

First, let's discuss this problem in the context of HTTP. We will write a `getBody` method that makes an HTTP GET request and returns the HTTP body response. Here's a first implementation:

```go
type handler struct {
    client http.Client
    url    string
}

func (h handler) getBody() (string, error) {
    resp, err := h.client.Get(h.url)          // Makes an HTTP
    if err != nil {                            // GET request
        return "", err
    }

    body, err := io.ReadAll(resp.Body)         // Reads resp.Body and
    if err != nil {                            // gets a body as a []byte
        return "", err
    }

    return string(body), nil
}
```

We use `http.Get` and parse the response using `io.ReadAll`. This method looks OK, and it correctly returns the HTTP response body. However, there's a resource leak. Let's understand where.

`resp` is an `*http.Response` type. It contains a `Body io.ReadCloser` field (`io.ReadCloser` implements both `io.Reader` and `io.Closer`). This body must be closed if `http.Get` doesn't return an error; otherwise, it's a resource leak. In this case, our application will keep some memory allocated that is no longer needed but can't be reclaimed by the GC and may prevent clients from reusing the TCP connection in the worst cases.

The most convenient way to deal with body closure is to handle it as a `defer` statement this way:

```go
defer func() {
    err := resp.Body.Close()
    if err != nil {
        log.Printf("failed to close response: %v\n", err)
    }
}()
```

In this implementation, we properly handle the body resource closure as a `defer` function that will be executed once `getBody` returns.

NOTE On the server side, while implementing an HTTP handler, we aren't required to close the request body because the server does this automatically.

We should also understand that a response body must be closed regardless of whether we read it. For example, if we are only interested in the HTTP status code and not in the body, it has to be closed no matter what, to avoid a leak:

```go
func (h handler) getStatusCode(body io.Reader) (int, error) {
    resp, err := h.client.Post(h.url, "application/json", body)
    if err != nil {
        return 0, err
    }

    defer func() {                    ⟵─┐  Closes the response body
        err := resp.Body.Close()           even if we don't read it
        if err != nil {
            log.Printf("failed to close response: %v\n", err)
        }
    }()

    return resp.StatusCode, nil
}
```

This function closes the body even though we haven't read it.

Another essential thing to remember is that the behavior is different when we close the body, depending on whether we have read from it:

- If we close the body without a read, the default HTTP transport may close the connection.
- If we close the body following a read, the default HTTP transport won't close the connection; hence, it may be reused.

Therefore, if `getStatusCode` is called repeatedly and we want to use keep-alive connections, we should read the body even though we aren't interested in it:

```go
func (h handler) getStatusCode(body io.Reader) (int, error) {
    resp, err := h.client.Post(h.url, "application/json", body)
    if err != nil {
        return 0, err
    }

    // Close response body

    _, _ = io.Copy(io.Discard, resp.Body)      ⟵─┐  Reads the
    return resp.StatusCode, nil                      response body
}
```

In this example, we read the body to keep the connection alive. Note that instead of using `io.ReadAll`, we used `io.Copy` to `io.Discard`, an `io.Writer` implementation. This code reads the body but discards it without any copy, making it more efficient than `io.ReadAll`.

When to close the response body

Fairly frequently, implementations close the body if the response isn't empty, not if the error is `nil`:

```
resp, err := http.Get(url)        ⎤  If the response
if resp != nil {             ◁─────┘  isn't nil ...
    defer resp.Body.Close()   ◁───┐  ... close the response
}                                 ┘  body as a defer function.

if err != nil {
    return "", err
}
```

This implementation isn't necessary. It's based on the fact that in some conditions (such as a redirection failure), neither `resp` nor `err` will be `nil`. But according to the official Go documentation (https://pkg.go.dev/net/http),

> On error, any Response can be ignored. A non-nil Response with a non-nil error only occurs when CheckRedirect fails, and even then, the returned Response.Body is already closed.

Therefore, the `if resp != nil {}` check isn't necessary. We should stick with the initial solution that closes the body in a `defer` function only if there is no error.

Closing a resource to avoid leaks isn't only related to HTTP body management. In general, all structs implementing the `io.Closer` interface should be closed at some point. This interface contains a single `Close` method:

```
type Closer interface {
    Close() error
}
```

Let's now see the impacts with `sql.Rows`.

10.5.2 *sql.Rows*

`sql.Rows` is a struct used as a result of an SQL query. Because this struct implements `io.Closer`, it has to be closed. The following example omits closing the rows:

```
db, err := sql.Open("postgres", dataSourceName)
if err != nil {
    return err
}

rows, err := db.Query("SELECT * FROM CUSTOMERS")    ◁──┐  Performs the
if err != nil {                                        ┘  SQL query
    return err
}

// Use rows

return nil
```

Forgetting to close the rows means a connection leak, which prevents the database connection from being put back into the connection pool.

We can handle the closure as a `defer` function following the `if err != nil` block:

```
// Open connection

rows, err := db.Query("SELECT * FROM CUSTOMERS")          Performs an
if err != nil {                                            SQL query
    return err
}
                         Closes
                         the rows
defer func() {
    if err := rows.Close(); err != nil {
        log.Printf("failed to close rows: %v\n", err)
    }
}()

// Use rows
```

Following the `Query` call, we should eventually close `rows` to prevent a connection leak if it doesn't return an error.

> **NOTE** As discussed in the previous section, the `db` variable (`*sql.DB` type) represents a pool of connections. It also implements the `io.Closer` interface. But as the documentation suggests, it is rare to close an `sql.DB` because it's meant to be long-lived and shared among many goroutines.

Next, let's discuss closing resources while working with files.

10.5.3 os.File

`os.File` represents an open file descriptor. Like `sql.Rows`, it must be closed eventually:

```
f, err := os.OpenFile(filename, os.O_APPEND|os.O_WRONLY, os.ModeAppend)
if err != nil {
    return err                                           Opens the file
}
                                   Closes the file
defer func() {                     descriptor
    if err := f.Close(); err != nil {
        log.Printf("failed to close file: %v\n", err)
    }
}()
```

In this example, we use `defer` to defer the call to the `Close` method. If we don't eventually close an `os.File`, it will not lead to a leak per se: the file will be closed automatically when `os.File` is garbage collected. However, it's better to call `Close` explicitly because we don't know when the next GC will be triggered (unless we manually run it).

There's another benefit of calling `Close` explicitly: to actively monitor the error that is returned. For example, this should be the case with writable files.

Writing to a file descriptor isn't a synchronous operation. For performance concerns, data is buffered. The BSD manual page for close(2) mentions that a closure can lead to an error in a previously uncommitted write (still living in a buffer) encountered during an I/O error. For that reason, if we want to write to a file, we should propagate any error that occurs while closing the file:

```go
func writeToFile(filename string, content []byte) (err error) {
    // Open file

    defer func() {                           ◁─┐ Returns the close error
        closeErr := f.Close()                  │ if the write succeeds
        if err == nil {
            err = closeErr
        }
    }()

    _, err = f.Write(content)
    return
}
```

In this example, we use named arguments and set the error to the response of f.Close if the write succeeds. This way, clients will be aware if something goes wrong with this function and can react accordingly.

Furthermore, success while closing a writable os.File doesn't guarantee that the file will be written on disk. The write can still live in a buffer on the filesystem and not be flushed on disk. If durability is a critical factor, we can use the Sync() method to commit a change. In that case, errors coming from Close can be safely ignored:

```go
func writeToFile(filename string, content []byte) error {
    // Open file

    defer func() {
        _ = f.Close()          ◁─┐ Ignores possible
    }()                          │ errors

    _, err = f.Write(content)
    if err != nil {
        return err
    }
                                 ┐ Commits the write
    return f.Sync()          ◁───┘ to the disk
}
```

This example is a synchronous write function. It ensures that the content is written to disk before returning. But its downside is an impact on performance.

To summarize this section, we've seen how important it is to close ephemeral resources and thus avoid leaks. Ephemeral resources must be closed at the right time and in specific situations. It's not always clear up front what has to be closed. We can only acquire this information by carefully reading the API documentation and/or through experience. But we should remember that if a struct implements the `io.Closer` interface, we must eventually call the `Close` method. Last but not least, it's essential to understand what to do if a closure fails: is it enough to log a message, or should we also propagate it? The appropriate action depends on the implementation, as seen in the three examples in this section.

Let's now switch to common mistakes related to HTTP handling: forgetting `return` statements.

10.6   #80: Forgetting the return statement after replying to an HTTP request

While writing an HTTP handler, it's easy to forget the `return` statement after replying to an HTTP request. This may lead to an odd situation where we should have stopped a handler after an error, but we didn't.

We can observe this situation in the following example:

```
func handler(w http.ResponseWriter, req *http.Request) {
    err := foo(req)
    if err != nil {
        http.Error(w, "foo", http.StatusInternalServerError)    ◁──┐ Handles
    }                                                               │ the error

    // ...
}
```

If `foo` returns an error, we handle it using `http.Error`, which replies to the request with the `foo` error message and a 500 Internal Server Error. The problem with this code is that if we enter the `if err != nil` branch, the application will continue its execution, because `http.Error` doesn't stop the handler's execution.

What's the real impact of such an error? First, let's discuss it at the HTTP level. For example, suppose we had completed the previous HTTP handler by adding a step to write a successful HTTP response body and status code:

```
func handler(w http.ResponseWriter, req *http.Request) {
    err := foo(req)
    if err != nil {
        http.Error(w, "foo", http.StatusInternalServerError)
    }

    _, _ = w.Write([]byte("all good"))
    w.WriteHeader(http.StatusCreated)
}
```

In the case `err != nil`, the HTTP response would be the following:

```
foo
all good
```

The response contains both the error and success messages.

We would return only the first HTTP status code: in the previous example, 500. However, Go would also log a warning:

```
2021/10/29 16:45:33 http: superfluous response.WriteHeader call
from main.handler (main.go:20)
```

This warning means we tried to write the status code multiple times and doing so was superfluous.

In terms of execution, the main impact would be to continue the execution of a function that should have been stopped. For example, if `foo` was returning a pointer in addition to the error, continuing execution would mean using this pointer, perhaps leading to a nil pointer dereference (and hence a goroutine panic).

The fix for this mistake is to keep thinking about adding the `return` statement following `http.Error`:

```
func handler(w http.ResponseWriter, req *http.Request) {
    err := foo(req)
    if err != nil {
        http.Error(w, "foo", http.StatusInternalServerError)
        return              ◁──┐  Adds the return
    }                          │  statement

    // ...
}
```

Thanks to the `return` statement, the function will stop its execution if we end in the `if err != nil` branch.

This error is probably not the most complex of this book. Yet, it's so easy to forget about it that this mistake occurs fairly frequently. We always need to remember that `http.Error` doesn't stop a handler execution and must be added manually. Such an issue can and should be caught during testing if we have decent coverage.

The last section of this chapter continues our discussion of HTTP. We see why production-grade applications shouldn't rely on the default HTTP client and server implementations.

10.7   *#81: Using the default HTTP client and server*

The `http` package provides HTTP client and server implementations. However, it's all too easy for developers to make a common mistake: relying on the default implementations in the context of applications that are eventually deployed in production. Let's look at the problems and how to overcome them.

10.7.1   *HTTP client*

Let's define what *default client* means. We will use a GET request as an example. We can use the zero value of an `http.Client` struct like so:

```
client := &http.Client{}
resp, err := client.Get("https://golang.org/")
```

Or we can use the `http.Get` function:

```
resp, err := http.Get("https://golang.org/")
```

In the end, both approaches are the same. The `http.Get` function uses `http.DefaultClient`, which is also based on the zero value of `http.Client`:

```
// DefaultClient is the default Client and is used by Get, Head, and Post.
var DefaultClient = &Client{}
```

So, what's the problem with using the default HTTP client?

First, the default client doesn't specify any timeouts. This absence of timeout is not something we want for production-grade systems: it can lead to many issues, such as never-ending requests that could exhaust system resources.

Before delving into the available timeouts while making a request, let's review the five steps involved in an HTTP request:

1 Dial to establish a TCP connection.
2 TLS handshake (if enabled).
3 Send the request.
4 Read the response headers.
5 Read the response body.

Figure 10.2 shows how these steps relate to the main client timeouts.

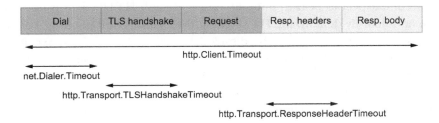

Figure 10.2   The five steps during an HTTP request, and the related timeouts

The four main timeouts are the following:

- `net.Dialer.Timeout`—Specifies the maximum amount of time a dial will wait for a connection to complete.
- `http.Transport.TLSHandshakeTimeout`—Specifies the maximum amount of time to wait for the TLS handshake.
- `http.Transport.ResponseHeaderTimeout`—Specifies the amount of time to wait for a server's response headers.
- `http.Client.Timeout`—Specifies the time limit for a request. It includes all the steps, from step 1 (dial) to step 5 (read the response body).

> **HTTP client timeout**
>
> You may have encountered the following error when specifying `http.Client`
> `.Timeout`:
>
> ```
> net/http: request canceled (Client.Timeout exceeded while awaiting
> headers)
> ```
>
> This error means the endpoint failed to respond on time. We get this error about
> headers because reading them is the first step while waiting for a response.

Here's an example of an HTTP client that overrides these timeouts:

```
client := &http.Client{
    Timeout: 5 * time.Second,              ◁──  Global request
    Transport: &http.Transport{                 timeout
        DialContext: (&net.Dialer{
            Timeout: time.Second,          ◁──  Dial timeout
        }).DialContext,
        TLSHandshakeTimeout:    time.Second,  ◁── TLS handshake
        ResponseHeaderTimeout: time.Second,   ◁──  timeout
    },                                          Response
}                                               header timeout
```

We create a client with a 1-second timeout for the dial, the TLS handshake, and read-ing the response header. Meanwhile, each request has a global 5-second timeout.

The second aspect to bear in mind about the default HTTP client is how connec-tions are handled. By default, the HTTP client does connection pooling. The default client reuses connections (it can be disabled by setting `http.Transport.Disable-KeepAlives` to `true`). There's an extra timeout to specify how long an idle connec-tion is kept in the pool: `http.Transport.IdleConnTimeout`. The default value is 90 seconds, which means the connection can be reused for other requests during this time. After that, if the connection hasn't been reused, it will be closed.

To configure the number of connections in the pool, we must override `http.Transport.MaxIdleConns`. This value is set to `100` by default. But there's some-thing important to note: the `http.Transport.MaxIdleConnsPerHost` limit per host, which by default is set to 2. For example, if we trigger `100` requests to the same host, only 2 connections will remain in the connection pool after that. Hence, if we trigger 100 requests again, we will have to reopen at least 98 connections. This configuration can also impact the average latency if we have to deal with a significant number of par-allel requests to the same host.

For production-grade systems, we probably want to override the default timeouts. And tweaking the parameters related to connection pooling can also have a signifi-cant impact on the latency.

10.7.2 *HTTP server*

We should also be careful while implementing an HTTP server. Again, a default server can be created using the zero value of `http.Server`:

```
server := &http.Server{}
server.Serve(listener)
```

Or we can use a function such as `http.Serve`, `http.ListenAndServe`, or `http`
`.ListenAndServeTLS` that also relies on the default `http.Server`.

Once a connection is accepted, an HTTP response is divided into five steps:

1 Wait for the client to send the request.
2 TLS handshake (if enabled).
3 Read the request headers.
4 Read the request body.
5 Write the response.

NOTE The TLS handshake doesn't have to be repeated with an already established connection.

Figure 10.3 shows how these steps relate to the main server timeouts. The three main timeouts are the following:

- `http.Server.ReadHeaderTimeout`—A field that specifies the maximum amount of time to read the request headers
- `http.Server.ReadTimeout`—A field that specifies the maximum amount of time to read the entire request
- `http.TimeoutHandler`—A wrapper function that specifies the maximum amount of time for a handler to complete

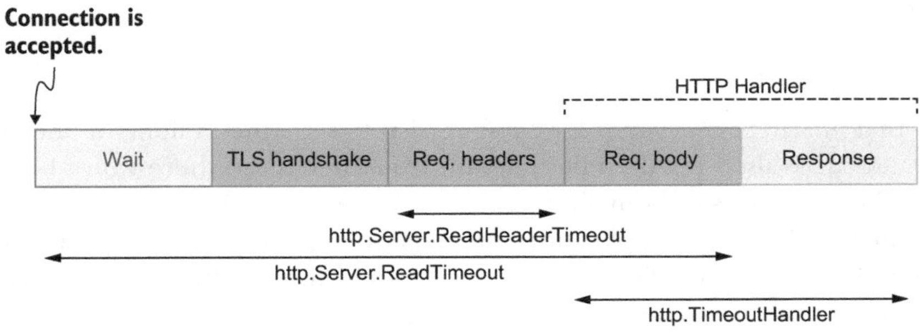

Figure 10.3   The five steps of an HTTP response, and the related timeouts

The last parameter isn't a server parameter but a wrapper on top of a handler to limit its duration. If a handler fails to respond on time, the server will reply 503 Service

Unavailable with a specific message, and the context passed to the handler will be canceled.

> **NOTE** We purposely omitted `http.Server.WriteTimeout`, which isn't necessary since `http.TimeoutHandler` was released (Go 1.8). `http.Server.Write-Timeout` has a few issues. First, its behavior depends on whether TLS is enabled, making it more complex to understand and use. It also closes the TCP connection without returning a proper HTTP code if the timeout is reached. And it doesn't propagate the cancellation to the handler context, so a handler may continue its execution without knowing that the TCP connection is already closed.

While exposing our endpoint to untrusted clients, the best practice is to set at least the `http.Server.ReadHeaderTimeout` field and use the `http.TimeoutHandler` wrapper function. Otherwise, clients may exploit this flaw and, for example, create never-ending connections that can lead to exhaustion of system resources.

Here's how to set up a server with these timeouts in place:

```
s := &http.Server{
    Addr:               ":8080",                                          Wraps the
    ReadHeaderTimeout: 500 * time.Millisecond,                            HTTP handler
    ReadTimeout:       500 * time.Millisecond,
    Handler:           http.TimeoutHandler(handler, time.Second, "foo"),  ◁
}
```

`http.TimeoutHandler` wraps the provided handler. Here, if `handler` fails to respond in 1 second, the server returns a 503 status code with `foo` as the HTTP response.

Just as we described regarding HTTP clients, on the server side we can configure the maximum amount of time for the next request when keep-alives are enabled. We do so using `http.Server.IdleTimeout`:

```
s := &http.Server{
    // ...
    IdleTimeout: time.Second,
}
```

Note that if `http.Server.IdleTimeout` isn't set, the value of `http.Server`
`.ReadTimeout` is used for the idle timeout. If neither is set, there won't be any timeouts, and connections will remain open until they are closed by clients.

For production-grade applications, we need to make sure not to use default HTTP clients and servers. Otherwise, requests may be stuck forever due to an absence of timeouts or even malicious clients that exploit the fact that our server doesn't have any timeouts.

Summary

- Remain cautious with functions accepting a `time.Duration`. Even though passing an integer is allowed, strive to use the time API to prevent any possible confusion.

- Avoiding calls to `time.After` in repeated functions (such as loops or HTTP handlers) can avoid peak memory consumption. The resources created by `time.After` are released only when the timer expires.

- Be careful about using embedded fields in Go structs. Doing so may lead to sneaky bugs like an embedded `time.Time` field implementing the `json.Marshaler` interface, hence overriding the default marshaling behavior.

- When comparing two `time.Time` structs, recall that `time.Time` contains both a wall clock and a monotonic clock, and the comparison using the `==` operator is done on both clocks.

- To avoid wrong assumptions when you provide a map while unmarshaling JSON data, remember that numerics are converted to `float64` by default.

- Call the `Ping` or `PingContext` method if you need to test your configuration and make sure a database is reachable.

- Configure the database connection parameters for production-grade applications.

- Using SQL prepared statements makes queries more efficient and more secure.

- Deal with nullable columns in tables using pointers or `sql.NullXXX` types.

- Call the `Err` method of `*sql.Rows` after row iterations to ensure that you haven't missed an error while preparing the next row.

- Eventually close all structs implementing `io.Closer` to avoid possible leaks.

- To avoid unexpected behaviors in HTTP handler implementations, make sure you don't miss the `return` statement if you want a handler to stop after `http.Error`.

- For production-grade applications, don't use the default HTTP client and server implementations. These implementations are missing timeouts and behaviors that should be mandatory in production.

Testing

This chapter covers

- Categorizing tests and making them more robust
- Making Go tests deterministic
- Working with utility packages such as `httptest` and `iotest`
- Avoiding common benchmark mistakes
- Improving the testing process

Testing is a crucial aspect of a project's lifecycle. It offers countless benefits, such as building confidence in an application, acting as code documentation, and making refactoring easier. Compared to some other languages, Go has strong primitives for writing tests. Throughout this chapter, we look at common mistakes that make the testing process brittle, less effective, and less accurate.

11.1 #82: Not categorizing tests

The testing pyramid is a model that groups tests into different categories (see figure 11.1). Unit tests occupy the base of the pyramid. Most tests should be unit tests: they're cheap to write, fast to execute, and highly deterministic. Usually, as we go further up the pyramid, tests become more complex to write and slower to run, and it is more difficult to guarantee their determinism.

A common technique is to be explicit about which kind of tests to run. For instance, depending on the project lifecycle stage, we may want to run only unit tests or run all the tests in the project. Not categorizing tests means potentially wasting time and effort and losing accuracy about the scope of a test. This section discusses three main ways to categorize tests in Go.

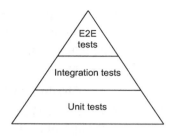

Figure 11.1   An example of the testing pyramid

11.1.1   Build tags

The most common way to classify tests is using build tags. A build tag is a special comment at the beginning of a Go file, followed by an empty line.

For example, look at this bar.go file:

```
//go:build foo

package bar
```

This file contains the foo tag. Note that one package may contain multiple files with different build tags.

> **NOTE**   As of Go 1.17, the syntax // +build foo was replaced by //go:build foo. For the time being (Go 1.18), gofmt synchronizes the two forms to help with migration.

Build tags are used for two primary use cases. First, we can use a build tag as a conditional option to build an application: for example, if we want a source file to be included only if cgo is enabled (cgo is a way to let Go packages call C code), we can add the //go:build cgo build tag. Second, if we want to categorize a test as an integration test, we can add a specific build flag, such as integration.

Here is an example db_test.go file:

```
//go:build integration

package db

import (
    "testing"
)

func TestInsert(t *testing.T) {
    // ...
}
```

Here we add the `integration` build tag to categorize that this file contains integration tests. The benefit of using build tags is that we can select which kinds of tests to execute. For example, let's assume a package contains two test files:

- The file we just created: db_test.go
- Another file that doesn't contain a build tag: contract_test.go

If we run `go test` inside this package without any options, it will run only the test files without build tags (contract_test.go):

```
$ go test -v .
=== RUN    TestContract
--- PASS: TestContract (0.01s)
PASS
```

However, if we provide the `integration` tag, running `go test` will also include db_test.go:

```
$ go test --tags=integration -v .
=== RUN    TestInsert
--- PASS: TestInsert (0.01s)
=== RUN    TestContract
--- PASS: TestContract (2.89s)
PASS
```

So, running tests with a specific tag includes both the files without tags and the files matching this tag. What if we want to run *only* integration tests? A possible way is to add a negation tag on the unit test files. For example, using `!integration` means we want to include the test file only if the `integration` flag is *not* enabled (contract_test.go):

```
//go:build !integration

package db

import (
    "testing"
)

func TestContract(t *testing.T) {
    // ...
}
```

Using this approach,

- Running `go test` with the `integration` flag runs only the integration tests.
- Running `go test` without the `integration` flag runs only the unit tests.

Let's discuss an option that works at the level of a single test, not a file.

11.1.2 *Environment variables*

As mentioned by Peter Bourgon, a member of the Go community, build tags have one main drawback: the absence of signals that a test has been ignored (see http://mng.bz/qYlr). In the first example, when we executed `go test` without build flags, it showed only the tests that were executed:

```
$ go test -v .
=== RUN    TestUnit
--- PASS: TestUnit (0.01s)
PASS
ok       db   0.319s
```

If we're not careful with the way tags are handled, we may forget about existing tests. For that reason, some projects favor the approach of checking the test category using environment variables.

For example, we can implement the `TestInsert` integration test by checking a specific environment variable and potentially skipping the test:

```
func TestInsert(t *testing.T) {
    if os.Getenv("INTEGRATION") != "true" {
        t.Skip("skipping integration test")
    }

    // ...
}
```

If the `INTEGRATION` environment variable isn't set to `true`, the test is skipped with a message:

```
$ go test -v .
=== RUN    TestInsert
    db_integration_test.go:12: skipping integration test      ◁─┐  Shows the test-
--- SKIP: TestInsert (0.00s)                                    │  skipped message
=== RUN    TestUnit
--- PASS: TestUnit (0.00s)
PASS
ok       db   0.319s
```

One benefit of using this approach is making explicit which tests are skipped and why. This technique is probably less widely used than build tags, but it's worth knowing about because it presents some advantages, as we discussed.

Next, let's look at another way to categorize tests: short mode.

11.1.3 Short mode

Another approach to categorize tests is related to their speed. We may have to dissociate short-running tests from long-running tests.

As an illustration, suppose we have a set of unit tests, one of which is notoriously slow. We would like to categorize the slow test so we don't have to run it every time (especially if the trigger is after saving a file, for example). Short mode allows us to make this distinction:

```
func TestLongRunning(t *testing.T) {     ┌  Marks the test
    if testing.Short() {           ◁─────┘  as long-running
        t.Skip("skipping long-running test")
    }
    // ...
}
```

Using `testing.Short`, we can retrieve whether short mode was enabled while running the test. Then we use `Skip` to skip the test. To run tests using short mode, we have to pass `-short`:

```
% go test -short -v .
=== RUN   TestLongRunning
    foo_test.go:9: skipping long-running test
--- SKIP: TestLongRunning (0.00s)
PASS
ok      foo  0.174s
```

`TestLongRunning` is explicitly skipped when the tests are executed. Note that unlike build tags, this option works per test, not per file.

In summary, categorizing tests is a best practice for a successful testing strategy. In this section, we've seen three ways to categorize tests:

- Using build tags at the test file level
- Using environment variables to mark a specific test
- Based on the test pace using short mode

We can also combine approaches: for example, using build tags or environment variables to classify a test (for example, as a unit or integration test) and short mode if our project contains long-running unit tests.

In the next section, we discuss why enabling the `-race` flag matters.

11.2   #83: Not enabling the -race flag

In mistake #58, "Not understanding race problems," we defined a data race as occurring when two goroutines simultaneously access the same variable, with at least one writing to the variable. We should also know that Go has a standard race-detector tool to help detect data races. One common mistake is forgetting how important this tool is and not enabling it. This section looks at what the race detector catches, how to use it, and its limitations.

In Go, the race detector isn't a static analysis tool used during compilation; instead, it's a tool to find data races that occur at runtime. To enable it, we have to enable the `-race` flag while compiling or running a test. For example:

```
$ go test -race ./...
```

Once the race detector is enabled, the compiler instruments the code to detect data races. *Instrumentation* refers to a compiler adding extra instructions: here, tracking all memory accesses and recording when and how they occur. At runtime, the race detector watches for data races. However, we should keep in mind the runtime overhead of enabling the race detector:

- Memory usage may increase by 5 to 10×.
- Execution time may increase by 2 to 20×.

Because of this overhead, it's generally recommended to enable the race detector only during local testing or continuous integration (CI). In production, we should avoid it (or only use it in the case of canary releases, for example).

If a race is detected, Go raises a warning. For instance, this example contains a data race because i can be accessed at the same time for both a read and a write:

```
package main

import (
    "fmt"
)

func main() {
    i := 0
    go func() { i++ }()
    fmt.Println(i)
}
```

Running this application with the -race flag logs the following data race warning:

```
==================
WARNING: DATA RACE
Write at 0x00c000026078 by goroutine 7:        ◁──   Indicates that
  main.main.func1()                                  goroutine 7 was writing
        /tmp/app/main.go:9 +0x4e

Previous read at 0x00c000026078 by main goroutine:   ◁──   Indicates that the main
  main.main()                                                goroutine was reading
        /tmp/app/main.go:10 +0x88

Goroutine 7 (running) created at:     ◁──   Indicates when
  main.main()                               goroutine 7 was created
        /tmp/app/main.go:9 +0x7a
==================
```

Let's make sure we are comfortable reading these messages. Go always logs the following:

- The concurrent goroutines that are incriminated: here, the main goroutine and goroutine 7.
- Where accesses occur in the code: in this case, lines 9 and 10.
- When these goroutines were created: goroutine 7 was created in main().

NOTE Internally, the race detector uses vector clocks, a data structure used to determine a partial ordering of events (and also used in distributed systems such as databases). Each goroutine creation leads to the creation of a vector clock. The instrumentation updates the vector clock at each memory access and synchronization event. Then, it compares the vector clocks to detect potential data races.

The race detector cannot catch a false positive (an apparent data race that isn't a real one). Therefore, we know our code contains a data race if we get a warning. Conversely, it can sometimes lead to false negatives (missing actual data races).

We need to note two things regarding testing. First, the race detector can only be as good as our tests. Thus, we should ensure that concurrent code is tested thoroughly against data races. Second, given the possible false negatives, if we have a test to check data races, we can put this logic inside a loop. Doing so increases the chances of catching possible data races:

```go
func TestDataRace(t *testing.T) {
    for i := 0; i < 100; i++ {
        // Actual logic
    }
}
```

In addition, if a specific file contains tests that lead to data races, we can exclude it from race detection using the `!race` build tag:

```go
//go:build !race

package main

import (
    "testing"
)

func TestFoo(t *testing.T) {
    // ...
}

func TestBar(t *testing.T) {
    // ...
}
```

This file will be built only if the race detector is disabled. Otherwise, the entire file won't be built, so the tests won't be executed.

In summary, we should bear in mind that running tests with the `-race` flag for applications using concurrency is highly recommended, if not mandatory. This approach allows us to enable the race detector, which instruments our code to catch potential data races. While enabled, it has a significant impact on memory and performance, so it must be used in specific conditions such as local tests or CI.

The following section discusses two flags related to execution mode: `parallel` and `shuffle`.

11.3   *#84: Not using test execution modes*

While running tests, the `go` command can accept a set of flags to impact how tests are executed. A common mistake is not being aware of these flags and missing opportunities that could lead to faster execution or a better way to spot possible bugs. Let's look at two of these flags: `parallel` and `shuffle`.

11.3.1 *The parallel flag*

Parallel execution mode allows us to run specific tests in parallel, which can be very useful: for example, to speed up long-running tests. We can mark that a test has to be run in parallel by calling `t.Parallel`:

```
func TestFoo(t *testing.T) {
    t.Parallel()
    // ...
}
```

When we mark a test using `t.Parallel`, it is executed in parallel alongside all the other parallel tests. In terms of execution, though, Go first runs all the sequential tests one by one. Once the sequential tests are completed, it executes the parallel tests.

For example, the following code contains three tests, but only two of them are marked to be run in parallel:

```
func TestA(t *testing.T) {
    t.Parallel()
    // ...
}

func TestB(t *testing.T) {
    t.Parallel()
    // ...
}

func TestC(t *testing.T) {
    // ...
}
```

Running the tests for this file gives the following logs:

```
=== RUN    TestA
=== PAUSE  TestA          <──┤  Pauses TestA
=== RUN    TestB
=== PAUSE  TestB        <──┤  Pauses TestB
=== RUN    TestC            <──┤  Runs TestC
--- PASS: TestC (0.00s)
=== CONT   TestA          <──┐  Resumes TestA
--- PASS: TestA (0.00s)      │  and TestB
=== CONT   TestB
--- PASS: TestB (0.00s)
PASS
```

`TestC` is the first to be executed. `TestA` and `TestB` are logged first, but they are paused, waiting for `TestC` to complete. Then both are resumed and executed in parallel.

By default, the maximum number of tests that can run simultaneously equals the `GOMAXPROCS` value. To serialize tests or, for example, increase this number in the context of long-running tests doing a lot of I/O, we can change this value using the `-parallel` flag:

```
$ go test -parallel 16 .
```

Here, the maximum number of parallel tests is set to 16.

Let's now see another mode while running Go tests: shuffle.

11.3.2 *The -shuffle flag*

As of Go 1.17, it's possible to randomize the execution order of tests and benchmarks. What's the rationale? A best practice while writing tests is to make them isolated. For example, they shouldn't depend on execution order or shared variables. These hidden dependencies can mean a possible test error or, even worse, a bug that won't be caught during testing. To prevent that, we can use the -shuffle flag to randomize tests. We can set it to on or off to enable or disable test shuffling (its disabled by default):

```
$ go test -shuffle=on -v .
```

However, in some cases, we want to rerun tests in the same order. For example, if tests fail during CI, we may want to reproduce the error locally. To do that, instead of passing on to the -shuffle flag, we can pass the seed used to randomize the tests. We can access this seed value when running shuffled tests by enabling verbose mode (-v):

```
$ go test -shuffle=on -v .
-test.shuffle 1636399552801504000      ⟵  Seed value
=== RUN    TestBar
--- PASS: TestBar (0.00s)
=== RUN    TestFoo
--- PASS: TestFoo (0.00s)
PASS
ok        teivah  0.129s
```

We executed the tests randomly, but go test printed the seed value: 1636399552801504000. To force the tests to be run in the same order, we provide this seed value to shuffle:

```
$ go test -shuffle=1636399552801504000 -v .
-test.shuffle 1636399552801504000
=== RUN    TestBar
--- PASS: TestBar (0.00s)
=== RUN    TestFoo
--- PASS: TestFoo (0.00s)
PASS
ok        teivah  0.129s
```

The tests were executed in the same order: TestBar and then TestFoo.

In general, we should be cautious about existing test flags and keep ourselves informed about new features with recent Go releases. Running tests in parallel can be an excellent way to decrease the overall execution time of running all the tests. And shuffle mode can help us spot hidden dependencies that may mean testing errors or even invisible bugs while running tests in the same order.

11.4   *#85: Not using table-driven tests*

Table-driven tests are an efficient technique for writing condensed tests and thus reducing boilerplate code to help us focus on what matters: the testing logic. This section goes through a concrete example to see why table-driven tests are worth knowing when working with Go.

Let's consider the following function that removes all the new-line suffixes (\n or \r\n) from a string:

```go
func removeNewLineSuffixes(s string) string {
    if s == "" {
        return s
    }
    if strings.HasSuffix(s, "\r\n") {
        return removeNewLineSuffixes(s[:len(s)-2])
    }
    if strings.HasSuffix(s, "\n") {
        return removeNewLineSuffixes(s[:len(s)-1])
    }
    return s
}
```

This function removes all the leading \r\n and \n suffixes recursively. Now, let's say we want to test this function extensively. We should at least cover the following cases:

- Input is empty.
- Input ends with \n.
- Input ends with \r\n.
- Input ends with multiple \n.
- Input ends without newlines.

The following approach creates one unit test per case:

```go
func TestRemoveNewLineSuffix_Empty(t *testing.T) {
    got := removeNewLineSuffixes("")
    expected := ""
    if got != expected {
        t.Errorf("got: %s", got)
    }
}

func TestRemoveNewLineSuffix_EndingWithCarriageReturnNewLine(t *testing.T) {
    got := removeNewLineSuffixes("a\r\n")
    expected := "a"
    if got != expected {
        t.Errorf("got: %s", got)
    }
}

func TestRemoveNewLineSuffix_EndingWithNewLine(t *testing.T) {
    got := removeNewLineSuffixes("a\n")
    expected := "a"
```

```
        if got != expected {
            t.Errorf("got: %s", got)
        }
    }

    func TestRemoveNewLineSuffix_EndingWithMultipleNewLines(t *testing.T) {
        got := removeNewLineSuffixes("a\n\n\n")
        expected := "a"
        if got != expected {
            t.Errorf("got: %s", got)
        }
    }

    func TestRemoveNewLineSuffix_EndingWithoutNewLine(t *testing.T) {
        got := removeNewLineSuffixes("a\n")
        expected := "a"
        if got != expected {
            t.Errorf("got: %s", got)
        }
    }
```

Each function represents a specific case that we want to cover. However, there are two main drawbacks. First, the function names are more complex (TestRemoveNewLine-Suffix_EndingWithCarriageReturnNewLine is 55 characters long), which can quickly affect the clarity of what the function is supposed to test. The second drawback is the amount of duplication among these functions, given that the structure is always the same:

1 Call removeNewLineSuffixes.
2 Define the expected value.
3 Compare the values.
4 Log an error message.

If we want to change one of these steps—for example, include the expected value as part of the error message—we will have to repeat it in all the tests. And the more tests we write, the more difficult the code becomes to maintain.

   Instead, we can use table-driven tests so we write the logic only once. Table-driven tests rely on subtests, and a single test function can include multiple subtests. For example, the following test contains two subtests:

```
func TestFoo(t *testing.T) {
    t.Run("subtest 1", func(t *testing.T) {          ◄─┐   Runs a first subtest
        if false {                                      │   called subtest 1
            t.Error()
        }
    })
    t.Run("subtest 2", func(t *testing.T) {          ◄─┐   Runs a second subtest
        if 2 != 2 {                                     │   called subtest 2
            t.Error()
        }
    })
}
```

The `TestFoo` function includes two subtests. If we run this test, it shows the results for both `subtest 1` and `subtest 2`:

```
--- PASS: TestFoo (0.00s)
    --- PASS: TestFoo/subtest_1 (0.00s)
    --- PASS: TestFoo/subtest_2 (0.00s)
PASS
```

We can also run a single test using the `-run` flag and concatenating the parent test name with the subtest. For example, we can run only `subtest 1`:

```
$ go test -run=TestFoo/subtest_1 -v        ◁─┐  Uses the -run flag
=== RUN   TestFoo                            │  to run only subtest 1
=== RUN   TestFoo/subtest_1
--- PASS: TestFoo (0.00s)
    --- PASS: TestFoo/subtest_1 (0.00s)
```

Let's return to our example and see how to use subtests to prevent duplicating the testing logic. The main idea is to create one subtest per case. Variations exist, but we will discuss a map data structure where the key represents the test name and the value represents the test data (input, expected).

Table-driven tests avoid boilerplate code by using a data structure containing test data together with subtests. Here's a possible implementation using a map:

```go
func TestRemoveNewLineSuffix(t *testing.T) {
    tests := map[string]struct {        ◁─┐  Defines the
        input    string                   │  test data
        expected string
    }{
        `empty`: {             ◁─┐  Each entry in the map
            input:    "",        │  represents a subtest.
            expected: "",
        },
        `ending with \r\n`: {
            input:    "a\r\n",
            expected: "a",
        },
        `ending with \n`: {
            input:    "a\n",
            expected: "a",
        },
        `ending with multiple \n`: {
            input:    "a\n\n\n",
            expected: "a",
        },
        `ending without newline`: {
            input:    "a",
            expected: "a",
        },
    }
                                      ┌  Iterates over
    for name, tt := range tests {   ◁─┘  the map
        t.Run(name, func(t *testing.T) {     ◁─┐  Runs a new subtest
            got := removeNewLineSuffixes(tt.input)  │  for each map entry
            if got != tt.expected {
```

```
            t.Errorf("got: %s, expected: %s", got, tt.expected)
        }
    })
    }
}
```

The `tests` variable is a map. The key is the test name, and the value represents test data: in our case, input and expected string. Each map entry is a new test case that we want to cover. We run a new subtest for each map entry.

This test solves the two drawbacks we discussed:

- Each test name is now a string instead of a PascalCase function name, making it simpler to read.
- The logic is written only once and shared for all the different cases. Modifying the testing structure or adding a new test requires minimal effort.

We need to mention one last thing regarding table-driven tests that can also be a source of mistakes: as we mentioned previously, we can mark a test to be run in parallel by calling `t.Parallel`. We can also do this in subtests inside the closure provided to `t.Run`:

```
for name, tt := range tests {
    t.Run(name, func(t *testing.T) {
        t.Parallel()                    ◁─┐ Marks the subtest
        // Use tt                          │ to be run in parallel
    })
}
```

However, this closure uses a loop variable. To prevent an issue similar to that discussed in mistake #63, "Not being careful with goroutines and loop variables," which may cause the closures to use a wrong value of the `tt` variable, we should create another variable or shadow `tt`:

```
for name, tt := range tests {
    tt := tt                            ◁─┐ Shadows tt to make it
    t.Run(name, func(t *testing.T) {      │ local to the loop iteration
        t.Parallel()
        // Use tt
    })
}
```

This way, each closure accesses its own `tt` variable.

In summary, if multiple unit tests have a similar structure, we can mutualize them using table-driven tests. Because this technique prevents duplication, it makes it simple to change the testing logic and easier to add new use cases.

Next, let's discuss how to prevent flaky tests in Go.

11.5   *#86: Sleeping in unit tests*

A *flaky* test is a test that may both pass and fail without any code change. Flaky tests are among the biggest hurdles in testing because they are expensive to debug and undermine our confidence in testing accuracy. In Go, calling `time.Sleep` in a test can be a signal of possible flakiness. For example, concurrent code is often tested using sleeps. This section presents concrete techniques to remove sleeps from tests and thus prevent us from writing flaky tests.

We will illustrate this section with a function that returns a value and spins up a goroutine that performs a job in the background. We will call a function to get a slice of `Foo` structs and return the best element (the first one). In the meantime, the other goroutine will be in charge of calling a `Publish` method with the first n `Foo` elements:

```go
type Handler struct {
    n         int
    publisher publisher
}

type publisher interface {
    Publish([]Foo)
}

func (h Handler) getBestFoo(someInputs int) Foo {
    foos := getFoos(someInputs)          // Gets a slice of Foo
    best := foos[0]                      // Keeps the first element (checking the length
                                         // of foos is omitted for the sake of simplicity)

    go func() {
        if len(foos) > h.n {             // Keeps only the
            foos = foos[:h.n]            // first n Foo structs
        }
        h.publisher.Publish(foos)        // Calls the Publish
    }()                                  // method

    return best
}
```

The `Handler` struct contains two fields: an n field and a `publisher` dependency used to publish the first n `Foo` structs. First we get a slice of `Foo`; but before returning the first element, we spin up a new goroutine, filter the `foos` slice, and call `Publish`.

How can we test this function? Writing the part to assert the response is straightforward. However, what if we also want to check what is passed to `Publish`?

We could mock the `publisher` interface to record the arguments passed while calling the `Publish` method. Then we could sleep for a few milliseconds before checking the arguments recorded:

```go
type publisherMock struct {
    mu  sync.RWMutex
    got []Foo
}

func (p *publisherMock) Publish(got []Foo) {
    p.mu.Lock()
    defer p.mu.Unlock()
    p.got = got
}

func (p *publisherMock) Get() []Foo {
    p.mu.RLock()
```

```
        defer p.mu.RUnlock()
        return p.got
}

func TestGetBestFoo(t *testing.T) {
    mock := publisherMock{}
    h := Handler{
        publisher: &mock,
        n:         2,
    }

    foo := h.getBestFoo(42)
    // Check foo

    time.Sleep(10 * time.Millisecond)  ←───  Sleeps for 10 milliseconds
    published := mock.Get()                   before checking the arguments
    // Check published                        passed to Publish
}
```

We write a mock of `publisher` that relies on a mutex to protect access to the `published` field. In our unit test, we call `time.Sleep` to leave some time before checking the arguments passed to `Publish`.

This test is inherently flaky. There is no strict guarantee that 10 milliseconds will be enough (in this example, it is likely but not guaranteed).

So, what are the options to improve this unit test? First, we can periodically assert a given condition using retries. For example, we can write a function that takes an assertion as an argument and a maximum number of retries plus a wait time that is called periodically to avoid a busy loop:

```
func assert(t *testing.T, assertion func() bool,
    maxRetry int, waitTime time.Duration) {
    for i := 0; i < maxRetry; i++ {
        if assertion() {       ←──┐  Checks the
            return                 │  assertion
        }
        time.Sleep(waitTime)   ←──┐  Sleeps
    }                             │  before retry
    t.Fail()   ←──┐  Fails eventually after
}              │  a number of retries
```

This function checks the assertion provided and fails after a certain number of retries. We also use `time.Sleep`, but we could use a shorter sleep with this code.

For example, let's go back to `TestGetBestFoo`:

```
assert(t, func() bool {
    return len(mock.Get()) == 2
}, 30, time.Millisecond)
```

Instead of sleeping for 10 milliseconds, we sleep each millisecond and configure a maximum number of retries. Such an approach reduces the execution time if the test succeeds because we reduce the waiting interval. Therefore, implementing a retry strategy is a better approach than using passive sleeps.

NOTE Some testing libraries, such as `testify`, offer retry features. For example, in `testify`, we can use the `Eventually` function, which implements assertions that should eventually succeed and other features such as configuring the error message.

Another strategy is to use channels to synchronize the goroutine publishing the `Foo` structs and the testing goroutine. For example, in the mock implementation, instead of copying the slice received into a field, we can send this value to a channel:

```go
type publisherMock struct {
    ch chan []Foo
}

func (p *publisherMock) Publish(got []Foo) {
    p.ch <- got      ⟵⎤ Sends the
}                        ⎦ arguments received

func TestGetBestFoo(t *testing.T) {
    mock := publisherMock{
        ch: make(chan []Foo),
    }
    defer close(mock.ch)

    h := Handler{
        publisher: &mock,
        n:         2,
    }
    foo := h.getBestFoo(42)
    // Check foo
                                          ⎤ Compares these
    if v := len(<-mock.ch); v != 2 {  ⟵⎦ arguments
        t.Fatalf("expected 2, got %d", v)
    }
}
```

The publisher sends the received argument to a channel. Meanwhile, the testing goroutine sets up the mock and creates the assertion based on the received value. We can also implement a timeout strategy to make sure we don't wait forever for `mock.ch` if something goes wrong. For example, we can use `select` with a `time.After` case.

Which option should we favor: retry or synchronization? Indeed, synchronization reduces waiting time to the bare minimum and makes a test fully deterministic if well designed.

If we can't apply synchronization, we should perhaps reconsider our design since we may have a problem. If synchronization is truly impossible, we should use the retry option, which is a better choice than using passive sleeps to eradicate non-determinism in tests.

Let's continue our discussion of how to prevent flakiness in testing, this time when using the time API.

11.6 *#87: Not dealing with the time API efficiently*

Some functions have to rely on the time API: for example, to retrieve the current time. In such a case, it can be pretty easy to write brittle unit tests that may fail at some point. In this section, we go through a concrete example and discuss the options. The goal is not to cover every use case and technique but rather to give directions about writing more robust tests of functions using the time API.

Let's say an application receives events that we want to store in an in-memory cache. We will implement a `Cache` struct to hold the most recent events. This struct will expose three methods that do the following:

- Append events
- Get all the events
- Trim the events for a given duration (we will focus on this method)

Each of these methods needs to access the current time. Let's write a first implementation of the third method using `time.Now()` (we will assume that all the events are sorted by time):

```go
type Cache struct {
    mu     sync.RWMutex
    events []Event
}

type Event struct {
    Timestamp time.Time
    Data string
}

func (c *Cache) TrimOlderThan(since time.Duration) {
    c.mu.RLock()
    defer c.mu.RUnlock()

    t := time.Now().Add(-since)        // Subtracts the given duration
                                       // from the current time
    for i := 0; i < len(c.events); i++ {
        if c.events[i].Timestamp.After(t) {
            c.events = c.events[i:]    // Trims
            return                     // the events
        }
    }
}
```

We compute a `t` variable that is the current time minus the provided duration. Then, because the events are sorted by time, we update the internal `events` slice as soon as we reach an event whose time is after `t`.

How can we test this method? We could rely on the current time using `time.Now` to create the events:

```go
func TestCache_TrimOlderThan(t *testing.T) {    // Creates events
    events := []Event{                          // using time.Now()
        {Timestamp: time.Now().Add(-20 * time.Millisecond)},
```

```
            {Timestamp: time.Now().Add(-10 * time.Millisecond)},
            {Timestamp: time.Now().Add(10 * time.Millisecond)},
    }
    cache := &Cache{}                                    Adds these events
    cache.Add(events)                              ◁──┘  to the cache
    cache.TrimOlderThan(15 * time.Millisecond)     ◁──┐ Trims the events since
    got := cache.GetAll()            ◁──┐              │ 15 milliseconds ago
    expected := 2                       │  Retrieves all
    if len(got) != expected {           │  the events
        t.Fatalf("expected %d, got %d", expected, len(got))
    }
}
```

We add a slice of events to the cache using `time.Now()` and add or subtract some small durations. Then we trim these events for 15 milliseconds, and we perform the assertion.

Such an approach has one main drawback: if the machine executing the test is suddenly busy, we may trim fewer events than expected. We might be able to increase the duration provided to reduce the chance of having a failing test, but doing so isn't always possible. For example, what if the timestamp field was an unexported field generated while adding an event? In this case, it wouldn't be possible to pass a specific timestamp, and one might end up adding sleeps in the unit test.

The problem is related to the implementation of `TrimOlderThan`. Because it calls `time.Now()`, it's harder to implement robust unit tests. Let's discuss two approaches to make our test less brittle.

The first approach is to make the way to retrieve the current time a dependency of the `Cache` struct. In production, we would inject the *real* implementation, whereas in unit tests, we would pass a stub, for example.

There are various techniques to handle this dependency, such as an interface or a function type. In our case, because we only rely on a single method (`time.Now()`), we can define a function type:

```
type now func() time.Time

type Cache struct {
    mu     sync.RWMutex
    events []Event
    now    now
}
```

The `now` type is a function that returns a `time.Time`. In the factory function, we can pass the actual `time.Now` function this way:

```
func NewCache() *Cache {
    return &Cache{
        events: make([]Event, 0),
        now:    time.Now,
    }
}
```

Because the now dependency remains unexported, it isn't accessible by external clients. Furthermore, in our unit test, we can create a `Cache` struct by injecting a *fake* implementation of `func() time.Time` based on a predefined time:

```
func TestCache_TrimOlderThan(t *testing.T) {
    events := []Event{                                           ⬅─┐ Creates events
        {Timestamp: parseTime(t, "2020-01-01T12:00:00.04Z")},    │ based on specific
        {Timestamp: parseTime(t, "2020-01-01T12:00:00.05Z")},    │ timestamps
        {Timestamp: parseTime(t, "2020-01-01T12:00:00.06Z")},    │
    }
    cache := &Cache{now: func() time.Time {              ⬅─┐ Injects a static function
        return parseTime(t, "2020-01-01T12:00:00.06Z")   │ to fix the time
    }}
    cache.Add(events)
    cache.TrimOlderThan(15 * time.Millisecond)
    // ...
}

func parseTime(t *testing.T, timestamp string) time.Time {
    // ...
}
```

While creating a new `Cache` struct, we inject the now dependency based on a given time. Thanks to this approach, the test is robust. Even in the worst conditions, the outcome of this test is deterministic.

> ### Using a global variable
> Instead of using a field, we can retrieve the time via a global variable:
>
> ```
> var now = time.Now      ⬅─┐ Defines a now
>                            │ global variable
> ```
>
> In general, we should try to avoid having such a mutable shared state. In our case, it would lead to at least one concrete issue: tests would no longer be isolated because they would all depend on a shared variable. Therefore, the tests couldn't be run in parallel, for example. If possible, we should handle these cases as part of struct dependencies, fostering testing isolation.

This solution is also extensible. For example, what if the function calls `time.After`? We can either add another `after` dependency or create one interface grouping the two methods: `Now` and `After`. However, this approach has one main drawback: the now dependency isn't available if we, for example, create a unit test from an external package (we explore this in mistake #90, "Not exploring all the Go testing features").

In that case, we can use another technique. Instead of handling the time as an unexported dependency, we can ask clients to provide the current time:

```
func (c *Cache) TrimOlderThan(now time.Time, since time.Duration) {
    // ...
}
```

To go even further, we can *merge* the two function arguments in a single `time.Time` that represents a specific point in time until which we want to trim the events:

```
func (c *Cache) TrimOlderThan(t time.Time) {
    // ...
}
```

It is up to the caller to calculate this point in time:

```
cache.TrimOlderThan(time.Now().Add(time.Second))
```

And in the test, we also have to pass the corresponding time:

```
func TestCache_TrimOlderThan(t *testing.T) {
    // ...
    cache.TrimOlderThan(parseTime(t, "2020-01-01T12:00:00.06Z").
        Add(-15 * time.Millisecond))
    // ...
}
```

This approach is the simplest because it doesn't require creating another type and a stub.

In general, we should be cautious about testing code that uses the `time` API. It can be an open door for flaky tests. In this section, we have seen two ways to deal with it. We can keep the `time` interactions as part of a dependency that we can fake in unit tests by using our own implementations or relying on external libraries; or we can rework our API and ask clients to provide us with the information we need, such as the current time (this technique is simpler but more limited).

Let's now discuss two helpful Go packages related to testing: `httptest` and `iotest`.

11.7 #88: Not using testing utility packages

The standard library provides utility packages for testing. A common mistake is being unaware of these packages and trying to reinvent the wheel or rely on other solutions that aren't as handy. This section examines two of these packages: one to help us when using HTTP and another to use when doing I/O and using readers and writers.

11.7.1 The httptest package

The `httptest` package (https://pkg.go.dev/net/http/httptest) provides utilities for HTTP testing for both clients and servers. Let's look at these two use cases.

First, let's see how `httptest` can help us while writing an HTTP server. We will implement a handler that performs some basic actions: writing a header and body, and returning a specific status code. For the sake of clarity, we will omit error handling:

```
func Handler(w http.ResponseWriter, r *http.Request) {
    w.Header().Add("X-API-VERSION", "1.0")
    b, _ := io.ReadAll(r.Body)
    _, _ = w.Write(append([]byte("hello "), b...))    ◁─┐ Concatenates hello
    w.WriteHeader(http.StatusCreated)                     with the request body
}
```

An HTTP handler accepts two arguments: the request and a way to write the response. The `httptest` package provides utilities for both. For the request, we can use `httptest.NewRequest` to build an `*http.Request` using an HTTP method, a URL, and a body. For the response, we can use `httptest.NewRecorder` to record the mutations made within the handler. Let's write a unit test of this handler:

```
func TestHandler(t *testing.T) {
    req := httptest.NewRequest(http.MethodGet, "http://localhost",   // Builds the request
        strings.NewReader("foo"))
    w := httptest.NewRecorder()   // Creates the response recorder
    Handler(w, req)   // Calls the handler

    if got := w.Result().Header.Get("X-API-VERSION"); got != "1.0" {   // Verifies the HTTP header
        t.Errorf("api version: expected 1.0, got %s", got)
    }

    body, _ := io.ReadAll(wordy)   // Verifies the HTTP body
    if got := string(body); got != "hello foo" {
        t.Errorf("body: expected hello foo, got %s", got)
    }

    if http.StatusOK != w.Result().StatusCode {   // Verifies the HTTP status code
        t.FailNow()
    }
}
```

Testing a handler using `httptest` doesn't test the transport (the HTTP part). The focus of the test is calling the handler directly with a request and a way to record the response. Then, using the response recorder, we write the assertions to verify the HTTP header, body, and status code.

Let's look at the other side of the coin: testing an HTTP client. We will write a client in charge to query an HTTP endpoint that calculates how long it takes to drive from one coordinate to another. The client looks like this:

```
func (c DurationClient) GetDuration(url string,
    lat1, lng1, lat2, lng2 float64) (
    time.Duration, error) {
    resp, err := c.client.Post(
        url, "application/json",
        buildRequestBody(lat1, lng1, lat2, lng2),
    )
    if err != nil {
        return 0, err
    }

    return parseResponseBody(resp.Body)
}
```

This code performs an HTTP POST request to the provided URL and returns the parsed response (let's say, some JSON).

What if we want to test this client? One option is to use Docker and spin up a mock server to return some preregistered responses. However, this approach makes the test slow to execute. The other option is to use `httptest.NewServer` to create a local HTTP server based on a handler that we will provide. Once the server is up and running, we can pass its URL to `GetDuration`:

```go
func TestDurationClientGet(t *testing.T) {
    srv := httptest.NewServer(                    // Starts the
        http.HandlerFunc(                         // HTTP server
            func(w http.ResponseWriter, r *http.Request) {
                _, _ = w.Write([]byte(`{"duration": 314}`))   // Registers the
            },                                                 // handler to serve
        ),                                                     // the response
    )
    defer srv.Close()                             // Shuts down
                                                  // the server

    client := NewDurationClient()
    duration, err :=
        client.GetDuration(srv.URL, 51.551261, -0.1221146, 51.57, -0.13)   // Provides the
    if err != nil {                                                        // server URL
        t.Fatal(err)
    }
                                                  // Verifies the
    if duration != 314*time.Second {              // response
        t.Errorf("expected 314 seconds, got %v", duration)
    }
}
```

In this test, we create a server with a static handler returning 314 seconds. We could also make assertions based on the request sent. Furthermore, when we call `Get-Duration`, we provide the URL of the server that's started. Compared to testing a handler, this test performs an actual HTTP call, but it executes in only a few milliseconds.

We can also start a new server using TLS with `httptest.NewTLSServer` and create an unstarted server with `httptest.NewUnstartedServer` so that we can start it lazily.

Let's remember how helpful `httptest` is when working in the context of HTTP applications. Whether we're writing a server or a client, `httptest` can help us create efficient tests.

11.7.2 The iotest package

The `iotest` package (https://pkg.go.dev/testing/iotest) implements utilities for testing readers and writers. It's a convenient package that Go developers too often forget.

When implementing a custom `io.Reader`, we should remember to test it using `iotest.TestReader`. This utility function tests that a reader behaves correctly: it accurately returns the number of bytes read, fills the provided slice, and so on. It also tests different behaviors if the provided reader implements interfaces such as `io.ReaderAt`.

Let's assume we have a custom `LowerCaseReader` that streams lowercase letters from a given input `io.Reader`. Here's how to test that this reader doesn't misbehave:

```go
func TestLowerCaseReader(t *testing.T) {
    err := iotest.TestReader(                              // Provides an
        &LowerCaseReader{reader: strings.NewReader("aBcDeFgHiJ")},   // io.Reader
```

```
        []byte("acegi"),    ←—| Expectation
    )
    if err != nil {
        t.Fatal(err)
    }
}
```

We call `iotest.TestReader` by providing the custom `LowerCaseReader` and an expectation: the lowercase letters `acegi`.

Another use case for the `iotest` package is to make sure an application using readers and writers is tolerant to errors:

- `iotest.ErrReader` creates an `io.Reader` that returns a provided error.
- `iotest.HalfReader` creates an `io.Reader` that reads only half as many bytes as requested from an `io.Reader`.
- `iotest.OneByteReader` creates an `io.Reader` that reads a single byte for each non-empty read from an `io.Reader`.
- `iotest.TimeoutReader` creates an `io.Reader` that returns an error on the second read with no data. Subsequent calls will succeed.
- `iotest.TruncateWriter` creates an `io.Writer` that writes to an `io.Writer` but stops silently after *n* bytes.

For example, let's assume we implement the following function that starts by reading all the bytes from a reader:

```
func foo(r io.Reader) error {
    b, err := io.ReadAll(r)
    if err != nil {
        return err
    }

    // ...
}
```

We want to make sure our function is resilient if, for example, the provided reader fails during a read (such as to simulate a network error):

```
func TestFoo(t *testing.T) {
    err := foo(iotest.TimeoutReader(          ←—⌐ Wraps the provided io.Reader
        strings.NewReader(randomString(1024)),   │ using io.TimeoutReader
    ))
    if err != nil {
        t.Fatal(err)
    }
}
```

We wrap an `io.Reader` using `io.TimeoutReader`. As we mentioned, the second read will fail. If we run this test to make sure our function is tolerant to error, we get a test failure. Indeed, `io.ReadAll` returns any errors it finds.

Knowing this, we can implement our custom `readAll` function that tolerates up to *n* errors:

```go
func readAll(r io.Reader, retries int) ([]byte, error) {
    b := make([]byte, 0, 512)
    for {
        if len(b) == cap(b) {
            b = append(b, 0)[:len(b)]
        }
        n, err := r.Read(b[len(b):cap(b)])
        b = b[:len(b)+n]
        if err != nil {
            if err == io.EOF {
                return b, nil
            }
            retries--
            if retries < 0 {          ◁───┐  Tolerates
                return b, err              │  retries
            }
        }
    }
}
```

This implementation is similar to io.ReadAll, but it also handles configurable retries. If we change the implementation of our initial function to use our custom readAll instead of io.ReadAll, the test will no longer fail:

```go
func foo(r io.Reader) error {
    b, err := readAll(r, 3)       ◁───┐  Indicates up to
    if err != nil {                    │  three retries
        return err
    }

    // ...
}
```

We have seen an example of how to check that a function is tolerant to errors while reading from an io.Reader. We performed the test by relying on the iotest package.

When doing I/O and working with io.Reader and io.Writer, let's remember how handy the iotest package is. As we have seen, it provides utilities to test the behavior of a custom io.Reader and test our application against errors that occur while reading or writing data.

The following section discusses some common traps that can lead to writing inaccurate benchmarks.

11.8   #89: Writing inaccurate benchmarks

In general, we should never guess about performance. When writing optimizations, so many factors may come into play that even if we have a strong opinion about the results, it's rarely a bad idea to test them. However, writing benchmarks isn't straightforward. It can be pretty simple to write inaccurate benchmarks and make wrong assumptions based on them. The goal of this section is to examine common and concrete traps leading to inaccuracy.

Before discussing these traps, let's briefly review how benchmarks work in Go. The skeleton of a benchmark is as follows:

```go
func BenchmarkFoo(b *testing.B) {
    for i := 0; i < b.N; i++ {
        foo()
    }
}
```

The function name starts with the `Benchmark` prefix. The function under test (`foo`) is called within the `for` loop. `b.N` represents a variable number of iterations. When running a benchmark, Go tries to make it match the requested benchmark time. The benchmark time is set by default to 1 second and can be changed with the `-benchtime` flag. `b.N` starts at 1; if the benchmark completes in under 1 second, `b.N` is increased, and the benchmark runs again until `b.N` roughly matches `benchtime`:

```
$ go test -bench=.
cpu: Intel(R) Core(TM) i5-7360U CPU @ 2.30GHz
BenchmarkFoo-4                73             16511228 ns/op
```

Here, the benchmark took about 1 second, and `foo` was executed 73 times, for an average execution time of 16,511,228 nanoseconds. We can change the benchmark time using `-benchtime`:

```
$ go test -bench=. -benchtime=2s
BenchmarkFoo-4               150             15832169 ns/op
```

`foo` was executed roughly twice more than during the previous benchmark.

Next, let's look at some common traps.

11.8.1 *Not resetting or pausing the timer*

In some cases, we need to perform operations before the benchmark loop. These operations may take quite a while (for example, generating a large slice of data) and may significantly impact the benchmark results:

```go
func BenchmarkFoo(b *testing.B) {
    expensiveSetup()
    for i := 0; i < b.N; i++ {
        functionUnderTest()
    }
}
```

In this case, we can use the `ResetTimer` method before entering the loop:

```go
func BenchmarkFoo(b *testing.B) {
    expensiveSetup()
    b.ResetTimer()          ◁─┐ Resets the
    for i := 0; i < b.N; i++ {  │ benchmark timer
        functionUnderTest()
    }
}
```

Calling `ResetTimer` zeroes the elapsed benchmark time and memory allocation counters since the beginning of the test. This way, an expensive setup can be discarded from the test results.

What if we have to perform an expensive setup not just once but within each loop iteration?

```
func BenchmarkFoo(b *testing.B) {
    for i := 0; i < b.N; i++ {
        expensiveSetup()
        functionUnderTest()
    }
}
```

We can't reset the timer, because that would be executed during each loop iteration. But we can stop and resume the benchmark timer, surrounding the call to `expensiveSetup`:

```
func BenchmarkFoo(b *testing.B) {
    for i := 0; i < b.N; i++ {
        b.StopTimer()          ⟵┐  Pauses the
        expensiveSetup()            benchmark timer
        b.StartTimer()    ⟵┐   Resumes the
        functionUnderTest()     benchmark timer
    }
}
```

Here, we pause the benchmark timer to perform the expensive setup and then resume the timer.

> **NOTE** There's one catch to remember about this approach: if the function under test is too fast to execute compared to the setup function, the benchmark may take too long to complete. The reason is that it would take much longer than 1 second to reach `benchtime`. Calculating the benchmark time is based solely on the execution time of `functionUnderTest`. So, if we wait a significant time in each loop iteration, the benchmark will be much slower than 1 second. If we want to keep the benchmark, one possible mitigation is to decrease `benchtime`.

We must be sure to use the timer methods to preserve the accuracy of a benchmark.

11.8.2 Making wrong assumptions about micro-benchmarks

A micro-benchmark measures a tiny computation unit, and it can be extremely easy to make wrong assumptions about it. Let's say, for example, that we aren't sure whether to use `atomic.StoreInt32` or `atomic.StoreInt64` (assuming that the values we handle will always fit in 32 bits). We want to write a benchmark to compare both functions:

```
func BenchmarkAtomicStoreInt32(b *testing.B) {
    var v int32
    for i := 0; i < b.N; i++ {
        atomic.StoreInt32(&v, 1)
```

```
    }
}

func BenchmarkAtomicStoreInt64(b *testing.B) {
    var v int64
    for i := 0; i < b.N; i++ {
        atomic.StoreInt64(&v, 1)
    }
}
```

If we run this benchmark, here's some example output:

```
cpu: Intel(R) Core(TM) i5-7360U CPU @ 2.30GHz
BenchmarkAtomicStoreInt32
BenchmarkAtomicStoreInt32-4         197107742              5.682 ns/op
BenchmarkAtomicStoreInt64
BenchmarkAtomicStoreInt64-4         213917528              5.134 ns/op
```

We could easily take this benchmark for granted and decide to use `atomic.Store-Int64` because it appears to be faster. Now, for the sake of doing a *fair* benchmark, we reverse the order and test `atomic.StoreInt64` first, followed by `atomic.StoreInt32`. Here is some example output:

```
BenchmarkAtomicStoreInt64
BenchmarkAtomicStoreInt64-4         224900722              5.434 ns/op
BenchmarkAtomicStoreInt32
BenchmarkAtomicStoreInt32-4         230253900              5.159 ns/op
```

This time, `atomic.StoreInt32` has better results. What happened?

In the case of micro-benchmarks, many factors can impact the results, such as machine activity while running the benchmarks, power management, thermal scaling, and better cache alignment of a sequence of instructions. We must remember that many factors, even outside the scope of our Go project, can impact the results.

> **NOTE** We should make sure the machine executing the benchmark is idle. However, external processes may run in the background, which may affect benchmark results. For that reason, tools such as `perflock` can limit how much CPU a benchmark can consume. For example, we can run a benchmark with 70% of the total available CPU, giving 30% to the OS and other processes and reducing the impact of the machine activity factor on the results.

One option is to increase the benchmark time using the -benchtime option. Similar to the law of large numbers in probability theory, if we run a benchmark a large number of times, it should tend to approach its expected value (assuming we omit the benefits of instructions caching and similar mechanics).

Another option is to use external tools on top of the classic benchmark tooling. For instance, the `benchstat` tool, which is part of the `golang.org/x` repository, allows us to compute and compare statistics about benchmark executions.

Let's run the benchmark 10 times using the -count option and pipe the output to a specific file:

```
$ go test -bench=. -count=10 | tee stats.txt
cpu: Intel(R) Core(TM) i5-7360U CPU @ 2.30GHz
BenchmarkAtomicStoreInt32-4        234935682              5.124 ns/op
BenchmarkAtomicStoreInt32-4        235307204              5.112 ns/op
// ...
BenchmarkAtomicStoreInt64-4        235548591              5.107 ns/op
BenchmarkAtomicStoreInt64-4        235210292              5.090 ns/op
// ...
```

We can then run `benchstat` on this file:

```
$ benchstat stats.txt
name                time/op
AtomicStoreInt32-4  5.10ns ± 1%
AtomicStoreInt64-4  5.10ns ± 1%
```

The results are the same: both functions take on average 5.10 nanoseconds to complete. We also see the percent variation between the executions of a given benchmark: ± 1%. This metric tells us that both benchmarks are stable, giving us more confidence in the computed average results. Therefore, instead of concluding that `atomic.StoreInt32` is faster or slower, we can conclude that its execution time is similar to that of `atomic .StoreInt64` for the usage we tested (in a specific Go version on a particular machine).

In general, we should be cautious about micro-benchmarks. Many factors can significantly impact the results and potentially lead to wrong assumptions. Increasing the benchmark time or repeating the benchmark executions and computing stats with tools such as `benchstat` can be an efficient way to limit external factors and get more accurate results, leading to better conclusions.

Let's also highlight that we should be careful about using the results of a micro-benchmark executed on a given machine if another system ends up running the application. The production system may act quite differently from the one on which we ran the micro-benchmark.

11.8.3 *Not being careful about compiler optimizations*

Another common mistake related to writing benchmarks is being fooled by compiler optimizations, which can also lead to wrong benchmark assumptions. In this section, we look at Go issue 14813 (https://github.com/golang/go/issues/14813, also discussed by Go project member Dave Cheney) with a population count function (a function that counts the number of bits set to 1):

```
const m1 = 0x5555555555555555
const m2 = 0x3333333333333333
const m4 = 0x0f0f0f0f0f0f0f0f
const h01 = 0x0101010101010101

func popcnt(x uint64) uint64 {
    x -= (x >> 1) & m1
    x = (x & m2) + ((x >> 2) & m2)
    x = (x + (x >> 4)) & m4
    return (x * h01) >> 56
}
```

This function takes and returns a `uint64`. To benchmark this function, we can write the following:

```
func BenchmarkPopcnt1(b *testing.B) {
    for i := 0; i < b.N; i++ {
        popcnt(uint64(i))
    }
}
```

However, if we execute this benchmark, we get a surprisingly low result:

```
cpu: Intel(R) Core(TM) i5-7360U CPU @ 2.30GHz
BenchmarkPopcnt1-4        1000000000                   0.2858 ns/op
```

A duration of 0.28 nanoseconds is roughly one clock cycle, so this number is unreasonably low. The problem is that the developer wasn't careful enough about compiler optimizations. In this case, the function under test is simple enough to be a candidate for *inlining*: an optimization that replaces a function call with the body of the called function and lets us prevent a function call, which has a small footprint. Once the function is inlined, the compiler notices that the call has no side effects and replaces it with the following benchmark:

```
func BenchmarkPopcnt1(b *testing.B) {
    for i := 0; i < b.N; i++ {
        // Empty
    }
}
```

The benchmark is now empty—which is why we got a result close to one clock cycle. To prevent this from happening, a best practice is to follow this pattern:

1 During each loop iteration, assign the result to a local variable (local in the context of the benchmark function).
2 Assign the latest result to a global variable.

In our case, we write the following benchmark:

```
var global uint64                              ◁──┐ Defines a global
                                                   │ variable
func BenchmarkPopcnt2(b *testing.B) {
    var v uint64                               ◁──┤ Defines a local variable
    for i := 0; i < b.N; i++ {
        v = popcnt(uint64(i))                  ◁──┐ Assigns the result
    }                                              │ to the local variable
    global = v       ◁──┐ Assigns the result
}                       │ to the global variable
```

`global` is a global variable, whereas `v` is a local variable whose scope is the benchmark function. During each loop iteration, we assign the result of `popcnt` to the local variable. Then we assign the latest result to the global variable.

> **NOTE** Why not assign the result of the `popcnt` call directly to `global` to simplify the test? Writing to a global variable is slower than writing to a local

variable (we discuss these concepts in mistake #95, "Not understanding stack vs. heap"). Therefore, we should write each result to a local variable to limit the footprint during each loop iteration.

If we run these two benchmarks, we now get a significant difference in the results:

```
cpu: Intel(R) Core(TM) i5-7360U CPU @ 2.30GHz
BenchmarkPopcnt1-4      1000000000          0.2858 ns/op
BenchmarkPopcnt2-4      606402058           1.993 ns/op
```

BenchmarkPopcnt2 is the accurate version of the benchmark. It guarantees that we avoid the inlining optimizations, which can artificially lower the execution time or even remove the call to the function under test. Relying on the results of Benchmark-Popcnt1 could have led to wrong assumptions.

Let's remember the pattern to avoid compiler optimizations fooling benchmark results: assign the result of the function under test to a local variable, and then assign the latest result to a global variable. This best practice also prevents us from making incorrect assumptions.

11.8.4 *Being fooled by the observer effect*

In physics, the observer effect is the disturbance of an observed system by the act of observation. This effect can also be seen in benchmarks and can lead to wrong assumptions about results. Let's look at a concrete example and then try to mitigate it.

We want to implement a function receiving a matrix of int64 elements. This matrix has a fixed number of 512 columns, and we want to compute the total sum of the first eight columns, as shown in figure 11.2.

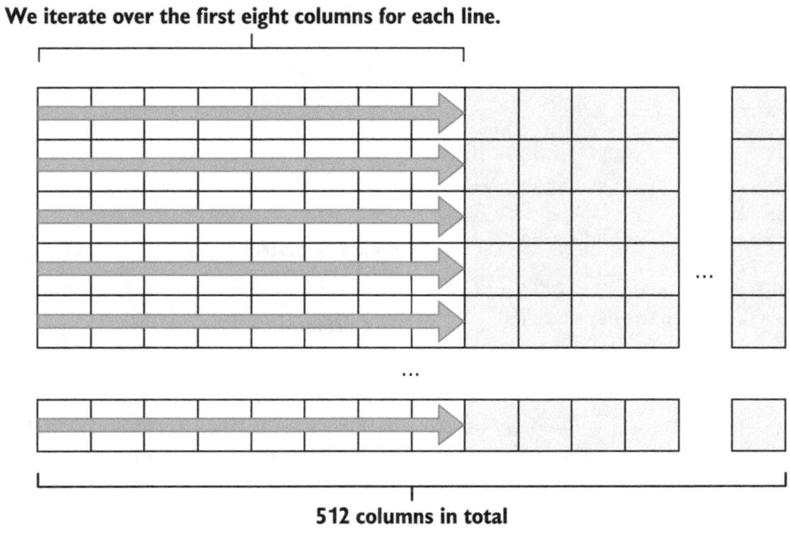

We iterate over the first eight columns for each line.

512 columns in total

Figure 11.2 Computing the sum of the first eight columns

For the sake of optimizations, we also want to determine whether varying the number of columns has an impact, so we also implement a second function with 513 columns. The implementation is the following:

```go
func calculateSum512(s [][512]int64) int64 {
    var sum int64
    for i := 0; i < len(s); i++ {        Iterates over
        for j := 0; j < 8; j++ {         each row
            sum += s[i][j]               Iterates over the
        }                                first eight columns
    }
    return sum                           Increments sum
}

func calculateSum513(s [][513]int64) int64 {
    // Same implementation as calculateSum512
}
```

We iterate over each row and then over the first eight columns, and we increment a sum variable that we return. The implementation in `calculateSum513` remains the same.

We want to benchmark these functions to decide which one is the most performant given a fixed number of rows:

```go
const rows = 1000

var res int64

func BenchmarkCalculateSum512(b *testing.B) {
    var sum int64
    s := createMatrix512(rows)        Creates a matrix
    b.ResetTimer()                    of 512 columns
    for i := 0; i < b.N; i++ {
        sum = calculateSum512(s)      Calculates
    }                                 the sum
    res = sum
}

func BenchmarkCalculateSum513(b *testing.B) {
    var sum int64
    s := createMatrix513(rows)        Creates a matrix
    b.ResetTimer()                    of 513 columns
    for i := 0; i < b.N; i++ {
        sum = calculateSum513(s)      Calculates
    }                                 the sum
    res = sum
}
```

We want to create the matrix only once, to limit the footprint on the results. Therefore, we call `createMatrix512` and `createMatrix513` outside of the loop. We may expect the results to be similar as again we only want to iterate on the first eight columns, but this isn't the case (on my machine):

```
cpu: Intel(R) Core(TM) i5-7360U CPU @ 2.30GHz
BenchmarkCalculateSum512-4          81854                 15073 ns/op
BenchmarkCalculateSum513-4         161479                  7358 ns/op
```

The second benchmark with 513 columns is about 50% faster. Again, because we iterate only over the first eight columns, this result is quite surprising.

To understand this difference, we need to understand the basics of CPU caches. In a nutshell, a CPU is composed of different caches (usually L1, L2, and L3). These caches reduce the average cost of accessing data from the main memory. In some conditions, the CPU can fetch data from the main memory and copy it to L1. In this case, the CPU tries to fetch into L1 the matrix's subset that `calculateSum` is interested in (the first eight columns of each row). However, the matrix fits in memory in one case (513 columns) but not in the other case (512 columns).

> **NOTE**   It isn't in the scope of this chapter to explain why, but we look at this problem in mistake #91, "Not understanding CPU caches."

Coming back to the benchmark, the main issue is that we keep reusing the same matrix in both cases. Because the function is repeated thousands of times, we don't measure the function's execution when it receives a plain new matrix. Instead, we measure a function that gets a matrix that already has a subset of the cells present in the cache. Therefore, because `calculateSum513` leads to fewer cache misses, it has a better execution time.

This is an example of the observer effect. Because we keep observing a repeatedly called CPU-bound function, CPU caching may come into play and significantly affect the results. In this example, to prevent this effect, we should create a matrix during each test instead of reusing one:

```
func BenchmarkCalculateSum512(b *testing.B) {
    var sum int64
    for i := 0; i < b.N; i++ {
        b.StopTimer()
        s := createMatrix512(rows)      ◁──┐ Creates a new matrix during
        b.StartTimer()                      │ each loop iteration
        sum = calculateSum512(s)
    }
    res = sum
}
```

A new matrix is now created during each loop iteration. If we run the benchmark again (and adjust `benchtime`—otherwise, it takes too long to execute), the results are closer to each other:

```
cpu: Intel(R) Core(TM) i5-7360U CPU @ 2.30GHz
BenchmarkCalculateSum512-4           1116                 33547 ns/op
BenchmarkCalculateSum513-4            998                 35507 ns/op
```

Instead of making the incorrect assumption that `calculateSum513` is faster, we see that both benchmarks lead to similar results when receiving a new matrix.

As we have seen in this section, because we were reusing the same matrix, CPU caches significantly impacted the results. To prevent this, we had to create a new matrix during each loop iteration. In general, we should remember that observing a function under test may lead to significant differences in results, especially in the context of micro-benchmarks of CPU-bound functions where low-level optimizations matter. Forcing a benchmark to re-create data during each iteration can be a good way to prevent this effect.

In the last section of this chapter, let's see some common tips regarding testing in Go.

11.9   *#90: Not exploring all the Go testing features*

When it comes to writing tests, developers should know about Go's specific testing features and options. Otherwise, the testing process can be less accurate and even less efficient. This section discusses topics that can make us more comfortable while writing Go tests.

11.9.1 *Code coverage*

During the development process, it can be handy to see visually which parts of our code are covered by tests. We can access this information using the -coverprofile flag:

```
$ go test -coverprofile=coverage.out ./...
```

This command creates a coverage.out file that we can then open using go tool cover:

```
$ go tool cover -html=coverage.out
```

This command opens the web browser and shows the coverage for each line of code.

By default, the code coverage is analyzed only for the current package being tested. For example, suppose we have the following structure:

```
/myapp
  |_ foo
    |_ foo.go
    |_ foo_test.go
  |_ bar
    |_ bar.go
    |_ bar_test.go
```

If some portion of foo.go is only tested in bar_test.go, by default, it won't be shown in the coverage report. To include it, we have to be in the myapp folder and use the -coverpkg flag:

```
go test -coverpkg=./... -coverprofile=coverage.out ./...
```

We need to remember this feature to see the current code coverage and decide which parts deserve more tests.

> **NOTE** Remain cautious when it comes to chasing code coverage. Having 100% test coverage doesn't imply a bug-free application. Properly reasoning about what our tests cover is more important than any static threshold.

11.9.2 Testing from a different package

When writing unit tests, one approach is to focus on behaviors instead of internals. Suppose we expose an API to clients. We may want our tests to focus on what's visible from the outside, not the implementation details. This way, if the implementation changes (for example, if we refactor one function into two), the tests will remain the same. They can also be easier to understand because they show how our API is used. If we want to enforce this practice, we can do so using a different package.

In Go, all the files in a folder should belong to the same package, with only one exception: a test file can belong to a _test package. For example, suppose the following counter.go source file belongs to the counter package:

```
package counter

import "sync/atomic"

var count uint64

func Inc() uint64 {
    atomic.AddUint64(&count, 1)
    return count
}
```

The test file can live in the same package and access internals such as the count variable. Or it can live in a counter_test package, like this counter_test.go file:

```
package counter_test

import (
    "testing"

    "myapp/counter"
)

func TestCount(t *testing.T) {
    if counter.Inc() != 1 {
        t.Errorf("expected 1")
    }
}
```

In this case, the test is implemented in an external package and cannot access internals such as the count variable. Using this practice, we can guarantee that a test won't use any unexported elements; hence, it will focus on testing the exposed behavior.

11.9.3 Utility functions

When writing tests, we can handle errors differently than we do in our production code. For example, let's say we want to test a function that takes as an argument a Customer struct. Because the creation of a Customer will be reused, we decide to create a specific createCustomer function for the sake of the tests. This function will return a possible error alongside a Customer:

```
func TestCustomer(t *testing.T) {
    customer, err := createCustomer("foo")      ◁─┐  Creates a customer
    if err != nil {                                │  and checks for errors
        t.Fatal(err)
    }
    // ...
}

func createCustomer(someArg string) (Customer, error) {
    // Create customer
    if err != nil {
        return Customer{}, err
    }
    return customer, nil
}
```

We create a customer using the `createCustomer` utility function, and then we perform
the rest of the test. However, in the context of testing functions, we can simplify error
management by passing the `*testing.T` variable to the utility function:

```
func TestCustomer(t *testing.T) {
    customer := createCustomer(t, "foo")        ◁─┐  Calls the utility
    // ...                                          │  function and provides t
}

func createCustomer(t *testing.T, someArg string) Customer {
    // Create customer
    if err != nil {
        t.Fatal(err)          ◁─┐  Fails the test directly if we
    }                            │  can't create a customer
    return customer
}
```

Instead of returning an error, `createCustomer` fails the test directly if it can't create a
`Customer`. This makes `TestCustomer` smaller to write and easier to read.

Let's remember this practice regarding error management and testing to improve
our tests.

11.9.4 *Setup and teardown*

In some cases, we may have to prepare a testing environment. For example, in integration tests, we spin up a specific Docker container and then stop it. We can call setup
and teardown functions per test or per package. Fortunately, in Go, both are possible.

To do so per test, we can call the setup function as a preaction and the teardown
function using `defer`:

```
func TestMySQLIntegration(t *testing.T) {
    setupMySQL()
    defer teardownMySQL()
    // ...
}
```

It's also possible to register a function to be executed at the end of a test. For example,
let's assume `TestMySQLIntegration` needs to call `createConnection` to create the

database connection. If we want this function to also include the teardown part, we can use `t.Cleanup` to register a cleanup function:

```
func TestMySQLIntegration(t *testing.T) {
    // ...
    db := createConnection(t, "tcp(localhost:3306)/db")
    // ...
}

func createConnection(t *testing.T, dsn string) *sql.DB {
    db, err := sql.Open("mysql", dsn)
    if err != nil {
        t.FailNow()
    }
    t.Cleanup(          Registers a function to be
        func() {        executed at the end of the test
            _ = db.Close()
        })
    return db
}
```

At the end of the test, the closure provided to `t.Cleanup` is executed. This makes future unit tests easier to write because they won't be responsible for closing the `db` variable.

Note that we can register multiple cleanup functions. In that case, they will be executed just as if we were using `defer`: last in, first out.

To handle setup and teardown per package, we have to use the `TestMain` function. A simple implementation of `TestMain` is the following:

```
func TestMain(m *testing.M) {
    os.Exit(m.Run())
}
```

This particular function accepts a `*testing.M` argument that exposes a single `Run` method to run all the tests. Therefore, we can surround this call with setup and teardown functions:

```
func TestMain(m *testing.M) {       Sets up
    setupMySQL()                    MySQL
    code := m.Run()     Runs the tests
    teardownMySQL()                 Tears down
    os.Exit(code)                   MySQL
}
```

This code spins up MySQL once before all the tests and then tears it down.

Using these practices to add setup and teardown functions, we can configure a complex environment for our tests.

Summary

- Categorizing tests using build flags, environment variables, or short mode makes the testing process more efficient. You can create test categories using build flags or environment variables (for example, unit versus integration tests) and differentiate short- from long-running tests to decide which kinds of tests to execute.

- Enabling the -race flag is highly recommended when writing concurrent applications. Doing so allows you to catch potential data races that can lead to software bugs.

- Using the -parallel flag is an efficient way to speed up tests, especially long-running ones.

- Use the -shuffle flag to help ensure that a test suite doesn't rely on wrong assumptions that could hide bugs.

- Table-driven tests are an efficient way to group a set of similar tests to prevent code duplication and make future updates easier to handle.

- Avoid sleeps using synchronization to make a test less flaky and more robust. If synchronization isn't possible, consider a retry approach.

- Understanding how to deal with functions using the time API is another way to make a test less flaky. You can use standard techniques such as handling the time as part of a hidden dependency or asking clients to provide it.

- The httptest package is helpful for dealing with HTTP applications. It provides a set of utilities to test both clients and servers.

- The iotest package helps write io.Reader and test that an application is tolerant to errors.

- Regarding benchmarks:
  - Use time methods to preserve the accuracy of a benchmark.
  - Increasing benchtime or using tools such as benchstat can be helpful when dealing with micro-benchmarks.
  - Be careful with the results of a micro-benchmark if the system that ends up running the application is different from the one running the micro-benchmark.
  - Make sure the function under test leads to a side effect, to prevent compiler optimizations from fooling you about the benchmark results.
  - To prevent the observer effect, force a benchmark to re-create the data used by a CPU-bound function.

- Use code coverage with the -coverprofile flag to quickly see which part of the code needs more attention.

- Place unit tests in a different package to enforce writing tests that focus on an exposed behavior, not internals.

- Handling errors using the *testing.T variable instead of the classic if err != nil makes code shorter and easier to read.

- You can use setup and teardown functions to configure a complex environment, such as in the case of integration tests.

Optimizations

This chapter covers

- Delving into the concept of mechanical sympathy
- Understanding heap vs. stack and reducing allocations
- Using standard Go diagnostics tooling
- Understanding how the garbage collector works
- Running Go inside Docker and Kubernetes

Before we begin this chapter, a disclaimer: in most contexts, writing readable, clear code is better than writing code that is optimized but more complex and difficult to understand. Optimization generally comes with a price, and we advocate that you follow this famous quote from software engineer Wes Dyer:

> *Make it correct, make it clear, make it concise, make it fast, in that order.*

That doesn't mean optimizing an application for speed and efficiency is prohibited. For example, we can try to identify code paths that need to be optimized because there's a need to do so, such as making our customers happy or reducing our costs. Throughout this chapter, we discuss common optimization techniques; some are specific to Go, and some aren't. We also discuss methods to identify bottlenecks so we don't work blindly.

12.1   *#91: Not understanding CPU caches*

Mechanical sympathy is a term coined by Jackie Stewart, a three-time F1 world champion:

> *You don't have to be an engineer to be a racing driver, but you do have to have mechanical sympathy.*

In a nutshell, when we understand how a system is designed to be used, be it an F1 car, an airplane, or a computer, we can align with the design to gain optimal performance. Throughout this section, we discuss concrete examples where a mechanical sympathy for how CPU caches work can help us optimize Go applications.

12.1.1   *CPU architecture*

First, let's understand the fundamentals of CPU architecture and why CPU caches are important. We will take as an example the Intel Core i5-7300.

Modern CPUs rely on caching to speed up memory access, in most cases via three caching levels: L1, L2, and L3. On the i5-7300, here are the sizes of these caches:

- L1: 64 KB
- L2: 256 KB
- L3: 4 MB

The i5-7300 has two physical cores but four logical cores (also called *virtual cores* or *threads*). In the Intel family, dividing a physical core into multiple logical cores is called Hyper-Threading.

Figure 12.1 gives an overview of the Intel Core i5-7300 (Tn stands for *thread n*). Each physical core (core 0 and core 1) is divided into two logical cores (thread 0 and thread 1). The L1 cache is split into two sub-caches: L1D for data and L1I for instructions (each 32 KB). Caching isn't solely related to data—when a CPU executes an application, it can also cache some instructions with the same rationale: to speed up overall execution.

The closer a memory location is to a logical core, the faster accesses are (see http://mng.bz/o29v):

- L1: about 1 ns
- L2: about 4 times slower than L1
- L3: about 10 times slower than L1

The physical location of the CPU caches can also explain these differences. L1 and L2 are called *on-die*, meaning they belong to the same piece of silicon as the rest of the

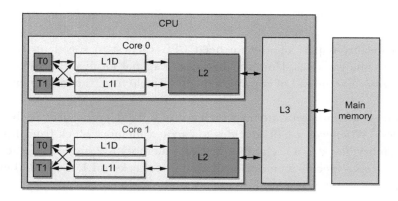

**Figure 12.1
The i5-7300 has three
levels of caches, two
physical cores, and four
logical cores.**

processor. Conversely, L3 is *off-die*, which partly explains the latency differences compared to L1 and L2.

For main memory (or RAM), average accesses are between 50 and 100 times slower
than L1. We can access up to 100 variables stored on L1 for the price of a single access
to the main memory. Therefore, as Go developers, one avenue for improvement is
making sure our applications use CPU caches.

12.1.2 Cache line

The concept of cache lines is crucial to understand. But before presenting what they
are, let's understand why we need them.

When a specific memory location is accessed (for example, by reading a variable),
one of the following is likely to happen in the near future:

- The same location will be referenced again.
- Nearby memory locations will be referenced.

The former refers to temporal locality, and the latter refers to spatial locality. Both are
part of a principle called *locality of reference.*

For example, let's look at the following function that computes the sum of an
`int64` slice:

```
func sum(s []int64) int64 {
    var total int64
    length := len(s)
    for i := 0; i < length; i++ {
        total += s[i]
    }
    return total
}
```

In this example, temporal locality applies to multiple variables: `i`, `length`, and `total`.
Throughout the iteration, we keep accessing these variables. Spatial locality applies to
code instructions and the slice `s`. Because a slice is backed by an array allocated

contiguously in memory, in this case, accessing s[0] means also accessing s[1], s[2], and so on.

Temporal locality is part of why we need CPU caches: to speed up repeated accesses to the same variables. However, because of spatial locality, the CPU copies what we call a *cache line* instead of copying a single variable from the main memory to a cache.

A cache line is a contiguous memory segment of a fixed size, usually 64 bytes (8 int64 variables). Whenever a CPU decides to cache a memory block from RAM, it copies the memory block to a cache line. Because memory is a hierarchy, when the CPU wants to access a specific memory location, it first checks in L1, then L2, then L3, and finally, if the location is not in those caches, in the main memory.

Let's illustrate fetching a memory block with a concrete example. We call the sum function with a slice of 16 int64 elements for the first time. When sum accesses s[0], this memory address isn't in the cache yet. If the CPU decides to cache this variable (we also discuss this decision later in the chapter), it copies the whole memory block; see figure 12.2.

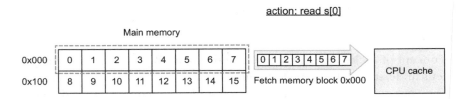

Figure 12.2   Accessing s[0] makes the CPU copy the 0x000 memory block.

At first, accessing s[0] results in a cache miss because the address isn't in the cache. This kind of miss is called a *compulsory miss*. However, if the CPU fetches the 0x000 memory block, accessing elements from 1 to 7 results in a cache hit. The same logic applies when sum accesses s[8] (see figure 12.3).

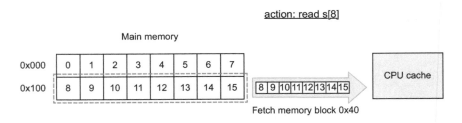

Figure 12.3   Accessing s[8] makes the CPU copy the 0x100 memory block.

Again, accessing s[8] results in a compulsory miss. But if the 0x100 memory block is copied into a cache line, it will also speed up accesses for elements 9 to 15. In the end, iterating over the 16 elements results in 2 compulsory cache misses and 14 cache hits.

CPU caching strategies

You may wonder about the exact strategy when a CPU copies a memory block. For example, will it copy a block to all the levels? Only to L1? In this case, what about L2 and L3?

We have to know that different strategies exist. Sometimes caches are inclusive (for example, L2 data is also present in L3), and sometimes caches are exclusive (for example, L3 is called a *victim cache* because it contains only data evicted from L2).

In general, these strategies are hidden by CPU vendors and not necessarily useful to know. So, we won't delve deeper into these questions.

Let's look at a concrete example to illustrate how fast CPU caches are. We will implement two functions that compute a total while iterating over a slice of int64 elements. In one case we will iterate over every two elements, and in the other case over every eight elements:

```go
func sum2(s []int64) int64 {
    var total int64
    for i := 0; i < len(s); i+=2 {      // Iterates over every
        total += s[i]                    // two elements
    }
    return total
}

func sum8(s []int64) int64 {
    var total int64
    for i := 0; i < len(s); i += 8 {    // Iterates over every
        total += s[i]                    // eight elements
    }
    return total
}
```

Both functions are the same except for the iteration. If we benchmark these two functions, our gut feeling may be that the second version will be about four times faster because we have to increment over four times fewer elements. However, running a benchmark shows that sum8 is only about 10% faster on my machine: still faster, but only 10%.

The reason is related to cache lines. We saw that a cache line is usually 64 bytes, containing up to eight int64 variables. Here, the running time of these loops is dominated by memory accesses, not increment instruction. Three out of four accesses result in a cache hit in the first case. Therefore, the execution time difference for these two functions isn't significant. This example demonstrates why the cache line matters and that we can easily be fooled by our gut feeling if we lack mechanical sympathy—in this case, for how CPUs cache data.

Let's keep discussing locality of reference and see a concrete example of using spatial locality.

12.1.3 *Slice of structs vs. struct of slices*

This section looks at an example that compares the execution time of two functions. The first takes as an argument a slice of structs and sums all the a fields:

```
type Foo struct {
    a int64
    b int64
}

func sumFoo(foos []Foo) int64 {          ◁──┐ Receives a
    var total int64                          slice of Foo
    for i := 0; i < len(foos); i++ {     ◁──┐ Iterates over each Foo
        total += foos[i].a                     and sums each a field
    }
    return total
}
```

sumFoo receives a slice of Foo and increments total by reading each a field.

The second function also computes a sum. But this time, the argument is a struct containing slices:

```
type Bar struct {
    a []int64          ◁──┐ a and b are
    b []int64              now slices.
}

func sumBar(bar Bar) int64 {          ◁──┐ Receives a
    var total int64                       single struct
    for i := 0; i < len(bar.a); i++ {  ◁──┐ Iterates over each
        total += bar.a[i]     ◁──┐ Increments  element of a
    }                              the total
    return total
}
```

sumBar receives a single Bar struct that contains two slices: a and b. It iterates over each element of a to increment total.

Do we expect any difference in terms of speed for these two functions? Before running a benchmark, let's visually look at the differences in memory in figure 12.4. Both cases have the same amount of data: 16

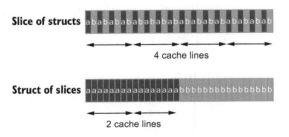

Figure 12.4 A struct of slices is more compact and therefore requires fewer cache lines to iterate over.

`Foo` elements in the slice and 16 elements in the slices of `Bar`. Each black bar represents an `int64` that is read to compute the sum, whereas each gray bar represents an `int64` that is skipped.

In the case of `sumFoo`, we receive a slice of structs containing two fields, a and b. Therefore, we have a succession of a and b in memory. Conversely, in the case of `sum-Bar`, we receive a struct containing two slices, a and b. Therefore, all the elements of a are allocated contiguously.

This difference doesn't lead to any memory compaction optimization. But the goal of both functions is to iterate over each a, and doing so requires four cache lines in one case and only two cache lines in the other.

If we benchmark these two functions, `sumBar` is faster (about 20% on my machine). The main reason is a better spatial locality that makes the CPU fetch fewer cache lines from memory.

This example demonstrates how spatial locality can have a substantial impact on performance. To optimize an application, we should organize data to get the most value out of each individual cache line.

However, is using spatial locality enough to help the CPU? We are still missing one crucial characteristic: predictability.

12.1.4 Predictability

Predictability refers to the ability of a CPU to anticipate what the application will do to speed up its execution. Let's see a concrete example where a lack of predictability negatively impacts application performance.

Again, let's look at two functions that sum a list of elements. The first iterates over a linked list and sums all the values:

```
type node struct {          ⟵──┐  Linked list
    value int64                 │  data structure
    next  *node
}

func linkedList(n *node) int64 {
    var total int64                    │  Iterates over
    for n != nil {          ⟵───────┘  each node
        total += n.value    ⟵──┐  Increments
        n = n.next             │  total
    }
    return total
}
```

This function receives a linked list, iterates over it, and increments a total.

On the other side, let's again take the `sum2` function that iterates over a slice, one element out of two:

```
func sum2(s []int64) int64 {
    var total int64                              │  Iterates over every
    for i := 0; i < len(s); i+=2 {    ⟵───────┘  two elements
```

```
        total += s[i]
    }
    return total
}
```

Let's assume that the linked list is allocated contiguously: for example, by a single function. On a 64-bit architecture, a word is 64 bits long. Figure 12.5 compares the two data structures that the functions receive (linked list or slice); the darker bars represent the int64 elements we use to increment the total.

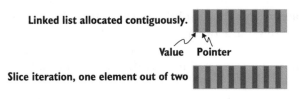

In both examples, we face similar compaction. Because a linked list is a succession of values and 64-bit pointer elements, we increment the sum using one element out of two. Meanwhile, the sum2 example reads only one element out of two.

Figure 12.5   **In memory, linked lists and slices are compacted in a similar manner.**

The two data structures have the same spatial locality, so we may expect a similar execution time for these two functions. But the function iterating on the slice is significantly faster (about 70% on my machine). What's the reason?

To understand this, we have to discuss the concept of striding. Striding relates to how CPUs work through data. There are three different types of strides (see figure 12.6):

- *Unit stride*—All the values we want to access are allocated contiguously: for example, a slice of int64 elements. This stride is predictable for a CPU and the most efficient because it requires a minimum number of cache lines to walk through the elements.

- *Constant stride*—Still predictable for the CPU: for example, a slice that iterates over every two elements. This stride requires more cache lines to walk through data, so it's less efficient than a unit stride.

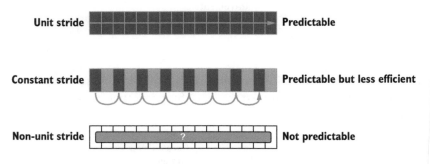

Figure 12.6   **The three types of strides**

- *Non-unit stride*—A stride the CPU can't predict: for example, a linked list or a slice of pointers. Because the CPU doesn't know whether data is allocated contiguously, it won't fetch any cache lines.

For sum2, we face a constant stride. However, for the linked list, we face a non-unit stride. Even though we know the data is allocated contiguously, the CPU doesn't know that. Therefore, it can't predict how to walk through the linked list.

Because of the different stride and similar spatial locality, iterating over a linked list is significantly slower than a slice of values. We should generally favor unit strides over constant strides because of the better spatial locality. But a non-unit stride cannot be predicted by the CPU regardless of how the data is allocated, leading to negative performance impacts.

So far, we have discussed that CPU caches are fast but significantly smaller than the main memory. Therefore, a CPU needs a strategy to fetch a memory block to a cache line. This policy is called *cache placement policy* and can significantly impact performance.

12.1.5 *Cache placement policy*

In mistake #89, "Writing inaccurate benchmarks," we discussed an example with a matrix in which we had to compute the total sum of the first eight columns. At that point, we didn't explain why changing the overall number of columns impacted the benchmark results. It might sound counterintuitive: because we need to read only the first eight columns, why does changing the total number of columns affect the execution time? Let's take a look in this section.

As a reminder, the implementation is the following:

```go
func calculateSum512(s [][512]int64) int64 {        ◁────┐  Receives a matrix
    var sum int64                                        │  of 512 columns
    for i := 0; i < len(s); i++ {
        for j := 0; j < 8; j++ {
            sum += s[i][j]
        }
    }
    return sum
}
                                                            Receives a matrix
                                                    ◁───┘  of 513 columns
func calculateSum513(s [][513]int64) int64 {
    // Same implementation as calculateSum512
}
```

We iterate over each row, summing the first eight columns each time. When these two functions are benchmarked each time with a new matrix, we don't observe any difference. However, if we keep reusing the same matrix, calculateSum513 is about 50% faster on my machine. The reason lies in CPU caches and how a memory block is copied to a cache line. Let's examine this to understand this difference.

When a CPU decides to copy a memory block and place it into the cache, it must follow a particular strategy. Assuming an L1D cache of 32 KB and a cache line of 64 bytes, if a block is placed randomly into L1D, the CPU will have to iterate over 512 cache lines in the worst case to read a variable. This kind of cache is called *fully associative*.

To improve how fast an address can be accessed from a CPU cache, designers work on different policies regarding cache placement. Let's skip the history and discuss today's most widely used option: *set-associative cache*, which relies on cache partitioning.

For the sake of clarity in the following figures, we will work with a reduced version of the problem:

- We will assume an L1D cache of 512 bytes (8 cache lines).
- The matrix is composed of 4 rows and 32 columns, and we will read only the first 8 columns.

Figure 12.7 shows how this matrix can be stored in memory. We will use the binary representation for the memory block addresses. Also, the gray blocks represent the first 8 `int64` elements we want to iterate over. The remaining blocks are skipped during the iteration.

Memory addresses

s[0][0] ... s[0][7]	0000000000000
s[0][8] ... s[0][15]	0001000000000
s[0][16] ... s[0][23]	0010000000000
s[0][24] ... s[0][31]	0011000000000
s[1][0] ... s[1][7]	0100000000000
s[1][8] ... s[1][15]	0101000000000
s[1][16] ... s[1][23]	0110000000000
s[1][24] ... s[1][31]	0111000000000
s[2][0] ... s[2][7]	1000000000000
s[2][8] ... s[2][15]	1001000000000
s[2][16] ... s[2][23]	1010000000000
s[2][24] ... s[2][31]	1011000000000
s[3][0] ... s[3][7]	1100000000000
s[3][8] ... s[3][15]	1101000000000
s[3][16] ... s[3][23]	1110000000000
s[3][24] ... s[3][31]	1111000000000

Cache

Figure 12.7 The matrix stored in memory, and an empty cache for the execution

Each memory block contains 64 bytes and hence 8 `int64` elements. The first memory block starts at 0x0000000000000, the second begins at 0001000000000 (512 in binary), and so on. We also show the cache that can hold 8 lines.

NOTE We will see in mistake #94, "Not being aware of data alignment," that a slice doesn't necessarily start at the beginning of a block.

With the set-associative cache policy, a cache is partitioned into sets. We assume the cache is two-way set associative, meaning each set contains two lines. A memory block can belong to only one set, and the placement is determined by its memory address. To understand this, we have to dissect the memory block address into three parts:

- The *block offset* is based on the block size. Here a block size is 512 bytes, and 512 equals 2^9. Therefore, the first 9 bits of the address represent the block offset (bo).

- The *set index* indicates the set to which an address belongs. Because the cache is two-way set associative and contains 8 lines, we have 8 / 2 = 4 sets. Furthermore, 4 equals 2^2, so the next two bits represent the set index (si).

- The rest of the address consists of the tag bits (tb). In figure 12.7, we represent an address using 13 bits for simplicity. To compute tb, we use 13 – bo – si. This means the two remaining bits represent the tag bits.

Let's say the function starts and tries to read s[0][0], which belongs to address 0000000000000. Because this address isn't present in the cache yet, the CPU calculates its set index and copies it to the corresponding cache set (figure 12.8).

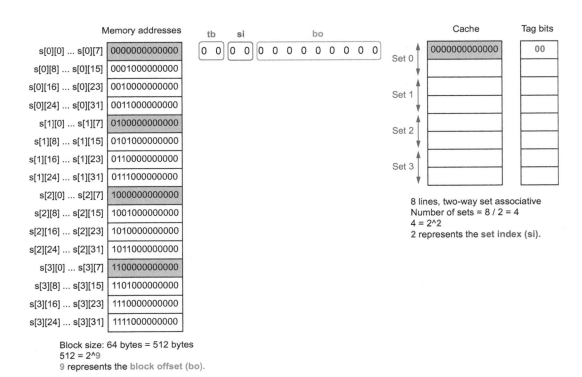

Figure 12.8   Memory address 0000000000000 is copied into set 0.

As discussed, 9 bits represent the block offset: it's the minimum common prefix for each memory block address. Then, 2 bits represent the set index. With address 0000000000000, si equals 00. Hence, this memory block is copied to set 0.

When the function reads from s[0][1] to s[0][7], the data is already in the cache. How does the CPU know about it? The CPU calculates the starting address of the memory block, computes the set index and the tag bits, and then checks whether 00 is present in set 0.

Next the function reads s[0][8], and this address isn't cached yet. So the same operation occurs to copy memory block 0100000000000 (figure 12.9).

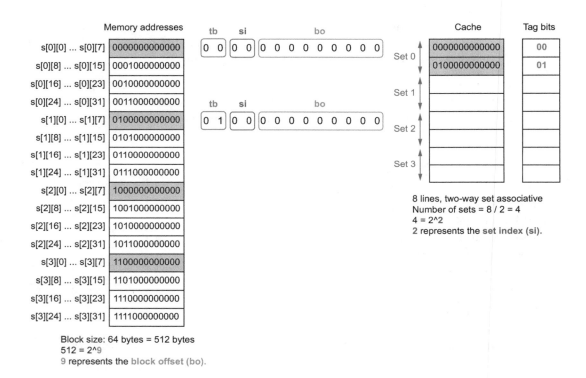

Figure 12.9   Memory address 0100000000000 is copied into set 0.

This memory has a set index equal to 00, so it also belongs to set 0. The cache line is copied to the next available line in set 0. Then, again, reading from s[1][1] to s[1][7] results in cache hits.

Now things are getting interesting. The function reads s[2][0], and this address isn't present in the cache. The same operation is performed (figure 12.10).

The set index is again equal to 00. However, set 0 is full—what does the CPU do? Copy the memory block to another set? No. The CPU replaces one of the existing cache lines to copy memory block 1000000000000.

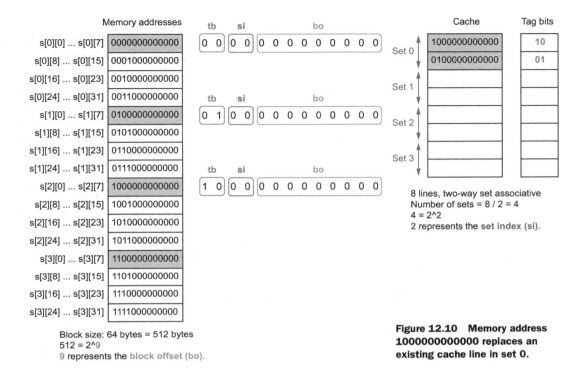

Block size: 64 bytes = 512 bytes
512 = 2^9
9 represents the block offset (bo).

Figure 12.10 Memory address 1000000000000 replaces an existing cache line in set 0.

The cache replacement policy depends on the CPU, but it's usually a pseudo-LRU policy (a real LRU [least recently used] would be too complex to handle). In this case, let's say it replaces our first cache line: 0000000000000. This situation is repeated when iterating on row 3: memory address 1100000000000 also has a set index equal to 00, resulting in replacing an existing cache line.

Now, let's say the benchmark executes the function with a slice pointing to the same matrix starting at address 0000000000000. When the function reads s[0][0], the address isn't in the cache. This block was already replaced.

Instead of using CPU caches from one execution to another, the benchmark will lead to more cache misses. This type of cache miss is called a *conflict miss*: a miss that wouldn't occur if the cache wasn't partitioned. All the variables we iterate belong to a memory block whose set index is 00. Therefore, we use only one cache set instead of having a distribution across the entire cache.

Previously we discussed the concept of striding, which we defined as how a CPU walks through our data. In this example, this stride is called a *critical stride*: it leads to accessing memory addresses with the same set index that are hence stored to the same cache set.

Let's come back to our real-world example with the two functions `calculate-Sum512` and `calculateSum513`. The benchmark was executed on a 32 KB eight-way set-associative L1D cache: 64 sets total. Because a cache line is 64 bytes, the critical stride equals 64 × 64 bytes = 4 KB. Four KB of `int64` types represent 512 elements.

Therefore, we reach a critical stride with a matrix of 512 columns, so we have a poor caching distribution. Meanwhile, if the matrix contains 513 columns, it doesn't lead to a critical stride. This is why we observed such a massive difference between the two benchmarks.

In summary, we have to be aware that modern caches are partitioned. Depending on the striding, in some cases only one set is used, which may harm application performance and lead to conflict misses. This kind of stride is called a critical stride. For performance-intensive applications, we should avoid critical strides to get the most out of CPU caches.

> **NOTE** Our example also highlights why we should take care with the results of a micro-benchmark if it's executed on a system other than production. If the production system has a different cache architecture, performance may be significantly different.

Let's continue discussing the impact of CPU caching. This time, we see concrete effects while writing concurrent code.

12.2   *#92: Writing concurrent code that leads to false sharing*

So far, we have discussed the fundamental concepts of CPU caching. We have seen that some specific caches (typically, L1 and L2) aren't shared among all the logical cores but are specific to a physical core. This specificity has some concrete impacts such as concurrency and the concept of false sharing, which can lead to a significant performance decrease. Let's look at what false sharing is via an example and then see how to prevent it.

In this example, we use two structs, `Input` and `Result`:

```
type Input struct {
    a int64
    b int64
}

type Result struct {
    sumA int64
    sumB int64
}
```

The goal is to implement a `count` function that receives a slice of `Input` and computes the following:

- The sum of all the `Input.a` fields into `Result.sumA`
- The sum of all the `Input.b` fields into `Result.sumB`

For the sake of the example, we implement a concurrent solution with one goroutine that computes `sumA` and another that computes `sumB`:

```
func count(inputs []Input) Result {
    wg := sync.WaitGroup{}
    wg.Add(2)

    result := Result{}          ◁──┐ Initializes the
                                    │ result struct
```

```
go func() {
    for i := 0; i < len(inputs); i++ {
        result.sumA += inputs[i].a        ⊲──┤ Computes sumA
    }
    wg.Done()
}()

go func() {
    for i := 0; i < len(inputs); i++ {
        result.sumB += inputs[i].b        ⊲──┤ Computes sumB
    }
    wg.Done()
}()

wg.Wait()
return result
}
```

We spin up two goroutines: one that iterates over each a field and another that iterates over each b field. This example is fine from a concurrency perspective. For instance, it doesn't lead to a data race, because each goroutine increments its own variable. But this example illustrates the false sharing concept that degrades expected performance.

Let's look at the main memory (see figure 12.11). Because sumA and sumB are allocated contiguously, in most cases (seven out of eight), both variables are allocated to the same memory block.

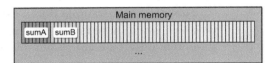

Figure 12.11 In this example, sumA and sumB are part of the same memory block.

Now, let's assume that the machine contains two cores. In most cases, we should eventually have two threads scheduled on different cores. So if the CPU decides to copy this memory block to a cache line, it is copied twice (figure 12.12).

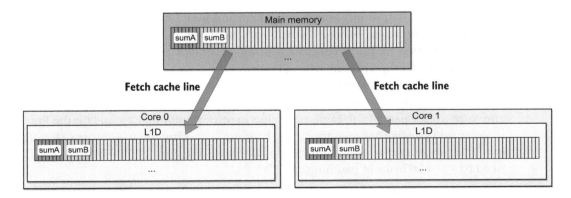

Figure 12.12 Each block is copied to a cache line on both core 0 and core 1.

Both cache lines are replicated because L1D (L1 data) is per core. Recall that in our example, each goroutine updates its own variable: sumA on one side, and sumB on the other side (figure 12.13).

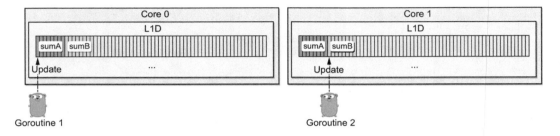

Figure 12.13   Each goroutine updates its own variable.

Because these cache lines are replicated, one of the goals of the CPU is to guarantee cache coherency. For example, if one goroutine updates sumA and another reads sumA (after some synchronization), we expect our application to get the latest value.

However, our example doesn't do exactly this. Both goroutines access their own variables, not a shared one. We might expect the CPU to know about this and understand that it isn't a conflict, but this isn't the case. When we write a variable that's in a cache, the granularity tracked by the CPU isn't the variable: it's the cache line.

When a cache line is shared across multiple cores and at least one goroutine is a writer, the entire cache line is invalidated. This happens even if the updates are logically independent (for example, sumA and sumB). This is the problem of false sharing, and it degrades performance.

> **NOTE** Internally, a CPU uses the MESI protocol to guarantee cache coherency. It tracks each cache line, marking it modified, exclusive, shared, or invalid (MESI).

One of the most important aspects to understand about memory and caching is that sharing memory across cores isn't real—it's an illusion. This understanding comes from the fact that we don't consider a machine a black box; instead, we try to have mechanical sympathy with underlying levels.

So how do we solve false sharing? There are two main solutions.

The first solution is to use the same approach we've shown but ensure that sumA and sumB aren't part of the same cache line. For example, we can update the Result struct to add *padding* between the fields. Padding is a technique to allocate extra memory. Because an int64 requires an 8-byte allocation and a cache line 64 bytes long, we need 64 − 8 = 56 bytes of padding:

```
type Result struct {
    sumA int64
```

```
_    [56]byte    ⟵┤ Padding
sumB int64
}
```

Figure 12.14 shows a possible memory allocation. Using padding, `sumA` and `sumB` will always be part of different memory blocks and hence different cache lines.

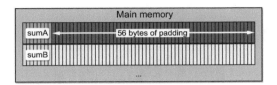

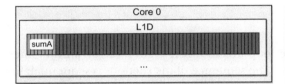
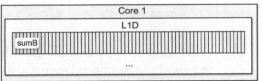

Figure 12.14   `sumA` and `sumB` are part of different memory blocks.

If we benchmark both solutions (with and without padding), we see that the padding solution is significantly faster (about 40% on my machine). This is an important improvement that results from the addition of padding between the two fields to prevent false sharing.

The second solution is to rework the structure of the algorithm. For example, instead of having both goroutines share the same struct, we can make them communicate their local result via channels. The result benchmark is roughly the same as with padding.

In summary, we must remember that sharing memory across goroutines is an illusion at the lowest memory levels. False sharing occurs when a cache line is shared across two cores when at least one goroutine is a writer. If we need to optimize an application that relies on concurrency, we should check whether false sharing applies, because this pattern is known to degrade application performance. We can prevent false sharing with either padding or communication.

The following section discusses how CPUs can execute instructions in parallel and how to leverage that capability.

12.3   *#93: Not taking into account instruction-level parallelism*

Instruction-level parallelism is another factor that can significantly impact performance. Before defining this concept, let's discuss a concrete example and how to optimize it.

We will write a function that receives an array of two `int64` elements. This function will iterate a certain number of times (a constant). During each iteration, it will do the following:

- Increment the first element of the array.
- Increment the second element of the array if the first element is even.

Here's the Go version:

```go
const n = 1_000_000

func add(s [2]int64) [2]int64 {        Iterates
    for i := 0; i < n; i++ {           n times
        s[0]++                         Increments s[0]
        if s[0]%2 == 0 {               Increments s[1]
            s[1]++                     if s[0] is even
        }
    }
    return s
}
```

The instructions executed within the loop are shown in figure 12.15 (an increment requires both a read and then a write). The sequence of instructions is sequential: first we increment `s[0]`; then, before incrementing `s[1]`, we need to read `s[0]` again.

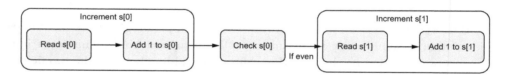

Figure 12.15   Three main steps: increment, check, increment

NOTE   This sequence of instructions doesn't match the granularity of the assembly instructions. But for clarity throughout this section, we use a simplified view.

Let's take a moment to discuss the theory behind instruction-level parallelism (ILP). A few decades ago, CPU designers stopped focusing solely on clock speed to improve CPU performance. They developed multiple optimizations, including ILP, which allows developers to parallelize the execution of a sequence of instructions. A processor that implements ILP in a single virtual core is called a *superscalar processor*. For example, figure 12.16 illustrates a CPU executing an application consisting of three instructions, `I1`, `I2`, and `I3`.

Executing a sequence of instructions requires different stages. In a nutshell, the CPU needs to decode the instructions and execute them. The execution is handled by the execution unit, which performs the various operations and calculations.

In figure 12.16, the CPU decided to execute the three instructions in parallel. Note that not all the instructions necessarily complete in a single clock cycle. For example, an instruction that reads a value already present in a register will finish in one clock cycle, but an instruction that reads an address that must be fetched from main memory may take dozens of clock cycles to complete.

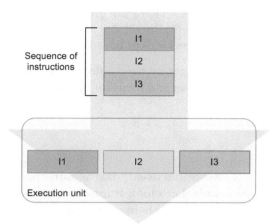

If executed sequentially, this sequence of instructions would have taken the following time (the function t(x) denotes the time the CPU takes to execute instruction x):

Figure 12.16 Despite being written sequentially, the three instructions are executed in parallel.

```
total time = t(I1) + t(I2) + t(I3)
```

Thanks to ILP, the total time is the following:

```
total time = max(t(I1), t(I2), t(I3))
```

ILP looks magic, theoretically. But it leads to a few challenges called *hazards*.

For example, what if I3 sets a variable to 42 but I2 is a conditional instruction (for example, if foo == 1)? In theory, this scenario should prevent executing I2 and I3 in parallel. This is called a *control hazard* or *branching hazard*. In practice, CPU designers solved control hazards using branch prediction.

For example, a CPU can count that the condition was true 99 of the last 100 times; therefore, it will execute both I2 and I3 in parallel. In case of a wrong prediction (I2 happens to be false), the CPU will flush its current execution pipeline, ensuring that there are no inconsistencies. This flush leads to a performance penalty of 10 to 20 clock cycles.

Other types of hazards can prevent executing instructions in parallel. As software engineers, we should be aware of that. For example, let's consider the two following instructions that update registers (temporary storage areas used to execute operations):

- I1 adds the numbers in registers A and B to C.
- I2 adds the numbers in registers C and D to D.

Because I2 depends on the outcome of I1 concerning the value of register C, the two instructions cannot be executed simultaneously. I1 must complete before I2. This is called a *data hazard*. To deal with data hazards, CPU designers have come up with a trick called *forwarding* that basically bypasses writing to a register. This technique doesn't solve the problem but rather tries to alleviate the effects.

NOTE There are also *structural hazards*, when at least two instructions in the pipeline need the same resource. As Go developers, we can't really impact these kinds of hazards, so we don't discuss them in this section.

Now that we have a decent understanding of ILP theory, let's get back to our initial problem and focus on the content of the loop:

```
s[0]++
if s[0]%2 == 0 {
    s[1]++
}
```

As we discussed, data hazards prevent instructions from being executed simultaneously. Let's look at the sequence of instructions in figure 12.17; this time we highlight the hazards between the instructions.

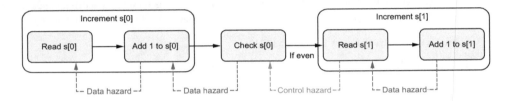

Figure 12.17   Hazard types between the instructions

This sequence contains one control hazard because of the `if` statement. However, as discussed, it's the scope of the CPU to optimize the execution and predict what branch should be taken. There are also multiple data hazards. As we discussed, data hazards prevent ILP from executing instructions in parallel. Figure 12.18 shows the sequence of instructions from an ILP standpoint: the only independent instructions are the `s[0]` check and the `s[1]` increment, so these two instruction sets can be executed in parallel thanks to branch prediction.

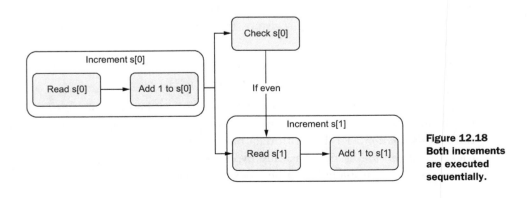

**Figure 12.18
Both increments
are executed
sequentially.**

What about the increments? Can we improve our code to minimize the number of data hazards?

Let's write another version (add2) that introduces a temporary variable:

```
func add(s [2]int64) [2]int64 {          ◁── First
    for i := 0; i < n; i++ {                   version
        s[0]++
        if s[0]%2 == 0 {
            s[1]++
        }
    }
    return s
}

func add2(s [2]int64) [2]int64 {       ◁── Second version
    for i := 0; i < n; i++ {
        v := s[0]                    ◁── Introduces a new variable
        s[0] = v + 1                     to fix the s[0] value
        if v%2 != 0 {
            s[1]++
        }
    }
    return s
}
```

In this new version, we fix the value of s[0] to a new variable, v. Previously we incremented s[0] and checked whether it was even. To replicate this behavior, because v is based on s[0], to increment s[1] we now check whether v is odd.

Figure 12.19 compares the two versions in terms of hazards. The number of steps is the same. The significant difference is regarding the data hazards: the s[0] increment step and the check v step now depend on the same instruction (read s[0] into v).

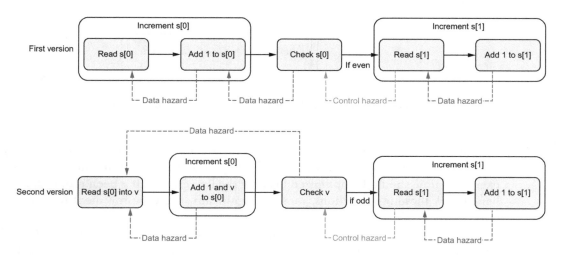

Figure 12.19   One significant difference: the data hazard for the v check step

Why does this matter? Because it allows the CPU to increase the level of parallelism (figure 12.20).

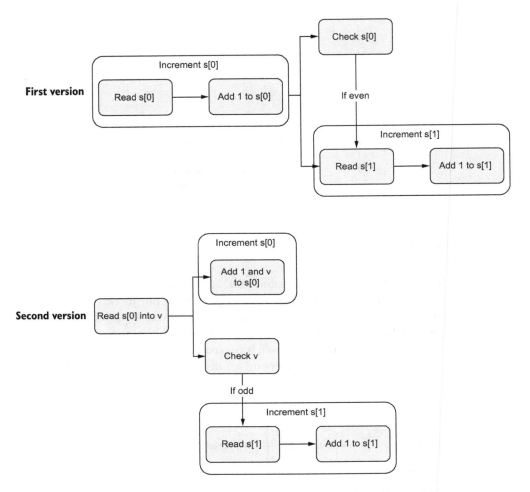

Figure 12.20   In the second version, both increment steps can be executed in parallel.

Despite having the same number of steps, the second version increases how many steps can be executed in parallel: three parallel routes instead of two. Meanwhile, the execution time should be optimized because the longest path has been reduced. If we benchmark these two functions, we see a significant speed improvement for the second version (about 20% on my machine), mainly because of ILP.

Let's take a step back to conclude this section. We discussed how modern CPUs use parallelism to optimize the execution time of a set of instructions. We also looked at data hazards, which can prevent executing instructions in parallel. And we optimized a Go example by reducing the number of data hazards to increase the number of instructions that can be executed in parallel.

Understanding how Go compiles our code into assembly and how to use CPU optimizations such as ILP is another avenue for improvement. Here, introducing a temporary variable resulted in a significant performance improvement. This example demonstrated how mechanical sympathy can help us optimize a Go application.

Let's also remember to remain cautious about such micro-optimizations. Because the Go compiler keeps evolving, an application's generated assembly may also change when the Go version is bumped.

The following section discusses the effects of data alignment.

12.4   #94: Not being aware of data alignment

Data alignment is a way to arrange how data is allocated to speed up memory accesses by the CPU. Not being aware of this concept can lead to extra memory consumption and even degraded performance. This section discusses this concept, where it applies, and techniques to prevent under-optimized code.

To understand how data alignment works, let's first discuss what would happen without it. Suppose we allocate two variables, an `int32` (32 bytes) and an `int64` (64 bytes):

```
var i int32
var j int64
```

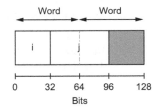

Without data alignment, on a 64-bit architecture, these two variables could be allocated as shown in figure 12.21. The `j` variable allocation could be spread over two words. If the CPU wanted to read `j`, it would require two memory accesses instead of one.

To prevent such a case, a variable's memory address should be a multiple of its own size. This is the concept of data alignment. In Go, the alignment guarantees are as follows:

Figure 12.21   `j` allocated on two words

- `byte, uint8, int8`: 1 byte
- `uint16, int16`: 2 bytes
- `uint32, int32, float32`: 4 bytes
- `uint64, int64, float64, complex64`: 8 bytes
- `complex128`: 16 bytes

All these types are guaranteed to be aligned: their addresses are a multiple of their size. For example, the address of any `int32` variable is a multiple of 4.

Let's get back to the real world. Figure 12.22 shows two different cases where `i` and `j` are allocated in memory.

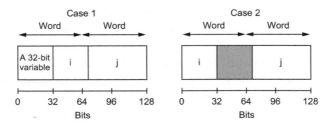

Figure 12.22 In both cases, j is aligned to its own size.

In the first case, a 32-bit variable was allocated just before i. Therefore, i and j were allocated contiguously. In the second case, the 32-bit variable wasn't allocated before i (for example, it was a 64-bit variable); so, i was allocated at the beginning of a word. To respect data alignment (an address that is a multiple of 64), j can't be allocated alongside i but to the next multiple of 64. The gray box represents 32 bits of padding.

Next, let's look at when padding can be an issue. We will consider the following struct containing three fields:

```
type Foo struct {
    b1 byte
    i  int64
    b2 byte
}
```

We have a byte type (1 byte), an int64 (8 bytes), and another byte type (1 byte). On a 64-bit architecture, the struct is allocated in memory as shown in figure 12.23. b1 is allocated first. Because i is an int64, its address must be a multiple of 8. Therefore, it's impossible to allocate it alongside b1 at 0x01. What's the next address that is a multiple of 8? 0x08. b2 is allocated to the next available address that is a multiple of 1: 0x10.

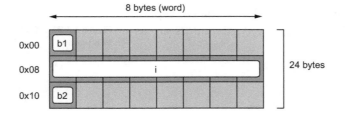

Figure 12.23 The struct occupies 24 bytes total.

Because a struct's size must be a multiple of the word size (8 bytes), its address isn't 17 bytes but 24 bytes total. During the compilation, the Go compiler adds padding to guarantee data alignment:

```
type Foo struct {
    b1 byte           Added by
    _  [7]byte    ◁── the compiler
```

```
    i  int64
    b2 byte
    _  [7]byte
}
```

Added by
the compiler

Every time a `Foo` struct is created, it requires 24 bytes in memory, but only 10 bytes contain data—the remaining 14 bytes are padding. Because a struct is an atomic unit, it will never be reorganized, even after a garbage collection (GC); it will always occupy 24 bytes in memory. Note that the compiler doesn't rearrange the fields; it only adds padding to guarantee data alignment.

How can we reduce the amount of memory allocated? The rule of thumb is to reorganize a struct so that its fields are sorted by type size in descending order. In our case, the `int64` type is first, followed by the two `byte` types:

```
type Foo struct {
    i  int64
    b1 byte
    b2 byte
}
```

Figure 12.24 shows how this new version of `Foo` is allocated in memory. `i` is allocated first and occupies a complete word. The main difference is that now `b1` and `b2` can live alongside each other in the same word.

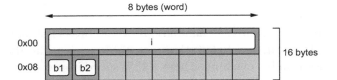

Figure 12.24 The struct now occupies 16 bytes in memory.

Again, the struct must be a multiple of the word size; but instead of occupying 24 bytes in memory, it occupies only 16 bytes. We saved 33% of the memory just by moving `i` to the first position.

What would be the concrete impacts if we used the first version of the `Foo` struct (24 bytes) instead of the compacted one? If the `Foo` structs were retained (for example, an in-memory `Foo` cache), our application would consume extra memory. But even if the `Foo` structs weren't retained, there would be other effects. For example, if we created `Foo` variables frequently and they were allocated to the heap (we discuss this concept in the next section), the result would be more frequent GCs, impacting overall application performance.

Speaking of performance, there's another effect on spatial locality. For example, let's consider the following `sum` function that takes a slice of `Foo` structs as an argument. This function iterates over the slice and sums all the `i` fields (`int64`):

```
func sum(foos []Foo) int64 {
    var s int64
```

```
for i := 0; i < len(foos); i++ {
    s += foos[i].i
}
return s
}
```

 Sums all
the i fields

Because a slice is backed by an array, it means a contiguous allocation of Foo structs.

Let's discuss the backing array for the two versions of Foo and check two cache lines of data (128 bytes). In figure 12.25, each gray bar represents 8 bytes of data, and the darker bars are the i variables (the fields we want to sum).

```
type Foo struct {
    b1 byte
    i int64
    b2 byte
}
```

Cache line   Cache line

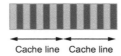

```
type Foo struct {
    i int64
    b1 byte
    b2 byte
}
```

Cache line   Cache line

Figure 12.25   Because each cache line contains more i variables, iterating over a slice of Foo requires fewer cache lines total.

As we can see, with the latest version of Foo, each cache line is more useful because it contains on average 33% more i variables. Therefore, iterating over a Foo slice to sum all the int64 elements is more efficient.

We can confirm this observation with a benchmark. If we run two benchmarks with the two versions of Foo using a slice of 10,000 elements, the version using the latest Foo struct is about 15% faster on my machine. That's a 15% speed improvement from changing the position of a single field in a struct.

Let's be mindful of data alignment. As we have seen in this section, reorganizing the fields of a Go struct to sort them by size in descending order prevents padding. Preventing padding means allocating more compact structs, possibly leading to optimizations such as reducing the frequency of GCs and better spatial locality.

The following section discusses the fundamental differences between stack and heap and why they matter.

12.5   *#95: Not understanding stack vs. heap*

In Go, a variable can be allocated either on the stack or on the heap. These two types of memory are fundamentally different and can significantly impact data-intensive applications. Let's examine these concepts and the rules the compiler follows to decide where a variable should be allocated.

12.5.1   *Stack vs. heap*

First, let's discuss the differences between the stack and the heap. The stack is the default memory; it's a last-in, first-out (LIFO) data structure that stores all the local variables for a specific goroutine. When a goroutine starts, it gets 2 KB of contiguous memory as its stack space (this size has evolved over time and could change again). However, this size isn't fixed at run time and can grow and shrink as necessary (but it always remains contiguous in memory, preserving data locality).

When Go enters a function, a stack frame is created, representing an interval in memory that only the current function can access. Let's look at a concrete example to understand this concept. Here, the main function will print the result of a sumValue function:

```go
func main() {
    a := 3
    b := 2

    c := sumValue(a, b)      // Calls the sumValue function
    println(c)               // Prints the result
}

//go:noinline                // Disables inlining
func sumValue(x, y int) int {
    z := x + y
    return z
}
```

There are two things to note here. First, we use the println built-in function instead of fmt.Println, which would force allocating the c variable on the heap. Second, we disable inlining on the sumValue function; otherwise, the function call would not occur (we discuss inlining in mistake #97, "Not relying on inlining").

Figure 12.26 shows the stack following a and b allocations. Because we executed main, a stack frame was created for this function. The two variables a and b were allocated to the stack in this stack frame. All the variables stored are valid addresses, meaning they can be referenced and accessed.

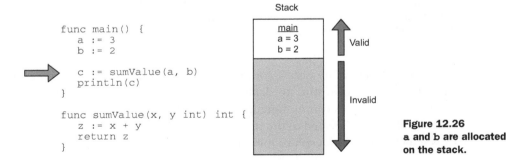

Figure 12.26
a and b are allocated
on the stack.

Figure 12.27 shows what happens if we enter into the sumValue function up to the return statement. The Go runtime creates a new stack frame as part of the current goroutine stack. x and y are allocated alongside z in the current stack frame.

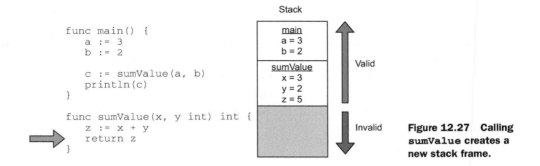

Figure 12.27 **Calling** `sumValue` **creates a new stack frame.**

The previous stack frame (`main`) contains addresses that are still considered valid. We can't access `a` and `b` directly; but if we had a pointer on `a`, for example, it would be valid. We discuss pointers shortly.

Let's move to the last statement of the `main` function: `println`. We exited the `sum-Value` function, so what happens to its stack frame? See figure 12.28.

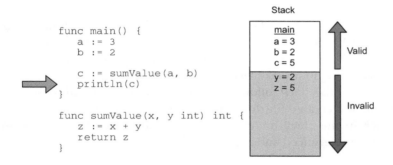

Figure 12.28 **The** `sumValue` **stack frame was deleted and replaced by variables from** `main`**. In this example,** `x` **has been erased by** `c`**, while** `y` **and** `z` **are still allocated in memory but unreachable.**

The `sumValue` stack frame wasn't completely erased from memory. When a function returns, Go doesn't take time to deallocate the variables to reclaim free space. But these previous variables can no longer be accessed, and when new variables from the parent function are allocated to the stack, they replace earlier allocations. In a sense, a stack is self-cleaning; it doesn't require an additional mechanism such as a GC.

Now, let's make a slight change to understand the stack's limitations. Instead of returning an `int`, the function will return a pointer:

```
func main() {
    a := 3
    b := 2
```

```
    c := sumPtr(a, b)
    println(*c)
}

//go:noinline
func sumPtr(x, y int) *int {          ◁─┐  Returns
    z := x + y                           │  a pointer
    return &z
}
```

The c variable in main is now a *int type. Let's move directly to the last println statement, following the call to sumPtr. What would happen if z remained allocated on the stack (which can't be the case)? See figure 12.29.

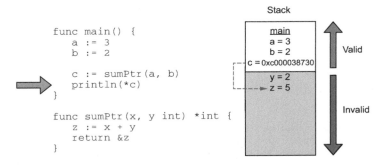

Figure 12.29 The c variable references an address that is no longer valid.

If c was referencing the address of the z variable, and that z was allocated on the stack, we would have a major problem. The address would no longer be valid, plus the stack frame of main would keep growing and erase the z variable. For that reason, the stack isn't enough, and we need another type of memory: the heap.

A memory heap is a pool of memory shared by all the goroutines. In figure 12.30, each of the three goroutines G1, G2, and G3 has its own stack. They all share the same heap.

In the previous example, we saw that the z variable couldn't live on the stack; therefore, it is *escaped* to the heap. If the compiler cannot prove that a variable *isn't* referenced after the function returns, the variable is allocated on the heap.

Why should we care? What's the point of understanding the differences between stack and heap? Because there's a significant impact in terms of performance.

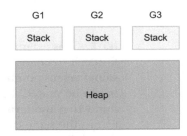

Figure 12.30 Three goroutines that have their own stacks but share the heap

As we said, a stack is self-cleaning and is accessed by a single goroutine. Conversely, the heap must be cleaned by an external system: the GC. The more heap allocations are made, the more we pressure the GC. When the GC runs, it uses 25% of the available CPU capacity and may create milliseconds of "stop the world" latency (the phase when an application is paused).

We must also understand that allocating on the stack is faster for the Go runtime because it's trivial: a pointer references the following available memory address. Conversely, allocating on the heap requires more effort to find the right place and hence takes more time.

To illustrate these differences, let's benchmark sumValue and sumPtr:

```
var globalValue int
var globalPtr *int

func BenchmarkSumValue(b *testing.B) {
    b.ReportAllocs()              ◁── Reports heap
    var local int                     allocations
    for i := 0; i < b.N; i++ {
        local = sumValue(i, i)   ◁── Sums by
    }                                 value
    globalValue = local
}

func BenchmarkSumPtr(b *testing.B) {
    b.ReportAllocs()              ◁── Reports heap
    var local *int                    allocations
    for i := 0; i < b.N; i++ {
        local = sumPtr(i, i)     ◁── Sums by
    }                                 pointer
    globalValue = *local
}
```

If we run these benchmarks (and still disable inlining), we get the following results:

```
BenchmarkSumValue-4    992800992    1.261 ns/op    0 B/op    0 allocs/op
BenchmarkSumPtr-4       82829653   14.84 ns/op     8 B/op    1 allocs/op
```

sumPtr is about an order of magnitude slower than sumValue, which is the direct consequence of using the heap instead of the stack.

> **NOTE** This example shows that using pointers to avoid a copy isn't necessarily faster; it depends on the context. So far in this book, we have only discussed values versus pointers via the prism of semantics: using a pointer when a value has to be shared. In most cases, this should be the rule to follow. Also bear in mind that modern CPUs are extremely efficient at copying data, especially within the same cache line. Let's avoid premature optimization and focus on readability and semantics first.

We should also note that in the previous benchmarks, we called b.ReportAllocs(), which highlights heap allocation (stack allocations aren't counted):

- `B/op`: how many bytes per operation allocated
- `allocs/op`: how many allocations per operation

Next, let's discuss the conditions for a variable to escape to the heap.

12.5.2 Escape analysis

Escape analysis refers to the work performed by the compiler to decide whether a variable should be allocated on the stack or the heap. Let's look at the main rules.

When an allocation cannot be done on the stack, it is done on the heap. Even though this sounds like a simplistic rule, it's important to remember. For example, if the compiler cannot prove that a variable isn't referenced after a function returns, this variable is allocated on the heap. In the previous section, this was the case with the `sumPtr` function returning a pointer to a variable created in the function's scope. In general, *sharing up* escapes to the heap.

But what about the opposite situation? What if we accept a pointer, as in the following example?

```
func main() {
    a := 3
    b := 2
    c := sum(&a, &b)
    println(c)
}


//go:noinline
func sum(x, y *int) int {          ◁─┐ Accepts
    return *x + *y                    │ pointers
}
```

`sum` accepts two pointers on variables created in the parent. If we move to the `return` statement in the `sum` function, figure 12.31 shows the current stack.

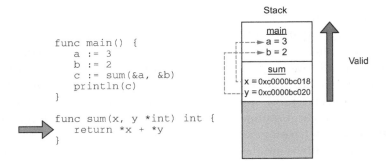

Figure 12.31   The x and y variables reference valid addresses.

Despite being part of another stack frame, the `x` and `y` variables reference valid addresses. Therefore, `a` and `b` won't have to be escaped; they can stay on the stack. In general, *sharing down* stays on the stack.

The following are other cases in which a variable can be escaped to the heap:

- Global variables, because multiple goroutines can access them.
- A pointer sent to a channel:

```
type Foo struct{ s string }
ch := make(chan *Foo, 1)
foo := &Foo{s: "x"}
ch <- foo
```

Here, foo escapes to the heap.

- A variable referenced by a value sent to a channel:

```
type Foo struct{ s *string }
ch := make(chan Foo, 1)
s := "x"
bar := Foo{s: &s}
ch <- bar
```

Because s is referenced by Foo via its address, it escapes to the heap in these situations.

- If a local variable is too large to fit on the stack.
- If the size of a local variable is unknown. For example, s := make([]int, 10) may not escape to the heap, but s := make([]int, n) will, because its size is based on a variable.
- If the backing array of a slice is reallocated using append.

Although this list gives us ideas for understanding the compiler's decisions, it's not exhaustive and may change in future Go versions. To confirm an assumption, we can access the compiler's decisions using -gcflags:

```
$ go build -gcflags "-m=2"
...
./main.go:12:2: z escapes to heap:
```

Here, the compiler informs us that the z variable will escape to the heap.

Understanding the fundamental differences between heap and stack is crucial in optimizing a Go application. As we have seen, heap allocations are more complex for the Go runtime to handle and require an external system with the GC to deallocate data. Heap management can account for up to 20% or 30% of the total CPU time consumed in some data-intensive applications. On the other hand, a stack is self-cleaning and local to a single goroutine, making allocations faster. Therefore, optimizing memory allocation can have a great return on investment.

It's also essential to understand the rules of escape analysis to write more efficient code. In general, sharing down stays on the stack, whereas sharing up escapes to the heap. This should prevent common mistakes such as premature optimizations where we want to return pointers, for example, "to avoid a copy." Let's focus on readability and semantics first and then optimize allocations if needed.

The following section discusses how to reduce allocations.

12.6   *#96: Not knowing how to reduce allocations*

Reducing allocations is a common optimization technique to speed up Go applications. This book has already covered a few approaches that reduce the number of heap allocations:

- Under-optimized string concatenation (mistake #39): using `strings.Builder` instead of the + operator to concatenate strings.
- Useless string conversions (mistake #40): whenever possible, avoid having to convert `[]byte` into strings.
- Inefficient slice and map initialization (mistakes #21 and #27): preallocate slices and maps if the length is already known.
- Better data struct alignment to reduce struct size (mistake #94).

As part of this section, we discuss three common approaches to reduce allocations:

- Changing our API
- Relying on compiler optimizations
- Using tools such as `sync.Pool`

12.6.1 *API changes*

The first option is to work carefully on the API we provide. Let's take as a concrete example the `io.Reader` interface:

```
type Reader interface {
    Read(p []byte) (n int, err error)
}
```

The `Read` method accepts a slice and returns the number of bytes read. Now, imagine if the `io.Reader` interface had been designed the other way around: passing an `int` representing how many bytes have to be read and returning a slice:

```
type Reader interface {
    Read(n int) (p []byte, err error)
}
```

Semantically, there is nothing wrong with this. But the returned slice would automatically escape to the heap in this case. We would be in the sharing-up case described in the previous section.

The Go designers used the sharing-down approach to prevent automatically escaping the slice to the heap. Therefore, it's up to the caller to provide a slice. That doesn't necessarily mean this slice won't be escaped: the compiler may have decided that this slice cannot stay on the stack. However, it's up to the caller to handle it, not a constraint caused by calling the `Read` method.

Sometimes even a slight change in an API can positively affect allocations. When designing an API, let's remain aware of the escape analysis rules described in the previous section and, if needed, use `-gcflags` to understand the compiler's decisions.

12.6.2 *Compiler optimizations*

One of the goals of the Go compiler is to optimize our code if possible. Here's a concrete example regarding maps.

In Go, we can't define a map using a slice as a key type. In some cases, especially in applications doing I/O, we may receive []byte data that we would like to use as a key. We are obliged to transform it into a string first, so we can write the following code:

```
type cache struct {
    m map[string]int          ◁─┐  Holds a map
}                                │  of strings

func (c *cache) get(bytes []byte) (v int, contains bool) {   ┐  Converts from
    key := string(bytes)                              ◁──────┘  []byte to string
    v, contains = c.m[key]        ◁─┐  Queries the map
    return                          │  using the string value
}
```

Because the get function receives a []byte slice, we convert it to a key string to query the map.

However, the Go compiler implements a specific optimization if we query the map using string(bytes):

```
func (c *cache) get(bytes []byte) (v int, contains bool) {
    v, contains = c.m[string(bytes)]   ◁─┐  Queries the map directly
    return                                │  using string(bytes)
}
```

Despite this being almost the same code (we call string(bytes) directly instead of passing a variable), the compiler will avoid doing this bytes-to-string conversion. Hence, the second version is faster than the first.

This example illustrates that two versions of a function that look similar may result in different assembly code following the Go compiler's work. We should also be aware of the possible compiler optimizations to optimize an application. And we need to watch future Go releases to check whether new optimizations are added to the language.

12.6.3 *sync.Pool*

Another avenue for improvement if we want to tackle the number of allocations is using sync.Pool. We should understand that sync.Pool isn't a cache: there's no fixed size or maximum capacity that we can set. Instead, it's a pool to reuse common objects.

Let's imagine that we want to implement a write function that receives an io.Writer, calls a function to get a []byte slice, and then writes it to the io.Writer. Our code looks like this (we omit error handling for the sake of clarity):

```
func write(w io.Writer) {     ┐  Receives a []byte
    b := getResponse()    ◁───┘  response
    _, _ = w.Write(b)        ◁─┐  Writes to
}                               │  the io.Writer
```

Here, getResponse returns a new []byte slice upon each call. What if we want to reduce the number of allocations by reusing this slice? We assume that all the responses have a max size of 1,024 bytes. In this situation, we can use sync.Pool.

Creating a sync.Pool requires a func() any factory function; see figure 12.32. sync.Pool exposes two methods:

- Get() any—Gets an object from the pool
- Put(any)—Returns an object to the pool

```
func factory() any {
    return ◯
}
```

Figure 12.32 Define a factory function that creates a new object upon each call.

Using Get either creates a new object if the pool is empty or reuses an object, otherwise. Then, after using the object, we can put it back into the pool using Put. Figure 12.33 shows an example with the previously defined factory with a Get when the pool is empty, a Put, and a Get when the pool isn't empty.

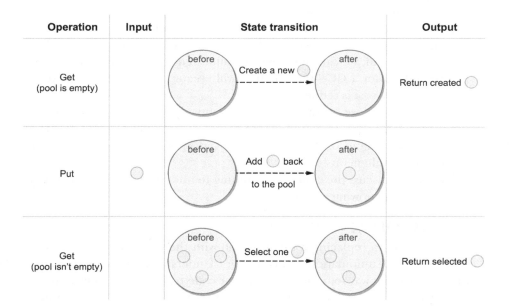

Figure 12.33 Get either creates a new object or returns one from the pool. Put returns the object to the pool.

When are objects drained from the pool? There's no specific method to do this: it relies on the GC. After each GC, objects from the pool are destroyed.

Back in our example, assuming that we can update the getResponse function to write data to a given slice instead of creating one, we can implement another version of the write method that relies on a pool:

```
var pool = sync.Pool{
    New: func() any {                    ◁──┐  Creates a pool and sets
        return make([]byte, 1024)           │  the factory function
    },
}
```

```
func write(w io.Writer) {                        ┌  Gets a []byte from the
    buffer := pool.Get().([]byte)       ◁──┘  pool or creates one
    buffer = buffer[:0]                 ◁──┤  Resets the buffer
    defer pool.Put(buffer)              ◁──────────┐  Puts the buffer
                                                   │  back into the pool
    getResponse(buffer)                ◁──┐  Writes the response
    _, _ = w.Write(buffer)                │  to the provided buffer
}
```

We define a new pool using the sync.Pool struct and set the factory function to create a new []byte with a length of 1,024 elements. In the write function, we try to retrieve one buffer from the pool. If the pool is empty, the function creates a new buffer; otherwise, it selects an arbitrary buffer from the pool and returns it. One crucial step is to reset the buffer using buffer[:0], as this slice may already have been used. Then we defer the call to Put to put the slice back into the pool.

With this new version, calling write doesn't lead to creating a new []byte slice for every call. Instead, we can reuse existing allocated slices. In the worst-case scenario—for example, after a GC—the function will create a new buffer; however, the amortized allocation cost is reduced.

In summary, if we frequently allocate many objects of the same type, we can consider using sync.Pool. It is a set of temporary objects that can help us prevent reallocating the same kind of data repeatedly. And sync.Pool is safe for use by multiple goroutines simultaneously.

Next, let's discuss the concept of inlining to understand that this computer optimization is worth knowing about.

12.7 #97: Not relying on inlining

Inlining refers to replacing a function call with the body of the function. Nowadays, inlining is done automatically by compilers. Understanding the fundamentals of inlining can also be a way to optimize particular code paths of an application.

Let's see a concrete example of inlining with a simple sum function that sums two int types:

```
func main() {
    a := 3
    b := 2
    s := sum(a, b)
    println(s)
}
                                        ┌  Inlines the
func sum(a int, b int) int {    ◁──┘  function
    return a + b
}
```

If we run `go build` using -gcflags, we access the decision made by the compiler regarding the sum function:

```
$ go build -gcflags "-m=2"
./main.go:10:6: can inline sum with cost 4 as:
    func(int, int) int { return a + b }
...
./main.go:6:10: inlining call to sum func(int, int) int { return a + b }
```

The compiler decided to inline the call to sum. Hence, the previous code is replaced by the following:

```
func main() {
    a := 3
    b := 2                    Replaces the call to
    s := a + b      <──┘      sum with its body
    println(s)
}
```

Inlining only works for functions with a certain complexity, also known as an *inlining budget*. Otherwise, the compiler will inform us that the function is too complex to be inlined:

```
./main.go:10:6: cannot inline foo: function too complex:
    cost 84 exceeds budget 80
```

Inlining has two main benefits. First, it removes the overhead of a function call (even though the overhead has been mitigated since Go 1.17 and register-based calling conventions). Second, it allows the compiler to proceed to further optimizations. For example, after inlining a function, the compiler can decide that a variable it was initially supposed to escape on the heap may stay on the stack.

The question is, if this optimization is applied automatically by the compiler, why should we care about it as Go developers? The answer lies in the concept of mid-stack inlining.

Mid-stack inlining is about inlining functions that call other functions. Before Go 1.9, only leaf functions were considered for inlining. Now, thanks to mid-stack inlining, the following foo function can also be inlined:

```
func main() {
    foo()
}

func foo() {
    x := 1
    bar(x)
}
```

Because the foo function isn't too complex, the compiler can inline its call:

```
func main() {                Replaced with
    x := 1      <──┘          the body of foo
    bar(x)
}
```

Thanks to mid-stack inlining, as Go developers, we can now optimize an application using the concept of fast-path inlining to distinguish between fast and slow paths. Let's look at a concrete example released in the `sync.Mutex` implementation to understand how this works.

Before mid-stack inlining, the implementation of the `Lock` method was the following:

```go
func (m *Mutex) Lock() {
    if atomic.CompareAndSwapInt32(&m.state, 0, mutexLocked) {
        // Mutex isn't locked
        if race.Enabled {
            race.Acquire(unsafe.Pointer(m))
        }
        return
    }

    // Mutex is already locked
    var waitStartTime int64
    starving := false
    awoke := false
    iter := 0
    old := m.state
    for {
        // ...           ◁——|  Complex logic
    }
    if race.Enabled {
        race.Acquire(unsafe.Pointer(m))
    }
}
```

We can distinguish two primary paths:

- If the mutex isn't locked (`atomic.CompareAndSwapInt32` is true), fast path
- If the mutex is already locked (`atomic.CompareAndSwapInt32` is false), slow path

However, regardless of the path taken, the function cannot be inlined because of its complexity. To use mid-stack inlining, the `Lock` method was refactored so that the slow path lives in a specific function:

```go
func (m *Mutex) Lock() {
    if atomic.CompareAndSwapInt32(&m.state, 0, mutexLocked) {
        if race.Enabled {
            race.Acquire(unsafe.Pointer(m))
        }
        return
    }
    m.lockSlow()        ◁——|  Path on which the mutex
}                              is already locked

func (m *Mutex) lockSlow() {
    var waitStartTime int64
    starving := false
```

```
    awoke := false
    iter := 0
    old := m.state
    for {
        // ...
    }

    if race.Enabled {
        race.Acquire(unsafe.Pointer(m))
    }
}
```

Thanks to this change, the `Lock` method can be inlined. The benefit is that a mutex that isn't already locked is now locked without paying the overhead of calling a function (speed improves around 5%). The slow path, when the mutex is already locked, didn't change. Previously it required one function call to execute this logic; it remains one function call, this time to `lockSlow`.

This optimization technique is about distinguishing between fast and slow paths. If a fast path can be inlined but not a slow one, we can extract the slow path inside a dedicated function. Hence, if the inlining budget isn't exceeded, our function is a candidate for inlining.

Inlining isn't just an invisible compiler optimization that we shouldn't care about. As seen in this section, understanding how inlining works and how to access the compiler's decision can be a road to optimization using the fast-path inlining technique. Extracting the slow path in a dedicated function prevents a function call if the fast path is executed.

The next section discusses common diagnostics tooling that can help us understand what should be optimized in our Go applications.

12.8   #98: Not using Go diagnostics tooling

Go offers a few excellent diagnostics tools to help us get insights into how an application performs. This section focuses on the most important ones: profiling and the execution tracer. Both tools are so important that they should be part of the core toolset of any Go developer who is interested in optimization. We'll discuss profiling first.

12.8.1   Profiling

Profiling provides insights into the execution of an application. It allows us to resolve performance issues, detect contention, locate memory leaks, and more. These insights can be collected via several profiles:

- `CPU`—Determines where an application spends its time
- `Goroutine`—Reports the stack traces of the ongoing goroutines
- `Heap`—Reports heap memory allocation to monitor current memory usage and check for possible memory leaks

- `Mutex`—Reports lock contentions to see the behaviors of the mutexes used in our code and whether an application spends too much time in locking calls
- `Block`—Shows where goroutines block waiting on synchronization primitives

Profiling is achieved via instrumentation using a tool called a profiler: in Go, `pprof`. First, let's understand how and when to enable `pprof`; then, we discuss the most critical profile types.

ENABLING PPROF

There are several ways to enable `pprof`. For example, we can use the `net/http/pprof` package to serve the profiling data via HTTP:

```
package main

import (
    "fmt"
    "log"
    "net/http"
    _ "net/http/pprof"          ◄─┐  Blank import
)                                  │  to pprof

func main() {
    http.HandleFunc("/", func(w http.ResponseWriter, r *http.Request) {  ◄──┐
        fmt.Fprintf(w, "")                                                  │
    })                                                           Exposes an │
    log.Fatal(http.ListenAndServe(":80", nil))                HTTP endpoint │
}
```

Importing `net/http/pprof` leads to a side effect that allows us to reach the `pprof` URL, http://host/debug/pprof. Note that enabling `pprof` is safe even in production (https://go.dev/doc/diagnostics#profiling). The profiles that impact performance, such as CPU profiling, aren't enabled by default, nor do they run continuously: they are activated only for a specific period.

Now that we have seen how to expose a `pprof` endpoint, let's discuss the most common profiles.

CPU PROFILING

The CPU profiler relies on the OS and signaling. When it is activated, the application asks the OS to interrupt it every 10 ms by default via a `SIGPROF` signal. When the application receives a `SIGPROF`, it suspends the current activity and transfers the execution to the profiler. The profiler collects data such as the current goroutine activity and aggregates execution statistics that we can retrieve. Then it stops, and the execution resumes until the next `SIGPROF`.

We can access the /debug/pprof/profile endpoint to activate CPU profiling. Accessing this endpoint executes CPU profiling for 30 seconds by default. For 30 seconds, our application is interrupted every 10 ms. Note that we can change these two default values: we can use the `seconds` parameter to pass to the endpoint how long the profiling should last (for example, /debug/pprof/profile?seconds=15), and we can change the interruption rate (even to less than 10 ms). But in most cases, 10 ms should be enough, and in decreasing this value (meaning increasing the rate), we should be careful not to harm performance. After 30 seconds, we download the results of the CPU profiler.

CPU profiling during benchmarks

We can also enable the CPU profiler using the `-cpuprofile` flag, such as when running a benchmark:

```
$ go test -bench=. -cpuprofile profile.out
```

This command produces the same type of file that can be downloaded via /debug/ pprof/profile.

From this file, we can navigate to the results using `go tool`:

```
$ go tool pprof -http=:8080 <file>
```

This command opens a web UI showing the call graph. Figure 12.34 shows an example taken from an application. The larger the arrow, the more it was a hot path. We can then navigate into this graph and get execution insights.

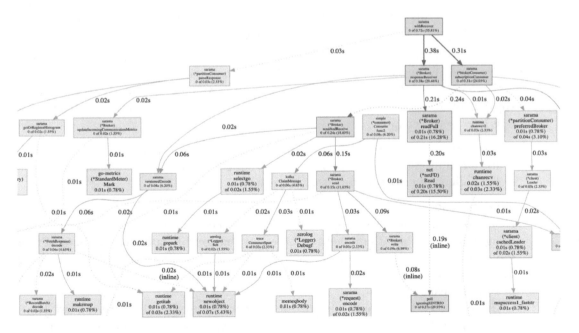

Figure 12.34 The call graph of an application during 30 seconds

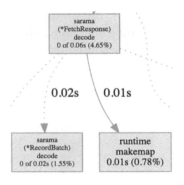

Figure 12.35   Example call graph

For example, the graph in figure 12.35 tells us that during 30 seconds, 0.06 seconds were spent in the decode method (`*FetchResponse` receiver). Of these 0.06 seconds, 0.02 were spent in `Record-Batch.decode` and 0.01 in `makemap` (creating a map).

We can also access this kind of information from the web UI with different representations. For example, the Top view sorts the functions per execution time, and Flame Graph visualizes the execution time hierarchy. The UI can even display the expensive parts of the source code line by line.

NOTE   We can also delve into profiling data via a command line. However, we focus on the web UI in this section.

Thanks to this data, we can get a general idea of how an application behaves:

- Too many calls to `runtime.mallogc` can mean an excessive number of small heap allocations that we can try to minimize.
- Too much time spent in channel operations or mutex locks can indicate excessive contention that is harming the application's performance.
- Too much time spent on `syscall.Read` or `syscall.Write` means the application spends a significant amount of time in Kernel mode. Working on I/O buffering may be an avenue for improvement.

These are the kinds of insights we can get from the CPU profiler. It's valuable to understand the hottest code path and identify bottlenecks. But it won't determine more than the configured rate because the CPU profiler is executed at a fixed pace (by default, 10 ms). To get finer-grained insights, we should use tracing, which we discuss later in this chapter.

NOTE   We can also attach labels to the different functions. For example, imagine a common function called from different clients. To track the time spent for both clients, we can use `pprof.Labels`.

HEAP PROFILING

Heap profiling allows us to get statistics about the current heap usage. Like CPU profiling, heap profiling is sample-based. We can change this rate, but we shouldn't be too granular because the more we increase the rate, the more effort heap profiling will require to collect data. By default, samples are profiled at one allocation for every 512 KB of heap allocation.

If we reach /debug/pprof/heap/, we get raw data that can be hard to read. However, we can download a heap profile using debug/pprof/heap/?debug=0 and then open it with `go tool` (the same command as in the previous section) to navigate into the data using the web UI.

Figure 12.36 shows an example of a heap graph. Calling the `MetadataResponse` `.decode` method leads to allocating 1536 KB of heap data (which represents 6.32% of the total heap). However, 0 out of these 1536 KB were allocated by this function directly, so we need to inspect the second call. The `Topic-Metadata.decode` method allocated 512 KB out of the 1536 KB; the rest—1024 KB— were allocated in another method.

This is how we can navigate the call chain to understand what part of an application is responsible for most of the heap allocations. We can also look at different sample types:

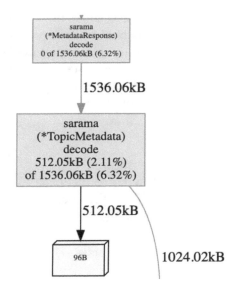

Figure 12.36   A heap graph

- `alloc_objects`—Total number of objects allocated
- `alloc_space`—Total amount of memory allocated
- `inuse_objects`—Number of objects allocated and not yet released
- `inuse_space`—Amount of memory allocated and not yet released

Another very helpful capability with heap profiling is tracking memory leaks. With a GC-based language, the usual procedure is the following:

1 Trigger a GC.
2 Download heap data.
3 Wait for a few seconds/minutes.
4 Trigger another GC.
5 Download another heap data.
6 Compare.

Forcing a GC before downloading data is a way to prevent false assumptions. For example, if we see a peak of retained objects without running a GC first, we cannot be sure whether it's a leak or objects that the next GC will collect.

Using `pprof`, we can download a heap profile and force a GC in the meantime. The procedure in Go is the following:

1 Go to /debug/pprof/heap?gc=1 (trigger the GC and download the heap profile).
2 Wait for a few seconds/minutes.
3 Go to /debug/pprof/heap?gc=1 again.
4 Use `go tool` to compare both heap profiles:

```
$ go tool pprof -http=:8080 -diff_base <file2> <file1>
```

Figure 12.37 shows the kind of data we can access. For example, the amount of heap memory held by the `newTopicProducer` method (top left) has decreased (−513 KB). In contrast, the amount held by `updateMetadata` (bottom right) has increased (+512 KB). Slow increases are normal. The second heap profile may have been calculated in the middle of a service call, for example. We can repeat this process or wait longer; the important part is to track steady increases in allocations of a specific object.

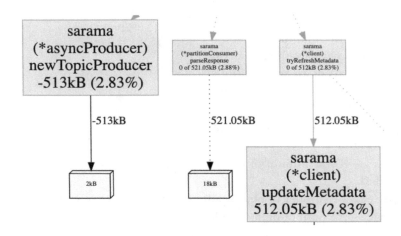

Figure 12.37   The differences between the two heap profiles

NOTE   Another type of profiling related to the heap is `allocs`, which reports allocations. Heap profiling shows the current state of the heap memory. To get insights about past memory allocations since the application started, we can use allocations profiling. As discussed, because stack allocations are cheap, they aren't part of this profiling, which only focuses on the heap.

GOROUTINES PROFILING

The `goroutine` profile reports the stack trace of all the current goroutines in an application. We can download a file using debug/pprof/goroutine/?debug=0 and use go tool again. Figure 12.38 shows the kind of information we can get.

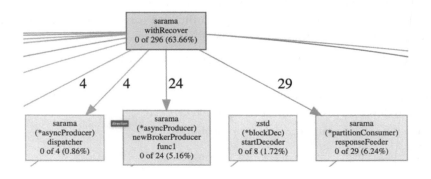

Figure 12.38 Goroutine graph

We can see the current state of the application and how many goroutines were created per function. In this case, `withRecover` has created 296 ongoing goroutines (63%), and 29 were related to a call to `responseFeeder`.

This kind of information is also beneficial if we suspect goroutine leaks. We can look at goroutine profiler data to know which part of a system is the suspect.

BLOCK PROFILING

The `block` profile reports where ongoing goroutines block waiting on synchronization primitives. Possibilities include

- Sending or receiving on an unbuffered channel
- Sending to a full channel
- Receiving from an empty channel
- Mutex contention
- Network or filesystem waits

Block profiling also records the amount of time a goroutine has been waiting and is accessible via debug/pprof/block. This profile can be extremely helpful if we suspect that performance is being harmed by blocking calls.

The `block` profile isn't enabled by default: we have to call `runtime.SetBlockProfileRate` to enable it. This function controls the fraction of goroutine blocking events that are reported. Once enabled, the profiler will keep collecting data in the background even if we don't call the debug/pprof/block endpoint. Let's be cautious if we want to set a high rate so we don't harm performance.

> ### Full goroutine stack dump
> If we face a deadlock or suspect that goroutines are in a blocked state, the full goroutine stack dump (debug/pprof/goroutine/?debug=2) creates a dump of all the current goroutine stack traces. This can be helpful as a first analysis step. For example, the following dump shows a Sarama goroutine blocked for 1,420 minutes on a channel-receive operation:
>
> ```
> goroutine 2494290 [chan receive, 1420 minutes]:
> github.com/Shopify/sarama.(*syncProducer).SendMessages(0xc00071a090,
>   {0xc0009bb800, 0xfb, 0xfb})
>     /app/vendor/github.com/Shopify/sarama/sync_producer.go:117 +0x149
> ```

MUTEX PROFILING

The last profile type is related to blocking but only regarding mutexes. If we suspect that our application spends significant time waiting for locking mutexes, thus harming execution, we can use mutex profiling. It's accessible via /debug/pprof/mutex.

This profile works in a manner similar to that for blocking. It's disabled by default: we have to enable it using `runtime.SetMutexProfileFraction`, which controls the fraction of mutex contention events reported.

Following are a few additional notes about profiling:

- We haven't mentioned the `threadcreate` profile because it's been broken since 2013 (https://github.com/golang/go/issues/6104).
- Be sure to enable only one profiler at a time: for example, do not enable CPU and heap profiling simultaneously. Doing so can lead to erroneous observations.
- `pprof` is extensible, and we can create our own custom profiles using `pprof.Profile`.

We have seen the most important profiles that we can enable to help us understand how an application performs and possible avenues for optimization. In general, enabling `pprof` is recommended, even in production, because in most cases it offers an excellent balance between its footprint and the amount of insight we can get from it. Some profiles, such as the CPU profile, lead to performance penalties but only during the time they are enabled.

Let's now look at the execution tracer.

12.8.2 *Execution tracer*

The execution tracer is a tool that captures a wide range of runtime events with `go tool` to make them available for visualization. It is helpful for the following:

- Understanding runtime events such as how the GC performs
- Understanding how goroutines execute
- Identifying poorly parallelized execution

Let's try it with an example given in mistake #56, "Thinking concurrency is always faster." We discussed two parallel versions of the merge sort algorithm. The issue with the first version was poor parallelization, leading to the creation of too many goroutines. Let's see how the tracer can help us in validating this statement.

We will write a benchmark for the first version and execute it with the `-trace` flag to enable the execution tracer:

```
$ go test -bench=. -v -trace=trace.out
```

NOTE We can also download a remote trace file using the /debug/pprof/trace?debug=0 pprof endpoint.

This command creates a trace.out file that we can open using `go tool`:

```
$ go tool trace trace.out
2021/11/26 21:36:03 Parsing trace...
2021/11/26 21:36:31 Splitting trace...
2021/11/26 21:37:00 Opening browser. Trace viewer is listening on
    http://127.0.0.1:54518
```

The web browser opens, and we can click View Trace to see all the traces during a specific timeframe, as shown in figure 12.39. This figure represents about 150 ms. We can see multiple helpful metrics, such as the goroutine count and the heap size. The heap size grows steadily until a GC is triggered. We can also observe the activity of the Go application per CPU core. The timeframe starts with user-level code; then a "stop the world" is executed, which occupies the four CPU cores for approximately 40 ms.

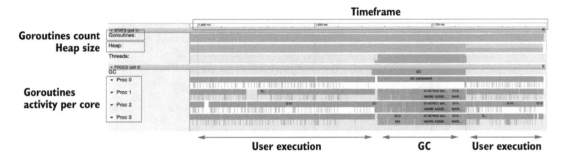

Figure 12.39   Showing goroutine activity and runtime events such as a GC phase

Regarding concurrency, we can see that this version uses all the available CPU cores on the machine. However, figure 12.40 zooms in on a portion of 1 ms. Each bar corresponds to a single goroutine execution. Having too many small bars doesn't look right: it means execution that is poorly parallelized.

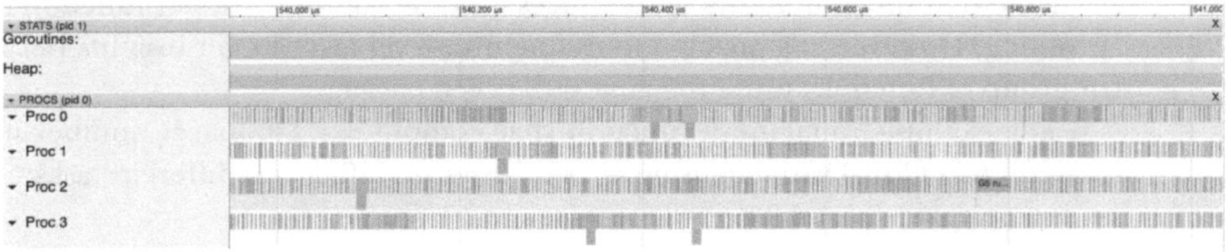

Figure 12.40   Too many small bars mean poorly parallelized execution.

Figure 12.41 zooms even closer to see how these goroutines are orchestrated. Roughly 50% of the CPU time isn't spent executing application code. The white spaces represent the time the Go runtime takes to spin up and orchestrate new goroutines.

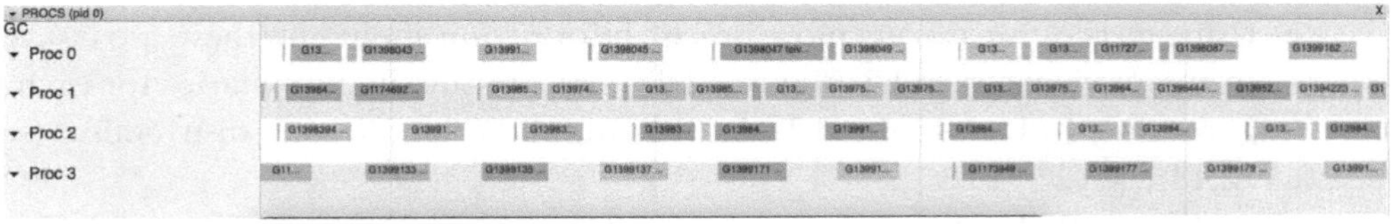

Figure 12.41   About 50% of CPU time is spent handling goroutine switches.

Let's compare this with the second parallel implementation, which was about an order of magnitude faster. Figure 12.42 again zooms to a 1 ms timeframe.

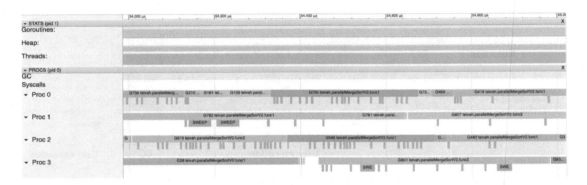

Figure 12.42   **The number of white spaces has been significantly reduced, proving that the CPU is more fully occupied.**

Each goroutine takes more time to execute, and the number of white spaces has been significantly reduced. Hence, the CPU is much more occupied executing application code than it was in the first version. Each millisecond of CPU time is spent more efficiently, explaining the benchmark differences.

Note that the granularity of the traces is per goroutine, not per function like CPU profiling. However, it's possible to define user-level tasks to get insights per function or group of functions using the `runtime/trace` package.

For example, imagine a function that computes a Fibonacci number and then writes it to a global variable using `atomic`. We can define two different tasks:

```
var v int64
ctx, fibTask := trace.NewTask(context.Background(), "fibonacci")    ◄──────────
trace.WithRegion(ctx, "main", func() {
    v = fibonacci(10)                                                   Creates a
})                                                                   fibonacci task
fibTask.End()
ctx, fibStore := trace.NewTask(ctx, "store")    ◄──   Creates a
trace.WithRegion(ctx, "main", func() {                store task
    atomic.StoreInt64(&result, v)
})
fibStore.End()
```

Using `go tool`, we can get more precise information about how these two tasks perform. In the previous trace UI (figure 12.42), we can see the boundaries for each task per goroutine. In User-Defined Tasks, we can follow the duration distribution (see figure 12.43).

We see that in most cases, the `fibonacci` task is executed in less than 15 microseconds, whereas the `store` task takes less than 6309 nanoseconds.

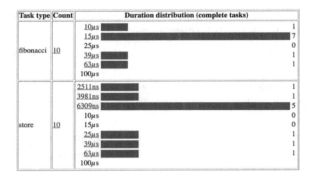

Task type	Count	Duration distribution (complete tasks)	
fibonacci	10	10µs	1
		15µs	7
		25µs	0
		39µs	1
		63µs	1
		100µs	
store	10	2511ns	1
		3981ns	1
		6309ns	5
		10µs	0
		15µs	0
		25µs	1
		39µs	1
		63µs	1
		100µs	

Figure 12.43 Distribution of user-level tasks

In the previous section, we discussed the kinds of information we can get from CPU profiling. What are the main differences compared to the data we can get from user-level traces?

- CPU profiling:
  - Sample-based.
  - Per function.
  - Doesn't go below the sampling rate (10 ms by default).

- User-level traces:
  - Not sample-based.
  - Per-goroutine execution (unless we use the `runtime/trace` package).
  - Time executions aren't bound by any rate.

In summary, the execution tracer is a powerful tool for understanding how an application performs. As we have seen with the merge sort example, we can identify poorly parallelized execution. However, the tracer's granularity remains per goroutine unless we manually use `runtime/trace` compared to a CPU profile, for example. We can use both profiling and the execution tracer to get the most out of the standard Go diagnostics tools when optimizing an application.

The next section discusses how the GC works and how to tune it.

12.9 #99: Not understanding how the GC works

The garbage collector (GC) is a critical piece of the Go language that simplifies the lives of developers. It allows us to track and free heap allocations that are no longer needed. Because we can't replace every heap allocation with a stack allocation, understanding how the GC works should be part of the Go developer's toolset to optimize applications.

12.9.1 Concepts

A GC keeps a tree of object references. The Go GC is based on the mark-and-sweep algorithm, which relies on two stages:

- *Mark stage*—Traverses all the objects of the heap and marks whether they are still in use

- *Sweep stage*—Traverses the tree of references from the root and deallocates blocks of objects that are no longer referenced

When a GC runs, it first performs a set of actions that lead to *stopping the world* (two stop-the-worlds per GC, to be precise). That is, all the available CPU time is used to perform the GC, putting our application code on hold. Following these steps, it starts the world again, resuming our application but also running a concurrent phase. For that reason, the Go GC is called *concurrent mark-and-sweep*: it aims to reduce the number of stop-the-world operations per GC cycle and mostly run concurrently alongside our application.

The Go GC also includes a way to free memory after consumption peak. Imagine that our application is based on two phases:

- An init phase that leads to frequent allocations and a large heap
- A runtime phase with moderate allocations and a small heap

How will Go tackle the fact that the large heap is only helpful when the application starts, not after that? This is handled as part of the GC with a so-called *periodic scavenger*. After a certain time, the GC detects that such a large heap is no longer necessary, so it frees some memory and returns it to the OS.

> **NOTE** If the scavenger isn't quick enough, we can manually force memory to be returned to the OS using `debug.FreeOSMemory()`.

The important question is, when will a GC cycle run? Compared to other languages such as Java, the Go configuration remains reasonably simple. It relies on a single environment variable: `GOGC`. This variable defines the percentage of the heap growth since the last GC before triggering another GC; the default value is 100%.

Let's look at a concrete example to be sure we understand. Let's assume a GC just got triggered and the current heap size is 128 MB. If `GOGC=100`, the next GC is triggered when the heap size reaches 256 MB. A GC is executed by default every time the heap size doubles. Also, if a GC hasn't been executed during the last 2 minutes, Go will force one to run.

If we profile our application with production loads, we can fine-tune `GOGC`:

- Reducing it will cause the heap to grow more slowly, increasing the pressure on the GC.
- Conversely, bumping it will cause the heap to grow faster, reducing the pressure on the GC.

GC traces

We can print the GC traces by setting the `GODEBUG` environment variable, such as while running a benchmark:

```
$ GODEBUG=gctrace=1 go test -bench=. -v
```

Enabling `gctrace` writes a trace to `stderr` each time the GC runs.

Let's go through some concrete examples to understand how the GC behaves in the event of a load increase.

12.9.2 Examples

Let's imagine that we expose some public services to users. During peak time at 12:00 PM, 1 million users connect. However, it's a steady increase in connected users. Figure 12.44 represents the average heap size and when a GC will be triggered if we keep GOGC set to 100.

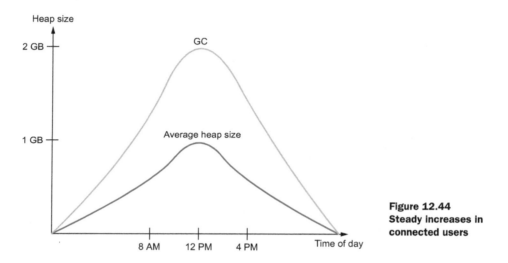

**Figure 12.44
Steady increases in
connected users**

Because GOGC is set to 100, the GC is triggered every time the heap size doubles. In these conditions, because the number of users steadily increases, we should face an acceptable number of GCs throughout the day (figure 12.45).

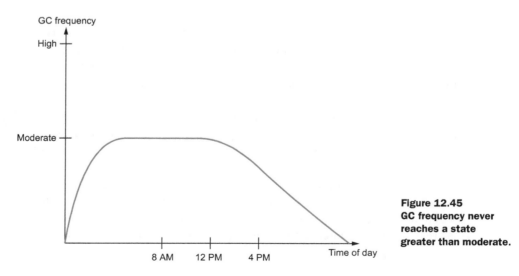

**Figure 12.45
GC frequency never
reaches a state
greater than moderate.**

We should have a moderate number of GC cycles at the beginning of the day. When we reach 12:00 PM, when the number of users starts to decrease, the number of GC cycles should also decrease steadily. In such a scenario, keeping GOGC to 100 should be fine.

Now, let's consider a second scenario where most of the 1 million users connect in less than an hour; see figure 12.46. At 8:00 AM, the average heap size grows rapidly, reaching its peak in about an hour.

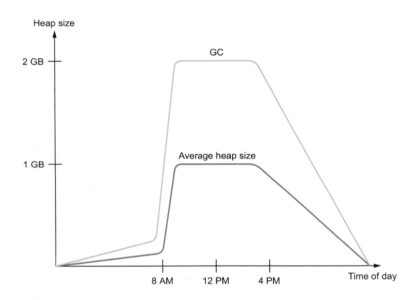

Figure 12.46   A sudden increase in users

The frequency of the GC cycles is heavily impacted during this hour, as shown in figure 12.47. Because of the significant and sudden bump of the heap, we face frequent GC cycles during a short period. Even though the Go GC is concurrent, this situation will lead to a significant number of stop-the-world periods and can cause impacts such as increasing the average latency seen by users.

In this case, we should consider bumping GOGC to a higher value to reduce the pressure on the GC. Note that increasing GOGC doesn't lead to linear benefits: the bigger the heap, the longer it will take to clean. Hence, using production load, we should be careful when configuring GOGC.

In exceptional conditions with a bump that is even more significant, tweaking GOGC may not be enough. For example, let's say that instead of going from 0 to 1 million users in an hour, we do so in a few seconds. During these seconds, the number of GCs may reach a critical state, causing the application to perform very poorly.

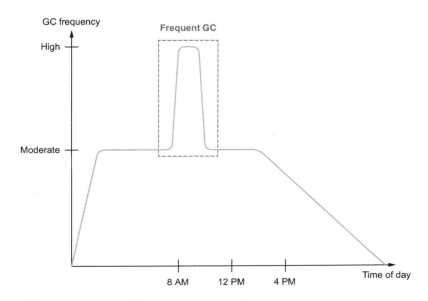

Figure 12.47   During one hour, we observe a high frequency of GCs.

If we know about the heap peak, we can use a trick that forces a large allocation of memory to improve the stability of the heap. For example, we can force the allocation of 1 GB using a global variable in main.go:

```
var min = make([]byte, 1_000_000_000) // 1 GB
```

What's the point of such an allocation? If GOGC is kept at 100, instead of triggering a GC every time the heap doubles (which, again, happens extremely frequently during these few seconds), Go will only trigger a GC when the heap reaches 2 GB. This should reduce the number of GC cycles triggered when all the users connect, reducing the impact on average latency.

We could argue that when the heap size decreases, this trick will waste a lot of memory. But that isn't the case. On most OSs, allocating this min variable won't make our application consume 1 GB of memory. Calling make results in a system call to mmap(), which leads to a lazy allocation. For example, on Linux, memory is virtually addressed and mapped through page tables. Using mmap() allocates 1 GB of memory in the virtual address space, not the physical space. Only a read or a write will cause a page fault leading to an actual physical memory allocation. So even if the application starts without any connected clients, it won't consume 1 GB of physical memory.

NOTE   We can validate this behavior using tools such as ps.

It's essential to understand how the GC behaves in order to optimize it. As Go developers, we can use GOGC to configure when the next GC cycle is triggered. In most cases, keeping it at 100 should be enough. However, if our application may face request peaks leading to frequent GC and latency impacts, we can increase this value. Finally, in the event of an exceptional request peak, we can consider using the trick of keeping the virtual heap size to a minimum.

The last section of this chapter discusses the impacts of running Go in Docker and Kubernetes.

12.10 #100: Not understanding the impacts of running Go in Docker and Kubernetes

Writing services with Go is the most common use, according to the 2021 Go developer survey (https://go.dev/blog/survey2021-results). Meanwhile, Kubernetes is the most widely used platform to deploy these services. It's important to understand the implications of running Go in Docker and Kubernetes, to prevent common situations such as CPU throttling.

We mentioned in mistake #56, "Thinking concurrency is always faster," that the GOMAXPROCS variable defines the limit of OS threads in charge of executing user-level code simultaneously. By default, it's set to the number of OS-apparent logical CPU cores. What does this mean in the context of Docker and Kubernetes?

Let's assume that our Kubernetes cluster is composed of eight-core nodes. When a container is deployed in Kubernetes, we can define a CPU limit to ensure that an application won't consume all the host's resources. For example, the following configuration limits the use of CPU to 4,000 millicpu (or millicores), so four CPU cores:

```
spec:
  containers:
  - name: myapp
    image: myapp
    resources:
      limits:
        cpu: 4000m
```

We may assume that when our application is deployed, GOMAXPROCS will be based on these limits and hence will have a value of 4. But that won't be the case; it is set to the number of logical cores on the host: 8. So, what's the impact?

Kubernetes uses Completely Fair Scheduler (CFS) as a process scheduler. CFS is also used to enforce CPU limits for Pod resources. When administrating a Kubernetes cluster, an administrator can configure these two parameters:

- cpu.cfs_period_us (global setting)
- cpu.cfs_quota_us (setting per Pod)

The former defines a period and the latter a quota. By default, the period is set to 100 ms. Meanwhile, the default quota value is how much CPU time the application can consume in 100 ms. The limit is set to four cores, which means 400 ms (4 × 100 ms). Therefore, CFS will ensure that our application never consumes more than 400 ms of CPU time for 100 ms.

Let's imagine a scenario where multiple goroutines are currently being executed on four different threads. Each thread is scheduled on a different core (1, 3, 4, and 8); see figure 12.48.

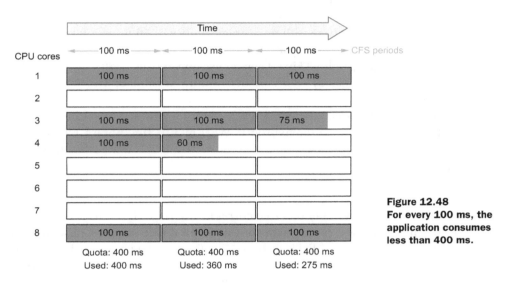

Figure 12.48
For every 100 ms, the application consumes less than 400 ms.

During the first period of 100 ms, four threads are busy, so we consume 400 out of 400 ms: 100% of the quota. During the second period, we consume 360 out of 400 ms, and so on. Everything is fine because the application consumes less than the quota.

However, let's remember that GOMAXPROCS is set to 8. Therefore, in the worst-case scenario, we can have eight threads, each scheduled on a different core (figure 12.49).

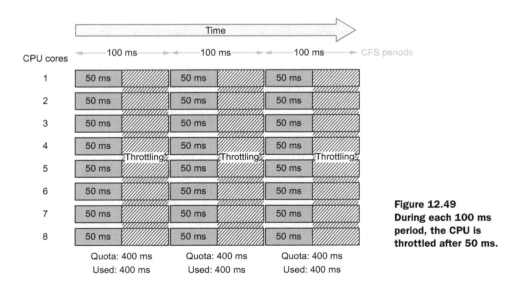

Figure 12.49
During each 100 ms period, the CPU is throttled after 50 ms.

CHAPTER 12 *Optimizations*

For every 100 ms, the quota is set to 400 ms. If the eight threads are busy executing goroutines, after 50 ms, we reach the quota of 400 ms (8 × 50 ms = 400 ms). What will be the consequence? CFS will throttle the CPU resource. Hence, no more CPU resources will be allocated until the start of another period. In other words, our application will be on hold for 50 ms.

For example, a service with an average latency of 50 ms can take up to 150 ms to complete. This is a possible 300% penalty on the latency.

So, what's the solution? First, keep an eye on Go issue 33803 (https://github.com/golang/go/issues/33803). Perhaps in a future version of Go, GOMAXPROCS will be CFS-aware.

A solution for today is to rely on a library made by Uber called automaxprocs (github.com/uber-go/automaxprocs). We can use this library by adding a blank import to go.uber.org/automaxprocs in main.go; it will automatically set GOMAXPROCS to match the Linux container CPU quota. In the previous example, GOMAXPROCS would be set to 4 instead of 8, so we wouldn't be able to reach a state where the CPU is throttled.

In summary, let's remember that currently, Go isn't CFS-aware. GOMAXPROCS is based on the host machine rather than on the defined CPU limits. Consequently, we can reach a state where the CPU is throttled, leading to long pauses and substantial effects such as a significant latency increase. Until Go becomes CFS-aware, one solution is to rely on automaxprocs to automatically set GOMAXPROCS to the defined quota.

Summary

- Understanding how to use CPU caches is important for optimizing CPU-bound applications because the L1 cache is about 50 to 100 times faster than the main memory.
- Being conscious of the cache line concept is critical to understanding how to organize data in data-intensive applications. A CPU doesn't fetch memory word by word; instead, it usually copies a memory block to a 64-byte cache line. To get the most out of each individual cache line, enforce spatial locality.
- Making code predictable for the CPU can also be an efficient way to optimize certain functions. For example, a unit or constant stride is predictable for the CPU, but a non-unit stride (for example, a linked list) isn't predictable.
- To avoid a critical stride, hence utilizing only a tiny portion of the cache, be aware that caches are partitioned.
- Knowing that lower levels of CPU caches aren't shared across all the cores helps avoid performance-degrading patterns such as false sharing while writing concurrency code. Sharing memory is an illusion.
- Use instruction-level parallelism (ILP) to optimize specific parts of your code to allow a CPU to execute as many parallel instructions as possible. Identifying data hazards is one of the main steps.
- You can avoid common mistakes by remembering that in Go, basic types are aligned with their own size. For example, keep in mind that reorganizing the

fields of a struct by size in descending order can lead to more compact structs (less memory allocation and potentially a better spatial locality).

- Understanding the fundamental differences between heap and stack should also be part of your core knowledge when optimizing a Go application. Stack allocations are almost free, whereas heap allocations are slower and rely on the GC to clean the memory.

- Reducing allocations is also an essential aspect of optimizing a Go application. This can be done in different ways, such as designing the API carefully to prevent sharing up, understanding the common Go compiler optimizations, and using `sync.Pool`.

- Use the fast-path inlining technique to efficiently reduce the amortized time to call a function.

- Rely on profiling and the execution tracer to understand how an application performs and the parts to optimize.

- Understanding how to tune the GC can lead to multiple benefits such as handling sudden load increases more efficiently.

- To help avoid CPU throttling when deployed in Docker and Kubernetes, keep in mind that Go isn't CFS-aware.

Final words

Congratulations for reaching the end of *100 Go Mistakes and How to Avoid Them*. I genuinely hope that you enjoyed reading this book and that it will help you with your personal and/or professional projects.

Remember that making mistakes is part of the learning process, and as I highlighted in the preface, it was also a significant source of inspiration for this book. What matters, in the end, is our capacity to learn from them.

If you want to continue the discussion, you can follow me on Twitter: @teivah.

index